DATE DUE

4-9

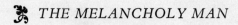 *THE MELANCHOLY MAN*

THE MELANCHOLY MAN

❧ A study of Dickens's novels

JOHN LUCAS

METHUEN & CO LTD
11 New Fetter Lane · London EC4

First published 1970
by Methuen & Co Ltd
11 New Fetter Lane London EC4
© 1970 John Lucas
Printed in Great Britain
by W & J Mackay & Co Ltd
Chatham, Kent

SBN 416 07340 9 Hardback
SBN 416 07350 6 Paperback

Distributed in the USA
by Barnes & Noble Inc

FOR PAULINE

✵ CONTENTS

ℋ INTRODUCTION

Dickens is an undisciplined genius. So much is commonplace and, within limits, so much is true. But where do the limits begin – or end? Can we always be sure that what we regard as undisciplined is not in fact answering to its own laws and requirements which we are reluctant to recognize because they go against the demands we usually lay down for the novel? And what are those demands? Such a question can easily resolve itself into the old problem, what is a novel. In theory the question seems difficult. In practice it seems easy. We all feel we know what a novel is. But the trouble with Dickens is that he seems to elude our idea of the novel so that we find ourselves saying either that in some ways he isn't a novelist – not a *real* novelist, not a *complete* one – or that he is a special case. Well, of course, he is. Because he is a great genius. And it looks a little odd to construct a theory of the novel that has to be strained to fit him in. But thinking of Dickens as a special case can also mean protecting him from criticism. And when we see this happening we are likely to feel that it will hardly do. If he is great, he should not need protecting.

Years ago Middleton Murry put his finger on the problem. In a little essay in *Pencillings*, Murry noted that 'Dickens is a baffling figure. There are moments when it seems that his chief purpose in writing is to put a spoke in the wheel of our literary aesthetics. We manage to include everybody but him.' Compared with when Murry wrote, there are few people nowadays who would exclude Dickens. But just how to include him remains a problem. Dickens, Murry goes on, has a 'curious trick of immortality. So we are beginning to discover that [he] was a genius, but, of course, only in parts. When we have discovered which are the parts we shall breathe again.'

But which *are* the parts? In view of all the criticism Dickens now receives it is inevitable that many are being discovered and put together, and from them we of course find out what we already knew, that the whole is greater than the sum of the parts. And we also find that what from one point of view does not look a part of the genius, does when it is seen from a different point of view. Someone somewhere must be writing a full-scale study called *Dickens and His Critics*. In the following book I shall have very little to say about other critics, not because there is no criticism of Dickens from which I have profited, but because I want to have my own say about him, and it seems best to do this by concentrating on my own point of view, indicating where *I* think the genius is to be found.

This brings me to the matter of the title. Why *The Melancholy Man*? It comes from Kant. In his *Observations on the Feeling of the Beautiful and the Sublime*, Kant sets out his definition of a type of man, many of whose features he took from Rousseau. On later occasions in the book I quote all or part of the passage, but it is perhaps a good thing to have it before us now.

> The man of melancholy disposition is little concerned with the judgement of others, with their opinion of what is good or true; he relies purely on his own insight. . . . He regards changes of fashion with indifference and their glitter with contempt. . . . He has a lofty sense of the dignity of human nature. He esteems himself and regards man as a creature deserving of respect. He suffers no abject subservience and breathes the noble air of freedom. To him all chains are abhorrent, from the gilded fetters worn at court to the heavy irons of the galley slave. He is a stern judge of himself as well as of others and is not infrequently disgusted with himself as well as with the world.

It is a great passage and it fits Dickens perfectly, even down to the idea that the melancholy man is a stern judge of himself. For we can hardly read *Great Expectations* without realizing what severity of self-judgement is implied in Dickens's study of Pip and his ambitious heart.

But there is another sense in which it is appropriate to call Dickens the Melancholy Man. 'He breathes the noble air of freedom,' Kant says of his man of melancholy disposition. Much of my book is taken up with the suggestion that for Dickens the noble air of freedom becomes more and more stifled and threatened by the social prison. Freedom becomes associated with the past. Now Dickens has a piercing sense of time passing, an acute and melancholic perception of how the past recedes, is destroyed, is lost. Often, his awareness of the past is connected with a personal landscape of memory. It is no accident that his imagination should have been so caught by Falstaff's great sad line, 'We have heard the chimes at midnight, Master Shallow.' But Dickens also regards the past as identified with personal and social freedom of a sort that the present seems absolutely to threaten. That is why his developing use of pastoralism is so important to a true understanding of his work. For it is through pastoral language and scenes that he works out an increasingly complex vision of the nature of freedom.

My way of putting the matter may suggest that in some sense Dickens recommends the past, much as Ruskin and Carlyle recommended it. And to an extent he does. But only to an extent, and only in the earlier work. In the great novels he turns away from such escapism (which is what it amounts to). For the great Dickens is a truly mimetic novelist. Although I shall try to keep *The Melancholy Man* as free as possible from technical terms – Dickens has put too many spokes in the wheel of literary aesthetics to make it of much use in any discussion of him, at least – I shall make use of the word mimetic, just as I shall make use of the word prescriptive. But the words should not cause any difficulties. On the contrary, I hope they will help bring Dickens's art into focus. For when I call him prescriptive I mean simply that he recommends, and when I call him mimetic I mean that he studies the social and human probabilities. Not that that is an easy matter. Indeed, Dickens seems to me the greatest of all English novelists because he manages to be more mimetic than any other, he sees more deeply into and renders more finely and

completely social and human probabilities than any of his great
rivals. But certainly he belongs with the developing strain of
realism that Erich Auerbach traces in the nineteenth-century
novel.

> The serious treatment of everyday reality, the rise of more
> extensive and socially inferior groups to the position of subject
> matter for problematical-existential representation, on the one
> hand; on the other, the embedding of random persons and events in
> the general course of contemporary history, the fluid historical
> background – these, we believe, are the foundations of modern
> realism, and it is natural that the broad and elastic form of the novel
> should increasingly impose itself for a rendering comprising so
> many elements.[1]

True, Auerbach adds that he finds in Dickens that 'there is, despite the strong social feeling and suggestive density of his
milieux, almost no trace of the fluidity of the political and historical background', but there is no point in quarrelling with that
verdict here, since the following pages take up the enormous
extent to which Dickens is concerned with the fluidity, not of
the background, but of the social and political process. I prefer
the word process to system or framework, let alone background,
because these suggest that Dickens sees society as mechanistic,
even fixed, whereas I think that we do him justice only if we
recognize how, in the great novels, he explores the different ways
in which social change occurs.

Social probabilities. Yes, Dickens is a great novelist in his
investigation of them. But social probabilities are inseparable
from human probabilities, and Dickens is equally great at
investigating these. In a famous and beautiful letter to his friend
George Russell, Yeats remarked, 'I think that a poet . . . becomes
a greater power from understanding all the great primary
emotions & these one only gets out of going through the common
experiences & duties of life.' I would not claim that we can find
all the great primary emotions in Dickens, but we find nearly all
of them, irradiated and given authority by his constant exposure

[1] *Mimesis*, 1957, pp. 433–4.

to and involvement with the common experiences and duties of life. In the last analysis, Dickens seems to me a great, sane and utterly central force, and to know more about life and in more ways than any other English novelist.

Of course, he has his faults. It is easy to point them out. 'The first thing we notice about *War and Peace* and *Madame Bovary*,' Randall Jarrell said, 'is how wonderful they are; the second thing we notice is how much they have wrong with them.' Much the same may be said of Dickens. But what is wrong with him frequently turns out to be so peripheral as not to matter – not when we realize how much he achieves. Which is not to say that we should ignore the faults, only that we should remember the scale and greatness of his accomplishment. 'Works of art,' Rilke noted, 'are with nothing so little to be reached as with criticism. Only love can grasp and hold and be just towards them.' I cannot pretend that *The Melancholy Man* is not a work of criticism, still less that it manages to be just towards so great a man as Dickens is. But I *have* written it out of love.

There are two very obvious points to be made about the *Pickwick Papers*, and since they inevitably condition the way we read the book it will be as well to note them at the outset of this chapter. The first point is that *The Posthumous Papers of the Pickwick Club* – to give the work its full title – is not really a novel at all, even though Dickens tries increasingly to give it shape and coherence. The second is, that the interpolated tales jar against the idyllic mode of the main narrative. It is of course this latter point which critics since Edmund Wilson have found more interesting. In his witty and provocative essay, 'Dingley Dell and the Fleet', Auden has argued that Mr Pickwick is a mythopeaic creation whom Dickens must cease to write about as soon as the fat gentleman fully comprehends that he has entered a fallen world. The book, Auden suggests, is really about a banishment from Eden; and the tales of horror which at first seem *merely* tales to Pickwick, are more and more brought into line with the real world. In other words, Pickwick finds that he does not live in an enclosed paradisal world but in a fallen world which naturally breeds the extreme, hideous emotions and human failings that the tales reveal.

But there is more to it than just that. For Pickwick deliberately chooses to enter the fallen world. He accepts guilt by renouncing his honour; in deciding to pay an unfairly imposed debt so that Mrs Bardell may go free from the Fleet, Pickwick acknowledges that he belongs to a world of evil. And once he has made his decision he enters a temporal world: the novel begins to move forward in time rather than circling atemporally as is possible in the Edenic world.

Auden's case is adroitly made and it pushes to an extreme the assumption most people make, or feel, about the *Pickwick Papers*, that Pickwick falls from idyllic contentment into a condition of experience and pain. My chief quarrel with the assumption is that it does not sufficiently reckon with the fact that the book is not, strictly speaking, a novel. The point needs some attention, I think, because although it is obvious its implications are not frequently grasped. Once they have been we shall see that Dickens himself is perhaps importantly present as manipulator of his book, trying to find a point of view or vision that will allow him to be a novelist of the 'real' world. Not that I want to pretend that the book in any way begins as a deliberate experiment or enquiry into the ability of fiction to encounter the world 'out there'. But I do believe that just occasionally the *Pickwick Papers* nearly develops into such an enquiry, and part of the fascination the book has for us comes from recognizing how Dickens begins here very dimly to perceive themes and problems of treating them that become central in his greatest works.

If I were to try and say what the *Pickwick Papers* is finally about, I think I could come close to it by agreeing with all that Auden has to say but at all times substituting Dickens for Pickwick. For surely it is the novelist himself who learns to break out of his hoped-for idyllic world, who learns to accept the fact of pain, of suffering and of evil – as of course he had accepted them in his *Sketches*. If we are honest we will have to admit that Pickwick's fall into a world of guilt is so slight a descent as to be hardly distinguishable for what Auden takes it to be. And certainly in view of the way Dickens treats it there is no hint that he had anything like a fall in mind. Auden's way of looking at the episode seems too much determined by the fictions of later novelists. It is almost as though he is projecting back on to Pickwick a drama of the agonized inner conscience, which might do nicely in a discussion of George Eliot or Henry James, but at this early stage of Dickens's career is pretty well beside the point. And indeed you have to stay a long way from the actual text of the *Papers* if you are to use words like guilt and fall of the scene in which Pickwick renounces his honour; the words are simply in excess of the experience we are offered.

On the other hand there can be no doubt that in the *Papers* we find a good many clues to suggest that Dickens increasingly comes to realize that a concern with human beings may well mean a concern with pain and suffering. The clues do not provide a vision of the real world, but they go some way towards composing such a vision, and only Dickens's constant interference as manipulator prevents them from forming a coherent picture of the world into which Auden sees Pickwick as descending. Dickens, that is, by several twists in the plotting of things turns away from the possibilities his own work opens up. And because the *Pickwick Papers* isn't a proper novel we cannot regard this as a flaw. It is up to Dickens to decide just how far he wants to go in letting the real world intrude, before regarding its threat as enough to require a withdrawal back into his fiction.

Perhaps I make it sound as though Dickens wants to have it both ways. And in a sense he does. For if the *Pickwick Papers* isn't a novel, it contains elements of two kinds of fiction. There is the prescriptive, in which we are offered an idyllic view of life as it should be; and the mimetic, in which we are given a realistic view of life as it is. But the mimetic is much less fully treated, for Dickens's confrontation with the real world is rarely more than tangential; the idyll predominates. Yet even so there are moments which I call clues and which hint no matter how faintly at Dickens's abiding concern to do justice as a novelist to the reality which he thinks fiction must confront and somehow come to terms with. To put it rather differently, already in the *Pickwick Papers* we get some indication of the future clashes that will take place between Dickens the entertainer and Dickens the great truth-teller and conscience of his age, and a faint hint that the consolations of fiction, beautiful and seductive though they are, prove finally unsatisfactory. But let me start with the consolations.

Most of the interpolated tales in the *Pickwick Papers* are pretty much 'freezers'. But one, 'The Bagman's Story', stands out as very different. The narrator was told it, so he says, by his uncle, and he repeats to the company a comic story about a widow who narrowly avoids making a bigamous marriage. She is saved from this fate by the story's hero, Tom Smart, who tells her the truth about her intended husband and marries her himself (Tom has heard the truth from an old chair on which the would-be bigamist has left his trousers containing a letter from his wife). After the bagman finishes his story the company discusses it:

> 'Everybody believed the story, didn't they?' said the dirty-faced man, refilling his pipe.
> 'Except Tom's enemies,' replied the bagman. 'Some of 'em said Tom invented it altogether; and the others said he was drunk and fancied it, and got hold of the wrong trousers before he went to bed. But nobody ever minded what *they* said.'
> 'Tom said it was all true?'
> 'Every word.'
> 'And your uncle?'
> 'Every letter.'
> 'They must have been very nice men, both of 'em,' said the dirty-faced man.
> 'Yes, they were,' replied the bagman; 'very nice men indeed!' (ch 14)[1]

I quote this story because it provides an almost perfect emblem of the consolatory powers of the story-teller, in which truth is consistent with happiness, the fraudulent get their just deserts and virtue is rewarded by success. In such a fictional world the story-teller becomes a benovelent God or at the least a very nice man. And clearly the *Pickwick Papers* itself is partly the work of a 'very nice man' who makes things come out well. That is its fiction. But because the real comes into it Dickens has to invent another very nice man who can carry the novelist's powers of making things come out well. Hence Sam Weller, who always proves equal to the purpose of making good prevail. And given the existence of this second very nice man, Gissing's generous praise of the *Papers* seems not quite accurate. 'The *Pickwick Papers* cannot be classed as a novel,' Gissing said in his shrewd and

[1] Throughout the book the text of Dickens I have used is the Oxford Illustrated Edition.

loving study of Dickens, 'it is merely a great book.' Yet in the end the *Papers* is more than merely a great book even if it is less than a novel. For it does begin to show signs of having the coherence and integrity that we expect from a novel (without getting too involved in generic definitions), and that it does so is largely due to the invention of Weller.

It is worth looking into why this should be. And in order to understand Sam's position we should notice that as he comes more and more into prominence so the interpolated tales drop away. The point is that with Weller beginning to occupy the large centre of the *Papers* Dickens has found a way of coping with evils that had previously to be confined to the tales so that they wouldn't disturb the idyllic mode of the main narrative. As the narrative proceeds evils begin to show themselves in it; and these evils represent a reality that can be confronted by Weller, since he embodies and champions the positive values of the idyll against whatever of the real world is allowed into the *Pickwick Papers*.

But where does the real intrude into the idyll? Auden would say that it enters with Mr Pickwick's payment of his debt, but the truth surely is that it is always getting in, though Dickens makes repeated efforts to convert the real back into the idyllic. Even Birmingham does not seriously disturb the mode:

> As they rattled through the narrow thoroughfares leading to the heart of the turmoil, the sights and sounds of earnest occupation struck more forcibly on the senses. The streets were thronged with working-people. The hum of labour resounded from every house, lights gleamed from the long casement windows in the attic stories, and the whirl of wheels and noise of machinery shook the trembling walls. The fires, whose lurid sullen light had been visible for miles, blazed fiercely up, in the great works and factories of the Town. The din of hammers, the rushing of steam, and the dead heavy clanking of engines, was the harsh music which arose from every corner. (ch 50)

Of course, for all the glow of enthusiasm which touches part of this passage – and we are also told of 'handsome and well-lighted shops' – the city is clearly not intended to be seen as an earthly paradise. Our attention is drawn to 'straggling cottages by the road-side, the dingy hue of every object visible, the murky atmosphere, the paths of cinder and brick-dust'. All the same the passage is likely to come as a surprise to someone acquainted only with Dickens's later fiction. For on the whole this is a rather dull description of what we are meant to see as a cheerful and prosperous place. Well, it is true that Birmingham *was* prosperous in the 1830s (I do not think we have to bother overmuch about the date at which the novel is ostensibly set). As Asa Briggs has pointed out, the city was far better placed to deal with the industrial boom than any of its rivals; it offered a wide diversity of occupation, the work tended to go on in small workshops rather than large factories so that relations between master and men were good, and since much of the labour force was skilled the introduction of machines did not mean that they were simply substituted for men, as happened in Manchester, for example.[1] Birmingham had its unpleasant side, which struck De Tocqueville so forcibly,[2] but obviously the city could be accommodated to the sort of image we are presented with in the *Pickwick Papers*. Yet in *Dombey and Son* Birmingham looks very different:

> Everything around is blackened. There are dark pools of water, muddy lanes, and miserable habitations far below. There are jagged walls and falling houses close at hand, and through the battered roofs and broken windows, wretched rooms are seen, where want and fever hide themselves in many wretched shapes, while smoke and crowded gables, and distorted chimneys, and deformity of brick and mortar penning up deformity of mind and body, choke the murky distance. (ch 20)

The point is not that Birmingham had changed but that Dickens had, and that by the time he came to write *Dombey and Son* he had moved to the forefront of his concern miseries that are almost kept out of the *Pickwick Papers*.

[1] *Victorian Cities*, 1963, pp. 188–9.
[2] Ibid. pp. 67–8.

Almost, but not quite. For those straggling cottages remain to trouble the picture, and so does the murky atmosphere, which hints at something the very opposite of idyllic. And once we notice this flaw in the idyll we are drawn to perceive others: the grasping vulgarity of non-conformist religion, the corruption of law, the cant of politics. Flaws such as these might upset the designs of the very nice man. But of course they don't. For if we notice their intrusions we can also hardly help noticing that they are soon swept aside or coped with or defeated, either by the writer himself or by Sam. Consider the rook-shooting incident:

> The old gentleman nodded; and two ragged boys who had been marshalled to the spot under the direction of the infant Lambert, forthwith commenced climbing up two of the trees.
> 'What are those lads for?' enquired Mr. Pickwick abruptly. He was rather alarmed; for he was not quite certain but that the distress of the agricultural interest, about which he had often heard a great deal, might have compelled the small boys attached to the soil to earn a precarious and hazardous subsistence by making marks of themselves for inexperienced marksmen.
> 'Only to start the game,' replied Mr Wardle, laughing. (ch 7)

The effect of this is to expunge not only Mr Pickwick's fears but ours also; the moment is sufficient to dissolve any possibility that agricultural distress could brutishly enter the idyllic world. And of course laughter in the *Pickwick Papers* time and again deflects Satan from Paradise; death may dwell in Arcady, but it makes no appearance in Dingley Dell. I do not think we have any right to object against Dickens's tactic, but we are bound to recognize that because of his decision to fend off brute reality he has no way of providing adequately for the keen and compassionate studies of suffering that feature so remarkably in the *Sketches* – as in, for example, the studies of the Pawn-Shop, the Gin-Shop, the Condemned Cell, and the beautiful and already utterly characteristic sketch of 'Shabby-Genteel People':

> But, if you see hurrying along a by-street, keeping as close as he can to the area-railing, a man of about forty or fifty, clad in an old rusty suit of threadbare black cloth which shines with constant

wear as if it had been bees-waxed – the trousers tightly strapped down, partly for the look of the thing and partly to keep his old shoes from slipping off at the heels, – if you observe, too, that his yellowish white neckerchief is carefully pinned up, to conceal the tattered garment underneath, and that his hands are encased in the remains of an old pair of beaver gloves, you may set him down as a shabby-genteel gentleman. A glance at that depressed face, and timorous air of conscious poverty, will make your heart ache – always supposing that you are neither a philosopher nor a political economist. (ch 10)

There is very little to match that order of beautifully attentive writing in the *Pickwick Papers*. Nor is there much to rival the psychological power of the conclusion to 'A Visit to Newgate', where the condemned man dreams of escape:

The night is dark and cold, the gates have been left open, and in an instant he is in the street, flying from the scene of his imprisonment like the wind. The streets are cleared, the open fields are gained and the broad wide country lies before him. Onward he dashes in the midst of darkness, over hedge and ditch, through mud and pool, bounding from spot to spot with a speed and lightness, astonishing even to himself. At length he pauses; he must be safe from pursuit now; he will stretch himself out on that bank and sleep till sunrise.

A period of unconsciousness succeeds. He wakes, cold and wretched. The dull gray light of morning is stealing into the cell, and falls upon the form of the attendant turnkey. Confused by his dreams, he starts up from his uneasy bed in momentary uncertainty. It is but momentary. Every object in the narrow cell is too frightfully real to admit of doubt or mistake. He is the condemned villain again, guilty and despairing; and in two hours will be dead.

Admittedly, this does not have the concentrated power of Crabbe's 'Prisons', in the *Borough*, from which Dickens's sketch almost certainly comes. It lacks the real shock that Crabbe springs in his final lines as the condemned man's dream is broken:

> 'Oh! horrible, a wave
> Roars as it rises – save me, Edward, save!'
> She cries. Alas, the watchman on his way
> Calls and lets in truth, terror and the day.

All the same, it was astute of Dickens to see what Crabbe had to offer him, and he makes marvellous use of the poet on later occasions. And in the *Sketches* themselves he works very near to Crabbe's sombre and unflinching steadiness of perception when he writes, as he so often does, about suffering and misery.

We cannot often find this sort of perception in the *Papers*, and we shall not find it at all in the interpolated tales. Of course, it is customary to say that the tales are a way of drawing off the darker side that Dickens couldn't allow into his idyll and I myself have spoken of their containing the evil that is automatically banished from the main narrative. But I want to add that this evil is a decidedly literary and inauthentic concoction. Even when the prose of one of the tales catches fire at all – and it does so remarkably infrequently – we do not go far from the derivative. The deluded visions of the drunkard in the 'Stroller's Tale' are a case in point:

> A short period of oblivion, and he was wandering through a tedious maze of low-arched rooms – so low, sometimes, that he must creep upon his his hands and knees to make his way along; it was close and dark, and every way he turned, some obstacle impeded his progress. There were insects too, hideous crawling things with eyes that stared upon him, and filled the very air around: glistening horribly amidst the thick darkness of the place. The walls and ceiling were alive with reptiles – the vault expanded to an enormous size – frightful figures flitted to and fro – and the faces of the men he knew, rendered hideous by gibing and mouthing, peered out from among them; they were searing him with heated irons, and binding his head with cords till the blood started; and he struggled madly for life. (ch 3)

That passage is as good as anything we can find in the tales and it seems to me not to be worthy of comparison with the one I have quoted from 'Shabby-Genteel People'. It does not owe its invention to what Dickens has seen of life but to what he has read of 'Monk' Lewis, whom he quotes in the tale of 'The Lamplighter'; and by the time we have reached such tales as 'A Madman's Manuscript' and 'The Convict's Return', with its clear debt to 'Ellen Orford', we have moved into a world of entirely literary inspiration. Indeed, the interpolated tales of the *Pickwick Papers* cannot seriously be felt as constituting a potential threat to the idyllic world from which they have therefore to be kept apart, because they are so contrived and otiose an expression of Dickens's imagination. If they accomplish anything, it is to help deflect attention away from where the more genuine suffering is to be found in the book – that is, in the narrative itself.

I have already pointed out that in the descriptions of Birmingham and the rook-shooting incident there are flaws to the idyll which are quickly smoothed away. Yet they keep cropping up. It is almost as though Dickens finds it necessary to fashion checks against his own beautifully realized nostalgia for a world that never was. And so we have Pickwick's sudden and unique reference to his age, 'I am growing older, and want repose and quiet. My rambles, Sam, are over!' (ch 56), which I do not think comes as a consequence of his fall into experience but is prompted by Dickens's own sense that time will not relent. Or consider Perker's remark about the apparently repentant Jingle and Trotter, made when Pickwick asks the lawyer if he thinks there is any chance of their being permanently reformed, as in an idyll they should be. '"Of course there is a chance," Perker says. "I hope it may prove a good one. They are unquestionably penitent now; but then, you know, they have the recollection of a very recent suffering fresh upon them. What they may become, when that fades away, is a problem that neither you nor I can solve."' (ch 53) Perker's speech is the more remarkable in that until he makes it he is presented as a straightforward comic figure. At this point he sounds a very different and almost melancholic note.

But the most arresting of all flaws in the idyll is the Fleet. Chapter 42 is taken up with describing Mr Pickwick's first experiences of his imprisonment and it is very revealing to note how Dickens's tone deepens and darkens as the chapter progresses. At first the note struck is one of brash contempt for self-deceivers within prison walls. And so when Mr Pickwick arranges for 'chummage' we get this:

Mr Pickwick had been eyeing the room, which was filthily dirty, and smelt intolerably close. There was no vestige of either carpet, curtain, or blind. There was not even a closet in it. Unquestionably there were but few things to put away, if there had been one; but however few in number, or small in individual amount, still remnants of loaves and pieces of cheese, and damp towels . . . and toasting-forks without prongs, *do* present somewhat of an uncomfortable appearance when they are scattered about the floor of a small apartment, which is the common sitting and sleeping room of three idle men. (ch 42)

We are bound to notice most about this passage Dickens's contempt for the men, and indeed it seems designed to guard him from having to view them sympathetically. He is not going to have his idyll broken by the brute facts of life. If people get into the Fleet they have only themselves to blame (how wonderfully prim and ill-judged the word 'idle' is). But because Dickens is Dickens he cannot merely write off the sufferings of debtors. Turn the page, therefore, and you come on this description of the Chancery prisoner:

He was a tall, gaunt, cadaverous man, in an old great-coat and slippers: with sunken cheeks, and a restless, eager eye. His lips were bloodless, and his bones sharp and thin. God help him! the iron teeth of confinement and privation had been slowly filing him down for twenty years.

And there, all at once, is the great Dickens. He is there in the marvellously alert prose that can note the man's incongruities – sunken cheeks versus restless, eager eye, hopelessness versus mad hope; and there also in the image of the rasp, which is by no means merely fanciful but so deeply and truly imaginative that it shocks us as nothing in the tales does (think of it working on those sharp, thin bones). There is nothing literary or self-regarding about such prose as this; on the contrary, it draws us to keen and painful contemplation of the person it describes.

And once Dickens has freed his imagination in this way, the chapter devotes itself to an intense study of the misery of the chained human spirit, as for example in the countryman:

flicking with a worn-out hunting-whip the top-boot that adorned his right foot; his left being (for he dressed by easy stages) thrust into an old slipper. Horses, dogs and drink, had brought him there, pell-mell. There was a rusty spur on the solitary boot, which he occasionally jerked into the empty air, at the same time giving the boot a smart blow, and muttering some of the sounds by which a sportsman encourages his horse. He was riding, in imagination, some desperate steeple-chase at that moment. Poor wretch! he never rode a match on the swiftest animal in his costly stud, with half the speed at which he had torn along the course that ended in the Fleet. (ch 42)

It isn't as good, admittedly. And undoubtedly in this passage Dickens's language begins to lose contact with the person it should be describing; it is too eager to point its moral and to force the analogy between riding to hounds and riding to ruin. And its limitations show up very exactly if we compare it with the great moment in *Little Dorrit* describing Fanny's mounting into her marriage-coach which 'after rolling for a few minutes smoothly over a fair pavement, had begun to jolt through a slough of despond, and through a long, long avenue of wrack and ruin'. There, the totally unexpected wit that moves so abruptly from the literal to the figurative mocks the conventionalities of descriptive prose and takes the opportunity to generalize Fanny's condition. Here the analogy is trite and comes too pat. Even so, the passage has about it a quality of compassion that also occurs in the description of the 'lean and haggard woman – a prisoner's wife – who was watering, with great solicitude, the wretched stump of a dried-up, withered plant, which, it was plain to see, could never send forth a green leaf again – too true an emblem, perhaps, of the office she had come there to discharge.'

The next five chapters continue to present images of misery and suffering and by and large the prose has a power and urgency to it which, no matter how often it slips towards crude rhetoric, never becomes as bad as the gothic-horror excesses of the interpolated tales. But of course the very fact that these chapters have such power creates an acute problem for Dickens, since they threaten the general tone of the *Pickwick Papers*. Once he has admitted this reality into the idyll he cannot convert it into anything else. The only way out of his difficulty, therefore, is to get Pickwick away from the Fleet, and the way he manages this is so adroitly done that it is liable to usurp all our attention. Indeed, we return to the fact of suffering only as Pickwick is on the point of saying farewell to the prison:

> At three o'clock that afternoon, Mr Pickwick took a last look at his little room, and made his way, as well as he could, through the throng of debtors who pressed eagerly forward to shake him by the hand, until he reached the lodge steps. He turned here, to look about him, and his eye lightened as he did so. In all the crowd of wan, emaciated faces, he saw not one which was not the happier for his sympathy and charity. (ch 47)

I suppose we have to say that it is the best Dickens could manage. under the circumstances. Even so, it inevitably seems inadequate and there is no help for it. Dickens has simply to do what he can to get out of a rather awkward spot, because he has not provided for such moments of reality as the prison scenes create. Of course Pickwick's benevolence, his charity and sympathy, are the complement of that laughter which elsewhere in the novel dispels or keeps at bay discordant notes, but individual goodness seems almost irrelevant once the scenes of misery are opened up to our gaze. Steven Marcus notes that

> Pickwick can allay his insulted sense of injustice by arraigning Dodson and Fogg, or he can withdraw from the dismal reality of the Fleet by locking himself in his room, disposing ultimately, of whatever he cannot reform by removing it from sight.[1]

But of course it is Dickens who manipulates Pickwick's withdrawal, Dickens who turns his eyes – and therefore ours – from what cannot be reformed by the touch of personal kindness and fellow-feeling. Personal goodness does well enough in the face of individual evils, but in the face of social evils it looks pretty small beer. Yet it is all Dickens has to offer, in the image of Mr

[1] *Dickens, from Pickwick to Dombey*, 1964, p. 48.

Pickwick's chinking waistcoat-pocket, and, much more power-fully, in Sam Weller. And this brings us back to the point I made earlier, about how Dickens capitalizes on his great invention.

Sam is the triumphant champion of goodness because his comic nature always defeats the enemy. When the artful Dodger remarks in *Oliver Twist* that this 'ain't the shop for justice', his remark strikes home, but injustice wins. When Sam is in the Fleet, he tells his cobbler acquaintance that there's 'very little trust at that shop' – meaning, the law. Yet Sam wins. He is, in fact, the novel's most persuasive image of that 'lighter and more kindly side of life', which Dickens in his Preface hoped that his readers might be willing to look upon. Sam defeats Buzfuz in one of the great comic exchanges of our literature; he manages to cause Dodson and Fogg the maximum discomfort with the minimum of effort; he gets even with Job Trotter and Jingle in irresistible style – ' "It won't do, Job Trotter . . . Come! None o' that 'ere nonsense. You ain't so wery handsome that you can afford to throw avay many o' your good looks" '; and he and his father rout the Rev. Stiggins. Repeatedly, Sam emerges as Dickens's spokesman, as in this passage, describing a meeting of the Brick Lane Branch of the United Grand Junction Ebenezer Temperance Association:

> Mr. Stiggins did not desire his hearers to be upon their guard against those false prophets and wretched mockers of religion, who, without sense to expound its first doctrines, or hearts to feel its first principles, are more dangerous members of society than the common criminal; imposing, as they necessarily do, upon the weakest and worst informed, casting scorn and contempt on what should be held most sacred, and bringing into partial disrepute large bodies of virtuous and well-conducted persons of many excellent sects and persuasions. But as he leant over the back of the chair for a considerable time, and closing one eye, winked a good deal with the other, it is presumed he thought all this, but kept it to himself.
>
> During the delivery of the oration, Mrs. Weller sobbed and wept at the end of the paragraphs; while Sam, sitting cross-legged on a

chair and resting his arms on the top-rail, regarded the speaker with great suavity and blandness of demeanour; occasionally bestowing a look of recognition on the old gentleman, who was delighted at the beginning, and went to sleep about half-way.

'Brayvo; wery pretty!' said Sam, when the red-nosed man having finished, pulled his worn gloves on: thereby thrusting his fingers through the broken tops till the knuckles were disclosed to view. 'Wery pretty.'

'I hope it may do you good, Samuel,' said Mrs. Weller solemnly.

'I think it vill, mum,' replied Sam. (ch 45)

Sam's laconic way of destroying Stiggins's cant is a good deal more effective than Dickens's own rather clumsy outbursts, and in general it is his wit and air of unruffled reasonableness that vindicate the views which Dickens wants to endorse. Sam, we implicitly believe, can see through any amount of 'gammon'.

But there is more to him than just his wit. He is also the good servant who can rescue his master from the many disasters that befall him. Everyone who reads the *Pickwick Papers* notices the Don Quixote-Sancho Panza nature of the relationship that exists between Pickwick and Sam, and I bring up the point here only because I want to suggest that Dickens can go much further in developing the relationship once he begins to see Pickwick as a good man. We know that when he first undertook the *Papers* he intended to make Pickwick vain, pompous and stupid; and it is clear that when we close the book our impression of Pickwick is of a kindly, warm-hearted and impulsively generous man. So much is obvious. What perhaps is not so obvious is that as he changes his mind about Pickwick, Dickens begins to discover where his true allegiances lie. In other words, the degree of involvement the writer comes to have with his central character makes possible his development as a novelist. And although the change of heart may seem trivial enough it is, I think, of really profound importance.

How, after all, does the *Pickwick Papers* start? As a thoroughly unconvincing series of echoes of earlier writers and as a pallid attempt to find a tone of voice that can align itself with late-

Augustan urbanity. There is the pastiche of Fielding, for example. 'That punctual servant of all work, the sun, had just risen, and begun to strike a light on the morning of the thirteenth of May, one thousand eight hundred and twenty seven, when Mr. Samuel Pickwick burst like another sun from his slumbers' (ch 2). There is the imitation of Peacock:

> Next came the three philosophers, highly delighted with their walk, and full of rapturous exclamations on the sublime beauties of the scenery.
>
> The Doctor shrugged up his shoulders, and confessed he preferred the scenery of Putney and Kew, where a man could go comfortably to sleep in his chaise, without being in momentary terror of being hurled headlong down a precipice.
>
> Mr. Milestone observed that there were great capabilities in the scenery, but it wanted shaving and polishing. If he could have it under his care for a single twelve month, he assured them no one would be able to know it again.
>
> Mr. Jenkinson thought the scenery just what it ought to be, and required no alteration.

That comes from *Headlong Hall* (ch 13). This comes from the *Pickwick Papers*:

> 'Magnificent ruin!' said Mr. Augustus Snodgrass, with all the poetic fervour that distinguished him, when they came in sight of the fine old castle.
>
> 'What a study for an antiquarian!' were the very words which fell from Mr. Pickwick's mouth, as he applied his telescope to his eye.
>
> 'Ah! fine place,' said the stranger, 'glorious pile . . .'
>
> 'Evidently a traveller in many countries, and a close observer of men and things,' said Mr. Pickwick.
>
> 'I should like to see his poem,' said Mr. Snodgrass. (ch 2)

But Dickens debases the Peacockian method, since his characters are mere pretenders to the ideas that Peacock is concerned with. The difference between Milestone and Snodgrass is quite simply that Milestone is a man of taste and that Snodgrass isn't. Making fun of Snodgrass and Pickwick is too easy, and I think we have to assume that Dickens undertook the task only because he wanted to present his own credentials of taste and urbanity. He had made a very similar effort in the *Sketches*. Look for instance at the closing paragraph to 'Sentiment', a tale of an imprudent marriage:

> Mr. and Mrs. Butler are at present rusticating in a small cottage at Ball's-Pond, pleasantly situated in the immediate vicinity of a brick-field. They have no family. Mr. Theodosius looks very important, and writes incessantly; but, in consequence of a gross combination on the part of publishers, none of his productions appear in print. His young wife begins to think that ideal misery is preferable to real unhappiness; and that a marriage, contracted in haste, and repented at leisure, is the cause of more substantial wretchedness than she ever anticipated.

What is Dickens doing, we ask, taking Jane Austen's line on marriage and in such faint echo of her tone? Yet he echoes her again and again, for instance in the sketch of 'Horatio Sparkins', where he describes a Mr Malderton, 'hospitable from ostentation, illiberal from ignorance, and prejudiced from conceit'; and in 'The Steam Excursion' where he introduces Mrs Taunton with the remark that she had 'the form of a giantess and the mind of a child. The pursuit of pleasure, and some means of killing time, were the sole means of her existence. She doted on her daughters, who were as frivolous as herself.'

Of course, the echoes are weak. But the very fact that they keep cropping up suggests how deeply Dickens is engaged in trying to discover his role as writer. The urbane pose sits ludicrously on him because he really knows nothing of the world that Jane Austen and Peacock inhabit. Nor does it matter. Indeed, Dickens becomes a great novelist when he realizes how necessary it is to abandon what are for him arbitrary and irrelevant standards of judgement. And the realization comes very quickly. Hence the change in point of view over Pickwick, and the famous Prefatorial defence:

> It has been observed of Mr. Pickwick, that there is a decided change in his character, as these pages proceed, and that he becomes

more good and more sensible. I do not think this change will
appear forced or unnatural to my readers, if they will reflect that
in real life the peculiarities and oddities of a man who has anything
whimsical about him, generally impress us first, and that it is not
until we are better acquainted with him that we usually begin to
look below these superficial traits, and to know the better part of
him.

It is easy enough to unpick the specious logic of this argument.
But it is more worthwhile to accept that when Dickens talks
about his readers he really means himself, that Pickwick's superficial traits are the ones which can be mocked from the 'urbane'
standpoint, and that in seeing the uselessness of such a standpoint
for himself Dickens makes a decisive breakthrough towards the
open-minded acceptance of very ordinary people that is so
essential to his greatness because it allows him to explore and
record the life of Victorian England with an intensity and range
that are unequalled in the English novel.

Dickens's 'better acquaintance' with Pickwick is a great
moment for English fiction. Yet it could cause an acute problem.
Sam the good servant gets his master out of scrapes, which is
perhaps as it should be, except that in 'real life' servants don't
always win with Sam's infallible wit and easy grace. But if by
and large we do not notice this as a problem it is partly the consequence of Dickens's plotting, whereby Sam and his master are
kept on the move, and partly also because of the *Pickwick Papers'*
social inexactness which, with rare exceptions, operates throughout. For we do not think of asking awkward questions about the
probability of Sam's successes, and this has much to do with
Dickens's way of presenting a vision of the real world which
only rarely becomes uncontrollable by art. Birmingham can be
controlled, and so can Bath. It is there that we meet Lord Mutanhed, who plainly has for fictional ancestor someone like Lord
Struttwell of *Roderick Random*. But whereas Smollett hates
Struttwell, Dickens is merely amused by Mutanhed.

'Gwacious heavens!' said his lordship, 'I thought evewebody
had seen the new mail cart; it's the neatest, pwettiest, gwacefullest

thing that ever wan upon wheels. Painted wed, with a cweam piebald.'

'With a real box for the letters, and all complete,' said the Honourable Mr. Crushton.

'And a little seat in fwont, with an iwon wail, for the dwiver,' added his lordship. (ch 35)

We are not meant to take this seriously, and because we don't have to we are the readier to accept Sam as the novel's triumphant hero. And even the more menacing figures, such as Dodson and Fogg, and institutions, such as the Fleet, are made to feel the less threatening because they are brought into the same world as Lord Mutanhed inhabits. Which is perhaps to say in a rather roundabout and laborious manner what everyone perfectly well recognizes; that the *Pickwick Papers* is for the most part a miraculous and quite inimitable triumph. For Dickens rarely demeans the strength of the intrusive forces into his idyllic world; and yet he never lets them take control and so wreck his work's unity. Only with the Fleet does he come really near to trouble and he does so there because he can throw no sort of gloss over suffering with which he feels such acute compassion.

Steven Marcus has said that at this moment of his career, Dickens found it possible to create 'in the company of the fortunate people who surround Pickwick the life promised by the Gospels; these meek ones have indeed inherited the earth – or at least as much of it as is contained within the borders of Richmond and Dingley Dell.'[1] But Dingley Dell is not of the earth at all and Richmond is no more 'real' than Birmingham and Bath. They are all part of a beautiful myth and the characters who inhabit their world are also mythic. The only spot of 'earth' in the entire book is the Fleet, which is precisely what the fortunate people *cannot* inherit. For their meekness and goodness can flourish only where and as the writer lets them; and Dickens makes the triumph of their virtues plausible because he does not allow them steadily to confront an earth where they would wither. That is why G. K. Chesterton was essentially right when

[1] Marcus, op. cit., p. 51.

he called the *Pickwick Papers* a 'supernatural story'. We may recoil a little from the fey implications of Chesterton's phrase, but it does remind us that Dickens's book is not really a mimetic work; and just because it isn't we do not have to fear that matters will work out badly. The *Pickwick Papers* is a beautiful dream of what might be. But Dickens's next work comes crashing down on to the earth itself and the dream of what might be is displaced by the nightmare of what in fact is.

Sketches by Boz gained most of its enormous reputation from the freshness of its comic studies of London life. Certainly, scenes such as 'The Parlour Orator' are outrageously funny, but they are matched by a very different sort of writing, as in the following passage from the 'Drunkard's Death':

> The alley into which he turned, might, for filth and misery, have competed with the darkest corner of this ancient sanctuary in its dirtiest and most lawless time. The houses, varying from two stories in height to four, were stained with every indescribable hue that long exposure to the weather, damp, and rottenness can impart to tenements composed originally of the roughest and coarsest materials. The windows were patched with paper, and stuffed with foulest rags; the doors were falling from their hinges; poles with lines on which to dry clothes, projected from every casement, and sounds of quarrelling or drunkenness issued from every room.

I quote this not because it is good – Dickens will plainly learn to do a greater deal better than content himself with such reach-me-down epithets – but because we too commonly make the mistake of forgetting how much of *Sketches by Boz* is taken up with scenes of the degradations of poverty and the sufferings of children. There is, for example, the famous 'Visit to Newgate', with its mention of a prostitute: 'one of those children, born and bred in neglect and vice, who have never known what childhood is'; and in the really magnificent 'Streets – Morning', Dickens mentions 'small office lads in large hats, who are made men before they are boys'. Or consider 'The Streets – Night', with its description of a wretched woman:

with the infant in her arms, round whose meagre form the remnant of her own scanty shawl is carefully wrapped [who] has been attempting to sing some popular ballad, in the hope of wringing a few pence from the compassionate passerby. A brutal laugh at her own weak voice is all she has gained. The tears fall thick and fast down her own pale face; the child is cold and hungry, and its low half-stifled wailing adds to the misery of its wretched mother, as she moans aloud, and sinks despairingly down, on a cold damp door-step.

Clearly, there would not be room for many such moments as these in the *Pickwick Papers*. But equally clearly, the note that Dickens sounds in the passages I have so far quoted would fit very well into *Oliver Twist*. What could not be found there is the sketch of a youthful offender in 'Criminal Courts':

A boy of thirteen is tried, say, for picking the pocket of some subject of his Majesty, and the offence is about as clearly proved as an offence can be. He is called upon for his defence, and contents himself with a little declamation about the jurymen and his country – asserts that all the witnesses have committed perjury, and hints that the police force generally have entered into a conspiracy 'again' him. However probable this statement may be, it fails to convince the Court, and some such scene as the following then takes place:

    Court: Have you any witnesses to speak to your character, boy?
    Boy: Yes, my Lord, fifteen gen'lm'n is a vaten outside, and vos a vaten all day yesterday, vich they told me the night afore my trial vos a comen' on.
    Court: Inquire for these witnesses.

Here, a stout beadle runs out, and vociferates for the witnesses at the very top of his voice; for you hear his cry grow fainter and fainter as he descends the steps into the court-yard below. After an absence of five minutes, he returns, very warm and hoarse, and informs the Court of what it had known perfectly well before – namely, that there are no such witnesses in attendance. Hereupon, the boy sets up a most awful howling; screws the lower part of the palms of his hands into the corners of his eyes; and endeavours to look the picture of injured innocence. The jury at once finds him 'guilty', and his endeavours to squeeze out a tear or two are re-doubled. The governor of the gaol then states, in reply to an inquiry from the bench, that the prisoner has been under his care twice before. This the urchin resolutely denies in some such terms as – 'S'elp me, gen'lm'n, I never vos in trouble afore – indeed, my Lord, I never vos. It's all a howen to my having a twin brother, vich has wrongfully got into trouble, and vich is so exactly like me, that no vun ever knows the difference atween us.'

This representation, like the defence, fails in producing the desired effect, and the boy is sentenced, perhaps, to seven years' transportation. Finding it impossible to excite compassion, he gives vent to his feelings in an imprecation bearing reference to the eyes of 'old big vig!' and as he declines to take the trouble of walking from the dock, is forthwith carried out, congratulating himself on having succeeded in giving everybody as much trouble as possible.

I have quoted this at length because I want to give the flavour of its comedy which, in the way it treats the boy criminal as quaintly funny, is aimed at a middle-class audience not likely to think of him as anything except deservedly punished. The boy bears of course a strong family resemblance to the artful Dodger and no doubt provided a source for Dickens when he came to the Dodger's own trial scene. But there is a crucial dif-ference between the trial of the *Sketches* and that of *Oliver Twist*, and we can indicate its nature by noting the Dodger's contemptu-ous remark that 'This ain't the shop for justice'. Those words blend with Dickens's own perception in the novel that justice is very much a class-matter, and although such a perception is occasionally hinted at in the *Sketches*, it is not present in the trial scene. Similarly, though the notion is fleetingly touched on in the *Pickwick Papers*, it is no part of Dickens's purpose there to investigate it. But as Arnold Kettle has pointed out, the percep-tion that justice is a class-matter becomes essential to the pattern of *Oliver Twist*, and because of it life's terrible disorders break in upon that enclosed world of fiction where justice can operate with rare impartiality. To risk putting it sensationally, the actuality of London destroys the dream of Dingley Dell, and where the *Pickwick Papers* was an idyll, *Oliver Twist* is Dickens's first sustained effort at realism.

I realize that to call *Oliver Twist* a realistic novel may seem merely perverse. There is after all some bad plotting to take account of, to say nothing of those excessive coincidences which give the novel a forced symmetry that is very unlike life. And in what sense can characters such as the Maylies, Losberne, Brownlow, Nancy, Monks, Oliver himself be thought of as realistic? Well, in some senses of course they are not realistic at all, and I admit that no matter how elastic the term may be it will hardly stretch enough to cover the Maylies, for example. This is a problem I shall take up later, but for now I want merely to suggest that *Oliver Twist* is a realistic novel in the very important sense that Dickens makes a deliberate effort to fashion an unliterary work. We may take our cue here from Harry Levin's essay on 'The Dissemination of Realism' which very sensibly argues that a great author may well start his career by producing a satire on previous writers in order to demonstrate their 'untruth'. And Levin goes on to say that where we encounter any such work we can regard it as essentially realistic, since

> while presenting its own substance as a guarantee of the factual ... [it] attacks the fictitious for having become synonymous with the untrue. It accuses literature of becoming too literary, of escaping into a sentimental daydream which cannot be dispelled except by shock treatments, sudden contacts with vulgar or brutal mundanities.[1]

Although Levin does not have *Oliver Twist* in mind, his description fits Dickens's novel particularly well. For in *Oliver Twist* Dickens attacks his own past writing, at least by implication. The novel offers no sure retreat from suffering as does the *Pickwick Papers*, and the Dodger's trial scene can justifiably be regarded as a truthful re-writing of the trial scene in the *Sketches*. But in addition, of course, *Oliver Twist* mounts a sustained attack on the Newgate novel.

[1] *Tri-Quarterly*, no 11, 1968, pp. 163–78.

There are two points common to most Newgate novels with which we need to concern ourselves. First, they present the criminal as at least partly created by society. Second, they romanticize the criminal. As Keith Hollingsworth points out in his study of the genre, Lytton's *Paul Clifford* is the first of the Newgate novels,[1] and in it we find law shown quite straightforwardly as an instrument of class-control; it makes criminals and then it punishes them. Lytton was particularly incensed by the fact that young offenders were treated in so brutal a fashion that they were literally forced into a life of crime. So, in chapter 8, he remarks that Paul has so far been

> honest in the face of circumstances. . . . Indeed, to let thee into a secret, it has been Paul's daring ambition to raise himself into a worthy member of the community. . . . Young people are apt, erroneously, to believe that it is a bad thing to be exceedingly wicked. The House of Correction is so called, because it is a place where so ridiculous a notion is invariably corrected.

Dickens would obviously sympathize with what Lytton says there. But he would hardly be likely to sympathize with the Newgate Novel's gambit of turning the criminal into a romantic hero, because such a trick is a way of allowing literature to impose on life. *Oliver Twist* is different from Newgate Novels because it tries to show the criminals for what and as they are, and if we may judge from the shock and discomfort of Dickens's first readers, he succeeded only too well. Henry Fox found the novel 'painful and revolting', and Lady Carlisle remarked, 'I know that there are such unfortunate beings as pick-pockets and street-walkers . . . but I own I do not much wish to hear what they say to one another.'[2] It is of course perfectly possible to protest that *Oliver Twist doesn't* tell you what the 'unfortunate beings' say to one another; the novel is by no means literal in its rendering of the Fagin gang's speeches, if only because it would not dare to be. On the other hand, I think most people will admit that the toning-down does not seriously interfere with the feeling

[1] *The Newgate Novel*, 1963, esp. pp. 69–71.
[2] Quoted by George H. Ford, *Dickens and his Readers*, 1965, p. 41.

of authenticity that Dickens communicates about the lives of Sikes, Charley Bates, the Dodger, and so on. From Sikes's oaths, for example, you can easily reconstruct the sort of thing he *would* have said.

Yet the odd thing is, that although many readers were shocked by the novel's realism, Thackeray claimed that it was not realistic enough. Indeed, he made exactly the charge against it that Dickens wanted to make against the Newgate novelists – of romanticizing the criminals. In *Catherine*, Thackeray allowed Issac (Ikey) Solomon – on whom Fagin had been based – to speak of the sentimental folly of those who think

> that in intellect and disposition all human beings are entirely equal, and that circumstance and education are the causes of the distinction and divisions that afterwards unhappily take place among them. . . . I, Ikey Solomons [*sic*], once had a dear little brother who could steal before he could walk. (ch 7)

Thackeray's attack might at this point seem to exclude Dickens, who certainly does not believe that Nancy and Sikes are equal, to say nothing of Oliver and the Dodger. All the same, we know that Thackeray had Dickens in mind, because in a passage that was cancelled when *Catherine* was published in book form, he said:

> No man has read that remarkable tale of *Oliver Twist* without being interested in poor Nancy and her murderer; and especially amused and tickled by the gambles of the Artful Dodger and his companions. The power of the writer is so amazing, that the reader at once becomes his captive, and must follow him withersoever he leads; and to what are we led? Breathlessly to watch all the crimes of Fagin, tenderly to deplore the errors of Nancy, to have for Bill Sikes a kind of pity and admiration, and an absolute love for the company of the Dodger. All these heroes stepped from the novel on to the stage; and the whole London public, from peers to chimney-sweeps, became interested about a set of ruffians whose occupation was thieving, murder, and prostitution. A most agreeable set of rascals, who have their virtues, too, but not good company for any man. We had better pass them by in decent silence; for as no writer can or dare tell the *whole* truth concerning them,

and faithfully explain their vices, there is no need to give *ex-parte* statements of their virtue.[1]

Thackeray's very oddly-phrased objection is essentially, I think, a response to Dickens's power. His argument is not that Dickens isn't realistic enough, even though occasionally he comes close to saying so; what really bothers him is that Dickens is too realistic for comfort. The criminals of *Oliver Twist* simply cannot be treated as dismissively as Lady Carlisle would wish. And indeed in the opening pages of *Catherine*, Thackeray complains about a clever class of novelists – and even if he mentions no names he has Dickens principally in mind – who 'create interest by making their rascals perform virtuous actions. Against these popular plans we here solemnly appeal. We say, let your rogues in novels act like rogues, and your honest men like honest men; don't let us have any juggling and thimble-rigging with virtue and vice . . .' Is Thackeray being ironic? Not at all. And yet his uncertainty of tone inevitably suggests that he himself half feels that Dickens may be right, and in its way his attack on *Oliver Twist* is an admission of the novel's ability to disturb its audience by means of a realism that destroys the comforting categories and evasions of literature.

Dickens himself, I think, knew how much he had achieved in the novel. That is why he offers his famous defence of Nancy (in the Preface to the 1841 edition):

> It is useless to discuss whether the conduct and character of the girl seems natural or unnatural, probable or improbable, right or wrong. It is true. Every man who has watched these melancholy shades of life knows it to be so. Suggested to my mind long ago – long before I dealt in fiction – by what I often saw of and read of in actual life around me, I have for years tracked it through many profligate and noisome ways, and found it still the same. From the first introduction of that poor wretch to her laying her bloody head upon the robber's breast, there is not one word exaggerated or overwrought. It is emphatically God's truth, for it is the truth he

[1] *Catherine* was first published in serial form in *Fraser's* (1839–40). The passage quoted comes from the concluding chapter for Jan–Feb, 1840.

leaves in such depraved and miserable hearts, the hope yet lingering behind, the last fair drop of water at the bottom of the dried-up weed-choked well. It involves the best and worst shades of our common nature, much of its ugliest hues and something of its most beautiful; it is a contradiction, an anomaly, an apparent impossibility, but it is a truth. I am glad to have had it doubted, for in that circumstance I find a sufficient assurance that it needed to be told.

Anyone determined to trip Dickens up could point out that in local details much is exaggerated and overwrought in the study of Nancy. Her mode of speech, for example, is often socially unplaced, as when she tells Rose that ' "When such as I, who have no certain roof but the coffin-lid, and no friend in sickness or death but the hospital nurse, set our rotten hearts on any man, and let him fill the place that has been a blank through our wretched lives, who can hope to cure us?" ' (ch 40) But underneath this melodramatic language there is usually a deep appeal to realism which sounds out as the girl says to Rose, ' "Oh, lady, lady! if there were more like you, there would be fewer like me – there would – there would!" ' Rose represents here the Pickwickian norm of the benevolent heart; but Pickwick never has to confront the sheer futility of benevolence. That, however, is what Nancy's words imply. They may carry praise for Rose, but more importantly they carry a condemnation of a society which creates criminals and against which the good individual is powerless. And with this point goes another, that Nancy's true nature is not the same as her class-identity. What she *is* differs from what she is seen to be. That is why, I think, she is given a manner of speech that belies her outer appearance. The same tactic applies to Oliver. And to object that Dickens is being unrealistic in employing such a tactic would be absurdly trivial – especially when we remember that what he is doing here is something quite new in the English novel.

Dickens's defence of Nancy is more than a defence of one character, however. At bottom, it amounts to the argument that the novel's readers simply will not accept that their discomfort with her – and for that matter with Sikes and Fagin – springs from a fundamental unwillingness to recognize what sort of a society they live in. And when Dickens says that he is certain that the truth about Nancy needs to be told, you almost hear the note of the crusading journalist determined to make his readers confront the truth. This is important. For *Oliver Twist* confronts its readers with a society which is rapidly becoming incapable of and unwilling to recognize itself and which in the process is becoming rapidly dehumanized. Dickens's readers are in the position of the respectable society of the novel itself. They are brought violently into contact with a world they would rather ignore; and the novelist comes near to anticipating Margaret Schlegel's cry, 'Do you see the connection? Stupid, hypocritical, cruel.' Some words of Mill's are relevant here. In *Civilization*, published in 1836, Mill remarked that one of the effects of civilization is that 'the spectacle, and even the very idea of pain, is kept more and more out of the sight of those classes who enjoy in their fulness the benefits of civilization'. And he goes on:

In our own time, the necessity of personal collision between one person and another is, comparatively speaking, almost at an end. All those necessary portions of the business of society which oblige any person to be the immediate agent or ocular witness of the infliction of pain, are delegated by common consent to peculiar and narrow classes: to the judge, the soldier, the surgeon, the butcher, and the executioner. To most people in easy circumstances, any pain (except accident, disease or emotional disturbance) is rather a thing known of than actually experienced. This is much more emphatically true in the more refined classes, and as refinement advances: for it is in keeping as far as possible out of sight, not actual pain, but all that can be offensive or disagreeable to the most sensitive person, that refinement exists. We may remark too, that this is possible only by a perfection of mechanical arrangement impracticable in any but a high state of civilization.[1]

If Dickens read that, as is at least possible, he would have derived a grim amusement from Mill's idea of high civilization, and even

[1] In *Essays on Politics and Culture*, ed. Himmelferb, 1963, p. 58.

more from the notion Mill advances a little later, that because the refined classes do not have to witness pain they are therefore 'more amiable and humane'. For Dickens, high civilization has much to do with the creation of pain because it is part of the process of class-separateness on which a great deal of pain is founded. And I do not think it excessive to suggest that most of Dickens's major writing is a prolonged attempt to bring his audience to confront – and at least vicariously experience – the pain it would otherwise know of only if it so desired (one thinks again of Lady Carlisle. How would Mill cope with her indifference to poverty and suffering?) The story of Dickens being smuggled into Hatton Garden Office so that he could study Mr Laing and then confront his readers with Fang, provides an instance of that reporter-turned-novelist who is determined to shock an audience in easy circumstances out of its complacency, to make it see connections and recognize responsibilities.

To speak of a novel in this way may seem to imply that it isn't a novel at all, but propaganda or mere journalism. Yet *Oliver Twist* is very certainly a novel. The point is that Dickens's method is possible because he had a relationship with his audience that is unique in the history of the novel and because he found marvellous ways of using that relationship to the full. And having said that much I want to turn and look much more closely at the novel itself.

In chapter 34, there is an incident which signifies a great deal about Dickens's deepest interests in *Oliver Twist*, and I shall have to quote from it at some length. Oliver at this moment is in his own room at the Maylie's house in the country:

> Oliver knew, perfectly well, that he was in his own little room, that his books were lying on the table before him, that the sweet air was stirring among the creeping plants outside. And yet he was asleep. Suddenly the scene changed; the air became close and confined; and he thought, with a glow of terror, that he was in the Jew's house again. There sat the hideous old man in his accustomed corner, pointing at him and whispering to another man, with his face averted, who sat beside him.

'Hush, my dear!' he thought he heard the Jew say; 'it is he, sure enough. Come away.'

'He!' the other man seemed to answer; 'could I mistake him, think you. . . . If you buried him fifty feet deep, and took me across his grave, I fancy I should know, if there wasn't a mark above it, that he lay buried there!'

The man seemed to say this with such a dreadful hatred that Oliver awoke with the fear and started up.

Good heaven! what was that which sent the blood tingling to his heart, and deprived him of his voice, and of power to move! There – there – at the window – close before him – so close that he could have almost touched him before starting back, with his eyes peering into the room and meeting his, there stood the Jew! And beside him, white with rage or fear, or both, were the scowling features of the very man who had accosted him in the churchyard. (ch 34)

It is not uncommon for critics to argue that this moment typifies Dickens's failure to control his plot. The argument runs that although the scene may have an immediate shock-effect, Dickens has to pay dearly for this when he comes at the end of the novel to try and tidy up the loose ends, since the best he can do is offer a very perfunctory explanation of how Fagin and Monks got where they did. But such an argument seems to me quite beside the point. And I do not find myself any more persuaded by an alternative critical approach, from which the scene is viewed as an indulgence in the Romantic interest in the waking dream, though I certainly think that without such an interest the episode could not have been invented. No, there are two very important ways in which this scene goes to the heart of the novel, and they deserve to be analysed a little.

In the first place, we may note that Oliver's dream of Fagin is the nearest he comes to corruption, in the sense – and it is a very oblique one – that it offers a hint that even in the country the boy's mind may be infected by Fagin's world. (Is Fagin *really* there or has he succeeded in stamping himself on Oliver's soul?) Elsewhere, of course, Oliver easily resists contamination. It is true that at the end of chapter 18 Dickens notes how 'the wily old Jew had the boy in his toils. Having prepared his mind, by solitude and gloom, to prefer any society to the companionship of his own sad thoughts in such a dreary place, he was now instilling into his soul the poison which he hoped would blacken it and change it for ever.' But Fagin's grip is remarkably inept, and at the end of the next chapter he is positively unmanned by seeing Oliver in a dreamless and innocent sleep, 'in the guise [the body] wears when life has just departed, when a young and gentle spirit has, but an instant, fled to Heaven, and the gross air of the world has not had time to breathe upon the changing dust it hallowed.' And later, Fagin admits that ' "I saw it was not easy to train him to the business . . . he was not like other boys in the same circumstances." ' Only in his waking dream is Oliver disturbed by the poison that Fagin has laboured to instil 'into his soul', and we might compare his disturbance with Eve's; they are both essentially innocent. Oliver, in fact, cannot be vitally corrupted; he knows evil for what it is and he knows it through good.

Here we come to another frequent objection against the novel. Granted that Oliver is essentially innocent, critics say, this only goes to show either that Dickens is seeing in him a justification for his own aloof attitude to the other boys at Warren's blacking factory, or that he is an unrealistic conception and Dickens stands convicted of exactly the charge that Thackeray brought against him. Plausible though it may at first seem, I think this objection can in some measure be met once we ask why Dickens should choose the particular moment he does to reveal that Oliver's soul cannot be harmed by evil. And we have to start by realizing that the novelist takes very seriously Oliver's being a child of nature. Nature is a word that receives a good deal of attention in *Oliver Twist* as it does in most of Dickens's novels, and later in the chapter I shall have something to say about Oliver as the natural child of a natural relationship. Here, however, I want to concentrate on Dickens's hero as a Rousseauistic child of nature.

To begin with, we must note that when Monks and Fagin appear to Oliver he is in the country and happier than he has

ever been. And this is not merely a matter of sweet air and climb-
ing plants; Dickens goes out of his way in this section of the book
to insist on the educative and healing powers of nature. No
doubt much of this passionate identification of Oliver and nature
goes back to the novelist's own childhood. Edgar Johnson calls
his chapter on the young Dickens at Rochester 'The Happy
Time', and he provides quite enough evidence of Dickens's
rambles with his father and delighted knowledge of the countryside to persuade us that those years were indeed happy.[1] They
must have looked particularly beautiful seen through a perspective created by the blacking factory, and there is a possible hint
of that retrospect when we read that 'Oliver, whose days had
been spent among squalid crowds and in the midst of noise and
brawling, seemed to enter on a new existence there.' (ch 32) But
no matter what autobiographical material may have been fed
into the study of Oliver, Dickens's interest in him is proper to
the novel. As a child of nature Oliver's new existence distin-
guishes him from those who live 'in the great city, pent 'mid
cloisters dim'. And as Coleridge promises his son that

> all seasons shall be sweet to thee,
> Whether the summer clothe the general earth
> With greenness, or the redbreast sit and sing
> Betwixt the tufts of snow on the bare branch
> Of mossy apple-tree, while the nigh thatch
> Smokes in the sun-thaw;

so Oliver finds the change of seasons equally sweet:

> Spring flew swiftly by, and summer came. If the village had been
> beautiful at first, it was now in the full glow and luxuriance of its
> richness. The great trees, which had looked shrunken and bare in
> the earlier months, had now burst into strong life and health and,
> stretching forth their green arms over the thirsty ground, converted
> open and naked spots into choice nooks, where there was a deep
> and pleasant shade from which to look upon the wide prospect,

[1] Edgar Johnson: *Charles Dickens: His Tragedy and Triumph* 2 vols (1952).
Vol. I, esp. pp. 14–19. Henceforward this will be referred to as *Johnson*.

steeped in sunshine, which lay stretched beyond. The earth had donned her mantle of brightest green, and shed her richest perfumes abroad. It was the prime and vigour of the year; all things were glad and flourishing. (ch 33)

Not very good, to be sure; in fact the diction of this passage is uncomfortably reminiscent of the 'Excelente Balade of Charitie': ' 'Twas now the pride, the manhood of the year,/And eke the ground was decked in its most deft aumere.' Had Dickens been reading Chatterton? Never mind, it is more important to notice how insistent he is that Oliver's nature is somehow made believable because of his contact with the natural world. As here:

Who can describe the pleasure and delight, the peace of mind and soft tranquillity, the sickly boy felt in the balmy air and among the green hills and rich woods of an inland village! Who can tell how scenes of peace and quietude sink into the minds of pain-worn dwellers in close and noisy places, and carry their own freshness deep into their jaded hearts!

Who can describe? Wordsworth, of course. Behind Dickens's words one hears very plainly indeed the famous lines about the forms of beauty that

> have not been to me,
> As is a landscape to a blind man's eye:
> But oft, in lonely rooms, and mid the din
> Of towns and cities, I have owed to them
> In hours of weariness, sensations sweet,
> Felt in the blood, and felt along the heart,
> And passing even into my purer mind
> With tranquil restoration: –

It is true that Wordsworth's involvement with the Wye leads him into areas of speculation where Dickens would not care to follow; but at the very least the two writers share a habit of identifying a profound spiritual health with a life that is lived away from the city. Just how Rousseauistic this is hardly needs emphasizing, nor how relevant to the total meaning of *Oliver Twist*. For Dickens's novel is in the last analysis about improper evaluations of human worth. 'What an excellent example of the power of dress, young Oliver Twist was! . . . he was badged and ticketted, and fell into his place at once . . .' (ch 1) Dress makes for the improper evaluation. The proper one is so strongly reminiscent of Rousseau that I think we need here to recall Kent's picture of the melancholy man, which, in quoting in the introduction, I pointed out owed much to Rousseau. The melancholy man is

> little concerned with the judgement of others, with their opinion of what is good or true . . . He regards changes of fashion with indifference and their glitter with contempt. He has a lofty sense of the dignity of human nature. He esteems himself and regards man as a creature deserving of respect. He suffers no abject subservience and breathes the noble air of freedom. To him all chains are abhorrent, from the gilded fetters worn at court to the heavy-irons of the galley-slave.[1]

In a very real sense Dickens is Kant's melancholy man, and his study of Oliver is the first in a long line of explorations of people whose true identity is denied by a society which heaps on them the chains of class-identity.

But more than that, Oliver is denied the noble air of freedom. The matter of education becomes important here, and although what Rousseau has to say on the subject obviously applies in greater part to the studies of Paul Dombey, Bitzer and Arthur Clennam, it is worth quoting here because perfectly relevant to Oliver. The child should be taught to be independent, Rousseau says:

> instead of making him serve the purposes of others, we should teach him to think of himself as an end and to act in accordance with this idea. Only when he has become in this sense inwardly free is he to enter society, and only then will he be able to contribute to it in the right way; for only the free man is the true citizen.[2]

[1] Quoted by E. Cassirer in *Rousseau, Kant and Goethe*, 1963, p. 12.
[2] Ibid., p. 32–3.

Is Oliver inwardly free? Yes, I think so. Or rather, his ability to correctly identify evil for what it is, is meant to suggest he cannot really be made to serve the purposes of others. (He is inept at doing anything that is evil, as Fagin admits, though we must accept that what Oliver and Dickens identify as evil is likely to be a product of a wicked society.) He is free because he is the child of nature, the boy whose true kinship is with the natural world.

One might of course object against what I have said that Rousseau's dream of freedom is essentially prescriptive and that though very desirable is also very unlikely, so that Oliver as child of nature emerges as a recommendation rather than a possibility. In other words, Oliver's role as I have been discussing it involves a lessening of the novel's realism. The objection can be met only if we recognize that Dickens himself is powerfully aware of the terrible vulnerability of the sort of innocence he wants his hero to embody. That is why Fagin and Monks appear to Oliver in the waking-dream; it is as though Dickens plays with the possibility of their having corrupted him, and while rejecting it none the less accepts their terrific power to reach out towards him. We might take the episode to imply that no matter how far you retreat from the rottenness you can never get right away from it. It is an idea that Dickens plumbs in novel after novel and always with an increasing subtlety and range of imaginative grasp, so that by the time he comes to *Little Dorrit* the noble air of freedom is itself merely a dream and there can be no pastoral retreat which images freedom from the city's spreading corruption. In *Oliver Twist* there is such a retreat, but the fact that it can be threatened makes the second point I want to attend to about the episode of Oliver's confrontation with Fagin and Monks. The boy's free world is always menaced.

But what is the free world? Clearly it isn't the one that Rousseau envisaged, for although it takes in the natural life it has become very much associated with middle-class values; the 'free' world is the world of the Maylies, of money that can buy a rural retreat far from the corruptions which even so come to threaten it. And in the notion of a 'safe' rural world which is inexplicably terrorized by Fagin and Monks' appearance it is perfectly possible to see a prolepsis of the dream of revolutionary horror that infects much of the literature of the 1840s.[1] Rousseau's prescription for avoiding corruption was to withdraw from society; Dickens's realism has much to do with his recognition that such a withdrawal is impossible. The evil that London embodies (and it is fair to see Dickens as taking London as the obvious Romantic image of social malaise as well as the plain fact) reaches even into the protected idyllic world of an inland village. In the world that *Oliver Twist* studies and presents, humanity must perforce prey on itself, and the natural child is threatened by Fagin and Monks, who are social beings.

The image of social malignity irresistibly spreading into the natural world is, of course, most marvellously presented in the episode of Sikes's and Oliver's journey from London to Chertsey, which is the more horrific because it is charted with such meticulous accuracy: Kensington, Hammersmith, Chiswick, Kew Bridge, Brentford, Hampton, Sunbury, Halliford, Shepperton – the list of towns the couple pass through make this a real horror, as opposed to mere fiction; and I am quite ready to believe the story of the man at Sunbury who became so caught up in his reading of the episode that he hastily drew the blinds in case Sikes should think of trying to break into his house. The episode is one of those many confrontations that the novel enacts; and it is followed by another one, equally important in the present context. After Oliver has been rescued from Sikes and is recovering from his injuries, he goes out riding with Losberne and suddenly recognizes the house where he had been taken by Sikes before the attempted robbery. Losberne runs to the door and begins hammering on it:

> 'Halloa?' said a little ugly hump-backed man, opening the door so suddenly that the doctor, from the very impetus of his last kick, nearly fell forward into the passage. 'What's the matter here?'

[1] I have written about this in my essay on 'Mrs. Gaskell and Brotherhood' in *Tradition and Tolerance in Nineteenth Century Fiction* (1966).

'Matter!' exclaimed the other, collaring him without a moment's reflection. 'A good deal. Robbery is the matter.'

'There'll be murder the matter, too,' replied the hump-backed man, coolly, 'if you don't take your hands off. Do you hear me?'

'I hear you,' said the doctor, giving his captive a hearty shake. 'Where's – confound the fellow, what's his rascally name – Sikes; that's it. Where's Sikes, you thief?'

The hump-backed man stared, as if in an excess of amazement and indignation; then, twisting himself dexterously from the doctor's grasp, growled forth a volley of horrid oaths and retired into the house. Before he could shut the door, however, the doctor had pressed into the parlour, without a word of parley. He looked anxiously around; not a vestige of anything, animate or inanimate; not even the description of the cupboards, answered Oliver's description. (ch 32)

Although the episode is never cleared up, I do not think we can feel the moment represents a failure on Dickens's part. For it seems remarkably symptomatic of the 'good' world's failure to control its fate. No matter how much Losberne may bluster, his impotence in the face of the enemy is what we become most aware of; the Quilp-like dwarf is terribly ominous because he is so mysteriously unknowable, and Dickens even derives a certain dark amusement from the doctor's raging stupidity. As a good middle-class man Losberne perhaps deserves to be victimized by the sort of world which he has helped to bring about. For *Oliver Twist* concerns itself with sets of worlds that threaten each other because, so it seems, they are creations of a society that has lost any sense of shared purpose or identity. Indeed, the novel is very close to the insight that we find in Blake's 'London' – as for that matter many of Dickens's novels are. As Blake's harlot is created by a class-ridden society and gives her disease back to the man who uses but does not marry her, so Fagin and Monks carry their diseased selves into a world which tries to deny them.

It is when we come to register Dickens's rendering of social apartness, its manifestations and consequences, that we inevitably come upon the most frequently noted characteristic of *Oliver*

Twist. The novel inaugurates what it is now customary to call Dickens's sense of an atomistic universe, of worlds that exist totally distinct from and unknown to each other. (Oliver's being led blindfold through the streets of London becomes the perfect image of how ignorant of each other the worlds are and what enormous distances separate them.) In this respect, the novel's topographical precision is important because by means of it Dickens localizes and makes realistic the different worlds and suggests the feel of their self-containment and mutual unknowability. (Lady Carlisle's wish not to know about pick-pockets and street-walkers neatly enough demonstrates Dickens's point.) But *Oliver Twist* is nevertheless determined to confront its audience with worlds that will not go away no matter how much they may be ignored. Eric Hobsbawm has pointed out that during the period 1820–40, urban development

> was a gigantic process of class segregation, which pushed the new labouring poor into great morasses of misery outside the centres of government and business and the newly specialised areas of the bourgeoisie. The almost universal European division of a 'good' west end and a 'poor' east end of large cities developed in this period.[1]

The picaresque element of *Oliver Twist* provides Dickens with the opportunities he needs for confronting his audience with those areas of society from which they have escaped or about which they are plainly ignorant. That is why Oliver is so important to the novel's purpose; he can introduce the reader to such different and concealed worlds as the poorhouse, Sowerberry's, Fagin's part of London, the courts, the condemned cell; and all with the innocent eye which guarantees truth and details the horror. As for example, when the Dodger first takes him to Fagin:

> A dirtier and more wretched place he had never seen. The street was very narrow and muddy, and the air was impregnated with filthy odours. There were a good many small shops; but the only

[1] E. J. Hobsbawm, *The Age of Revolution*, 1964, p. 242.

stock in trade appeared to be heaps of children, who, even at that time of night, were crawling in and out at the doors, or screaming from the inside. (ch 8)

Of course, the eye isn't quite as innocent as it should be; Oliver would hardly be in a position to express shock over children playing 'at that time of night'. Even so, episode after episode testifies to Dickens's wish to confront his readers with horrors that the pattern of their lives has made it easy for them to avoid. And he also confronts them with individuals for whom there can be no escape from the horror. One of the most moving moments in the novel is when Nancy tries to get away from her world:

When the girl got into the open street, she sat down upon a doorstep and seemed, for a few moments, wholly bewildered and unable to pursue her way. Suddenly she arose, and hurrying on, in a direction quite opposite to that in which Sikes was awaiting her return, quickened her pace until it gradually resolved into a violent run. After completely exhausting herself she stopped to take breath and, as if suddenly recollecting herself, and deploring her inability to do something she was bent upon, wrung her hands and burst into tears.

It might be that her tears relieved her, or that she felt the full hopelessness of her condition; but she turned back, and hurr[ied] with nearly as great rapidity in the contrary direction. (ch 39)

It is a brilliant image whose meaning is made explicit later when Nancy admits that ' "I am chained to my old life." '

But as I have already pointed out, the life to which Nancy is chained does not truly identify her worth. And yet how shall her worth be identified? By a selfless devotion that proves the very opposite of looking after number one, we may say; and it is true that the girl is an important image of good struggling to assert itself over evil circumstances that are none of its making. But Dickens knows that to present Nancy sympathetically is to invite the scepticism of his audience. That is why, I think, he confronts them with dress as the badge of worth which they would be so ready to accept. 'Society is founded upon cloth'

Tëufelsdrock remarks in *Sartor Resartus*, and one of the achievements of *Oliver Twist* is to give an entirely new credibility to his
assertion. Oliver is 'an excellent example of the power of dress'
whose worth is denied by the badge of his cloth. And from the
gentleman who is identified only by his white waistcoat, through
the doctor whose boots creak in 'a very important and wealthy
manner', to Bumble whose virility is identified with his cocked
hat, gold-laced coat and staff, and who is unmanned when he
loses them, society is identified by its clothes. And so it can quite
justifiably be victimized:

> 'Stop a minute, my dear,' said the Jew, producing a little
> covered basket. 'Carry that in one hand. It looks more respectable,
> my dear.'
> 'Give her a door-key to carry in her t'other one, Fagin,' said
> Sikes, 'it looks real and genivine like.'
> 'Yes, yes, my dear, so it does,' said the Jew, hanging a large
> street-door key on the forefinger of the young lady's right hand.
> 'There; very good! Very good indeed, my dear!' said the Jew,
> rubbing his hands. (ch 13)

If the clothes imagery of the novel is obvious it is no more so
than the animal imagery. For as respectable society exists by
cloth so it becomes dehumanized, incapable of recognizing and
therefore living by the sort of humane values that Nancy struggles to assert. Hence we find a magistrate called Fang, Sowerberry of the vixenish countenance, Sikes who looks like his dog,
Fagin, who seems 'like some loathsome reptile, engendered in
the slime and darkness through which he moved, crawling forth,
by night, in search of some rich offal for a meal' (ch 19). I do not
think we need to worry over the obviousness of such imagery.
Nor do we need to apologize for it. It is a perfectly acceptable,
highly intelligent and resourceful way of identifying the
horror of a society which has so lost its capacity for human inter-
dependence that it hunts, savages, destroys. I think of the crowd
that chases Oliver, that bays for Sikes's blood, that brings down
Fagin:

'The officers fought like devils, or they'd have torn him away. He was down once, but they made a ring round him, and fought their way along. You should have seen how he looked about him, all muddy and bleeding, and clung to them as if they were his dearest friends. I can see 'em now, not able to stand upright with the pressing of the mob, and dragging him along amongst 'em; I can see the people jumping up, one behind the other, and snarling with their teeth and making at him; I can see the blood upon his hair and beard, and hear the cries with which the women worked themselves into the centre of the crowd at the street corner, and swore they'd tear his heart out!' (ch 50)

This image of humanity preying on itself is central to the novel and is reinforced by the persistent images of stealth, secrecy and darkness. Fagin moves about at night, 'gliding stealthily along'; Sikes and Oliver creep towards Chertsey; Nancy moves stealthily to her night-appointment with Rose, and Noah even more stealthily follows her. Again, this imagery is perfectly obvious and has often been pointed out. But it deserves comment, both because of its genuine poetic intensity – and if we do not call it that I don't know what we *can* call it – and also because it cumulatively builds up a suggestion of a vital corruption of human relationships, which can be called obvious only in the sense of the terrific force with which Dickens communicates it. Time and again in *Oliver Twist* love and friendship are brought down to a matter of self-interest. At one extreme there is the grotesque comedy of Bumble wondering whether he should marry Mrs Corney:

Mr Bumble's conduct on being left to himself was rather inexplicable. He opened the closet, counted the tea-spoons, weighed the sugar-tongs, closely inspected a silver milk-pot to ascertain that it was of the genuine metal, and having satisfied his curiosity on these points, put on his cocked hat corner-wise, and danced with much gravity four distinct times round the table. Having gone through this very extraordinary performance, he took off the cocked hat again and, spreading himself before the fire with his back towards it, seemed to be mentally engaged in taking an exact inventory of the furniture. (ch 23)

And although there is no point in detailing all the various examples that the novel has to offer of this corruption of relationships, we may at least notice the hideous extreme of the old woman who confesses on her death-bed to having robbed Oliver's mother on *her* death-bed, ' "I robbed her, so I did! She wasn't cold – I tell you she wasn't cold, when I stole it!" ' (ch 24).

Marriage, love, friendship, parents and children – the abiding Dickens concern that has its first utterance in *Oliver Twist* – it hardly matters where we turn in the novel, we find the same horror of people selling themselves into bondage, or being sold into it. Oliver has no parents but he has any number of surrogate fathers, including Bumble, Sowerberry, Fagin, Gamfield and the Board; and all of them see in him the chance of money.

> 'So you won't let me have him, gen'lmen?' said Mr. Gamfield, pausing at the door.
> 'No,' replied Mr. Limbkins; 'at least, as it's a nasty business, we think you ought to take something less than the premium offered.'
> Mr. Gamfield's countenance brightened as, with a quick step, he returned to the table and said:
> 'What'll you give, gen'lmen? Come! Don't be too hard on a poor man. What'll you give?'
> 'I should say, three pound ten was plenty,' said Mr. Limbkins.
> 'Ten shillings too much,' said the gentleman in the white waistcoat.
> 'Come!' said Gamfield; 'say four pound, gen'lmen. Say four pound, and you've got rid of him for good and all. There!'
> 'Three pound ten,' repeated Mr. Limbkins, firmly.
> 'Come! I'll split the difference, gen'lmen,' urged Mr. Gamfield. 'Three pound fifteen.'
> 'Not a farthing more,' was the firm reply of Mr. Limbkins. (ch 3)

What is worth noting about the sheer inhumanity of this barter is the concentrated power of Dickens's sense of outrage that communicates itself through the dialogue and the whiplash contempt that comes through in Mr Limbkins's 'firm reply'. There's courage and probity for you!

Elsewhere the concern with the prostitution of human relationships can be scaldingly funny. ' "I sold myself," said Mr.
Bumble, "for six teaspoons, a pair of sugar-tongs, and a milk-pot,
with a small quantity of second-hand furniture and twenty
pound in money. I went very reasonable. Cheap, dirt cheap!" '
(ch 37) Indeed, if Nancy is the most obvious example of personal
relationships reduced to money, we should notice that Dickens
uses her to force the paradox, that 'respectable' society has little of
her sense of love and loyalty. ' "There are many of us," ' she
tells Brownlow, ' "who have kept the same courses together,
and I'll not turn upon them who might – any of them – have
turned upon me, but didn't, bad as they are." ' (ch. 46)

Again, it is hardly worth while detailing the different kinds
and sheer weight of unnatural relationships in *Oliver Twist*: Sikes
and Nancy, Fagin and his boys, Noah and Charlotte, Bumble
and Mrs Corney; in their different ways they all embody the
theme, and at its centre are Monks and Oliver, the Cain and Abel
of the novel. When Brownlow confronts Monks and unravels
the plot to destroy Oliver, he quite plainly becomes Dickens's
spokesman:

> I know that of the wretched marriage into which family pride, and
> the most sordid and narrowest of all ambition, forced your un-
> happy father when a mere boy, you were the sole and most
> unnatural issue . . . I also know the misery, the slow torture, the
> protracted anguish of that ill-assorted union. I know how list-
> lessly and wearily each of that wretched pair dragged on their
> heavy chain through a world that was poisoned to them both. I
> know how cold formalities were succeeded by open taunts, how
> indifference gave place to dislike, dislike to hate, and hate to
> loathing, until at last they wrenched the clanking bond asunder
> and, retiring a wide space apart, carried each a galling fragment, of
> which nothing but death could break the rivets, to hide it in a new
> gaiety beneath the gayest looks they could assume. (ch 49)

Monks symbolizes the plague that blights the marriage-hearse.
He is one 'in whom all evil passions, vice, and profligacy festered
till they found a vent in a hideous disease' which makes his face

'an index' to his mind. Even his assumed name, with its gothic-horror echo, hints at perverted sexual desires concealed under the cloak of celibacy. And in his spectacular disease, Monks helps direct our attention to one of the novel's most notable features, its obsession with death.

It is the unnaturalness of death in *Oliver Twist* which is so striking. One thinks, for example, of the workhouse hags watching over the dying woman who stole from Oliver's dying mother:

> 'Did she drink the hot wine the doctor said she was to have?' demanded the first.
>
> 'I tried to get it down,' rejoined the other. 'But her teeth were tight set, and she clenched the mug so hard that it was as much as I could do to get it back again. So *I* drank it, and it did me good!' . . .
>
> 'I mind the time,' said the first speaker, 'when she would have done the same, and made rare fun of it afterwards.' (ch 24)

Or there is the calculated brutality of the scene where Oliver as an undertaker's apprentice has to witness death:

> 'I tell you,' said the man, clenching his hands, and stamping furiously on the floor – 'I tell you I won't have her put into the ground. She couldn't rest there. The worms would worry her – not eat her – she is so worn away.'
>
> The undertaker offered no reply to this raving, but producing a tape from his pocket, knelt down for a moment by the side of the body.
>
> 'Ah!' said the man, bursting into tears and sinking on his knees at the feet of the dead woman; 'kneel down, kneel down – kneel round her, every one of you, and mark my words! I say she was starved to death. I never knew how bad she was till the fever came upon her, and then her bones were starting through the skin. There was neither fire nor candle; she died in the dark – in the dark! She couldn't even see her children's faces, though we heard her gasping out their names. I begged for her in the streets and they sent me to prison. When I came back she was dying; and all the blood in my heart has dried up, for they starved her to death. I swear it before the God that saw it! They starved her!' He twined his hands in his

hair and, with a loud scream, rolled grovelling upon the floor, his eyes fixed, and the foam covering his lips.

The terrified children cried bitterly; but the old woman, who had hitherto remained as quiet as if she had been wholly deaf to all that passed, menaced them into silence. Having unloosed the cravat of the man who still remained extended on the ground, she tottered towards the undertaker.

'She was my daughter,' said the old woman, nodding her head in the direction of the corpse and speaking with an idiotic leer, more ghastly than even the presence of death in such a place. 'Lord, lord! Well, it *is* strange that I who gave birth to her, and was a woman then, should be alive and merry now, and she lying there, so cold and stiff! Lord, lord! – to think of it; it's as good as a play – as good as a play!' (ch 5)

I would not defend every word in that scene, but even so it seems to me a great one and also entirely new to the English novel. Its radical quality does not lie in its exactness of social detail, but in the terrific imaginative insight by which Dickens perceives the malign horror of life as pointless suffering and forces his audience to perceive it. Dodger's contemptuous remark, 'This ain't the shop for justice', recalls us to Fang, to the silly old magistrate who quite by chance sees that Oliver is terrified of Gamfield, and to Beadledom; but above all it recalls us to the man who cries 'I begged for her in the streets and they sent me to prison.' Dickens compels his audience to confront the horror of that, and the equal horror of the old woman whose condition has drained her of humanity. What Engels was to say in *The Condition of the Working Class in England in 1844* applies perfectly to the hidden world that Dickens here rips open.

'In the working-man's dwellings', Engels wrote:

no cleanliness, no convenience, and consequently no comfortable family life is possible; . . . in such dwellings only a physically degenerate race, robbed of all humanity, degraded, reduced morally and physically to bestiality, could feel comfortable and at home.[1]

---

[1] *The Condition of the Working Class* (edn of 1892), p. 76.

Given the presentation of the old crone who cackles ' "It's as good as a play – as good as a play!" ' it is perhaps not surprising that Marx should praise Dickens to Engels as a novelist 'whose graphic and eloquent pages have issued to the world more political and social truths than have been uttered by all the professional politicians, publicists, and moralists put together.'[1] And yet the real audacity of Dickens's imagination lies in the exact words that the old woman is made to use. She romanticizes life into art, just as the Newgate novelists do, and one senses that hovering behind her exclamation is Dickens's own sardonic challenge to his audience to try and turn the reality he is showing them into art.

The challenge goes out again when we come to Nancy's death, the most brutal thing in the novel. The detail is unsparing. 'He struck a light, kindled a fire, and thrust the club in to it. There was hair upon the end, which blazed and shrunk into a light cinder and, caught by the air, whirled up the chimney.' (ch 48) Sikes's flight and suffering are no more than he deserves and we may sit back to enjoy his just punishment. Yet when we come face to face with the man's anguish, we find ourselves confronted with mental torment of so extreme a kind that we are compelled to recognize how human the murderer in fact is. And we are shocked out of any feelings of moral complacency into a fearfully disquieting recognition that he cannot simply be disowned:

> If he shut out the sight, there came the room with every well-known object – some, indeed, that he would have forgotten if he had gone over its contents from memory – each in its accustomed place. The body was in *its* place, and its eyes were as he saw them when he stole away. He got up, and rushed into the field without. The figure was behind him. He re-entered the shed, and shrunk down once more. The eyes were there, before he had laid himself along. (ch 48)

There is nowhere in English fiction that Dickens could have gone for that. True, there was a well-established literature of gallows-repentence, but it is either crudely moralistic or irreverently

[1] Quoted in Peter Demetz's *Marx, Engels and the Poets*, 1956, p. 45.

ribald and of no use whatsoever to somebody who wants to explore the nature of mental suffering. The only writer who could have been of use was Crabbe, with whose work Dickens was obviously familiar and who had dealt powerfully and at length with the mental agonies of a murderer in his study of Peter Grimes. The passage where Grimes tells of how he is haunted by the ghosts of his father and the apprentices for whose deaths he was responsible is certainly very remarkable, and I think there is a good chance that it provided Dickens with something like a source for Sikes's sufferings. Yet to say this is not to deny the force of the novelist's originality. If anything the comparison between Grimes and Sikes helps to underline Dickens's radical greatness. For Crabbe is reasonably sure that Grimes deserves to suffer, and although the murderer's agonies may move us to pity there is nothing in the poem to hint that they are not just. But with Sikes we are made terribly uncomfortable by our discovery of his capacity for suffering. If only he could simply be written off as one of those 'degraded, reduced morally and physically to bestiality'. But he can't, and the result is that when the mob comes for him we are in no position to feel satisfaction at the conventional propriety of a murderer brought to justice. On the contrary, we are appalled at the mindless brutality of those – including Losberne – who take pleasure in so relentlessly pursuing him. 'Some roared to those who were nearest to set the house on fire; others roared to the officers to shoot him dead. . . . 'They have him now,' cried a man on the nearest bridge. 'Hurrah!' (ch 50) Sikes's sufferings may be just, but we cannot possibly identify ourselves with the mob that wants him to suffer. Our sympathies and allegiances are confused and shaken, and that they should be is a triumph for Dickens's art of confrontation.

In contrast, Rose Maylie's recovery from a near-certain death is open to a good deal of criticism. It may well be, of course, that the decision to let her recover was partly influenced by Mary Hogarth's sudden and shattering death, and Edgar Johnson says firmly that the novelist 'found himself unable to carry out his original intention of having Rose Maylie die. He could not bear to describe the fair young creature breathing her last amid the blossoms of May.'[1] I do not know, however, whether we can justly accuse Dickens of changing his mind, because Rose's recovery fits very snugly into the theme of the persistent and indomitable powers of life in a 'natural' context which I have already suggested as lying behind Oliver's recuperation. But we can certainly protest that the girl's recovery is too obvious a piece of symbolism: society creates death; nature is life-enhancing. This may seem an odd protest since I have previously praised much of the novel's obviousness, but the point is that although dress and animal imagery, unnatural relations and unnatural deaths are in themselves obvious features of the novel and are handled with a certain starkness, taken altogether they build into a complex study of what Carlyle had called the 'Physical derangements of Society', whereas the symbolism of nature's recuperative powers comes in a bit too pat. At the very least, we have to say that the prescriptiveness of Rose's recovery feels a bit forlorn.

But what then of Oliver's powers of life? Some critics find him too obviously symbolic to be either true or interesting, but I am not sure that this is fair. For although the symbolism of his being the product of a natural union *is* obvious – his father, we are told, was 'the object of the first, true, ardent, only passion of a guileless girl', and Oliver himself is an 'innocent and unoffending child' – we are surely shown enough in the way of unnatural unions for us to accept that Dickens has put Oliver in justifiable symbolic opposition to Monks, the man associated with death and disease. And since Oliver's mother was Rose Maylie's sister, the boy is linked to the one other person in the novel who withstands all the pressures of evil. Monks's mother cannot destroy Rose. ' "There was some cursed spell, I think, against us; for in spite of all our efforts she . . . was happy" ' (ch 51). And honourable, of course. Belarius's words can be applied to both Oliver and Rose; an invisible instinct frames them to honour

[1] *Johnson*, Vol. I, p. 201.

untaught, civility not seen from other. Nature has indeed meal and bran, contempt and grace.

Not surprisingly, perhaps, the novel ends with a marriage of love between Rose and Harry, which is seen in terms of a return to nature and as offering of a way out of the terrible and destructive falseness of class-considerations. So Harry is made to tell Rose:

> 'When I left you last, I left you with a firm determination to level all fancied barriers between yourself and me; resolved that if my world could not be yours, I would make yours mine; that no pride of birth should curl the lip at you, for I would turn from it. This I have done. Those who have shrunk from me because of this, have shrunk from you, and proved you so far right. Such power and patronage, such relatives of influence and rank, as smiled upon me then, look coldly now; but there are smiling fields and waving trees in England's richest county, and by one village church – mine, Rose, my own! – there stands a rustic dwelling which you can make me prouder of than all the hopes I have renounced, measured a thousandfold. This is *my* rank and station now, and here I lay it down.' (ch 51)

It is, of course, appalling. And we have to face here a problem I raised earlier in the chapter, since it is difficult to see any way in which the marriage can be taken to belong to the novel's realism. And this is more than just a matter of surface texture. Real housebreakers didn't say 'Wolves tear your throats',[1] yet such oaths do not compromise the sureness of Dickens's understanding of what Sikes is. But when Harry says that he has exchanged all his ambitions for a village church we are bound to recognize that Dickens has momentarily lost his grip on the realities his novel has been exploring. For *Oliver Twist* is after all about society, its parish-boy's pilgrimage at least partly a fable of the journey through contemporary life (the echo of Bunyan in the novel's subtitle is presumably important). But the marriage which concludes the novel is an escape from that life and the horrors attendant on it, and it emerges as a 'recommendation'

[1] The original 'gallows throats' is hardly more probable. But for Dickens's 'toning-down' of Sikes's oaths, see the Clarendon *Oliver Twist*, ed. K. Tillotson, 1967, esp. p. xxxii.

of such incredibly dilute Rousseauistic prescriptiveness that it comes near to making a mockery of the novel's mimetic power in its treatment of a corrupt and corrupting society. And we have either to see Rose and Harry's marriage as an individual solution, unrelated to the novel's typical representativeness; or we have to recognize that it masquerades as a daydream of the classless idyll that *Pickwick* had entertained, whilst in fact being rooted in class (even village churches weren't *that* easy to come by). Or, at worst, we must admit that it is a fainthearted exercise in romance, and is so ineptly written that it leaves us persuaded that Dickens probably didn't believe a word of it himself. As indeed, he didn't, for we cannot ignore another obvious feature of the novel, that with the partial exception of Oliver all the good people come out as bloodless abstractions; and this suggests that they are the official representatives of Dickens's schematic concern with a 'natural' life into whose bases he has hardly bothered to enquire, so that the badness of his writing about them is almost a tacit admission of a failure of imaginative intelligence. It is the unoffocial representatives who in fact have all the life:

> When the breakfast was cleared away, the merry old gentleman and the two boys played at a very curious and uncommon game . . . [Fagin] would look constantly around him, for fear of thieves, and would keep slapping all his pockets in turn, to see that he hadn't lost anything, in such a very funny and natural manner, that Oliver laughed till the tears ran down his face. (ch 9)

I don't want to make too much out of what may be a casual phrase, but Fagin's natural manner does point unerringly to the fact that, in common with the Dodger and Charley Bates, he has a vitality which owes much to his marvellous ribald contempt for the officially good world that Oliver later joins. The boy laughs at what to all intents and purposes in an imitation of Brownlow.

But how can we reconcile the natural Fagin with the slimy reptile that Dickens also describes? The answer is that we cannot. Fagin is out of focus, as Thackeray of course recognized and as

I think most readers would acknowledge. Later in his career
Dickens will learn to shift the focus on a character to the sudden
discomfort of his audience (Uriah Heep is perhaps the first
fully-exploited example of a person treated in this way). Something of this shift happens in the presentation of Sikes, although
it is perhaps fairer to say that Dickens discovers that he himself
has more to learn about Sikes after the man has committed his
murder, and that he makes us learn with him. But unlike Sikes,
Fagin is treated inconsistently. And I suggest that the flaw in his
presentation springs directly from Dickens's inability or unwillingness to face up to his own deep indifference to the respectable
world of the Maylies and the trite dream of classlessness which
clearly bored him even though he couldn't bring himself to
admit as much.

I recognize that the argument I am putting forward may look
suspiciously like special pleading, but there is one piece of evidence that convinces me that I am right. Why, after all, is Fagin
hung? We know that his crime was one that was no longer
punishable by death, and Dickens also knew this – he could
hardly not know it. Philip Collins has suggested that Hugo's
Last Days of a Condemned Man may have much to do with
Dickens's decision. 'Condemned to death! These five weeks I
have dwelt with the idea.' This is a promising idea, Collins
suggests, 'for any writer interested in extreme sensations'.[1] And
over a hundred years earlier Richard 'Orion' Horne had made
much the same suggestion.[2] The notion is plausible enough, but
it does not explain why Oliver should be present to witness
Fagin's last ravings and pray for him. And we have either to see
in this a really monumental tastelessness, or to take it as evidence
that even Dickens could be touched by the current moral and
religious style (which comes to more or less the same thing as
tastelessness), or to recognize in the episode a final and appalling
confrontation, which is how I think we should regard it. For
without doubt these two coming face to face as they do is

[1] *Dickens and Crime*, 1965, p. 40.
[2] In his article on Dickens in *The New Spirit of the Age*, 1844.

terrible, especially since Fagin has in the past been willing to offer Oliver companionship and even gaiety. Of course, the companionship is deeply tainted and Fagin treats Oliver badly, but this can be seen as an inevitable part of the inconsistency with which he is presented. We may try to explain the final scene as the consequence of Dickens's deep and ambiguous feelings about the blacking factory where he so insistently kept his distance from the other boys and where his best friend was called Bob Fagin, or we may say that it works out a theme that is recurrent in the novels, of the child who is better than the parent – so that Fagin's humility before Oliver introduces an idea that finds ultimate expression in Mr Doll's humility before Jenny Wren, and which may be based on Dickens's problematic relations with his own father, whom he both despised and loved. But however we may try to explain the scene, there is no escaping the fact that the confrontation between Oliver and Fagin in the condemned cell is a hideous enactment of Paul Clifford's remark that the only two laws of society are those which make the criminal and those which catch him. Never mind intention or subconscious motive, what we notice most about the scene is the ludicrous and indeed insulting inadequacy of Oliver's offer of prayers for the condemned man. The monumental tastelessness is the whole point:

> 'The papers,' said Fagin, drawing Oliver towards him, 'are in a canvas bag, in a hole a little way up the chimney in the top front-room. I want to talk to you, my dear. I want to talk to you.'
>
> 'Yes, yes,' returned Oliver. 'Let me say a prayer. Do! Let me say one prayer. Say only one, upon your knees, with me, and we will talk till morning.'
>
> 'Outside, outside,' replied Fagin, pushing the boy before him towards the door, and looking vacantly over his head. 'Say I've gone to sleep – they'll believe *you*. You can get me out, if you take me so. Now then, now then!'
>
> 'Oh! God forgive this wretched man!' cried the boy with a burst of tears. (ch 52)

In Fagin's cry 'they'll believe *you*' and in his going to a death that is uncalled for by his crime we hear for the last time the novel's major statement that 'this ain't the shop for justice'. And as the agent of respectable society, Oliver has to face the helpless and entirely human rage of a world his society has had its share in creating but for which it denies all responsibility. For what makes the scene more memorable than any other in the novel – at least if I may judge from my own experience – is precisely the horror of Fagin's being unable to escape from death, although he is most intensely alive in his mind and although we are aware that he does not deserve the punishment he is to receive. Fagin's death is the final unnatural act of the novel, and as such it provides a bleakly terrible comment on the prayers of the middle-class boy, which is what Oliver has become and why I speak of 'his' society. And I think we have to acknowledge that Dickens's ability to make us confront Fagin's condition is an essential part of his greatness. Some words of Camus help us define the nature of the achievement. The artist's true vocation, Camus said, 'is to open the prisons and to give a voice to the sorrows and joys of all. This is where art, against its enemies, justifies itself, by proving that it is no one's enemy'. My own feeling is that Dickens shows the 'strong affection and humanity of heart' which he recommends at the end of the novel far more when he writes of Sikes and Fagin than when he writes of the natural world where he believes the qualities are to be found. The really marvellous things in *Oliver Twist* spring from Dickens's willingness to open the prisons and give a voice to the sorrows and joys of such as Nancy, Sikes and Fagin. The bad things result from the fact that he compromises his own deep insight into how the prison comes to be the token for a social malaise that touches everybody. And the failures do not depend on whether we think that what Dickens says about society is true (it is certainly very persuasive). What goes wrong with *Oliver Twist* is not that it occasionally lapses into inaccuracy but that it becomes inconsistent. Still, what goes right is more important, for in spite of the criticisms we may bring against the novel, it remains a very remarkable achievement, the finest of all the early works.

🦁 3 · NICHOLAS NICKLEBY
TO BARNABY RUDGE

I NICHOLAS NICKLEBY

Nicholas Nickleby is a novel which strikes us as remarkable for its random energies. That at least is the most generous way of putting the case for it. More bluntly, however, we might say that there are occasions on which the novel really becomes something of an incoherent muddle, and if this statement seems unfairly emphatic, it is at least one way of correcting the very uncritical acceptance of Dickensian worlds that has become so fashionable among recent studies of the novels. Of course, *Nicholas Nickleby* is Dickens's first full-scale novel and we can see that in it he is serving his apprenticeship; but although this may be some excuse, it does not alter the fact that much of the plot and narrative are mismanaged, that the presentation of some of the characters is grievously inconsistent, that there are too many conflicting tones, and that the proliferating interests strain so hard against each other that they threaten to blow the novel apart at its seams. And yet it is also true that the novel's faults are what make it interesting, since *Nicholas Nickleby* is clearly a work which betrays its author's obsession with certain themes which more or less erupt into the novel, in spite of what he tries consciously to achieve. Such themes become dominant and creatively explored in the great novels, and I shall have something more to say about them a little later. But I want first to investigate what is wrong with *Nicholas Nickleby*.

One of the most notable features of the novel is its author's aggressive self-confidence. Perhaps this is not altogether surprising. With the publication of The *Pickwick Papers* and *Oliver*

Twist Dickens had become something of a national hero, and he must have felt that he had achieved his rocketting fame against all the odds. So that when Mrs Wittiterly tells Sir Mulberry Hawk that she finds so much more interest in Shakespeare's plays 'after having been to that dear little dull house he was born in', it is not difficult to feel that the wry laconicism lying behind what Dickens has her say is of decidedly personal application. And the novel has other such moments. There is, for example, the very funny parody of silver-fork novels: 'At this instant, . . . the Lady Flabella yet inhaled that delicious fragrance by holding the *mouchoir* to her exquisite, but thoughtfully-chiselled nose'; there is the swift contempt with which Dickens puts down the literary gentleman who adapts Shakespeare (again, this has a personal bearing: Dickens was being much adapted, pirated, imitated); there is the joke about Literary Annuals, 'Lines on Contemplating the Portrait of Lady Mulberry Hawk. By Sir Dingleby Dabber'; and there is the smack at Newgate-romances: 'A thief in fustian is a vulgar character, scarcely to be thought of by persons of refinement; but dress him in green velvet, with a high-crowned hat, and change the scene of his operations, from a thickly peopled city to a mountain road, and you shall find in him the very soul of poetry and adventure.' (ch 18)

I do not object against the sort of moments I have here outlined; indeed, in view of what the *Sketches, Pickwick Papers* and *Oliver Twist* achieve, Dickens has earned the right to speak out as a professional writer. But we have surely to admit that the confidence he shows in his own powers is responsible for what in many ways is the most undisciplined of all his novels. It is not just a matter of the interpolated tales, irritating though they are, nor of the Boz-like sketches, as for instance that which opens chapter 22. Such offences are only minor, if real enough. But there are much more fundamental problems. First, the mismanagement of plot which produces the Cheerybles half-way through the book, and as a result of which Nicholas's fortune is guaranteed so early that interest in the rest of the novel has to be kept up by some fairly desperate manoeuvres, in particular Mrs

Nickleby's romance with the old madman and Arthur Gride's attempt to marry Madeline Bray. Even if we say that Gride's affair leads into an obsessive theme of young girls at the mercy of old men – which becomes central to the *Old Curiosity Shop* – we have still to admit that in *Nicholas Nickleby* the obsession is merely intrusive. How else account for the very old Lord who visits Madame Mantolini's to buy dresses for his very young bride, and of whom Madame remarks, ' "how he ever gets into a carriage without thinking of a hearse, *I* can't think." ' (ch 18) And why else should we have the scene of Ralph's accompanying Kate to the Mantolinis' and Dickens's comment that 'among all the wily plots and calculations of the old man, [it was wonderful that] there should not be one word or figure denoting thought of death or of the grave'. (ch 10) No matter how sympathetically we may regard Dickens's emotional disturbance following the death of Mary Hogarth, it is impossible not to see that the occasions he takes for berating the old who do not think of death (when younger and more beautiful have died) are quite irrelevant, and thrust into the novel both because the novelist himself has not yet accepted the discipline of relevance that he needs in order to become truly great, and also because his belief in his powers has shot ahead of his deeper responsibility to his art. The interpolated tale of 'The Five Sisters of York' is perhaps the most excusable outlet for Dickens's grief and clearly an attempt to come to terms with the horror of Mary's death. At its conclusion, one of the listeners remarks that 'it is a tale of life, and life is made up of such sorrows'. (ch 6) Yet the device of the tale is undeniably crude; and its being sealed-off from the rest of the novel does not gain it total immunity from the justifiable demand of relevance which it cannot meet.

Dickens's picture of the very old Lord is not, however, entirely dross. Although he occupies no more than three or four sentences, the taut prose with which Dickens describes how he 'tottered downstairs to the door, where his sprightly body was hoisted into the carriage by two stout footmen', suggests possibilities from which will grow those magnificent studies of aristocratic senility that we find in Mrs Skewton and Sir Leicester Dedlock. Similarly, we may note that the obsession with young girls corrupted by old men – Mary was at least spared that – looks towards the analyses of old people tyrannizing over the young which become so marked a feature of the later novels.

Even Nicholas himself embodies an idea which is developed in *Martin Chuzzlewit*. But in *Chuzzlewit* Dickens sees through the sort of hero he celebrates in *Nicholas Nickleby*. For there is no doubt that the novelist is fully identified with Nicholas's aggressive self-confidence, whereas Martin has to learn that he cannot put the world to rights by a few well-aimed blows, let alone a belief in his own worth. Nicholas is the novel's hero, but I doubt if he is one with whom many people would choose completely to sympathize. Consider his interview with Sir Mulberry Hawk. ' "I am the son of a country gentleman . . . your equal in birth and education, and your superior I trust in everything besides." ' (ch 32) It is a distressingly vulgar moment and one that comes very close to Dickens's own desire to be known as a gentleman. In later novels he learns to control and marvellously satirize this desire, but in *Nicholas Nickleby* his yearning for social standing produces some very striking failures in sympathy and novelistic tact, as for example the scene in the General Agency Office, where Nicholas enquires if there are any posts to be had as secretary to a gentleman:

> 'Any such!' rejoined the mistress, 'a dozen such. An't there, Tom?'
> '*I* should think so,' answered that young gentleman; and as he said it, he winked towards Nicholas with a degree of familiarity which he, no doubt, intended for a rather flattering compliment, but with which Nicholas was most ungratefully disgusted. (ch 16)

There are enough of these moments to make us feel that the Cheerybles must be monsters of imperceptiveness to reward Nicholas as they do.

On the other hand, Nicholas is the man who puts down Squeers, and in so far as he manages that we have less difficulty in seeing him as on the side of the angels. And yet problems loom up over Nicholas's action. We know that Dickens's journey to Greta Bridge in the company of Hablot Browne told him a good deal about the infamous Yorkshire schools and we sympathize with his rage over their continued existence. The trouble is that no matter how many schoolmasters received the thrashings they undoubtedly deserved, such punishments were not likely to make the schools disappear; and one does have the feeling that Dickens's bursting self-confidence rather takes control of his critical sense when Nicholas beats Squeers. Momentarily satisfying though the thrashing may be, it solves nothing; and indeed the problem of the Yorkshire schools, which was at least one starting point for the novel, is pushed out of sight as Nicholas heads back towards London. As a matter of fact, I do not think this a particularly great problem, for we can reasonably maintain that Nicholas's action isn't meant to solve anything, it is merely a very natural expression of outraged sensibilities. Even so, we are bound to recognize that in later novels Dickens shows us that individual action is helplessly ill-equipped to destroy the forces of evil, whereas in *Nicholas Nickleby* there is an implicit feeling that one strong right arm can smash down the worst of oppositions (it is a novel remarkable for its fights and beatings).

But how evil is Squeers? This may seem a silly question in view of the schoolmaster's viciousness. Squeers is almost as famous a Dickens figure as Fagin and we automatically associate him with terrible cruelty. But the odd thing is that when you look at the text Squeers turns out to be presented in a very disturbing way. It does not matter over-much that he is a Rowlandson-like parody of a mean-minded bully rather than a more sober study, of the sort we find in Creakle. What does matter is that Squeers is outrageously funny. True, we are brought face to face with the wretched boys, 'pale and haggard faces, lank and bony figures, children with the countenances of old men, deformities with irons upon their limbs, boys of stunted growth, and others whose long meagre legs would hardly bear their bodies'. But we are also brought face to face with the fact that this scene, painful as it was, had its grotesque features, which, in a less interested observer than Nicholas, might have provoked a smile. Mrs. Squeers stood at one of the desks, presiding over an immense basin of brimstone and treacle, of which delicious compound she administered a large instalment to each boy in succession: using for the purpose a common wooden spoon, which might have been originally manufactured for some gigantic top, and which widened every young gentleman's mouth considerably: they being all obliged, under heavy corporal penalties, to take in the whole of the bowl at a gasp. (ch 8)

'A less interested observer'. But who can be less interested than Nicholas? Not the reader surely, who has been forced to see the broken boys of Squeers' School? And we cannot argue that the grotesqueness belongs merely to the scene itself, for it is also written into Dickens's response. There is no avoiding the facetiousness of phrases like 'delicious compound' and 'young gentleman'. Dickens is all but writing for easy laughs, and there is a violent discrepancy between the tone in which he reports Mrs Squeers's feeding of the boys and the boys themselves. How to account for it? It is a difficult question. We may say that Dickens is tactlessly running together his two roles as novelist of protest and of comedy, but it seems a rather feeble explanation. It may make more sense to point out that he is bound to be in some difficulties when he comes to write about Dotheboys Hall, because once he has registered his protest there is not much more he can say, even though the school is part of the setting and plot. Elsewhere in the novel Dickens enters specific protests against social injustices; in chapter 17, for example, he sounds out against the plight of milliners. But such a protest does not enter the life of the novel, whereas Dotheboys Hall does. And since Dickens hasn't actually any more to do *than* protest about the school, the only way he can keep the novel going while Nicholas is there is to divert attention away from the boys towards the Squeers family, which allows his comic genius to take over but only at the expense of disastrously compromising his sombre prose about the boys' hell. We simply cannot reconcile Smike's fate and Squeers's practical mode of teaching. ' "C-l-e-a-n, clean, verb active, to make bright, to scour. W-i-n, win, d-e-r, der, winder, a casement. When the boy knows this out of the book, he goes and does it." ' (ch 8) And what of Fanny's letter to Ralph describing Nicholas's attack on the Squeers family? 'Me and my brother were then the victim of his feury since which we have suffered very much which leads us to the arrowing belief that we have received some injury in our insides, especially as no marks of violence are visible externally.' (ch 15) How can we be expected to take seriously the fact that Nicholas takes the letter seriously? In short, the attack on the Yorkshire schools, powerful though it may be on rare occasions, cannot be sustained without serious irrelevancies, discrepancies and plain inconsistencies of tone. One of the most remarkably inept moments comes when Dickens tells us of the 'host of unpleasant misgivings, which had been crowding upon Nicholas during the whole journey' to Dotheboys Hall. (ch 7) Since Nicholas and we have already seen Squeers's recruiting methods, his brutish gluttony and his savage treatment of small boys, Nicholas's misgivings come a bit late in the day, to put it mildly, and at the very least they suggest what difficulties Dickens was having with his narrative. The difficulties force themselves on our attention throughout the novel, for it is far too ready to fall back on limp explanations of how people came to be where they were on particular occasions, or what caused them to think their various thoughts, or not think them. The result of these many failures is that *Nicholas Nickleby* is the flabbiest and least dramatic of all Dickens's novels, and the one where we most clearly see that he is serving his apprenticeship to the art of writing fiction.

Did he perhaps over-reach himself in trying to build a novel out of the Yorkshire schools? Does the reporter-like desire to confront his audience with shocking and hidden truths outstrip his abilities in this instance? But as soon as we ask the question it is apparent that we must answer no, because the subject of Dotheboys Hall, no matter how crudely treated, releases a theme which had been first stated in *Oliver Twist* and which becomes central to the great novels. Here is its starting point:

> 'At midsummer,' muttered Mr. Squeers . . . 'I took down ten
> boys; ten twentys is two hundred pound. I go back at eight o'clock
> to-morrow morning, and have got only three – three oughts is an
> ought – three twos is six – sixty pound. What's come of all the
> boys? What's parents got in their heads? what does it all mean?'
> (ch 4)

It is the theme of lives sacrificed to financial interest which gives
Nicholas Nickleby such coherence as it has. For the novel is very
loosely organized around a basic opposition of natural versus
unnatural behaviour, where 'unnatural' may be defined in terms
of all those people who are willing to sacrifice themselves and
others for money or a place in society (for which money is the
customary passport). And in this context Squeers and Dotheboys
Hall take on metaphoric power; they become the image of a
necessary ulcer into which the infections of a society can drain.
Indeed, it would be pleasant to suggest that the novel takes up
that theme of society's tainting of nature which I suggested was
crucial in *Oliver Twist*. But the truth is that if we except Smike's
being followed into Devon and the presentation of John Brow-
die (who barely passes muster as the 'natural' good man), Dickens
makes very little of society's malevolent effect on the world of
natural values. What he does do, albeit clumsily, is show us
Squeers as the acquaintance of respectable society – of Ralph and
Snawley, for example – so that he can explore his interest in how
the rage for respectability creates evils that have either to be kept
out of sight or, where they emerge into the light of day, have to
be glossed as perfectly proper. Squeers is the necessary horror
that is thrown up by all those who seek to purchase respectability;
and it is one of the novel's better jokes that he himself is not just
totally disreputable but also plug-ugly and uncouth. In one
brilliant moment we are told that he is 'ill at ease in his clothes,
and as if he were in a perpetual state of astonishment at finding
himself so respectable'. (ch 4)

The destructive pressures of respectability provide one of the novel's main themes. And inevitably, it seems, we find an important sub-theme in the unnatural relationships between parents and children, for which again Dotheboys Hall becomes an apt metaphor. Mrs Squeers, we are told, is ' "more than a mother to them [boys]; ten times more." ' (ch 8) The point is rammed home when one of the Cheerybles remarks that ' "Parents who never showed their love, complain of want of natural affection in their children." ' (ch 46) And the statement reaches out to touch most of the parent-child relationships in the novel.

But at this point I want to notice that it is not only parent-child relationships that are sacrificed to respectability. In *Nicholas Nickleby*, as in most of Dickens's novels, all kinds of relationships are open to corruption: friendships are bought for money, marriages are made for money, blood relations are abandoned for money. And once we have grasped this fact we can see how the novel looks forward to the much greater, more systematic and comprehensive studies of corruption that we begin to find in *Dombey and Son*, and which occupy Dickens in all the later novels. There is at least one moment in *Nicholas Nickleby* when it looks as though he is going to tackle the theme head-on. It comes when Nicholas is reflecting on his position under Squeers:

> The cruelty of which he had been an unwilling witness, the coarse and ruffianly behaviour of Squeers even in his best moods, the filthy place, the sights and sounds about him, all contributed to [his] state of feeling; but when he recollected that, being there as an assistant, he actually seemed – no matter what unhappy train of circumstances had brought him to that pass – to be the aider and abettor of a system which filled him with honest disgust and indignation, he loathed himself, and felt, for the moment, as though the mere consciousness of his present situation must, through all time to come, prevent his raising his head again. (ch 8)

Although this is gawkily phrased, the passage is still of great interest because it clearly points towards something that comes to occupy Dickens in later novels and which, after all, is a central fact of modern life. Nicholas at Dotheboys Hall anticipates the conditions of such people as James Carker, Vholes, Pancks – of all those whose freedom of action and gesture are denied them by the social trap in which they find themselves and of which they are victims, no matter how they may have conspired to become so. Nicholas's moment of self-loathing comes very near to providing the sort of insight that in later novels helps to identify the centrality of Dickens's greatness, his ability to drive deep into the causes, explanations and difficulties of the conditions in which modern men exist.

But *Nicholas Nickleby* soon takes its hero away from the horror which at the one moment I have pointed to seems so inescapable. The novel does not pause to investigate in any detail the money-taint that Nicholas agonizes over. Even so, there are fine touches. One thinks, for example, of the relationship between Ralph and Newman Noggs. ' "He is useful enough, poor creature – useful enough," ' Ralph remarks of his clerk, and how dehumanizing 'use' is may be seen at the moment when Ralph tells Noggs to go home, 'looking round at the clerk as if he were his dog. The words were scarcely uttered when Newman darted across the road, slunk among the crowd, and disappeared in an instant.' (ch 3) We have to wait until *Our Mutual Friend* for the full statement about the fact of 'use', but it has its beginnings in *Nicholas Nickleby*. And because of such moments as the ones I have been pointing to it, is possible to remark that the novel has an intermittent intensity, especially when it concerns itself with the ways in which lives are bought and people destroy themselves or are destroyed in the pursuit of money.

Ralph is, of course, the centre of the corruption. For him all relationships are in the way of providing business, and through him Dickens sounds his first protest against that limitation of Bentham's philosophy which he enquires into far more severely in the character of Dombey and which Mill had identified as being the mistake of supposing 'that the *business* part of human affairs was the whole of them'. Ralph's readiness to sell Madeline and Kate for money, his relationships with his family and with Noggs and Verisopht, his use of Squeers, all testify to his taking business for the whole of human affairs. In fact, it would be easy to speak about Ralph in such a way as to persuade the unwary that he is as great a study as Dombey. But this would be absurd, for Ralph represents nothing like the scale of achievement we find in the later novel, and it is worth indicating why this should be.

The truth is, that although Ralph is presented with some power, he and his associates are not placed with any social exactness. We do not, for example, bother ourselves with how he comes to be the familiar of Hawk and Verisopht because they are such crudely parodic versions of the aristocracy that there is no need for us to speculate on the social implications of their relationship with each other and with Ralph. As their names clearly indicate, they derive from a broad Smollettian tradition of blunderbuss satire. The manner in which they are presented is nearly indistinguishable from that which produced young Lord Mutanhed, although there is occasionally a quite new razor-like contempt which points to Dickens's growing radicalism and which also flashes out in his vignette of the politician Gregsbury, who turns his eyes to the blue expanse above him and exclaims ' "Thank Heaven, I am a Briton." ' (ch 16)

I see no reason to protest about Dickens's mode of treating his aristocrats, but I think that as in the case of Newman Noggs, whose origins are strictly incredible, he has not troubled to identify them with any social specificity, so that his vision of them and of Ralph belongs more to the world of simple moral fable than to any profound analysis of contemporary society. One could, of course, argue that plenty of aristocrats were as near-idiotic as Verisopht and as dissolute and vicious as Hawk, but it would be impossible to argue that the qualities that Dickens chooses to identify them by are in any way socially representative. And when Hawk has killed Verisopht, Dickens's comment is socially quite inapt:

> So died Lord Verisopht, by the hand which he loaded with gifts, and clasped a thousand times; by the act of him, but for whom, and others like him, he might have lived a happy man, and died with children's faces round his bed. (ch 50)

And yet although many of Ralph's familiars do not belong to a socially specified world, we have also to accept that Dickens's feeling for the intricacies of the social web is liable to break through at various moments in the novel. His identification of the Kenwigs and Wittiterlys is very different from his identification of Verisopht and Hawk:

> 'I remember my niece,' said Mr. Lillyvick, surveying his audience with a grave air; 'I remember her, on that very afternoon, when she first acknowledged to her mother a partiality for Kenwigs. "Mother," she says, "I love him." . . . "What do I hear?" cried her mother; and instantly falls into strong conwulsions.'
> A general exclamation of astonishment burst from the company.
> 'Into strong conwulsions,' repeated Mr. Lillyvick, regarding them with a rigid look. 'Kenwigs will excuse my saying, in the presence of friends, that there was a very great objection to him, on the ground that he was beneath the family, and would disgrace it. You remember, Kenwigs?'
> 'Certainly,' replied that gentleman, in no way displeased at the reminiscence, in as much as it proved, beyond all doubt, what a high family Mrs. Kenwigs came of. (ch 14)

And there is the brilliant description of Cadogan Place, where the Wittiterlys live:

> Cadogan Place is the one slight bond that joins two great extremes; it is the connecting link between the aristocratic pavements of Belgrave Square, and the barbarism of Chelsea. It is in Sloane Street, but not of it. The people in Cadogan Place look down upon Sloane Street, and think Brompton low. They affect fashion too, and wonder where the New Road is. Not that they claim to be on precisely the same footing as the high folks of Belgrave Square and Grosvenor Place, but that they stand, with reference to them, rather in the light of those illegitimate children of the great who are content to boast of their connexions, although their connexions disavow them. (ch 21)

How much that tells us of the infinite gradations of class and social pretension, how both it and the passage about the Kenwigs suggest a novel remarkable for its grasp of social actuality. But then, of course, the presentation of Ralph, Hawk, Verisopht suggests a very different kind of novel. And how are we to take the presentation of Mantalini?:

> His name was originally Muntle; but it had been converted, by an easy transition, into Mantalini: the lady rightly considering that an English appellation would be of serious injury to the business. He had married on his whiskers; upon which property he had previously subsisted, in a genteel manner, for some years; and which he had recently improved, after patient cultivation, by the addition of a moustache, which promised to secure him an easy independence . . . (ch 10)

We may say that this takes up the dress theme of *Oliver Twist* and points the way towards its later development. But then we have only to consider Dickens's handling of the Lammles to realize how little he takes possession of the theme in *Nicholas Nickleby*, since Mantalini simply is not seen in terms of the social actualities that give the theme its deepest significance. Again, I do not see that we can protest about this, but we have to recognize that the genially comic way in which Mantalini is handled, and by means of which he can be reduced to a basement and a mangle, is consistent with an easy-going moralizing about pretenders who get their come-uppance but which is inconsistent with the presentation of other characters. Mantalini, Hawk and Verisopht belong, indeed, to the world of the Crummles, where people adopt 'false hair, false colour, false calves, false muscles' and so 'become different beings'. (ch 24) And I do not think that we can call the acting episodes a parody of social pretensions we are shown elsewhere in the novel, for the very good reason that in many cases the pretenders are themselves parodies.

I have no wish merely to attack *Nicholas Nickleby*. I would much rather pay tribute to its powers. But at the very least I think we must accept that two important consequences follow from the novel's large social inexactness. First, that the good people have little difficulty in emerging triumphant, and second, that Dickens finds it almost fatally easy to manufacture an escape from the world of social considerations into a 'natural' classless world.

It may seem odd to say that the good people triumph without much difficulty. After all, *Nicholas Nickleby* does demonstrate something of the atomistic universe which critics have learned to identify in most of the novels, and characters are certainly isolated from each other. But I think it will be agreed that separation is more typically brought about by the arbitrary mechanics of the plot rather than by its attempts to render the actuality of social pressures. Nicholas has his moment of anguish over being compromised by money, but he can soon cheer himself up with the reflection that 'The world is before me'; and Miss La Creevy, Miss Petowker, and Newman Noggs are hindered from finding solace in human relationships merely as the plot dictates. The only truly isolated figures are those who choose to remain so, as for example, Ralph, the powerfully emblematic Crowl, a 'hard-featured, square-faced man', who is the 'very epitome of selfishness', and Gride, who lives in 'an old house, dismal, dark and dusty, which seemed to have withered, like himself, and to have grown shrivelled in hoarding him from the sight of day'. (ch 51) And although when Miss La Creevy weeps before Newman we are told that it 'was the first opportunity she had had of opening her heart', it is fair to think of Miss Tox and recognize again how much more deeply the characters of *Dombey and Son* are bedded in social reality. It would be quite impossible to maintain that Miss La Creevy's loneliness is seen as anything like the inescapable fact that Miss Tox's is.

Even so, it is worth mentioning Miss Tox in the present context, for she is certainly foreshadowed in the presentation of Miss La Creevy and also of Miss Petowker. Admittedly, Dickens spoils his study of Miss Petowker because in pursuing the entirely irrelevant theme of marriages made by old men, he turns her into a comically grotesque harridan who wrecks Lillyvick's peaceful days. The nonsensical alteration in her character is doubly irritating because it comes near to undoing the touching and considerate moment in which she confesses her isolation:

> 'If I was blessed with a – a child' said Miss Petowker, blushing, 'of such genius, as that, I would have her out at the Opera instantly.'
>
> Mrs. Kenwigs sighed, and looked at Mr. Kenwigs, who shook his head, and observed that he was doubtful about it.
>
> 'Kenwigs is afraid,' said Mrs. K.
>
> 'What of?' inquired Miss Petowker, 'not of her failing?'
>
> 'Oh, no,' replied Mrs. Kenwigs, 'but if she grew up what she is now, – only think of the young dukes and marquises.'
>
> 'Very right,' said the collector.
>
> 'Still,' submitted Miss Petowker, 'if she took a proper pride in herself, you know – '
>
> 'There's a good deal in that,' observed Mrs. Kenwigs, looking at her husband.
>
> 'I only know – ' faltered Miss Petowker, – 'it may be no rule to be sure – but *I* have never found any inconvenience or unpleasantness of that sort.' (ch 14)

The moment is, of course, uniquely Dickensian in its compassion and decency, and those are the qualities which also characterize his presentation of Miss La Creevy, whom he admires for a reason that emerges when she remarks that her house may be robbed while she is out ' "though what there is to take away, besides tables and chairs, I don't know, except the miniatures: and he is a clever thief who can dispose of them to any great advantage, for *I* can't, I know, and that's the honest truth.' " (ch 38) Behind the miniature-painter's self-deprecatory words we detect the resilience that enables her to carry on a life of no expectations. And in this she has to be contrasted with Kenwigs, who announces a theme which is as central as any to Dickens's novels, when, hearing of Lillyvick's marriage to Miss Petowker, he cries about his new baby, ' "Let him die! He has no expectations, no property to come into. We want no babies here," said Mr. Kenwigs recklessly. "Take 'em away, take 'em away to the foundling!" ' (ch 36) At this point in the novel, Kenwigs becomes the object of some decidedly acid satire, which he hardly seems to deserve, and which is certainly inconsistent with the way in which he is earlier presented. And Dickens's changed attitude to him can be explained – though not justified – only when we register how intensely he hates the notion of great expectations. And against this, his love and admiration are freely called out for those people who have the courage and self-sufficient durability that enable them to cope with their own and other lives – for it is the resilient ones who choose to break out of the prison of self into a world of relationships which make them more human and therefore more vulnerable. The interpolated tale of 'the Baron of Grogzwig' is a comic fable about the need to choose life and live (to adapt Robert Lowell).

Yet the fact that the tale so obviously supplies a focus for the theme, inevitably demonstrates a failure in the novel. For very little in *Nicholas Nickleby* goes beyond the obvious moral point that the tale makes when the Baron says that he will brood over miseries no longer, but put on a good face. (ch 6) Putting on a good face is not the test that it might be in the novel because miseries can so comfortably be avoided; the good so easily triumphs, the benevolent so infallibly assume control. It is almost as though the novel says that those who don't entertain great expectations will be rewarded by having some come true anyway. On the other hand, dreadful though the Cheerybles and Tim Linkinwater undoubtedly are, they are less troublesome than they would be in a novel which was more concerned with social realities, for then they would represent a quite intolerable intrusion. As it is they come near to being one, but *Nicholas Nickleby* has enough of the moral fable about it for the do-gooder to be able to reward the deserving without our entirely losing patience. Still, it is worth pointing out that as Dickens develops his art towards the rendering of social actualities, benevolence will come to have increasingly limited powers; from the Cheerybles to the Boffins is a long and terrible way.

But the major point to make about the Cheerybles is, I think, that when they appear a world freed from any social pressures appears with them (although as with the Maylie world it is not so classless as Dickens would have us think; Tim Linkinwater knows his place as Smike knows his). Obviously such a world returns us to the idyllic mode of the *Pickwick Papers*, but there is now something decidedly odd about it. As here:

> 'A fine morning, Mr. Linkinwater!' said Nicholas, entering the office.
>
> 'Oh!' replied Tim, 'talk of the country, indeed! What do you think of this now, for a day – a London day – eh?'
>
> 'It's a little clearer out of town,' said Nicholas.
>
> 'Clearer?' echoed Tim Linkinwater. 'You shall see it from my bed-room window.'
>
> 'You should see it from *mine*,' replied Nicholas, with a smile.
>
> 'Pooh! pooh!' said Tim Linkinwater. 'Don't tell me. Country! (Bow was quite a rustic place to Tim.) 'Nonsense! What can you get in the country but new-laid eggs and flowers? I can buy new-laid eggs in Leadenhall market, any morning before breakfast. And as to flowers, it's worth a run upstairs to smell my mignonette, or to see the double-wallflower in the back-attic window, at no 6, in the court.' (ch 50)

The strangeness of this moment lies in the impression it gives that under the Cheerybles' influence London has become a sort of Dingley Dell or Chertsey; one touch of kin makes the whole world nature. Stranger still, is the fact that such a view of London has nothing whatsoever to do with the glimpses of the capital which the novel offers throughout. How can Tim's London be reconciled, for example, with the London Kate sees as she goes to work, a city peopled by 'many sickly girls, whose business, like that of the poor worm, is to produce, with patient toil, the finery that bedecks the thoughtless and luxurious' (ch 17); or the London of 'slipshod feet, and the chilly cry of the poor sweep as he crept, shivering, to his early toil' (ch 22); or the London which harbours dingy fowls 'sent, like many of the neighbouring children to get a livelihood in the streets' (ch 14); or the London of Snow Hill where 'four, six, or eight strong men at a time, have been hurried violently and swiftly from the world, when the scene has been rendered frightful with the excess of human life; when curious eyes have glared from casement, and housetop,

and wall and pillar; and when, in the mass of white and up-
turned faces, the dying wretch, in his all-comprehensive look of
agony, has met not one – not one – that bore the impress of pity
or compassion?' (ch 4) These views of London are totally opposed
to Tim's. And I think we have to say that the idyll to which his
view of London introduces us is part of the attempt to dispel the
moments of horror and actuality the novel renders elsewhere. It
is not simply that the city looks good to the good, but that it
becomes good because of the good. I feel very strongly that
when we reach Tim's encomium to his London we have come to
a point where the split between the fable and the mimetic widens
to an intolerable degree. For although the novel is not typically
concerned with social representativeness, its occasional presence
is bound to conflict with the presentation of various of the
characters as special cases or moral types – let alone those who
slip from one mode of presentation to another. Given even such
social actualities as the novel entertains, its moral recommendations become something of an intrusion. However we may try
to explain the different ways in which the novel works – by
suggesting, for example, that Dickens's desire to report the ills of
early Victorian England runs into his sense of the comic and also
into his deep involvement with characters whom he can't bring
himself to let suffer – we cannot avoid recognizing that such very
different ways weaken the novel.

Yet having said all this I want also to say that I do not think
we should make too much of the flaws of *Nicholas Nickleby*.
Important though it is to recognize them, it is more important
to recognize that the novel is still deeply interesting, both in what
it achieves and what it suggests. It is not nearly so good as *Oliver
Twist*, but it is perhaps more closely linked to the great novels
because it offers the first tentative statement of many of the
themes that become central to what they achieve. In the end its
faults spring from Dickens's attempt to combine views of
England under two heads: as it is and as it might be. Although
the attempt fails, we have at least to see in it a large readiness of
purpose by which he tries to accept to the full the responsibility

for art – meaning the novel – to become the central consciousness of its age. Such an acceptance has important implications for
his later works.

II THE OLD CURIOSITY SHOP

In some ways the *Old Curiosity Shop* is more of a muddle than
Nicholas Nickleby, and although its weaknesses and failures are so
obvious that they hardly need detailing, there is something to be
gained from trying to account for them. We know, of course,
that the novel was begun in more than usual haste, and that
Dickens was forced into this action in an attempt – which proved
highly successful – to boost the alarming fall in sales of *Master
Humphrey's Clock*, the periodical he had started in April 1840.
We know also that the *Old Curiosity Shop* was expanded almost
by accident from a short story into novel length. And a mere
glance at the book is enough to tell us that it very clearly makes
an effort to come to terms with Mary Hogarth's tragic death. It is
saturated in speculations about death's finality and sting, and
how it may be robbed of its victory; and the novel frequently
feels as though it exists merely to provide the opportunities for
such speculation.

The *Old Curiosity Shop* represents Dickens's attempt to explain death to himself, and the way it goes about its task is
strongly reminiscent of Ernst Cassirer's suggestion of how myth
'explains away' the fact of death. 'In mythical thought,' Cassirer
says, 'the mystery of death is "turned into an image" – and by
this transformation, death ceases being a hard unbearable physical
fact; it becomes understandable and supportable.'[1] Without
doubt, the air of myth hangs heavily over Dickens's novel, and
it is linked to that near-mythic early Victorian obsession with the
young girl who proves or is made to be too good for life. Nell
combines Pippa's gift for passing on with Evelyn Hope's triumph
of passing away. Only by dying young can she avoid Mildred's
fate in *A Blot in the 'Scutcheon*, expressed in words which so

[1] Ernst Cassirer, *The Myth of the State*, 1966, p. 49.

moved Dickens: ' "I had no mother; God forgot me: so I fell." '
Gabriel Pearson has written excellently about Dickens's struggle
to make death meaningful and bearable in the *Old Curiosity Shop*,
and there is nothing that can valuably be added to what he has
said.[1] On the other hand, I do not think that we have exhausted
the novel's interest when we have accounted for its obsessive
concern with death, for it also takes up themes that are more substantial and constant in Dickens's career, and although these are
often entangled in – and sometimes virtually submerged under –
the novel's obsession, they show themselves often enough to be
worth considering a little.

Here I should note that the themes I have in mind are most
certainly not expressed in the satires on Miss Monflathers and
Little Bethel. The point that Dickens makes against Miss Monflathers is merely a point; she is not involved in the novel, and
indeed it has to be said that the involvement of many characters is
peculiarly difficult in a novel which is so loosely structured, so
whimsically picaresque:

> 'Don't you feel how naughty it is of you,' [said] Miss Mon-
> flathers, 'to be a wax-work child, when you might have the proud
> consciousness of assisting, to the extent of your infant powers, the
> manufactures of your country; of improving your mind by the
> constant contemplation of the steam-engine; and of earning a com-
> fortable and independent subsistence of from two-and-ninepence
> to three shillings per week? Don't you know that the harder you
> are at work, the happier you are?' (ch 31)

It simply will not do to pretend that this is considered social
satire, for the very obvious reason that there is nothing in the
novel on either side of the speech that can give Miss Monflather's
words any dramatic appropriateness. She comes on, makes her
remark and goes off. And that is that.

The satire on Little Bethel is equally random, since Mrs
Nubbles, far from being in any way influenced by her religious
persuasions, is shown as a good woman who merely provides

[1] See his essay in *Dickens and the Twentieth Century*, 1962.

Dickens with the opportunity to take a few jabs at the cant of nonconformist religion and the style of its preaching:

> 'Stay, Satan, stay!' roared the preacher again. 'Tempt not the woman that doth incline her ear to thee, but hearken to the voice of him that calleth. He hath a lamb from the fold!' cried the preacher, raising his voice still higher and pointing to the baby. 'He beareth off a lamb, a precious lamb! He goeth about like a wolf in the night season, and inveigleth the tender lambs.' (ch 41)

Funny though this undoubtedly is, the target is a sitting duck; for Dickens to knock down the Rev. Cummings and his ilk can hardly be called a significant achievement.

Yet putting a finger on what *is* significant in the *Old Curiosity Shop* is remarkably difficult because the novel's most worthwhile concerns are quite likely to be overlaid by intrusive matter or muddled by uncertainties of direction. It may be fairest to remark that the most significant feature of the novel is precisely its air of uncertainty, the feeling it communicates that Dickens himself is far from sure just what he should be doing. The result is that we are reduced to searching for clues so that we can reconstruct the novel's possible interests – interests, that is, apart from the obsession with death.

And first of all there is the title. Surely the *Old Curiosity Shop* is the least apposite or relevant of titles, especially for a novelist who worried as much about titles as Dickens did? True, when he was mulling over the original plans for what was then to be a short story he considered calling it the *Old Curiosity Dealer and the Child*, but he soon rejected that idea. The peculiarity of the title he eventually chose is that it has little to do with the book as we have it. Or so it seems. Consider, however, the last sentences of the novel, which tell of Kit's taking his children to the street where Nell had lived:

> But new improvements had altered it so much, it was not the same. The old house had been long ago pulled down, and a fine broad road was in its place. At first he would draw with his stick upon the ground to show them where it used to stand. But he soon

became uncertain of the spot, and could only say that it was there-
abouts, he thought, and that these alterations were confusing.

Such are the changes which a few years bring about, and so do
things pass away, like a tale that is told!

Throughout the novel Dickens has of course been much exercised with how the dead are remembered and it is clear that the
closing sentences hark back to the burden of a passage in which
Nell and a sexton – who cleans his spade with a piece of slate,
and scrapes off 'the essence of Heaven knows how many Becky
Morgans' – talk of the flowers put on graves and, in answer to
Nell's grieving for how soon they are neglected, the old man
says:

'Ah! so say the gentlefolks who come down here to look at
them . . . but I say otherwise. "It's a pretty custom you have in
this part of the country," they say to me sometimes, "to plant the
graves, but it's melancholy to see these things all withering or
dead." I crave their pardon and tell them that, as I take it, 'tis a
good sign for the happiness of the living. And so it is. It's nature.'
(ch 54)

From the very beginning of the *Old Curiosity Shop* Kit has vowed
undying allegiance to little Nell; and his determination to serve
her in spite of the fact that she is out of his sight suggests that she
is never out of his mind. Yet the end of the novel makes it clear
that she does go out of mind, and the last sentences imply that
his failure of memory is a good thing; 'it's nature'. Men and
women must grow away from morbid or obsessive loves if they
are to achieve emotional health. And here I may note paren-
thetically that in the relationship of old Trent and Nell and
initially of Abel Garland and his parents – though nothing comes
of it – the *Old Curiosity Shop* inaugurates the theme of obsessive
love that is taken up much more fully in *David Copperfield*, in the
relationship of Wickfield and Agnes, and which it is reasonable
to suppose was urgently prompted by Dickens's own relationship with Mary Hogarth.

Yet having pointed to Dickens's attempt to indicate the natural
irony implicit in the novel's last sentences, I think we must note

that they are not simply concerned with Nell's inevitable fading from memory. For the old curiosity shop is also obliterated by passing time. It is as though Nell is linked to a way of life that is now nothing more than a legend. And the 'fine broad road' anticipates the exploration of the effects of time passing that we find in Dickens's writing about Staggs's Gardens in *Dombey and Son*, and, in the same novel, his study of Sol Gill's shop, the Wooden Midshipman, and its identification with a dying way of life. In other words, the past as we are given it in the *Old Curiosity Shop* does not merely offer a way of speaking about the death of individuals; it also has a social application.

There is another clue we may notice here. In chapter 17, Nell talks to an old woman who has come to put flowers on her husband's grave. The scene as a whole is a very remarkable and moving one, and I am not doing it justice in extracting one moment from it for comment, but it does reveal something of great value for our present purpose:

> [Nell] was looking at a humble stone which told of a young man who had died at twenty-three years old, fifty-five years ago, when she heard a faltering step approaching, and looking round saw a feeble woman bent with the weight of years, who tottered to the foot of that same grave and asked her to read the writing on the stone. The old woman thanked her when she had done, saying that she had had the words by heart for many a long, long year but could not see them now.
> 'Were you his mother?' said the child.
> 'I was his wife, my dear.'
> She as the wife of a young man of three-and-twenty! Ah, true! It was fifty-five years ago. (ch 17)

That moment suddenly and quite astonishingly opens up a perspective on to the past; it penetrates far back behind the world of the present which the child inhabits and in its manner of showing a deep rift in that apparently solid world it is inevitably reminiscent of a great moment in *Henry IV* Pt 2. Shallow asks Falstaff whether Jane Nightwork still holds her own well.

> *Fal.* Old, old, Master Shallow.
> *Shal.* Nay, she must be old; she cannot choose but be old; certain
> she's old; and had Robin Nightwork, by old Nightwork, before
> I came to Clement's Inn.
> *Sil.* That's fifty-five year ago.
> *Shal.* Ha, cousin Silence, that thou hadst seen that this knight and
> I have seen! Ha, Sir John, said I well?
> *Fal.* We have heard the chimes at midnight, Master Shallow.
> (III, ii)

Is the echo of Shakespeare insignificant? I do not think so. It is my very strong impression that Silence's words came into Dickens's mind because there is in his novel a confused, cloudily expressed but none the less crucial effort to oppose the past and present worlds, and to identify the past with a natural world – where 'natural' has the double meaning of what is rural and what is humanly healthy. In contrast, the present is connected with the city. As the scene in Gloucestershire in *Henry IV* upsets the perspective of a present world of wars and court activities, so in Dickens's novel the shop itself and all that is identified with it oppose the world of Quilp and money. But of course Shakespeare is in command of his material, whereas Dickens is not. (There is no doubt that Falstaff's great line had an especially piercing and almost private meaning for him.) That is why we must speak of clues. Here is another one:

> The town was glad with morning light: places that had shown ugly and distrustful all night long, now wore a smile; and sparkling sunbeams dancing on the chamber windows, and twinkling through blind and curtain before sleepers' eyes, shed light even into dreams, and chased away the shadows of the night. Birds in hot rooms, covered up close and dark, felt it was morning, and chafed and grew restless in their little cells; bright-eyed mice crept back to their tiny homes and nestled timidly together; the sleek house-cat, forgetful of her prey, sat winking at the rays of the sun starting through key-hole and cranny in the door, and longed for her stealthy run and warm sleek bask outside. The nobler beasts confined in dens stood motionless behind their bars, and gazed on fluttering boughs and sunshine peeping through some little win-

dow, with eyes in which old forests gleamed – then trod impa-
tiently the track their prisoned feet had worn – and stopped and
gazed again. (ch 15)

In spite of all the straining after poetic affect, this passage is
important because it provides a metaphor of caged vitality, and
is immediately associated with the city. For the paragraph I have
quoted comes at the beginning of the chapter that deals with Nell
and her grandfather's escape from Quilp and imprisonment. A
little later the old man 'waving his hand towards the city' tells
Nell that ' "Thou and I art free of it now." ' In the country,
there you feel free. But before we get to that we have had a
detailed description of

> mean houses parcelled off in rooms, and windows patched with
> rags and paper. . . . The shops sold goods that only poverty
> could buy, and sellers and buyers were pinched and gripped alike.
> Here were poor streets where faded gentility essayed . . . to make
> its last feeble stand, but tax gatherer and creditor came there as
> elsewhere, and the poverty that yet faintly struggled was hardly
> less squalid and manifest than that which had long ago submitted
> and given up the game. . . . Damp rotten houses . . . lodgings,
> where it would be hard to tell which needed pity most, those who
> let or those who came to take – children, scantily fed and clothed,
> spread over every street, and sprawling in the dust – scolding
> mothers, stamping their slipshod feet with noisy threats upon the
> pavement – shabby fathers hurrying with dispirited looks to the
> occupation which brought them 'daily bread' and little more –
> mangling-women, washerwomen, cobblers, tailors, chandlers,
> driving their trades in parlours and kitchens and back rooms and
> garrets, and sometimes all of them under the same roof – brick-
> fields, skirting gardens paled with staves of old casks, or timber
> pillaged from houses burnt down and blackened and blistered by
> the flames – mounds of dockweed, nettles, coarse grass and oyster-
> shells, heaped in rank confusion – small Dissenting chapels to teach,
> with no lack of illustration, the miseries of Earth, and plenty of
> new churches, erected with a little superfluous wealth, to show the
> way to Heaven.

This passage amounts to much more than a Boz-like sketch. For in the context of Nell and Trent's escape it means that they are fleeing not only from Quilp, but from a world of values with which he is linked and which are peculiarly associated with the city: of poverty, misery, stunted lives, and a mean ugliness that destroys all vitality and has no use for light (one of the novel's key words). And these values are meant to be definitive; the description of the city works by accumulating detail into a comprehensive statement – which is why I have had to quote it at such length.

The world that Nell and her grandfather escape to is one where

> the freshness of the day, the singing of the birds, the beauty of the waving grass, the deep green leaves, the wild flowers, and the thousand exquisite scents and sounds that floated in the air . . . sank into their hearts and made them very glad. (ch 15)

Such a passage is entirely typical of the descriptions of rural life with which the book is studded. It is very bad. It is moreover oddly generalized. We have only to compare the 'mounds of dockweed, nettles, coarse grass and oyster-shells' with the 'waving grass, the deep green leaves, the wild flowers' to see how superbly Dickens can write about the city, how ineptly about the country. His view of nature is sentimental not only because he doesn't see it accurately – what kind of leaves were they, what kind of flowers? – but because he wants it to be associated with values that the city lacks. For the Dickens of the *Old Curiosity Shop* nature means freedom, spontaneity, warm-heartedness, all those values in short which he sees as humanly natural, which he suggests are threatened by the city and which therefore require that he turn rural England into a vision of what never was on sea or land – as his reading of Crabbe should have told him.

And nature is associated with the past. At all events I do not see how else we can explain the presence of the poor schoolmaster who, if he does not come straight out of Goldsmith, can certainly claim a close literary relationship with the nostalgic creation of that village master who was 'kind, or if severe in

aught,/The love he bore to learning was in fault'. Goldsmith's
condescension, no matter how sympathetically intended, finds
its exact counterpart in Dickens's writing of the unworldly
teacher, appointed to his village school at, 'five-and-thirty pounds
a year. Five-and-thirty pounds!' (ch 46) Less even than Goldsmith's vicar received. No wonder he takes Nell and her grandfather to a village where they live in two old houses 'with sunken
windows and oaken doors' and can admire

> the old grey porch, the mullioned windows, the venerable grave-
> stones dotting the green churchyard, the ancient tower, the very
> weathercock; the brown thatched roofs of cottage, barn, and
> homestead, peeping from among the trees; the stream that rippled
> by the distant watermill; the blue Welsh mountains far away.
> (ch 46)

This is cockney pastoralism, and the aura of its nostalgic condescension is so strong that we inevitably feel it a mark almost of
Dickens's inability to think of the natural world as having any
present possibility at all. Rural England provides a myth of a
past that is irrecoverably lost and with its loss go the larger hopes
for the triumph of natural human values.

It is tempting to convict Dickens of intolerable sentimentality
and let the matter rest there. But in two ways his presentation of
the natural scene prevents us from merely dismissing what he is
trying to do. In the first place, we have to notice that in linking
Nell to nature Dickens is trying, no matter how clumsily, to
penetrate beyond the literal to a deeper level of meaning. We
have two clues:

> A change had been gradually stealing over her, in the time of her
> loneliness and sorrow. With failing strength and heightening
> resolution, there had sprung up a purified and altered mind; there
> had grown in her bosom blessed thoughts and hopes, which are
> the portion of few but the weak and drooping. There were none to
> see the frail, perishable figure, as it glided from the fire and leant
> pensively at the open casement, none but the stars, to look into the
> upturned face and read its history. (ch 52)

Impossible to miss the echo. Nell is the maid who dwells among untrodden ways, whom there are none to praise and very few to love, and who grows in sun and shower. In the following passage there is surely an under-echo of 'A Slumber Did My Spirit Seal':

> She was dead. No sleep so beautiful and calm, so free from trace of pain, so fair to look upon. She seemed a creature fresh from the hand of God, and waiting for the breath of life; not one who had lived and suffered death. (ch 61)

Nell seems a thing that cannot feel the touch of earthly years. But what are we to make of these Wordsworthian echoes? Do they amount merely to the fact that Mary is in her grave and, oh, the difference to Dickens? Not quite, I think. Though that element is certainly there, it is accompanied by a stronger concern to search out and identify the natural rhythms of life, uncontaminated by human touch or the touch of years. The concern is far from successful, and indeed Dickens later rejects the notion that you can ever think of a life as fulfilled if it is lived in isolation, housed at a distance from its kind. But it is possible to feel that at this point in his development he is trying to estimate the worth of his notion that life is ineluctably corrupted – perhaps – by the city. It hardly needs remarking that this notion comes within hailing distance of the considered withdrawal from life that is contemplated in much of Wordsworth's work. Dickens muddles the notion, however, because when he thinks of city life corrupting natural values what he half-means is that he doesn't want Nell's virginal innocence corrupted by Quilp's sexual taint (how he wounds himself over Quilp's sleeping in her bed). She has to stay pure even if the only way to do it is to die. Even so, Nell is in some ways the metaphor for natural values which must flee the city as a place of terrible corruption and death; and most of the city-dwellers we see *are* corrupted, warped, maimed.

There is another reason for our taking seriously Dickens's use of nature in the *Old Curiosity Shop*. No matter how Nell may want to escape into it, the fact is that its pristine innocence is remarkably difficult to discover, or to find permanent refuge in once it has been discovered. The natural world is constantly invaded by citizens of the corrupt world, and in trying to flee from them Nell is liable to be brought back to the city. Birmingham, for example:

> On every side, and as far as the eye could see into the heavy distance, tall chimneys crowded on each other, and presented that endless repetition of the same dull, ugly form, which is the horror of oppressive dreams, poured out their plague of smoke, obscured the light, and made foul the melancholy air. (ch 45)

The description goes on for a good while and then modulates into an account of 'night-time in this dreadful spot', with bands of 'unemployed labourers', 'maddened men, armed with sword and firebrand', carts that rumble by 'filled with rude coffins', orphans crying, women shrieking, and so on. (ch 45) I do not particularly want to stress what is the fairly loose symbolism of the *Old Curiosity Shop*, but we cannot avoid noticing that the city is associated with images of dark, the rural world with images of light. And the significance of those associations does not need explaining.

I do, however, want to notice how the corruptions of city life taint nature. In *Oliver Twist* Fagin unaccountably turns up miles from London, and in the *Old Curiosity Shop* Quilp does exactly the same thing. We note also that Codlin and Short pretend to a friendship for Nell that they do not really feel, because they see in her the chance of making money, and that old Trent is lured back into his gambling ways by the chance encounter with some gipsies. Nature is not the safe and enclosed world that Nell obscurely hopes it will prove to be. Even if it is itself associated with innocence and goodness it is powerless to resist the taint that spreads into it from the city. As the mention of Quilp, Codlin, the gipsies and Trent's mania imply, the chief taint is money.

In his descriptions of cities in the novel from which I have so far quoted, it is clear that Dickens is choosing to focus on the horror and misery of people forced to live in poverty. And many of the isolated scenes in the *Old Curiosity Shop* provide what we might call emblematic instances of money-ills. They do not join up to form a consistent or realized theme, but they occur often enough in the novel for us to feel that intermittently they force themselves on Dickens's attention in a way that should not be confused with his interest in the chance they give him to examine the fate of Nell as the near-holy child. Here is an example. Nell knocks on the door of a 'wretched hovel':

> 'What would you have here?' said a gaunt miserable man, opening it.
> 'Charity. A morsel of bread.'
> 'Do you see that?' returned the man hoarsely, pointing to a kind of bundle on the ground. 'That's a dead child. I and five hundred men were thrown out of work three months ago. That is my third dead child, and last. Do you think I have charity to show, or a morsel of bread to spare?' (ch 45)

It is striking and bizarre, the way a door can open to provide an example of horrific suffering. And although the novel does not try to analyse money-ills, it does attempt to identify and instance them.

> Why had they come to this noisy town when there were peaceful country places, in which, at least, they might have hungered and thirsted, with less suffering than in its squalid strife! They were but an atom here, in a mountain heap of misery, the very sight of which increased their hopelessness and suffering. (ch 44)

Nobody would pretend that the *Old Curiosity Shop* presents its readers with a mountain heap of misery, but it certainly shows a number of people who are corrupted or destroyed by their lack of cash or by their desire for it. And although these people make abrupt appearances and disappearances, their presence in the novel gives it some thematic coherence. In different ways Fred, Dick, old Trent, Brass, Codlin and Short all fail the test of the natural human claims that are made of them. 'Codlin's the friend, remember – not Short.' It is obvious enough, but it makes its point, as does

Fred's willingness to sell his sister to Dick so that they can get their hands on Trent's fortune. We may note that the desire for hard cash easily slips into the great expectations on which Fred, Dick and Trent all live. Fred has an expectation of fortune, Quilp introduces Dick to Brass as 'a gentleman of good family and great expectations' (ch 33), and very early in the novel Trent tells the narrator that Nell will 'be rich one of these days, and a fine lady'. (ch 1) The destruction of expectations is one of the novel's obvious motifs, and it works by means of an emblematic terseness well exemplified in the name and disposition of Sampson Brass, who in his subjection to Quilp willingly surrenders manhood for money. Quilp's taunting of Brass is a superb comic image of the lunatic indignities that the desire for money can create:

> It was not precisely the kind of weather in which people usually take tea in summer-houses, far less in summer-houses in an advanced state of decay, and overlooking the slimy banks of a great river at low water. Nevertheless, it was in this choice retreat that Mr. Quilp ordered a cold collation to be prepared, and it was beneath its cracked and leaky roof that he in due course of time received Mr. Sampson and his sister Sally.
> 'You're fond of the beauties of nature,' said Quilp with a grin. 'Is this charming, Brass? Is it unusual, unsophisticated, primitive?'
> 'It's delightful indeed, sir,' replied the lawyer.
> 'Cool?' said Quilp.
> 'N-not particularly so, I think, sir,' rejoined Brass, with his teeth chattering in his head.
> 'Perhaps a little damp and ague-ish?' said Quilp.
> 'Just damp enough to be cheerful, sir,' rejoined Brass. 'Nothing more, sir, nothing more.' (ch 51)

Quilp of course is a marvellous creation. And yet because of him we are brought face to face with perhaps the most teasing problem that the novel poses. I have said that the *Old Curiosity Shop* does not attempt to analyse the 'mountain heap of misery' which Dickens locates in the city. I hope it does not seem like quibbling if I say that he nevertheless tries to account for the corruption within the novel. For this is undoubtedly what he does, at least in so far as he locates the root cause of evil in the spirit of Quilp.

If we choose our moments carefully we can abstract enough from the novel to make Quilp appear a very impressive image or embodiment of the infallible cancer of money-interest. In the first place, he is particularly associated with the dark, even to the point of seeming like the devil hot from hell: 'he lighted his pipe, and smoked against the chimney until nothing of him was visible through the mist but a pair of red and highly inflamed eyes, with sometimes a dim vision of his head and face, as, in a violent fit of coughing, he slightly stirred the smoke and scattered the heavy wreaths by which they were obscured.' (ch 50) In the second place, Quilp's 'bachelor hall' is a debasing parody of pastoral values, as the scene I have already quoted, where he taunts Sampson Brass, makes clear. His summer-house provides the anti-pastoral element of the novel, and that this should be so reinforces the concept of Quilp as supremely unnatural, which his deformity and grotesque manners also indicate. Yet again, Quilp is an image of irresistible power. In spite of his incredible ugliness he is sexually attractive. His wife says to her friends that ' "Quilp has such a way with him when he likes, that the best-looking woman here couldn't refuse him if I was dead, and she was free, and he chose to make love to her . . . Mother knows . . . that what I say is quite correct, for she often said so before we were married. Didn't you say so, mother?" ' (ch 4) Even Casanova could conceive of no greater triumph than having a mother and daughter in love with him at the same time. With Quilp, sex emphasizes unnatural relationships. It is hinted that the Marchioness may be his illegitimate daughter. Not that the hint is cleared up (perhaps because since the Marchioness turns out well, Dickens couldn't think of giving her so awful a father), but at the end of the novel Dick entertains 'sundry misgivings whether [Quilp], in his lifetime, might not also have been able to solve the riddle, had he chosen'. (ch *The Last*). Is the Marchioness Sally's daughter by Quilp? At all events, that he should know the truth about her testifies to Quilp's omniscience. He knows whose daughter she is, just as he knows about Fred's plan to get rich, Dick's unhappy love-affair, Trent's secret, and the Brass's lodger. Quilp is also omnipresent. He turns up at Little Bethel, Kit's house, takes possession of Trent's shop, and is seen deep in the country. He is omnipotent: he owns Tom Scott, old Trent, Brass, Dick (he gets him employed and then dismissed), controls his wife and her mother, arranges Kit's imprisonment (significantly Kit is 'tainted' through money – accused of stealing from Brass). He is even immortal. After he is presumed missing and drowned, he turns up to terrify and taunt his mourners. In short, it is possible to make out a good case for the authority of Dickens's handling of the malign dwarf. Possible, too, to show him in a line running from Ralph Nickleby towards Carker. When Brass says that Quilp has never treated him 'otherwise than as a dog', we might recall Ralph's looking round at Noggs 'as if he were his dog'. And in Quilp's dominance over Tom Scott we might point to James Carker's control over the terrified Rob Toodle.

But of course it will not do. For no matter how we may work out a neat composite image of Quilp as the inhuman but irresistibly powerful embodiment of the soul of business, we know very well that he is quite incapable of bearing the weight that Dickens loads on to him. This is partly because his role of financial shark has little to do with his role as sexual aggressor (where Carker's lubricity is legitimately made an expression of his power as a man of business, Quilp's is mysterious and prompted by Dickens's deep and unconscious disquiet about Mary Hogarth's unassailed virginity – supposing she had matured, then who might *not* have had her?). But more important, the means whereby Quilp is made the all-powerful figure are decidedly crude, since they depend on a series of outrageous coincidences whose very blatancy belie his power. Without the novelist's interference Quilp could never succeed. This is not to say that the use of coincidence in Dickens's novels is always inexcusable, merely that as it occurs in the *Old Curiosity Shop* it is likely to be bad, because it so betrays Dickens's determination to invest Quilp with the sort of power that the dwarf cannot really embody. Intermittently, the novel tries to locate the disease of money-lust in the character of Quilp, but Dickens is not equal to the task.

I do not want to seem heavy-handed. What Dickens had in mind for Quilp is extremely intelligent, involving, as it does, the dwarf's presentation as the emblem of business affairs in a way that goes beyond what had been attempted in Ralph Nickleby. For Quilp is – at least by implication – linked to vast and troubling social actualities. The problem is that Dickens's intention runs smack into the pastoralism in the novel which is meant as some sort of escape from what – if we take Quilp as the embodiment of money-ills – is also suggested as inescapable, and, more seriously, that there is no secure tone by which Quilp can be held in focus. There is a really marvellous comic exuberance about him: 'he ate hard eggs, shell and all, devoured gigantic prawns with the heads and tails on . . . drank boiling tea without winking, bit his fork and spoon till they bent again.' (ch 5) I think we would all be prepared to admit that as a comic fiend Quilp is a huge success, a sort of Jonsonian rogue who spends most of his time wrecking the plans of those who are stupid or vicious enough to put themselves in his power. In his treatment of Fred and of Sampson Brass, Quilp earns the ambiguous approval that we give to Subtle and Face in their gulling of Mammon and Tribulation. But Quilp also releases in Dickens a viciousness of condemnation that seems totally disproportionate to what the dwarf is, and I think we can explain this only as we register that it is prompted by Dickens's stirrings of hatred against 'the mountain heap of misery' which, I imagine, he wanted to have destroyed just as he wanted to have Dotheboys Hall destroyed along with all that it stood for. When the notary explains how Kit's 'crime' was arranged by Quilp and describes the dwarf as 'a villain of the name of Quilp, the prime mover of this whole diabolical device', and when in death he is even more horribly maimed than he had been in life, the savagery of language offers itself as a clue to Dickens's desire to avenge those many diseased and poverty-stricken figures whose final and incurable ill is that they are victims of the money-god:

> [The water] toyed and sported with its ghastly freight, now bruising it against the slimy piles, now hiding it in mud or long rank grass, now dragging it heavily over rough stones and gravel, now feigning to yield it to its own element, and in the same action luring it away, until, tired of the ugly plaything, it flung it on a swamp – a dismal place where pirates had swung in chains, through many a wintry night – and left it there to bleach.
>
> And there it lay, alone. The sky was red with flame, and the water that bore it there had been tinged with the sullen light as it flowed along. The place the deserted carcase had left so recently, a living man, was now a blazing ruin. There was something of the glare upon its face. The hair, stirred by the damp breeze, played in a kind of mockery of death – such mockery as the dead man himself would have revelled in when alive – about its head, and its dress fluttered idly in the wind. (ch 67)

Does Quilp warrant such a death? Hardly, I think. Dickens's almost Quilp-like delight in making the dwarf suffer perhaps springs from an obscure desire to get even with life for Mary's death, but I think it owes most to his baffled feeling that in savaging Quilp he is attacking the cause of all the horrors that he so keenly registers throughout the novel.

I am not here trying to make do with unwarrantable assertion, because Dickens drops a very important clue that leads us to connect Quilp with the inhuman horrors of the city. Quilp is a creature of the dark, and he dies in the dark; and in the manner of his drowning it is even tempting to see Dickens playing with an anti-pastoralism; this river does not purify or return the body to the processes of nature. But that is no more than a possible clue. The real one comes when we read about the sky 'red with flame', for the words inevitably recall us to the view of Birmingham at night, 'when smoke was changed to fire; when every chimney spirited up its flame; and places, that had been dark vaults all day, now shone red hot, with figures moving to and fro within their blazing jaws'. More particularly, we remember Nell's strange friend, whose only solace is the fire:

'You don't know how many strange faces and different scenes I trace in the red-hot coals. It's my memory, that fire, and shows me all my life.'

The child, bending down to listen to his words, could not help remarking with what brightened eyes he continued to speak and muse.

'Yes,' he said, with a faint smile, 'it was the same when I was quite a baby, and crawled about it, till I fell asleep. My father watched it then.'

'Had you no mother?' asked the child.

'No, she was dead. Women work hard in these parts. She worked herself to death they told me, and, as they said so then, the fire has gone on saying the same thing ever since. I suppose it was true. I have always believed it.'

'Were you brought up here, then?' said the child.

'Summer and winter,' he replied. 'Secretly at first, but when they found it out, they let him keep me here. So the fire nursed me – the same fire. It has never gone out.'

'You are fond of it?' said the child.

'Of course I am. He died before it. I saw him fall down – just there, where those ashes are burning now – and wondered, I remember, why it didn't help him.' (ch 44)

If it is necessary to talk of the symbolism of fire in the novel – and I do not see how we can avoid it – it is even more necessary to add that the symbolism points precisely to what is inadequate or muddled in Dickens's presentation of Quilp and all that he is meant to embody. For *only* by symbol can he somehow be connected with and in some way made accountable for the lonely, scarcely-human figure in the ashes.

I have no wish to underrate the emblematic power of this figure. The image is a stunning one and as terrific in its unexpectedness as we know Birmingham was to Dickens in 1838, with its 'miles of cinder-paths and blazing furnaces and roaring steam engines', and such a mass of 'dirt gloom and misery as I never before witnessed'.[1] And presumably his shock was renewed when he visited the city again just after *Master Humphrey's Clock*

[1] *The Letters of Charles Dickens*, ed. House and Storey, Vol. I, 1965, p. 447.

had got under way. The savagery with which he destroys Quilp feels like the action of a man who is trying to find something he can blame and punish for the horror of suffering which his knowledge of London and visits to Birmingham had exposed him to. To say as much is to suggest that the pastoral world of the *Old Curiosity Shop* is obscurely identified with a retreat from the present of vast and hideous unnaturalness, of which Quilp becomes the emblem.

Yet the novel is not as schematic as my account so far implies. The present is at least free from the glories of Good Queen Bess's reign, when a grey-haired lady 'had been hanged and drawn and quartered' for 'succouring a wretched priest who fainted of thirst and hunger at her door' (ch 54); and if its horrors are contained within the city, then it has also to be said that the Nubbles are city-dwellers. Even the curiosity shop is replaced by a 'fine broad road'. In other words, Dickens tries to guard against any runaway lament for the past, and the Nubbles family is crucial to his attempt. They are the first in a line that includes the Toodles, Bagnets, Plornishes and Boffins, and they represent a very important step beyond the presentation of someone like Tim Linkinwater. For Dickens makes no attempt to assimilate them to the pastoral world; and the fact that they embody values he admires and which he places in the context of the city – the present – marks a significant step in his development. On the other hand it has to be admitted that the Nubbles family are not put under any great pressure by the force of the city world, so that whatever open-mindedness may be implied in their resilient goodness does not come under severe stress. (Though what stress there is, is Quilp's doing.) But Dickens leaves himself plenty of room to praise the Nubbles and let them emerge triumphant. Later, of course, the open-mindedness will be put under very great strain. But the *Old Curiosity Shop* keeps the way open for a more cheerful view than is implied if we concentrate solely on the meanings of Quilp and Nell that I have been trying to tease out.

Tease is the important word. For all too clearly I cannot claim that the novel is unambiguously or coherently *about* past and present. On the other hand, I do think that if we follow up enough clues we can reassemble a possible scheme for the *Old Curiosity Shop*, and that by means of it we shall be able to make sufficient sense of the novel to explain elements that are otherwise totally inexplicable. If we do this we can also see how it fits into Dickens's developing interests and concerns.

III BARNABY RUDGE

Once we have grasped that the *Old Curiosity Shop* voices in a muffled way concern about the new world and its threat to the past, we shall be in a better position to understand *Barnaby Rudge*. Like the *Old Curiosity Shop*, *Barnaby Rudge* is a novel that deserves sympathetic criticism. Too often critics either ignore it, brush it off as Dickens's attempt to allegorise the problems of chartism, refer to it as a mere pot-boiler, or excuse it as a misguided attempt to write a costume drama in the manner of Lytton or Ainsworth. Steven Marcus, it is true, takes the novel more seriously, but his investigation of *Barnaby Rudge* as a psychological study in father–son relationships does not do justice to its real worth. Not that I would deny that there is an important concern with father–son relationships in the novel; but I think it absolutely essential that we see in Dickens's handling of these relationships an extremely clever way of trying to make palpable the aggressive and oppressive influence of the past upon the present, of the old order against the new.

Barnaby Rudge is a much better novel than the *Old Curiosity Shop*. It is an altogether more balanced, articulate and considered work. The Gordon Riots offer Dickens both the opportunity to investigate how an explosive social situation comes into existence, and a chance to test out his own allegiances; and this second matter is by no means an open and shut affair. Indeed one of the novel's most brilliant achievements is its complex presentation of values so that they do not divide into the sort of sharp alternatives that he comes perilously near to entertaining in the *Old Curiosity Shop*. In *Barnaby Rudge* Dickens's concern with past and present does not produce any simple alignments. One reason for this is that the novel is clearly the work of a man who has brooded deeply on the nature of social movements and change, another is that he had been poring over Carlyle's studies of the *French Revolution* and *Chartism*, and a third is his determination to outdo Scott as an historical novelist (this determination is further proof of that aggressive self-confidence whose presence I noted in *Nicholas Nickleby*). And in far and away the best essay on the novel, Jack Lindsay has pointed out how all three reasons help to influence its final shape and scope.[1] I find myself in disagreement with Lindsay on several matters, but he is quite right in seeing that *Barnaby Rudge* is a very original and intelligent novel, and in particular an extremely impressive study of the nature of social change.

Since Dickens is primarily interested in enquiring into how change comes about and discovering where his own sympathies lie, it is obvious that *Barnaby Rudge* works best when it shows private lives caught up into public affairs, and is at its least impressive when dealing with the merely private. Indeed, the merely private is more or less irrelevant to the novel, which explains why its women are so tiresome and for the most part rendered in Dickens's worst prose. They represent his concession to audience expectations which he has little chance to satisfy, since *Barnaby Rudge* is not really about love at all. Mrs Varden is his last and for the most part inept effort to follow Jane Austen (the debt to Mrs Bennet is both obvious and strikingly to Dickens's disadvantage), Dolly is presumably another tribute to Mary and is plain awful, Miss Miggs is funny but unnecessary, and Emma is simply pallid. If we add to the novel's unsatisfactory studies of the women some hasty telescoping of the plot and the awkwardly bridged time-gap between the opening and the Riots themselves, we have made most of the obvious criticisms that can fairly be brought against *Barnaby Rudge*. Compared with what it achieves they seem very slight.

[1] In *Dickens and the Twentieth Century*.

A more serious criticism may be that in the end Dickens's effort to preserve an open-minded imaginative enquiry is unbalanced by the undeserved weight of approval he gives to some of the representatives of the passing social order. But I am not sure how heavily such criticism should weigh, because I think that in *Barnaby Rudge* he tries strenuously to avoid falling into emotional prejudice, and without doubt he works brilliantly to thicken his view of the social situation in order to resist any simple attitudes of approval and disapproval. The presentation of character and incident in *Barnaby Rudge* is such as to deny us any easy certainty of response. The novel's first chapter perfectly exemplifies Dickens's method.

It opens with a scene at the Maypole Inn at Chigwell, situated some twelve miles from London but still very much part of the pastoral world. The Inn is owned by the Haredale family, whose last male representative lives with his niece at the family's great house, a mile or so from the Maypole. In other words, we have an obvious image of a stable social order rooted in the past. What is far from obvious is Dickens's attitude to the order. The Maypole, we are told, is 'a very old house' and

> With its overhanging stories, drowsy little panes of glass, and front bulging out and projecting over the pathway, the old house looked as if it were nodding in its sleep. Indeed, it needed no very great stretch of fancy to detect in it other resemblances to humanity. The bricks of which it was built had originally been a deep dark red, but had grown yellow and discoloured like an old man's skin; the sturdy timbers had decayed like teeth; and here and there the ivy, like a garment to comfort it in its age, wrapt its green leaves closely round the time-worn walls. (ch 1)

It is a marvellously suggestive passage, controlled by a tone whose poise is typical of the entire effort of *Barnaby Rudge*, to register, enquire, judge, without hastening or thinning out any part of the process. I find very impressive the fact that any tendency towards sentimental or nostalgic affection that the first sentence releases (with the 'drowsy little panes of glass'), is fully balanced by the later images of decrepitude. The house is moribund; not just old, but decayed as well. What had once been fine about it may no longer be so. And if it seems to exist in harmony with nature – and therefore suggest a sort of unchallengeable rightness both in itself and in its dependence on the great house – we need to recognize that the ivy which comforts it is also an agent of destruction. For the ivy works naturally as an agent of time to destroy the house. In short, the opening sentences present us with a poetic image of a way of life that has grown old and apparently deserves to die, if only in the process of time.

Yet the next sentences suggest a considerable modification of what has so far been said:

> It was a hale and hearty age though, still: and in the summer or autumn evenings, when the glow of the setting sun fell upon the oak and chestnut trees of the adjacent forest, the old house, partaking of its lustre, seemed their fit companion, and to have many good years of life in him yet.

Not as moribund as all that, perhaps. And not so ready to be superseded, either. But the summer or autumn evenings, the setting sun. Images of fullness, without doubt, but also of the coming dark of winter and night. In the *Old Curiosity Shop*, I suggested, the pastoral world is associated with light, glad day; here light is to lose out to the dark, and again the implication is that this is in the natural course of things.

But Dickens has not done. The natural and certain course may itself be dislocated, thrown into doubt. For following immediately on the sentences I have just quoted, we have this:

> The evening with which we have to do, was neither a summer nor an autumn one, but the twilight of a day in March, when the wind howled dismally among the bare branches of the trees, and [rumbled] in the wide chimneys and [drove] the rain against the windows of the Maypole Inn.

The time is unpropitious, the weather uncertain; March suggests the hope of new life but the storm suggests a threat. Promise or threat. It could be either or both. In *Barnaby Rudge* the pastoral world is frequently seen by night.

But darkness is within as well as without. In the opening chapter we are told that the proprietor of the Inn is John Willet, 'a burly, large-headed man with a fat face, which betokened profound obstinacy and slowness of apprehension, combined with a very strong reliance upon his own merits'. It is possible to see in the landlord's name the clue to his belief that he can pre-serve the way of life he is identified with simply by willing that it should be so. Certainly, the full implications of his stupidity come out in a remark made to him by his son, Joe, whom he keeps in a state of total subservence. '"Look at other young men of my age. Have they no liberty, no will, no right to speak?"' Gabriel Varden, who is present during the row between father and son, suggests to John Willet that Joe 'should not be ruled with too tight a hand', and suggests to Joe that 'he should bear with his father's caprices, and rather turn them aside by temperate remonstrance than by ill-timed rebellion'. (ch. 2) When we read Varden's words we recognize how finely Dickens uses the father–son relationship as a metaphor rooted in social actuality, of the stupidities of the old order which prompt the new to rebel-lion.

The old order is collapsing into worthlessness:

> And maybe the great-grandson of that house,
> For all its bronze and marble, 's but a mouse.

The Maypole itself may not have bronze and marble, but it serves the great house, The Warren, which 'fifteen or twenty years ago stood in a park five times as broad, which with other and richer property has bit by bit changed hands and dwindled away'. (ch 1) And of the Inn's best room we are told that it

> had a melancholy aspect of grandeur in decay, and was much too vast for comfort. Rich rustling hangings, waving on the walls; and, far better, the rustling of youth and beauty's dress; the light of women's eyes, outshining the tapers and their own rich jewels; the sound of gentle tongues, and music, and the tread of maiden feet, had once been there and filled it with delight. But they were gone, and with them all its gladness. (ch 10)

Yet Willet is proud of the room: he clings to the empty form, to – dare one say – the marvellous empty sea-shell, from which all life, purpose, intrinsic value may well have departed.

Both Willet and his Inn and The Warren and its owner, Geoffrey Haredale, a lonely recluse, represent grandeur in decay. But for grandeur at its most decadent we have to go to the study of Sir John Chester (the country gentleman and John Bull-like brute who terrifies Barnaby and his mother – see ch 47 – is finely caught by Dickens's contemptuous prose but is an unintegrated image of such decadence). Dickens is not entirely successful in his manner of presenting Chester. For one thing he simply cannot resist the chance of cocking a snook at the aristocracy, and there are occasions when he uses Chester in much the same way as he used Mutanhed and Hawk. For another, the note of moral hectoring that accompanies much that he has to say of Chester as dissolute rake is wrongly limiting (the man's name, of course, shows him to be the spiritual heir of Lord Chesterfield). But when we have said this much, it is possible to add that we have in Sir John Chester a really remarkable and subtle study.

The main point about Chester is that he is the man in whom we can identify a tradition that has so obviously dwindled into irresponsibility that he hurries up its death. In one highly telling moment he glances 'approvingly at an elegant little sketch, entitled "Nature"'. (ch 15) In Chester, nature becomes a parody of intrinsic value (indeed like *Oliver Twist, Barnaby Rudge* often feels to be a novel which is built round a set of elaborate puns on the concept of nature). He is 'soft-spoken, delicately made, precise and elegant', and he always preserves 'a calm and placid smile'. (ch 11) But though he insists on the role of the gentleman, of the importance of breeding, of observing all the forms of the social order to which he belongs, its substance has so little meaning for him that he is willing to help destroy it. For it is he, as Sir John Chester M.P., who connives at the burning of the Warren; and in doing so he makes clear just how self-destructively irresponsible is his attitude to his own heritage.

In offering this view of Chester, Dickens is, of course, aligning himself with attitudes of a sort that are familiarly present in Carlyle and Ruskin. When, a year after the writing of *Barnaby Rudge*, Carlyle told his unworking aristocracy that 'you *are* bound to furnish guidance and governance to England! That is the law of your position on this God's Earth',[1] he was arguing in sheer desperation that if the governance was not forthcoming then 'the old System of Society is done, is dying and fallen into dotage'.[2] Chester M.P. is a parody of governance, and Dickens goes one step better by the quite brilliant stroke of having him disown his two sons, Edward and Hugh. Chester does not threaten his order by mere irresponsibility, he brings closer its downfall by the wilful destruction of lineage. Edward is thrown off because of the 'folly of [his] nature' in wanting to marry Emma Haredale. Chester informs him that since '"you intend to mar my plans for your establishment in life, and the preservation of that gentility and becoming pride, which our family have so long sustained"' then he has no alternative but to curse his son and let him go. (ch 32) Yet the marriage would at least have guaranteed the family's continuing to exist, so that Chester's action is both despicable and downright stupid, for with Edward gone there is no family to sustain. Not Edward's nature but his father's threatens to destroy the 'natural' order of society; and this is reinforced by the presence of Hugh, Chester's natural son.

Echoes of *King Lear* apart, the true brilliance of Dickens's invention of Hugh is that it gives him exactly the right opportunity to dramatize and explore his awareness of the gentry destroying itself through its own failures of responsibility. For it is Hugh's metaphoric meaning which signifies the extent to which *Barnaby Rudge* is probing at the complex nature of and reasons for social change. Chester uses Hugh to lead the destruction of Maypole and the Warren, those symbols of an old and ordered society. And to Hugh the destruction does not matter since he has

[1] *Past and Present*, Centenary Edn., Vol. X, p. 176.
[2] Ibid., p. 188.

been denied any proper social status. He does not even have a name, he is merely Maypole Hugh. This is how we see him:

> Loosely attired, in the coarsest and roughest garb, with scraps of straw and hay – his usual bed – clinging to him here and there, and mingling with his uncombed locks, he had fallen asleep in a posture as careless as his dress. (ch 11)

And our attention is repeatedly drawn to the 'negligence and disorder of the whole man'. Hugh, indeed, seems scarcely human, just because he is not socially identifiable. According to John Willet:

> 'that chap that can't read nor write, and has never had much to do with anything but animals, and has never lived in any way but like the animals he has lived among, *is* a animal. And,' said Mr. Willet, arriving at his logical conclusion, 'is to be treated accordingly.' (ch 11)

Hugh is allowed to live as an animal, and as a result he is quite willing to destroy the society by which he has been created and which disowns him. When he and Dennis the hangman are awaiting execution, he tells him ' "If there was but a little more sun to bask in than can find its way into this cursed place, I'd lie in it all day, and not trouble myself to sit or stand up once. That's all the care I have for myself. Why should I care for *you*?" ' (ch 74) It is a superb touch. Hugh's absolute carelessness comes straight out of the manner of his creation. Although it is Dickens who speaks through Hugh when the bastard refers to his father as ' "that black tree, of which I am the ripened fruit" ', the point remains a perfectly valid one and the image finely apt. Hugh is the final product of a way of life that has fallen into its dotage. He is a brilliantly complex and highly satisfying image by means of which Dickens can explore and present something of his concern with social decay.

The person to whom Hugh is most closely linked – the only person, indeed, with whom he feels any real allegiance – is Barnaby, who is the 'natural' (i.e. idiot) son of another wicked father. But where Chester is the bad master, Rudge is the bad servant. He kills Geoffrey Haredale's elder brother, whose steward he is. The metaphoric implications of the novel deepen now, because with this new element it is possible to see the old system of society as much threatened from without as from within. Barnaby becomes caught up in the riots; and as revolutionary leader he provides an obvious image of the irrationality of violence. He is the exact complement to Hugh because the revolutionary situation in which they both willingly participate is, it is implied, brought about by the sins of fathers who selfishly mutilate the traditional order of society and whose selfishness damages the future through their sons every bit as much as it destroys the past.

Barnaby's inherited corruption is pointed out not merely by the mark he bears but by his muddled desire for gold. And so he says to his mother:

> 'A brave evening, mother! If we had, chinking in our pockets, but a few specks of that gold which is piled up yonder in the sky, we should be rich for life.'
> 'We are better as we are,' returned the widow . . .
> 'Ay!' said Barnaby . . . 'that's well enough, mother; but gold's a good thing to have. I wish that I knew where to find it. Grip and I could do much with gold, be sure of that.'
> 'What would you do?' she asked.
> 'What! a world of things. We'd dress finely . . . keep horses, dogs, wear bright colours and feathers, do no more work, live delicately and at our ease. Oh, we'd find uses for it, mother, and uses that would do us good. I would I knew where gold was buried. How hard I'd work to dig it up!' (ch 45)

I think we are to see in Barnaby's last words a distorted or muffled envy or money-lust of the sort that drove his father to commit murder. 'How hard I'd work to dig it up' can easily pass into a revolutionary cry, and Dickens uses Barnaby to dramatize a possible cause of revolution. But there is nothing particularly simplistic about this. Envy is only one cause; it does not lie beneath every revolutionary impulse, as Hyacinth Robinson is later to think (in James's *Princess Casamassima*). Certainly envy has nothing to do with Hugh's reason for joining the riots.

This brings us to an important point. We need to notice that there is a crucial difference between the conception of the two natural men, and in trying to bring out what it is I shall also be attempting to reveal how much Dickens is seeking within himself points of balance between opposing convictions. For Hugh testifies to the hard radicalism of his creator's mind, whereas Barnaby signifies how very strong a conservative streak there is to Dickens. When the idiot and his father come face to face:

> Barnaby [struggled] with his imperfect memory, and [wondered] where he had seen that face before. He was not uncertain long, for suddenly he laid hands upon him, and striving to bear him to the ground, cried:
>
> 'Ah! I know! You are the robber!'
>
> He said nothing in reply at first, but held down his head, and struggled with him silently. Finding the younger man too strong for him, he raised his face, looked close into his eyes, and said,
>
> 'I am your father.' (ch 62)

As so often when Dickens is writing well, this moment provides the perfect image for an important theme. And surely we are meant to feel that the unnatural horror of Barnaby fighting his own father offers a metaphor of the radical disorders that stem from a refusal to acknowledge the social *status quo* (which can therefore be passed off, perhaps, as natural):

> Take but degree away, untune that string,
> And hark what discord follows! . . .
> Strength should be lord of imbecility,
> And the rude son should strike his father dead;
> Force should be right; or, rather, right and wrong –
> Between whose endless jar justice resides –
> Should lose their names, and so should justice too.
>
> (*Troilus and Cressida*, I, iii)

Impossible to resist quoting Ulysses's words, they so perfectly fit the situation which Dickens dramatizes in *Barnaby Rudge*. Strength – whether physical force or public assent – *is* the lord of imbecility, as Barnaby demonstrates and as does Lord George

Gordon, 'this poor crazy lord' as Dickens calls him. Even though Barnaby does not strike his father dead he certainly comes very close to doing so.

At this point it is perhaps necessary to say that, for all the imaginative intelligence that lies behind his invention, Barnaby strikes me as something of an unsatisfactory figure. I do not think he fails for the reason that Jack Lindsay gives – that he is too much the 'folk-fool' of the medieval world – but because, given his centrality, he is too obviously a reductive symbol of the chaotic forces that may be let loose once order is abandoned. Even his irrational lust for gold points too easily in the direction of a criticism that the mature Dickens would repudiate as cant; and as an embodiment both of irrational envy and mad destructiveness, Barnaby represents something of a withdrawal on Dickens's part from the contemplation of a revolutionary situation, not because envy and destructiveness may not play their part but because in *Barnaby Rudge* they are moved too swiftly to the centre of affairs.

A similar criticism can be brought against Sim Tappertit. Sim is shown as vain, weak and stupid, but he is also made a representative figure of revolt and violence. The plain fact is that Sim is too stupid to be as influential as Dickens would have us believe. He testifies, I think, to that conservative side of Dickens's thought which operates elsewhere in the novel and which, if it is not always unjustified, is so in the present instance because in making Sim a comic grotesque Dickens weakens his own enquiry into the possibility that 'force is right'. Tappertit is an apprentice to Gabriel Varden and also captain of a group called the 'Prentice Knights', whose elaborate forms of initiation provide an obvious parody of Unionism in the 1830s. Yet the group's essentially trivial reasons for wishing death to the masters can hardly be equated with Unionistic ambitions. Instead, they reveal Dickens's own fear that revolutionary attitudes are merely selfish and fashioned out of ignorance feeding on stupidity; and the ease with which Sim comes over to Lord George Gordon's side helps to demonstrate as much. After all, the anti-Popery riots aren't Sim's concern, nor can they be of much interest to him. And of course the riots themselves are spurious. Dickens notes of them that 'it was a most exquisite satire upon the false religious cry which had led to so much misery, that some of these [condemned rioters] owned themselves to be Catholics, and begged to be attended by their own priests'. (ch 77)

It is customary to say that when Dickens wrote about the Gordon Riots he was imaging his own deep disquiet about the potentially revolutionary situation existing in England in the 1840s. This may well be so, but I am not at all convinced that the threats of either Chartism or Unionism were uppermost in his mind. Or rather, if they were, it is because he saw in them eloquent testimony to the sort of malaise that Carlyle had pointed to in 'Signs of the Times'. Carlyle was convinced that 'the Metaphysical and Moral Sciences are falling into decay', that the age typically thinks that 'our happiness [depends] entirely on external circumstances', and that 'Unbelief' of a more fundamental character 'than intellectual dissent from the church . . . every man may see prevailing, with scarcely any but the faintest contradiction, all around him'. For Carlyle such signs were ominous portents for the future; but for Dickens they are, I think, elements he tries to trace back to the 1780s and for which the essentially irreligious nature of the no-Popery riots provides a clue of great importance, not merely because they are irreligious but because they expose a fundamental sickness existing in society, a mindless urge to destroy. For we can hardly avoid noticing that the riots in *Barnaby Rudge* are not brought about by what is bad in the past and its heritage, and Chester can manipulate Hugh only because the revolutionary situation already exists.

Here we come to a very important criticism of the novel. The fact is that a very real hiatus exists between Dickens's rendering of the order which is dying or has fallen into its dotage, and his rendering of the causes of the riots; and no amount of Marxist sophistication about the 'wild confusion' of a 'future striving to be born' can paper over the crack.[1] But then what can explain it?

[1] See Lindsay's essay, which for all its virtues becomes too schematic an account to be fair to the problems the novel raises.

Only, I suggest, Dickens's instinctive recoil from the fear of what revolution might prove to be, not just in terms of the immediate social horrors – though he was certainly very much impressed by the human tragedies of the French revolution as Carlyle recorded them, and might reasonably have seen them as providing a pattern for future disasters – but more fundamentally in terms of the destruction of social identity, and therefore of the contraction of those dimensions of time that give a spaciousness and, it seems, a significance to human life. 'Seems, I know not seems,' the revolutionary may reply. But one of Dickens's deepest feelings is his fear that the past, both social and personal, may be lost to men, and I suggested how this fear affects the writing of the *Old Curiosity Shop*. It is indeed one of his life-long concerns. The past that Dickens cares for is not a selfishly guarded and ossified set of prejudices, nor a collection of meaningless rituals and signs; it is a living and organic principle of identity. Such talk may seem unwarrantably cloudy, yet if we think for a moment of the comic genealogies he provides for such places as Staggs's Gardens and Bleeding-Heart Yard we shall recognize that on such occasions he is working a vein that for him has a unique richness. I see nothing wrong in arguing that Dickens could not bear the possibility that such richness might be destroyed by social actualities. In a very important way he sets his face against a concept of time that is new to the nineteenth century and which Hans Meyerhoff pins down when he remarks that in Victorian England time became regarded as a commodity and that accordingly the past was thought of as a waste of time:

> Thus the temporal perspective in human lives shrank, because the past was essentially stupid and useless. Only scholars, cranks, and reactionaries were interested in preserving it. . . . Previous generations *knew* much less about the past than we do, but perhaps *felt* a much greater sense of identity and continuity with it because of the fixity, stability and relative permanence of their social stature.[1]

[1] Hans Meyerhoff, *Time in Literature*, 1960, pp. 108–9.

The greatest treatment of time as commodity in nineteenth-century English literature is to be found in *Dombey and Son*, but it is surely implicit in *Barnaby Rudge*. For Dickens attributes the wilful destruction of the existing order to the selfish indifference or ignorance about the past of such people as Tappertit, Chester, Gashford (Gordon's unscrupulous secretary who brings about the worst excesses of the riots from purely personal and selfish motives), Hugh and Barnaby. And what makes all of them capable of such destructiveness is that for one reason or another they are alienated from an identity grounded in the social structure which they want to smash.

There is a further point. Dickens's most intense hatred is directed against the guardians of the social structure who are too stupid to undertake the safeguarding of what for him is finally still in 'hale and hearty age'. It seems to me undeniable that no matter how splendidly he strives for a balanced view he cannot finally wish to see the past and its heritage destroyed. In *Barnaby Rudge* Dickens shows himself as a great novelist at least to the extent that his exploration of the revolutionary condition is so much more profound than any of his contemporaries could manage. But for all that, when he writes about the destructiveness of the riots we sense how, as he piles detail on detail, he is lacerating himself in an agony of determination to know – and make us know – the worst. Nothing in the novel is more shocking than the force with which Dickens makes us see what destruction actually *is* (as opposed to what it may mean or promise). There is for example the demolition of Mansfield's house, which is set fire to by a mob. That Dickens should use the word mob emphasizes his sense of the crowd's basic irrationality, and what it destroys makes clear his detestation of its ways. Among the ruins are

> the whole of the costly furniture, the plate and jewels, a beautiful gallery of pictures, the rarest collection of manuscripts ever possessed by any one private person in the world, and worse than all, because nothing could replace this loss, the great Law Library, on almost every page of which were notes in the Judge's own hand,

of inestimable value – being the results of the study and experience of his whole life. (ch 66)

There is in addition the description of the looting of the Warren, far too long to quote here since Dickens takes several pages over it, but which in its remorseless attention to detail proves how determined he is that we shall be spared nothing of the pain of despoliation.

The destruction of the Warren, we should note, takes place at night. The wrecking of the great house is accomplished by the light of flames in which 'the more the fire crackled and raged, the wilder and more cruel the men grew'. (ch 55) The symbolism of the fire recalls us to the *Old Curiosity Shop*, where it is linked to the dark side of man's nature, to all the horrors from which Dickens so strongly recoils. But the darkness is most hideously apparent in the destruction of the Maypole, for whose owner the world has quite simply come to an end. John Willet

> was perfectly contented to sit there, staring at [the scene of destruction], and felt no more indignation or discomfort in his bonds than if they had been robes of honour. So far as he was personally concerned, old Time lay snoring, and the world stood still. (ch 55)

That the inherited glory of the rich is in bad hands could scarcely be brought out more succinctly than in Willet's total inability to grasp what is happening to him. Even so, the destruction of the heritage is dreadful, and in the energy that Dickens's prose takes on when he writes of the smashing of the Maypole we may see his terrible rage at what he regards as an offence against nature. I think we may also see that in choosing to make more of the destruction of the Maypole than of any other house, he is determined to show his audience that the average as well as the exceptional must suffer from revolution. It is hardly too much to suggest that the Inn represents a middle way of life that is just as much forfeit to the madness of revolution as is the great house.

> Men darting in and out, by door and window, smashing the glass, turning the taps, drinking liquor out of China punchbowls, sitting astride of casks, smoking private and personal pipes, cutting

down the sacred grove of lemons, hacking and hewing at the celebrated cheese, breaking open inviolable drawers, putting things in their pockets which didn't belong to them, dividing [John's] money before his own eyes, wantonly wasting, breaking, pulling down, and tearing up: nothing quiet, nothing private: men everywhere – above, below, overhead, in the bedrooms, in the kitchen, in the yard, in the stables – clambering in at windows when there were doors wide open; dropping out of windows when the stairs were handy; leaping over the banisters into chasms of passages: new faces and figures presenting themselves every instant – some yelling, some singing, some fighting, some breaking glass and crockery, some laying the dust with liquor they couldn't drink, some ringing the bells till they pulled them down, others beating them with pokers till they beat them into fragments: more men still – more, more, more – swarming in like insects: noise, smoke, light, darkness, frolic, anger, laughter, groans, plunder, fear, and ruin! (ch 54)

Even in this chaotic scene, Dickens shows how aware he is that Willet, as an embodiment on the 'fixed' order of things, has brought disaster on himself. 'Sacred', 'celebrated', 'inviolable': in the ironic use of such words we are directed towards Willet's stupidity in thinking himself and his order as beyond touch. Besides, there is a sort of holiday-spirit in the irreverance of those who drop out of windows when doors are handy; it is a witty detail of the disordering of custom.

All the same, what counts for most in the passage is its awareness of 'ruin'. It is therefore inevitable that the novel's heroes should be the conciliators, Varden, Joe and Edward Chester, who align themselves with the old system though they know its terrible limitations, Varden because of his encounters with Sir John Chester and his understanding of what that gentleman is, Joe and Edward because they are unjustifiably thrown off by their fathers. When Varden warns Joe against ill-timed rebellion he is making Dickens's point, that rebellion is always ill-timed. In Joe's decision to join the army and Edward's active desire to thwart the rioters' worst plans we see the 'average' or ordinary citizens who are prepared to honour the social order, no matter how it may be dishonoured by those whom it most favours or who are its official guardians. There is a great difference between Joe and Edward and the frightened Lord Mayor and panicking House of Commons, yet in the end they are on the same side. The young men want to save Barnaby, but they are determined to bring the rioters to justice even if that means destroying him.

I do not want to give the impression, however, that Dickens falls back on any simple set of oppositions. The brilliance of *Barnaby Rudge* depends on his determination to test to the full his allegiances, and this is shown in the really great scene where Varden refuses to hand over the key that will open up Newgate. At this moment the idea of the locksmith as unofficial guardian of the stable order is troubled by deep and very radical doubts. May it not be that the cost of championing the old order is too great in human terms? For many of the Newgate prisoners are unjustly thrown into prison by the inhuman lack of justice of the old order itself. And in what way is Varden different from Dennis the hangman, who does not want the condemned men released, since he 'had been bred and matured in the good old school, and had administered the good old laws on the good old plan'? (ch 65) There is no mistaking Dickens's icy contempt for Dennis, who exists in abject and broken adherence to an order which has dehumanized him. Against Dennis, indeed, Hugh emerges as a sort of hero, for it is he who frees the men:

> 'Halloa!' cried Hugh, who was the first to look into the dusky passage. 'Dennis before us! Well done, old boy. Be quick, and open here, for we shall be suffocated in the smoke, going out.'
>
> 'Go out at once, then,' said Dennis. 'What do you want here?'
>
> 'Want!' echoed Hugh. 'The four men.'
>
> 'Four devils!' cried the hangman. 'Don't you know they're left for death on Thursday? Don't you respect the law – the constitootion – nothing? Let the four men be.' (ch 65)

Dennis's remarks raise an important question. Who could respect a law of which he is representative and guardian? The disquieting answer is that Varden can, for he also wants to keep

the prison closed. Hugh challenges Akerman, the head jailor, to
deliver up some friends from Newgate, and Akerman refuses:

> 'Mr. Akerman,' cried Gabriel, 'Mr. Akerman.'
>
> 'I will hear no more from any of you,' replied the governor,
> turning towards the speaker, and waving his hand.
>
> 'But I am not one of them,' said Gabriel. 'I am an honest man,
> Mr. Akerman; a respectable tradesman – Gabriel Varden, the
> locksmith. You know me?'
>
> 'You among the crowd!' cried the governor in an altered voice.
>
> 'Brought here by force – brought here to pick the lock of the
> great door for them,' rejoined the locksmith. 'Bear witness for me,
> Mr. Akerman, that I refuse to do it; and that I will not do it, come
> what may of my refusal. If any violence is done to me, please to
> remember this.'
>
> 'Is there no way of helping you?' said the governor.
>
> 'None, Mr. Akerman. You'll do your duty and I'll do mine.
> Once again, you robbers and cut-throats,' said the locksmith,
> turning round upon them, 'I refuse. Ah! howl till you're hoarse. I
> refuse.' . . .
>
> 'Where is that man,' said the keeper anxiously, 'who spoke to
> me just now?'
>
> 'Here!' Hugh replied.
>
> 'Do you know what the guilt of murder is, and that by keeping
> the honest tradesman at your side you endanger his life!'
>
> 'We know it very well,' he answered, 'for what else did we
> bring him here? Let's have our friends, master, and you shall have
> your friend. Is that fair, lads?'
>
> The mob replied to him with a loud Hurrah!
>
> 'You see how it is, sir?' cried Varden. 'Keep 'em out, in King
> George's name. Remember what I have said. Good night!' (ch 64)

True, the conflict of allegiances doesn't emerge quite directly
because Varden is under the extra pressure of having had his
daughter kidnapped. Still, the fact that the kidnapping should
have been introduced may itself suggest some form of special
pleading on Dickens's part (that's the sort of thing the rioters
descend to). But anyway it hardly blinds us to the dubious worth
of Varden's loyalty. It is very hard to avoid feeling that his

request to 'Keep 'em out, in King George's name' is wickedly ironic. What cannot be avoided is the sense the scene gives, of representing a terrific effort of confrontation where values and allegiances can be fully exposed and tested. And it is because of such confrontations that *Barnaby Rudge* becomes a triumphant example of intellectual courage and honesty. One more point and I have done.

In his essay Jack Lindsay claims that with the exception of Varden, 'the persons in the novel who define the acceptance of the *status quo* are all . . . despicable.' But this is not so. Quite apart from Edward and Joe, who find reasons to accept an order to which personally they owe no allegiance, there is also the purely emblematic figure of the officer of the Foot Guards who arrests Barnaby:

> They were not long in reaching the barracks, for the officer who commanded the party was desirous to avoid rousing the people by the display of military force in the streets, and was humanely anxious to give as little opportunity as possible for any attempt at rescue; knowing that it must lead to bloodshed and loss of life, and that if the civil authorities by whom he was accompanied, empowered him to order his men to fire, many innocent persons would probably fall, whom curiosity and idleness had attracted to the spot. (ch 58)

Dickens, indeed, goes out of his way to commend the officer's 'merciful prudence' and 'wise proceeding', and the passage as a whole reads like a celebration of wisely paternal authority. At the very least, it acts as a check to those stark images of the dereliction of responsibility, Sir John Chester and the Lord Mayor. The city and what it contains is not necessarily hell, just as the country – given Willet and what he represents – is not necessarily paradise. But the passage I have just quoted needs to be set against the description of the scene prior to the executions of Barnaby, Hugh and Dennis:

> A fairer morning never shone. From the roofs and upper stories of these buildings, the spires of city churches and the great cathedral

dome were visible, rising up beyond the prison into the blue sky, and clad in the colour of light summer clouds, and showing in the clear atmosphere their every scrap of tracery and fret-work, and every niche and loophole. All was brightness and promise, excepting in the street below, into which (for it yet lay in shadow) the eye looked down as into a dark trench, where, in the midst of so much life, and hope, and renewal of existence, stood the terrible instrument of death. It seemed as if the very sun forbore to look at it.

But it was better, grim and sombre in the shade, than when, the day being advanced, it stood confessed in the full glare and glory of the sun, with its black paint blistering, and its nooses dangling in the light like loathsome garlands. It was better in the solitude and gloom of midnight with a few forms clustering about it, than in the freshness and stir of morning: the centre of an eager crowd. (ch 77)

At this point the passage rather trails off into an attack on public executions which we know Dickens loathed. But what I have quoted is extremely disquieting, especially if we pay attention to the imagery and its implications. For Dickens is attempting to assimilate the city into the natural order of things. In the *Old Curiosity Shop* the pastoral world had been associated with light, but now it is London that is linked to life-giving properties. Such properties have clear political overtones. We can hardly come upon the phrase 'life, and hope, and renewal of existence', without feeling that it somehow signifies a morning of social-political promise. The day of calm follows the night of storm (most of the novel's action takes place at night).

Although Dickens is prepared to see the city in terms of a natural order, healed or healthy, which promises continuity and vitality (witness the spires of city churches and cathedral dome that rise into the blue sky and are the 'colour of light summer clouds'), he also knows that it is a place of death. The gallows is, after all, a ghastly parody of the natural order, with nooses like 'loathsome garlands'. That image viciously mocks the optimism that associates the city with natural health. To put it as plainly as is fair: Dickens makes a real effort to see the city as equated with authority and the *status quo* and yet equated also with promise for the future, and he tries to make this promise palpable by the use of images that go with the rural scene he has mostly associated with time past and a valuably natural way of life. In short, the passage as a whole is an attempt to anneal past and future and country and city, and represents the novel's last effort to balance out allegiances and values.

It is an impressive attempt but it fails and for what is, I imagine, a fairly obvious reason. For it typifies Dickens's readiness in *Barnaby Rudge* to render a sense of social change and its causes almost entirely in terms of symbol and poetic image; and the result is that too little of the novel is seen in precise objective terms. No matter how brilliant in themselves Hugh, Barnaby, Chester, Varden, and the Maypole are, taken altogether they weaken the novel's force. Jack Lindsay puts his finger on what is wrong when he remarks that if an historical novel is to be a fully realized work it 'requires somewhere in it a more objective assessment of the social forces involved'. Dickens does not dare the objective assessment, I think, because it would disturb his attempt to prescribe a healthy process of social change as involving the adherence to much of the past (the officer is praised not just for doing the right thing but for being on the right side). In the end, *Barnaby Rudge* brings out into the open allegiances, which in the *Old Curiosity Shop* had been concealed or muffled. But the novel is remarkable for the sheer intelligence with which Dickens tests out and explores the implications of his allegiances, even if his way with language is finally too allusive and therefore evasive. The evasiveness probably results from his attempting to preserve an open-endedness that we also find at the end of the *Old Curiosity Shop*. That the attempt should have been made at all is a matter for considerable praise. It proves that Dickens had qualities of mind that he is not usually given credit for possessing.

⅔ 4 · FROM CHUZZLEWIT TO DOMBEY

I

I have brought two novels together in this chapter, because I think it important to discuss the considerable leap that Dickens takes in moving from one to the other. In particular, I want to discuss the limits of inspiration that are reached in *Martin Chuzzlewit*, since it is in this novel that Dickens's fabulous imaginative gifts are put under the severest strain and finally crack. *Martin Chuzzlewit*, indeed, is a crucial novel in Dickens's development. To speak plainly, it is a crisis novel. The evidence of the subsequent novels shows that after *Chuzzlewit* Dickens was determined that never again would he compose in so slapdash a way, be so prodigal with his material, or allow himself to waste his genius instead of taxing and extending it.

We know that from *Dombey and Son* onwards Dickens began to plan his novels with great care, and I do not think anyone would doubt that his decision was a wise one. Oddly, however, the implications for *Martin Chuzzlewit* have not been accepted. At least, with the exception of Barbara Hardy I do not know of any contemporary critic honest enough to admit that *Chuzzlewit*, marvellous though it undoubtedly is in parts, is something of a marvellous mess. The early and manifestly just criticisms of the novel's 'fast writing and careless composition', and lack of 'artistic craft' in the management of plot, have been conveniently ignored or forgotten.[1]

But how much of a mess *is Martin Chuzzlewit*? Is it a mess at

[1] For the reception of *Martin Chuzzlewit*, see Ford, *Dickens and his Readers*, esp. pp. 44–8.

all? Surely the novel has a perfectly plain subject, Self; or, to put it rather more fully, it is about the dire consequences of acting in the interests of Self, and these consequences stem mostly from seeing self-success in terms of financial acquisition and cover a whole range of personal disasters, failures of human relationship (marriage, friendship, etc), the follies of great expectations, and so on and so on. This sort of account of the novel's meaning is common in recent criticism, and since Dickens himself said that *Martin Chuzzlewit* was about Self, and since it is by no means difficult to build up an abstract scheme that will find a place for most of the novel's characters and plots, it may seem churlish to doubt its success. Yet the fact is that as soon as we begin to ask how adequately the scheme is worked out, we have to face some very disquieting answers.

I shall be attending to the answers shortly, but let me first clear up a possible misunderstanding. I do not think *Martin Chuzzlewit* is a bad novel. On the contrary, it has about it the air of being very nearly a great one, or at least possessing qualities that one would think necessary to greatness. Yet somehow or other they do not cohere. The result is that when we try to define *Martin Chuzzlewit*'s nature we find ourselves faced with great difficulties. I think it important to investigate what these difficulties are and how they arise, which means that I must try to set out what goes wrong. The problem is that in drawing attention to the novel's flaws I shall be guilty of a distortion of emphasis, so it is perhaps necessary to say here that in what follows I am not really trying to arrive at a balanced estimate of *Martin Chuzzlewit*, because to some extent at least I shall take its virtues for granted. They do not commonly lack for praise.

If we try to locate the failures in *Martin Chuzzlewit* we at once recognize that some are so trivial that they do not deserve to have much time spent on them and certainly should not be allowed to damn the novel. For example, a whole cluster of faults arise from Dickens's inability to control the vast sprawl of his narrative. Yet the very fact that the narrative is so enormously rich is as much a tribute to Dickens's ingenuity as a sign of weakness.

What other English novelist can engage so many characters, so many divergent interests, and make such bravura efforts to tie the whole lot together? Merely to watch how Dickens copes with the proliferating demands of his plots is pleasurable enough. But there are stray ends and they detract from our pleasure; the magic bundle threatens to come loose. It is mildly irritating, for instance, to have all Jonas's hole-and-corner plotting about his wife's life-insurance policy and then find that nothing comes of it. In giving Jonas this added touch of villainy Dickens is clearly working on the contemporary fascination with wife-murder, and Jonas may easily be imagined as the emblem of Self who kills for money. Only he doesn't kill Mercy. He doesn't even try to. The whole business is forgotten. So, too, is young Martin's letter to the Board of School Governors, explaining that it is his and not Pecksniff's architectural plans for a new school which they have accepted (I pass by the outrageous coincidence that on the very day Mark and Martin get back to England they should see Pecksniff in the act of receiving homage for Martin's invention of a grammar school). There are other acts of forgetfulness on Dickens's part and with them may go young Bailey's 'death' and restoration to life, and the reappearance of the couple Mark and Martin had left for as good as dead in Eden. All these are spots on the novel, but they do not amount to serious blemishes.

The confusions over the timing of events that pile up towards the end of the novel are, however, a more serious matter. It is perhaps all very well to have a sort of double time-scheme whereby events happen slowly in America and quickly in England, but as the novel draws to its close Dickens so bungles the timing of Tigg's murder and the events around it that he destroys the very suspense that he himself has been labouring to build. To set out the details of this mis-management would be a tedious exercise, but it is necessary to point out that when Pecksniff declares himself ruined by the fall of Tigg's business, Dickens's zeal for moral tit-for-tat has got well ahead of the possibilities. Because for Pecksniff to have been ruined would have required him to have handed over his money to Tigg and for it to then have been misappropriated. Yet Pecksniff only agrees to the deal on the evening of Tigg's murder, so that any actual financial transaction would have been out of the question. This may seem trivial enough. On the other hand it points towards what is perhaps the most crucial problem of all with the novel, for Dickens never quite makes up his mind whether he is writing a realistic study or a moral and prescriptive fable. Pecksniff's loss belongs to the fable. But the effort to make it fully realistic – and the failure to bring it off – amounts to a hesitancy of purpose that we find echoed again and again in the novel. Let me give another example, before I broaden the discussion. When old Antony Chuzzlewit dies, Dickens creates a quite superb image of the man's unnaturalness which finally catches up with him:

> He had fallen from his chair in a fit, and lay there, battling for each gasp of breath, with every shrivelled vein and sinew starting in its place, as if it were bent on bearing witness to his age, and sternly pleading with Nature against his recovery. It was frightful to see how the principle of life, shut up within his withered frame, fought like a strong devil, mad to be released, and rent its ancient prison-house. A young man in the fulness of his vigour, struggling with so much strength of desperation, would have been a dismal sight; but an old, old, shrunken body, endowed with preternatural might, and giving the lie in every motion of its every limb and joint to its enfeebled aspect, was a hideous spectacle indeed.

And almost with his last breath he tries to communicate and cannot:

> He spoke to them: in something of his own voice too, but sharpened and made hollow, like a dead man's face. What he would have said, God knows. He seemed to utter words, but they were such as man had never heard. And this was the most fearful circumstance of all, to see him standing there, gabbling in an unearthly tongue. (ch 18)

As an image of the utter incommunicable loneliness of Self, this seems to me quite magnificent. It has all the true imaginative power of Dickens at his best, able to find exactly the image that embodies his theme. When we add that we are meant to think Antony is dying because Jonas has poisoned him, the final chilling touch is given to the destructiveness of Self (for living by the principle of self-interest means dying by it: Antony teaches self-interest to Jonas who rewards his father by killing him out of self-interest).

Yet at the end of the novel Chuffey gives a quite different account of Antony's death. According to Chuffey's version, Antony had known that Jonas was trying to poison him and, although accepting that he deserved such a fate, died of a broken heart:

> 'It was only a few days, but he had never changed so much in twice the years. "Spare him, Chuff!" he said, before he died. They were the only words he could speak. "Spare him Chuff!" I promised him I would. I've tried to do it. He's his only son.' (ch 51)

My objection against the two very different versions of Antony's death is not that we are unfairly tricked into thinking the old man poisoned, but that in providing Chuffey's account Dickens damages his own theme. The point of Antony's death must be to pin down the destructive consequences of Self; turning it into a conventional broken-hearted ending is both vulgar and also fractures any consistency in Antony's presentation and the theme he helps embody. *Antony* to die of a broken heart? Nor can we mend matters by suggesting that Chuffey's account plays up Jonas's selfishness or that it continues the suspense (will Jonas now get clear of the law or will the murder of Tigg be laid at his door?), for the sacrifice simply is not worth what is gained. Jonas's selfishness hardly needs to be more insisted on than it already has been, and the drawing-out of the suspense is merely a trite and mechanical gimmick.

I have drawn attention to the discrepancy in the accounts of Antony's death because it directs us to something that is radically wrong with *Martin Chuzzlewit*. To put it as briefly as possible, I think that the novel suffers from Dickens's inability to decide how he shall render his chosen theme of Self. This inability has an adverse affect on both structure and the presentation of character. By and large *Martin Chuzzlewit* seems to deal in characters as types: Pecksniff, for example, is Hypocrisy, Antony and Jonas are Self, young Martin and Chevy Slyme are Great Expectations, Tom and Mark are Selflessness, Tigg is Cloth and Respectability. Faced with such a manner of presenting characters, we may think of *Martin Chuzzlewit* as a moral fable. Yet the more we examine these characters the less do they appear consistently rendered; some change from types into more individual studies (Mercy and Tigg are obvious examples) and some change from one type to another (Mrs Todgers is a case in point). Besides, some characters in the novel are seen mostly as individuals, with the result that it is difficult to take seriously the type-moralizing that is foisted on to them. Do we really believe that Mrs Gamp is a type of Self? Later on, I shall try to lay bare the nature of the inconsistencies I am indicating; for the moment I want merely to note that because they exist the novel becomes something of a muddle. And there is a related reason for its messiness. Because although it is possible to abstract the type-characters from any environmental considerations so that moral judgement is not in any sense conditioned by social factors, other characters *are* judged according to how and where they live. Mrs Todgers we learn, 'was poor, and [her goodness] had sprung up in her from among the sordid strivings of her life'. (ch 37) This remark, well enough though it may apply to Mrs Todgers, feels oddly incongruous in a novel which is surely the least socially focused of any in the canon.

I think that one important cause of the muddles I am pointing to is Dickens's involvement with his characters. It is, of course, a commonplace of criticism to remark how uniquely Dickens experiences his characters' lives, but this need not imply that the novels suffer as a result. But *Martin Chuzzlewit* does, for the simple reason that Dickens becomes so interested in his characters that he lets them take over the novel and therefore destroy any consistent rendering of his theme. They quite upset the moral pattern. Yet criticism of the sort that I am making is nearly inseparable from praise, since the fact that Dickens is prepared to free his characters from the grip of his abstract scheme testifies to that ceaseless curiosity about human affairs which is an essential part of his genius. He even becomes so fascinated by Tigg and Jonas that he quite forgets what he *should* be showing of them, in the interest of discovering what fascinates him about them. The case of Mercy, however, is the better one to start with.

Mercy and Charity are 'not unholy names I hope'. Thus Pecksniff, and for much of the time Dickens shows us the girls as comic extensions of their father's hypocrisy. They begin as types and Charity remains one to the very end. But Mercy is suddenly transformed, with the result that when she and Charity meet towards the close of the novel, the effect is unintentionally ridiculous, even though Dickens works manfully to disguise his difficulties by letting Charity do all the talking. It is not just that the girls come to belong to different worlds. More significantly they come to belong to different novelistic modes. The moment of Mercy's transition from one mode to another comes when Dickens tells us that she 'really had her share of good humour'. (ch 11) Nothing has prepared us for the remark, and indeed given what we have so far seen of her it is strictly incredible. The point is that Dickens wants to plot her walking into Jonas's marriage-trap, and as he does that he begins to feel a corresponding growth of sympathy for her. Besides, if she isn't capable of suffering, then Jonas's brutishness will be muffled. So Dickens changes his mind and Mercy changes her role. A mistake, of course, and yet without it we would not have the brilliant conversation between Mercy and old Martin, which occurs shortly before her wedding:

'When are you to be married?'

'Oh! dear Mr. Chuzzlewit, my goodness me! I'm sure I don't know. Not yet awhile, I hope.'

'You hope?' said the old man.

It was very gravely said, but she took it for banter, and giggled excessively.

'Come!' said the old man, with unusual kindness, 'you are

young, good-looking, and I think good-natured! Frivolous you
are, and love to be undoubtedly; but you must have some heart.'

'I have not given it all away, I can tell you,' said Merry, nodding
her head shrewdly, and plucking up the grass.

'Have you parted with any of it?'

She threw the grass about, and looked another way, but said
nothing.

Martin repeated his question.

'Lor, my dear Mr. Chuzzlewit! really you must excuse me!
How very odd you are.'

'If it be odd in me to desire to know whether you love the young
man whom I understand you are to marry, I *am* very odd,' said
Martin. 'For that is certainly my wish.'

'He's such a monster, you know,' said Merry, pouting.

'Then you don't love him?' returned the old man. 'Is that your
meaning?'

'Why, my dear Mr. Chuzzlewit, I'm sure I tell him a hundred
times a day that I hate him. You must have heard me tell him that.'

'Often,' said Martin.

'And so I do,' cried Merry. 'I do positively.'

'Being at the same time engaged to marry him,' observed the
old man.

'Oh yes,' said Merry. 'But I told the wretch – my dear Mr.
Chuzzlewit, I told him when he asked me – that if I ever did marry
him, it should only be that I might hate and tease him all my life.'
(ch 24)

Writing of this order requires no justification, and yet, marvellous though the dialogue is and wonderfully though Dickens
convinces us that Mercy is a silly, frivolous, but humanly interesting girl, there is very little room for him to develop his interest
in her. As Jonas's wife she lapses into a stock figure of suffering
who at best provides further evidence of her husband's brutality
– evidence which is hardly needed.

A similar problem arises with Tigg. Like Mercy, Tigg really
splits into two people. For much of the novel he is a superbly
comic creation, a fraud and trickster – 'The name Montague
Tigg will perhaps be familiar to you, in connexion with the most

remarkable events of the Peninsular War' – whose reversal of name and dress offers one more example of Dickens's concern with 'clothes-philosophy'. And a brilliant example it is, too. Tigg's meteoric rise to social eminence is very funny, very adroitly handled and earns Dickens the chance of parodying what is itself a parody in Bailey's 'rise' from Mrs Todger's jack-of-all-jobs to Tigg's man. Bailey belongs to the novel's comic genius, and *Martin Chuzzlewit* is without doubt packed with more comic brio than any other novel in the language. Consider this scrap of Bailey's conversational powers – powers of which, since he is in the service of a great man, Tigg, he is very mindful:

> 'Well, how are you?'
> 'Oh! I'm pretty well,' said Poll. He answered the question again because Mr. Bailey asked it again; and Mr. Bailey asked it again, because – accompanied with a straddling action of the white cords, a bend of the knees, and a striking forth of the top-boots – it was an easy, horse-fleshy, turfy sort of thing to do.
> 'Wot are you up to, old feller?' added Mr. Bailey, with the same graceful rakishness. He was quite the man-about-town of the conversation, while the easy-shaver was the child.
> 'Why, I am going to fetch my lodger home,' said Paul.
> 'A woman!' cried Mr. Bailey, 'for a twenty-pun' note.' (ch 26)

Bailey is quite stupendously funny as, for example, when he remarks of Mrs Gamp that ' "there's the remains of a fine woman about Sairah, Poll" ', or whenever he is providing his version of man-about-town conversation. Therefore his reported 'death' from a fall off his horse is absurdly moralistic (no need to say which moral tag it is meant to illustrate).

All the same, Bailey belongs more to the world of moral fable than social mimesis, because we cannot take seriously his act of gentility. This is also true of Tigg. Neither would be capable of deceiving the worlds over which we are to believe they triumph. Tigg is like Ralph Nickleby in that he embodies an abstract moral concept rather than illuminating any considered social criticism on Dickens's part. It is only necessary to think of

Carker and Merdle to see how little Dickens accomplishes as a
significant social novelist in his study of Tigg. We need not complain of that. There is no point in wondering just where Tigg got
his money from, how he earned such respect, why his Anglo-
Bengalee Company is taken at all seriously, because we are not
dealing with a world in which these questions raise themselves.
Similarly, we can admire Dickens's ingenuity in bringing Jonas
and Tigg together so that Tigg can be brought into contact with
Pecksniff, while realizing that it is done simply to ram home a
moral lesson. Pecksniff is to be ruined by a trickster as thoroughly
skilled in the arts of deception as he himself is. Even so, we are
bound to recognize that Dickens goes too far in insisting on
Pecksniff's downfall, not only for the reason I have already
given, but because he so obviously wants to knock Pecksniff
down. As Jonas pretends to fend off inquiries about the company

> the more solicitous, therefore, Mr. Pecksniff became to be initiated
> into the golden mysteries at which he had obscurely glanced. Why
> should there be cold and worldly secrets, he observed, between
> relations? What was life without confidence? If the chosen husband
> of his daughter, the man to whom he had delivered her with such
> pride and joy, such bounding and such beaming joy: if he was not
> a green spot in the barren waste of life, where was that Oasis to be
> found.
>
> Little did Mr. Pecksniff think on what a very green spot he
> planted one foot at that very moment! Little did he foresee when
> he said, 'All is but dust!' how very shortly he would come down
> with his own! (ch 44)

For all the rich comedy of the language, the lovely pun on 'golden
mysteries', the absurdity of Pecksniff's alchemic conversion of
sordor into the language of legend and holy writ, and the ripe
nonsense of his bounding and beaming joy, the fact remains that
Dickens's determination to make the Anglo-Bengalee Company
cause Pecksniff's downfall belongs so stridently to the world of
moral fable that it throws an odd and unbelievable light on those
moments when we are required to see Tigg as in some way
socially placed. Although these moments are not frequent their

very existence is problematic. Tigg acquires a change of name
and dress. 'His clothes, symmetrically made, were of the newest
fashion and costliest kind . . . The brass was burnished, lac-
quered, newly stamped; yet it was the true Tigg metal notwith-
standing.' (ch 27) That sentence seems to invite us to take Tigg
seriously, and not just as a moral type but as a social probability.
Yet the use made of Tigg destroys any chance that we could take
him either seriously or as socially probable.

But there is a deeper criticism. For Tigg does not in fact remain true Tigg metal to the end of the novel. Tigg the comic
trickster suddenly changes into Tigg the frightened victim, and
just as suddenly we see into his mind and become privy to his
truly terrifying nightmare and mental suffering. This switch
seems to me utterly implausible and one has to assume that
Dickens made it because he wanted the chance to explore states
of mind bordering on guilty panic. Hence Tigg's dream of
trying to keep a terrible creature locked up, working with others
to strengthen a door with iron plates and nails:

> but though they worked never so hard, it was all in vain, for the
> nails broke, or changed to soft twigs, or what was worse to worms,
> between their fingers; the wood of the door splintered and crum-
> bled, so that even nails would not remain in it; and the iron plates
> curled up like hot paper. All this time the creature on the other
> side – whether it was in the shape of man or beast, he neither knew
> nor sought to know – was gaining on them. But his greatest terror
> was when the man with the bloody smear upon his head demanded
> of him if he knew the creature's name, and said that he would
> whisper it. At this the dreamer fell upon his knees, his whole blood
> thrilling with inexplicable fear, and held his ears. But looking at
> the speaker's lips, he saw that they formed the utterance of the
> letter 'J'; and crying out aloud that the secret was discovered, and
> they were all lost, he awoke.
>
> Awoke to find Jonas standing at his bedside watching him.
> (ch 42)

The master of horror and fantasy at his best. And of course the
passage has that genuine concern with mental extremes which

Dickens repeatedly demonstrates. The trouble is that it has nothing to do with Tigg as he has been shown up till now, and in order to get to the moment at all Dickens has to resort to some extremely crude devices to make Jonas appear the sort of threatening figure of whom Tigg might be afraid. One of them completely misfires. Jonas looks at one of the doctor's 'shining little instruments', and scrutinizes it 'with a look as sharp and eager as its own bright edge'. (ch 41) But since Tigg is not even in the room at this moment, it is *we* rather than Jonas's intended victim who are given a hint of his villainous plan. Given that, Tigg's sudden panic becomes even less plausible.

The same sort of criticism applies even to Jonas. Marvellously as Dickens writes about his terror after he has murdered Tigg, the immediate change from blustering bully to panic-stricken coward creates a new dimension in his manner of presentation that has not been allowed for. It would be tedious to quote from the novel at length as I would have to do in order to demonstrate the point. Enough, I think, to add Jonas to the list of the novel's inconsistencies. While we are about it, Nadgett should also be mentioned. He is introduced to us as a 'short, dried-up, withered old man, who seemed to have secreted his very blood; for nobody would have given him credit for the possession of six ounces of it in his whole body'. (ch 27) On the strength of this, Nadgett belongs to the Misers and Self-seekers with which the novel deals. The language which describes him also condemns him. He is clearly one of the nasty characters who so distressed Victorian readers of *Martin Chuzzlewit*. Yet by the end of the novel Nadgett has turned into a decent and humane detective, notable for his 'anxious face and bloodshot eyes'. (ch 51) He is now the devoted guardian of law and justice.

G. K. Chesterton put his finger on the weaknesses I have been analysing when he said that 'the best figures are at their best when they have least to do'. He then went on to spoil the remark by turning it into a generalization about all the novels. 'Dickens's characters,' he says, 'are perfect if he can keep them out of his stories.' This is nonsense, but it is true that in *Martin Chuzzlewit* the demands of plot and narrative destroy the consistency of the characters, and Chesterton hits the mark exactly when he says that 'while Pecksniff is the best thing in the story, the story is the worst thing in Pecksniff'.[1] It is a perfectly just criticism and it points to the radical fault with *Martin Chuzzlewit*, which is that it is really directionless; it simply isn't going anywhere in particular. Hence the troubles with plot and with character. Hence, too, the American section, which, for all the reasons that can be advanced for its inclusion, surely remains something of an embarrassment. We may refer to the falling-off in sales of the serial parts and Dickens's traumatic experience on his tour of the United States as reasons for the insertion of the section, but this does not excuse its faults. In particular we have surely to admit that once the American scenes come into the novel, Dickens's control of the time-scale more or less deserts him, and that in addition young Martin is altered from a placed character to one who can provide the authorial point of view. He becomes yet another of the characters to be inconsistently presented.

Are the American scenes a mistake then? We may think so, and yet it would be difficult to wish them away. For they provide some extremely funny and accurate moments and the use that Dickens makes of Eden is another stroke of genius. 'Dickens,' James remarked curtly, 'was an improvisatore; the practice, for him, was a lawless revel of the imagination.'[2] Well, it is true of *Martin Chuzzlewit*, and of the American scenes in particular. But how brilliantly he turns his invention of Eden to account. In the first place, the misery and squalor of the place bring inescapably home to Martin that his dream of great expectations is finally meretricious, and that no matter how eagerly he pursues fortune he can never escape himself. Although his illness and slow recovery of health bring about a degree of self-perception that is fairly simply sketched-in, it is not inadequately treated and it does prepare the way for far greater explorations of the same theme in the late novels. It has as well a certain force that is

[1] *Charles Dickens*, 1913 edn., pp. 113–14.
[2] *French Poets and Novelists*, 1964, p. 213.

acceptable enough in so far as *Martin Chuzzlewit* is a moral fable.

More deeply, and perhaps less satisfactorily, Eden symbolizes what we have to call the bourgeois dream of freedom, of escape from social involvement and social identity by means of a return to a 'purer' identity. In setting himself against this dream Dickens is trying, I think, to stabilize his awareness that men are social beings whose various identities are in some manner inseparable from the historical moment in which they live. All of which no doubt seems rather portentous, especially since I have implied that this aspect of Eden is less satisfactory. But it is in this area of the novel that we come upon the most interesting and rewarding features of *Martin Chuzzlewit*, and I want to try and track down what these are. In order to do so I shall have to show Eden in contrast with the rural England of the novel.

In my experience, *Martin Chuzzlewit* feels as though it has more set descriptions of the countryside than any other Dickens novel. Whether it actually does have is open to question, but I suggest that the descriptive passages of *Martin Chuzzlewit* feel so prominent because they are not really absorbed into the novel. Indeed, there are occasions when they feel quite irrelevant (I note, more or less at random, passages that can be found in chapters 2, 5, 20, 36). The interesting question of course is why are they in the novel at all, and I shall have frankly to admit that the answer I give is in the nature of a guess. But let me begin by trying to make some connections between *Martin Chuzzlewit* and other, roughly contemporary, writing of Dickens.

The Battle of Life was Dickens's Christmas Book for 1846 and it is a decidedly undistinguished story. What makes it of interest to us is that it is set in eighteenth-century pastoral England, and that its pastoralism is of an altogether different kind from that of *Barnaby Rudge*. For the *Battle of Life* is totally simplistic in its attitude to the past. Doctor Jeddler, one of the story's central characters, is a very crude version of an Augustan rationalist who looks 'upon the world as a gigantic joke; as something too absurd to be considered seriously, by any rational man'. But Dickens is patronizingly cheerful about him, and such an attitude is bound to strike us as sharply at odds with his attitude to Sir John Chester. Jeddler, we have to assume, is all right because he belongs to a world that is no more – a world identified in terms of its natural rhythms and which blots out the memory of man-made battles fought on the spot where Jeddler now lives.

> The Seasons in their course, however, though they passed as lightly as the summer clouds themselves, obliterated, in the lapse of time [all] remains of the old conflict; and wore away such legendary traces of it as the neighbouring people carried in their minds, until they dwindled into old wives' tales, dimly remembered round the winter fire, and waning every year. (Part the First)

This is a past released from history, a timeless 'natural' world which Dickens invents, I imagine, from nostalgia or, more probably and deeply, from a dark and inchoate sense of loss. It is worth quoting his description of an inn:

> How beautiful the landscape kindling in the light, and that luxuri-ant influence passing on like the celestial presence, brightening everything! . . .
>
> At such a time, one little roadside Inn, snugly sheltered behind a great elm-tree with a rare seat for idlers encircling its capacious bole, addressed a cheerful front towards the traveller, as a house of entertainment ought, and tempted him with many mute but signi-ficant assurances of a comfortable welcome. The ruddy signboard perched up in the tree, with its golden letters winking in the sun, ogled the passer by, from among the green leaves, like a jolly face, and promised good cheer. The horse-trough, full of fresh clear water, and the ground below it sprinkled with droppings of frag-rant hay, made every horse that passed, prick up his ears. The crimson curtains in the lower rooms, and the pure white hangings in the little bed-chamber above, beckoned, Come in! (Part the Third)

The landlord's name is Benjamin Britain, and the reason for that is distressingly obvious.

If we make the inevitable comparison between Britain's Inn and the Maypole in *Barnaby Rudge* we shall of course see how slack Dickens's imaginative grip on the past is in his story. But

Britain's Inn is not all that unlike the Blue Dragon of *Martin Chuzzlewit*, with its 'rosy hostess', Mrs Lupin, who has a 'face of clear red and white, which, by its jovial aspect, at once bore testimony to her hearty participation in the good things of the larder and cellar'. (ch 3) The Blue Dragon, it will be remembered, eventually acquires a new landlord, Mark Tapley, and a new name, 'The Jolly Tapley'.

By and large, the good characters of *Martin Chuzzlewit* respond to the beauties of pastoral England, while the bad characters have souls deadened to natural beauty. Thus Tom Pinch goes walking on a frosty morning:

> The crust of ice on the else rippling brook was so transparent and so thin in texture, that the lively water might of its own free will have stopped – in Tom's glad mind it had – to look upon the lovely morning. (ch 5)

In contrast, Jonas sees nothing worthwhile about the natural scene:

> It was a lovely evening in the spring-time of the year; and in the soft stillness of the twilight, all nature was very calm and beautiful. The day had been fine and warm; but at the coming on of night, the air grew cool, and in the mellowing distance smoke was rising gently from the cottage chimneys. There were a thousand pleasant scents diffused around, from young leaves and fresh buds; the cuckoo had been singing all day long, and was but just hushed; the smell of earth newly-upturned, first breath of hope to the first labourer after his garden withered, was fragrant in the evening breeze. It was a time when most men cherish good resolves, and sorrow for the wasted past; when most men, looking on the shadows as they gather, think of that evening which must close on all, and that to-morrow which has none beyond.
>
> 'Precious dull,' said Mr. Jonas, looking about. 'It's enough to make a man go melancholy mad.' (ch 20)

I do not think Jonas is putting here the eighteenth-century case against solitude. He is simply dull of soul.

Ostensibly the scene which he passes up is of the countryside around Salisbury, and it is therefore worthwhile noting just how unrealistic Dickens's pastoralism is. We can compare the passage above with one written some fifteen years earlier, and about precisely the same area:

> From Salisbury up to very near Heytesbury, you have the valley . . . Here is water, here are meadows; plenty of fresh-water fish; hares and partridge in abundance, and it is next to impossible to destroy them. Here are shooting, coursing, hunting; hills of every height, size, and form; valleys, the same; lofty trees and rookeries in every mile; roads always solid and good; always pleasant for exercise; and the air must be the best in the world. Yet it is manifest, that four-fifths of the mansions have been swept away. There is a parliamentary return, to prove that nearly a third of the parsonage-houses have become beggarly holes or have disappeared. I have now been in nearly three score villages, and in twenty or thirty or forty hamlets of Wiltshire; and I do not know that I have been in one, in which I did not see a house or two, and sometimes more, either tumbled down, or beginning to tumble down. It is impossible for the eyes of man to be fixed on a finer country than that between the village of CODFORD and the town of WAR-MINSTER; and it is not very easy for the eyes of man to discover labouring people more miserable.[1]

That Cobbett's attention should be drawn to the inescapable fact of human misery in this landscape might lead us to think that Dickens would also insist on it. Because he doesn't we are forced to realize that the pastoral landscapes of *Martin Chuzzlewit* are not really views of rural England at all. As I remarked earlier, this novel is the least socially focused of all Dickens's novels, and as in the *Battle of Life* so in *Martin Chuzzlewit* nature is essentially mythic; it testifies to an order of life that is irreconcilable with Self and the chief expression of Self, money-interest or capitalism. In other words, Jonas's impercipience does not merely demonstrate that Dickens has absorbed the sort of associationist theorizing that filters through Romanticism from starting-points such as Archibald Alison's observation that for a man of business,

[1] *Rural Rides*, 1967, pp. 332–4.

'a beautiful scene in nature would produce . . . no other association than its value';[1] more importantly, it suggests that a world of natural and human values is becoming lost in the new society of capitalist enterprise. Jonas has learnt in a harsh school. 'The very first word he learnt to spell was "gain," and the second (when he got into two syllables) "money" '; and he has also been taught to 'over-reach everybody' and to consider 'everything as a question of property'. (ch 8) No wonder he cannot heed any lesson that the impulse from a vernal wood might have to offer him. Nor can his partner, Tigg. When Tigg goes down into the wood where he is to be murdered, 'The glory of the departing sun was on his face. The music of the birds was in his ears. Sweet wild flowers bloomed about him.' But unfortunately for him 'He had never read the lesson which these things conveyed.' (ch 47)

It may, of course, be objected against what I am saying that even if the natural descriptions are linked with natural human values, the connections are casual rather than organized, and suggest only that Dickens was quite ready to make use of a trite reach-me-down romanticism whenever he felt so inclined. I think the objection makes a valid point and clearly Dickens uses the appeal to nature as a thumbnail way of identifying heroes and villains. Yet casual and unorganized though his use of pastoralism is in *Martin Chuzzlewit*, it undoubtedly adds to the rough pattern that begins with the *Pickwick Papers* and stretches through *Oliver Twist* into the *Old Curiosity Shop* and, more problematically, into *Barnaby Rudge*. For in these novels the pastoral world is directly linked with humane values, and indeed at no point is it entirely clear whether Dickens is writing about what he thinks pastoral England actually is like or fashioning a mythic pastoralism which stands for and identifies with values he admires. In the *Old Curiosity Shop*, I suggested, the natural scene amounts to no more than a cockney pastoralism, an easy prescription for the good life. In *Barnaby Rudge* the matter has become more complex.

[1] Alison, *Essays in the Nature and Principles of Taste*, 1790, quoted in E. Tuveson, *The Imagination as a Means of Grace*, 1960, p. 186.

In *Martin Chuzzlewit*? Nature now has two functions. On the one hand it offers Dickens the chance to indulge a simple nostalgia or sentimental Sunday-outing affection for the natural scene. On the other hand, and more importantly, it serves to release his deeply-rooted fear of what the new world may mean. That these functions are blurred and not always easily to be distinguished from one another explains why the descriptions of the natural scene are not really assimilated into the novel. But if we use some tact the functions can be identified. There is no doubt that Dickens sees the new world of capitalism as measured and judged by its indifference to 'natural' human values. Crude though the device may seem, the indifference of Jonas and Tigg towards nature is meant to provide a crucial insight into the new world of money-interest.

The standards of measurement may seem simplistic and the related oppositions of natural and unnatural too obvious (even, perhaps, sentimental): Tom against Pecksniff, Mark against Martin, Ruth against Charity. Yet in fairness we have also to admit that much of the novel's strength stems from these oppositions, and that Dickens can be superb at providing memorable images of people whose identities are subdued to the elements they live in. Antony, Jonas, and Tigg, for example, are all seen as unnatural 'things', created by money-lust, and destroyed by it – literally and figuratively. They prey on each other and warp their own and others' lives, as the case of Chuffey brilliantly demonstrates:

> 'Three score and ten,' said Chuffey, 'ought and carry seven. Some men are so strong that they live to four score – four times ought's an ought, four times two's an eight – eighty. Oh! why-why-why didn't he live to four times ought's an ought, and four times two's an eight, eighty!' (ch 19)

Chuffey is a victim, and the audacity of Dickens's prose presents us with a terrific image of a man destroyed by his work, made totally unnatural.

At this point we come back to Eden. For Eden is an image of a

destroyed paradise, resting perhaps unsatisfactorily on the simplistic opposition to which I have drawn attention, and implying
also, I think, a relaxed vision of the past, for if the new is bad
then the good has somehow to inhere in the old. But of itself,
Eden is a stunningly brilliant device which hints at a second and
irrecoverable fall directly comparable with the disfiguring money-
lust of the English society of the novel (the 'new' can become
a conceptual pun on the New land and the New England).

Martin listens in on the conversation of American gentleman:

> It was rather barren of interest, to say the truth; and the greater
> part of it may be summed up in one word. Dollars. All their cares,
> hopes, joys, affections, virtues, and associations, seemed to be
> melted down into dollars. Whatever the chance contributions that
> fell into the slow cauldron of their talk, they made the gruel thick
> and slab with dollars. Men were weighed by their dollars, measures
> gauged by their dollars; life was auctioneered, appraised, put up,
> and knocked down for its dollars. (ch 16)

Therefore Eden.

> As they proceeded further on their track, and came more and
> more towards their journey's end, the monotonous desolation of
> the scene increased to that degree, that for any redeeming feature
> it presented to their eyes, they might have entered, in the body, on
> the grim domains of Giant Despair. A flat morass, bestrewn with
> fallen timber; a marsh on which the good growth of the earth
> seemed to have been wrecked and cast away, that from its decom-
> posing ashes vile and ugly things might rise; where the very trees
> took the aspect of huge weeds, begotten of the slime from which
> they sprung, by the hot sun that burnt them up; where fatal mala-
> dies, seeking whom they might infect, came forth at night in misty
> shapes, and creeping out upon the surface of the water, hunted
> them like spectres until day; where even the blessed sun, shining
> down on festering elements of corruption and disease, became a
> horror; this was the realm of Hope through which they moved.
>
> At last they stopped. At Eden too. The waters of the Deluge
> might have left it but a week before: so choked with slime and
> matted growth was the hideous swamp which bore that name.
> (ch 23)

The horror of this does not merely depend on its being a grotesque parody of the fairy-tale journey to a promised land,
though Dickens does engage the folk-tale device in order to
satirize Martin's great expectations. More fundamentally, the
terrific power of the description comes from Dickens's disgust
at a world gone crazy over money and its consequent destruction
of natural values. And indeed disgust is a notable feature of much
that goes into *Martin Chuzzlewit*. George Ford has usefully
pointed out that Victorian readers were deeply offended by the
novel, and he quotes as a typical reaction Crabb Robinson's
remark that he never wanted to re-read the novel, 'so generally
disgusting are the characters and incidents of the tale'.[1] But the
disgust is properly functional; it is part of Dickens's sense of
moral outrage over a system or growing interest which he sees as
totally inhumane and whose fit image is Eden.

The inhumane is frequently presented to us. Consider Ruth
Pinch's employers. Tom cries

> 'You have no right to employ her.'
> 'No right!' cried the brass-and-copper founder.
> 'Distinctly not,' Tom answered. 'If you imagine that the pay-
> ment of an annual sum of money gives it to you, you immensely
> exaggerate its power and value. Your money is the least part of
> your bargain in such a case. You may be punctual in that to half a
> second on the clock, and yet be Bankrupt.' (ch 36)

If we took this dialogue as indicative of the novel's deepest
concerns, we might say that *Martin Chuzzlewit* was about a set
of people whose lives are bankrupt, inhuman, unnatural, and
another set whose lives are rich in human worth. And in a sense
this *is* what the novel is about. But only in a sense. For the
awkward fact is that Dickens does not fully take possession of his
own theme and his genius is liable to run irresponsibly counter
to it. In the last few pages I have been using some big words:
capitalism, the new England, money-interest, the new world.
But I shall have to admit that the words suggest a pattern and
area of concern that the novel only hints at in a shadowy sort of

[1] *Dickens and his Readers*, p. 44.

way. We come back here to my opening remarks, and I can justify them best perhaps by glancing at Mrs Gamp and what George Gissing so astutely noted about her. Mrs Gamp, he says, is obviously the sort of creation we meet with only in the greatest writers. But who and what is she?

> Well, a sick nurse, living in Kingsgate Street, Holborn, in a filthy room somewhere upstairs, and summoned for nursing of all kinds by persons more or less well-to-do, who are so unfortunate as to know of no less offensive substitute. We are told, and can believe, that in the year 1844 . . . few people did know of any substitute for Mrs. Gamp; and that she was an institution; that she carried her odious vices and criminal incompetence from house to house in decent parts of London. Dickens knew her only too well; had observed her at moments of domestic crisis; had learnt her language and could reproduce it (or most of it) with surprising accuracy. In plain words, then, we are speaking of a very loathsome creature; a sluttish, drunken, avaricious, dishonest woman. Meeting her in the flesh, we should shrink disgusted, so well does the foulness of her person correspond with the baseness of her mind. Hearing her speak, we should turn away in half-amused contempt. Yet, when we encounter her in the pages of Dickens, we cannot have too much of Mrs. Gamp's company; her talk is an occasion of up-roarious mirth, we never dream of calling her to moral judgement, but laugh the more, the more infamously she sees fit to behave. Now, in what sense can this figure in literature be called a copy of the human original?[1]

Of course, Gissing is not entirely right. For Dickens does call Mrs Gamp to moral judgement. Old Martin, with the author's obvious approval, tells Poll Sweedlepipe to offer Mrs Gamp a few words of advice, such as:

> 'hinting at the expediency of a little less liquor, and a little more humanity, and a little less regard for herself, and a little more regard for her patients, and perhaps a trifle of additional honesty. Or when Mrs. Gamp gets into trouble, Mr. Sweedlepipe, it had better not be at a time when I am near enough to the Old Bailey to volunteer myself as a witness to her character.' (ch 52)

[1] *Charles Dickens*, p. 89.

Yet Martin's words inevitably strike us as absurdly out of key with the presentation of Mrs Gamp. Gissing is essentially right; Mrs Gamp is a great comic creation, and only by abrupt changes of tone can she be fitted to the themes of Self and of money-interest. Saying which brings us to George Orwell's remark, 'wonderful gargoyles, rotten architecture'. That neat judgement is very close to the one of Chesterton's which I have already noted, and it fits *Martin Chuzzlewit* uncomfortably well. The case of Mrs Gamp is perhaps particularly revealing, for she ought to present exactly the opportunity for Dickens to create an image of social malaise (the unnatural nurse for an unnatural society). Gissing is clearly puzzled by the fact that Dickens does not take his opportunity.

But it may be that his question is not accurate enough. For to ask in what sense Mrs Gamp is a copy of a human original is to ignore the possibility that for all her comic nature Dickens wants to make her a moral type – recognizably possessed of certain qualities but not pinned down with any social exactness. Certainly critics have tried to fit her to the theme that is announced so early on. ' "Oh self, self, self! At every turn nothing but self!" ' The words are old Martin's, and they may offer to lead us into the heart of the novel. Yet he is talking only about his family: ' "Brother against brother, child against parent, friends treading on the faces of friends, this is the social company by whom my way has been attended." ' (ch 3) And this brings us to the last major difficulty we have with the novel.

Martin's words aim, I think, for a certain typicality. There are other elements in the novel also which reinforce the generalizing possibilities of his remarks. I think, for example, of Eden, that emblem of money interest, and of Mould, who might be said to emblematize the inevitable parasitic growths that feed off bourgeois society: 'the laying out of money with a well-conducted establishment, where the thing is performed upon the very best scale, binds the broken heart, and sheds balm upon the wounded spirit.' Dickens's vision, in other words, struggles to transcend the local and familial. The first chapter, with its comic genealogy of the Chuzzlewit family is probably intended to prevent us from regarding them as a special case. Old Martin's cry about the social company 'by whom my way has been attended' is very probably meant to remind us of Wordsworth:

> The Youth, who daily further from the east
> Must travel, still is Nature's Priest,
> And by the vision splendid
> Is on his way attended.

Martin is the priest of anti-nature. Yet for all Dickens's ingenuity, the Chuzzlewit family cannot compose a vision of any genuine typicality; hence the desperate plotting to keep members in touch with each other and with the various other characters of the novel. Nor need this matter in so far as the novel is a moral fable about Self. But in so far as it is also a moral fable about money-interest and the spreading power of capitalism it does most certainly matter. The big words sketch in a plan which is never put into operation. Instead, the novel fragments into moments which we may say Dickens tries desperately to bind together by means either of abstract term or narrative. But in the end things fly apart, the centre will not hold. You cannot have a novel that is as socially unfocused as *Martin Chuzzlewit* is, and also pretend that it is somehow a central statement about capitalism.

All of which composes a rather severe criticism of the novel. I think such criticism is necessary, but I do not want to be identified with the critics who think that *Martin Chuzzlewit* really blows the gaffe on Dickens as a great novelist, even if it reveals the fact that he had an instinctive genius. Barbara Hardy's cool view of the novel is welcome but not her remark that its faults stem in part, at least, from Dickens's 'lack of intellectual quality'.[1] In my view, one reason for being severe on *Martin Chuzzlewit* is that it helps us to define the sudden composed greatness of *Dombey and Son*, which is not only the first of Dickens's indubitably great novels, but which as far as I am concerned is the first to

[1] *Dickens and the Twentieth Century*, p. 108.

reveal him as far and away the most intelligent of all English novelists.

II

Before I say anything about *Dombey and Son* I want briefly to consider the *Christmas Carol*. The *Carol* was the first of Dickens's Christmas Books, and was written in 1843 while he was working on *Chuzzlewit*. It requires no great ingenuity to see that there are similarities between the two works, the most important being the theme of Self. But in the *Christmas Carol*, Self is quite nakedly identified with Utilitarianism, and indeed the story is in some respects a fable about those human deficiencies in Utilitarian philosophy to which Mill had already drawn attention. Bentham's system of ethics, Mill says, 'does not pretend to aid individuals in the formation of their own character', and it 'recognises no such wish as that of self-culture'. In addition, Mill remarks, the Utilitarian ethic can do 'nothing for the spiritual interests of society'. What it can do, is 'teach the means of organizing and regulating the merely *business* parts of social arrangements'. But Bentham unfortunately made the mistake of 'supposing that the *business* part of human affairs was the whole of them'.[1] Thus sprang Scrooge. He is asked to contribute to a charity fund for the poor:

> 'I wish to be left alone,' said Scrooge. 'Since you ask me what I wish, gentlemen, that is my answer. I don't want to make merry myself at Christmas and I can't afford to make idle people merry. I help to support the establishments I have mentioned – they cost enough; and those who are badly off must go there.'
> 'Many can't go there; and many would rather die.'
> 'If they would rather die,' said Scrooge, 'they had better do it, and decrease the surplus population. Besides – excuse me – I don't know that.'
> 'But you might know it,' observed the gentleman.
> 'It's not my business,' Scrooge returned. 'It's enough for a man

[1] *Essays on Politics and Culture*, ed. Himmelfarb, pp. 100–2.

to understand his own business, and not to interfere with other people's. Mine occupies me constantly. Good afternoon, gentlemen.' (Stave 1)

The establishments to which Scrooge as a good Utilitarian gives support are the prisons and the Union workhouses, which in an important sense regulate the merely business part of social arrangements. And that this won't do, Marley's ghost reveals:

> 'Oh! captive, bound, and double-ironed,' cried the phantom, 'not to know that ages of incessant labour by immortal creatures for this earth must pass into eternity before the good of which it is susceptible is all developed. Not to know that any Christian spirit working kindly in its little sphere, whatever it may be, will find its mortal life too short for its vast means of usefulness. Not to know that no space of regret can make amends for one's opportunity misused! Yet such was I! Oh! such was I!'
> 'But you were always a good man of business, Jacob,' faltered Scrooge, who now began to apply this to himself.
> 'Business!' cried the Ghost, wringing its hands again. 'Mankind was my business. The common welfare was my business; charity, mercy, forbearance, and benevolence, were all my business. The dealings of my trade were but a drop of water in the comprehensive ocean of my business.' (Stave 1)

Neat though the play on 'business' is, if the attack on Malthusian and Utilitarian ideas were all that Dickens gave us in the *Christmas Carol* the story would be essentially the same as his next Christmas Book, the *Chimes*. But whereas the *Chimes* settles into a weary and threadbare denunciation of those who 'heap up facts on figures, facts on figures, facts on figures, mountains high and dry', and who try to persuade people that 'they have no right or business to be married' or to be alive (*The Chimes*, First Quarter), the *Christmas Carol* has a marvellously fierce vitality that comes from the concentrated power of Dickens's images and the way he takes full possession of his theme. As a result we are taken far beyond the abstract registering of protest against a body of ideas the novelist happens to dislike into a very real human awareness of what happens to people who try to live by those ideas. Given the medium of the fantastic tale, Marley is a brilliant comic-grotesque image, a fettered spirit, chained to a way of life that denies freedom and the naturalness of unrestrained human relationships. But the tale's great triumph is Scrooge (and for all that has been said in praise of Dickens's inventiveness with names, Scrooge is still one to marvel at). It is easy enough to point out that Mill's criticisms of Bentham and Carlyle's insistence on the failure of 'brotherhood' in the modern world amount to much the same sort of indictment that Dickens makes against Scrooge; but *A Christmas Carol* is persuasive as neither Mill nor Carlyle could hope to be, just because Dickens's fable has the sort of compressed intensity that in the literature of the past two hundred years is rivalled only perhaps by the 'Songs of Experience'. As here, where the real meaning of Self comes out:

> And now Scrooge looked on more attentively than ever, when the master of the house, having his daughter leaning fondly on him, sat down with her and her mother at his own fireside; and when he thought that such another creature, quite as graceful and as full of promise might have called him father, and been a springtime in the haggard winter of his life, his sight grew very dim indeed.
>
> 'Belle,' said the husband, turning to his wife with a smile, 'I saw an old friend of yours this afternoon.'
>
> 'Who was it?'
>
> 'Guess!'
>
> 'How can I! Tut, don't I know?' she added in the same breath, laughing as he laughed. 'Mr. Scrooge.'
>
> 'Mr. Scrooge it was. I passed his office window; and as it was not shut up, and he had a candle inside, I could scarcely help seeing him. His partner lies upon the point of death, I hear; and there he sat alone. Quite alone in the world, I do believe.'
>
> 'Spirit!' said Scrooge in a broken voice, 'remove me from this place.' (Stave 3)

What chiefly engages Dickens in the *Carol* is the horror of isolation, and Scrooge is the image of such horror, 'Hard and sharp as a flint, from which no steel had ever struck out generous fire; secret, and self-contained, and solitary as an oyster'. The image of the flint seems at first mere cliché, but the more you consider it the better it becomes, especially in the witty notion of Scrooge as so absurdly hugging self-containment that he won't even perform the functions one might expect of him.

In contrast, the Cratchits provide an image of successful human relationships, and the image seems to me completely acceptable. We are likely to call it sentimental only because we do not like admitting how moved we are by the pressure of Dickens's writing. There is no point in quoting, because to get the sense of how he succeeds with the family you have to read the entire tale, but it is worth remarking that both with the Cratchits and with Scrooge he achieves a degree of pared-down relevance that is absent from *Martin Chuzzlewit*. No doubt this has much to do with the matter of comparative length; but I think also that when Dickens came to write *A Christmas Carol*, he knew exactly what he wanted to do. He had found a theme that he had been trying to mine from the depths of the big novel but which wouldn't come out cleanly there.

A Christmas Carol is a fable, and it has an unmistakable gusto and buoyancy about it. Dickens can afford to be comic about Scrooge, that 'squeezing, wrenching, grasping, clutching, covetous, old sinner', because he can be altered for the better. But in the next novel the basic themes of the *Carol* come up for re-examination and now with a good deal more sombreness and even distress. For *Dombey and Son* does what *Martin Chuzzlewit* only hazily tried to do; it confronts the new England of the 1840s and squarely faces up to issues which were only glanced at in the previous novel. And accordingly there is a radical shift of tone. Dickens cannot afford to be comic about Dombey. When Scrooge sees Tim, he can be brought to acknowledge the malign absurdity of his notion that the surplus population should be left to die. He is the fable's reformed sinner. But Dombey?

'You have a son, I believe?' said Mr. Dombey.

'Four of 'em, Sir. Four hims and a her. All alive!'

'Why, it's as much as you can afford to keep them!' said Mr. Dombey.

'I couldn't hardly afford but one thing in the world less, Sir.'
'What is that?'
'To lose, 'em, Sir.' (ch 2)

Toodle may be in the right, but Dombey's impercipience is a much more terrifying possibility than Scrooge's skin-flint growl, for Dombey is conceived of as a representative figure in a novel which itself aims to be fully representative or mimetic.

Taken together, however, *Martin Chuzzlewit* and *A Christmas Carol* are clearly crucial for the genesis of *Dombey and Son*, the one because it hints at the social scope and breadth that is to be more surely contained and given focus in the later work, the other because it provides a controlling idea that can become resonant or richly metaphoric of the condition that affects the society which Dickens now sets out to investigate. And the real wonder of *Dombey and Son* is that it is so vast in range and yet so coherent. To say that it is about England under Utilitarian ideas would be absurd, but it is not absurd to say that the novel is about England at a particular moment in time and that the Utilitarian spirit is profoundly symbolic of what is happening to life in that England. Nor is it absurd to point out that Dickens's exploration of the effect of this spirit takes up ideas of self, great expectations, money-interest and makes a wonderfully complex and persuasively comprehensive statement. With *Dombey and Son* Dickens becomes, I think, a really great creative critic of the modern world. He also becomes the incomparably great master of the English novel.

I have written once before about *Dombey and Son* and I find it therefore a matter of some embarrassment to repeat arguments which I have already stated. On the other hand, since there is no reason to suppose that anybody reading this book will be familiar with my previous essay, and since my sense of *Dombey and Son*'s greatness continues to grow at the same pace as my sense of the inadequacy of my former remarks, it is pleasant to have the chance of once more trying to do the novel justice.[1]

---

[1] 'Dickens and Dombey and Son' in *Tradition and Tolerance in Nineteenth Century Fiction*.

To begin with, I want to note the sheer brilliance of the novel's plotting. For out of his narrative Dickens fashions analogous patterns of relationships, reverberative images, symbolic echoes, which bind together the novel's vast social range. Hardly any of the narrative is irrelevant to the novel's concerns. Instead of making tortuous and implausible connections of characters through the family unit as he had done in *Martin Chuzzlewit*, he lets patterns of behaviour and language suggest connections more deeply insistent than those of blood-ties; and by doing this he can imply a statement of such comprehensiveness that we might even see *Dombey and Son* as very nearly a definitive exploration of English society. Of course, it is not that; but this quite new method of plotting, which he takes further still in *Bleak House* and *Little Dorrit*, has so much confidence about it that we are struck by the novel's feeling of being a central statement. The social range extends from Mrs Skewton to Good Mrs Brown, from a fading aristocracy to the flotsam of the industrialized or dispossessed working-class. Both the range itself and the richness with which it is filled in, suggest how intense and varied an imaginative enquiry the novel makes into the sort of society that is possible for the new England which the novel sets out to identify and render.

In my previous essay, 'Past and Present Imperfect', I drew attention to what I felt then and feel even more now is Dickens's formidable intelligence in exploring the conditions and nature of the emergent society with which *Dombey and Son* is concerned. Much of that intelligence goes into the remarkable effort of open-mindedness which is so distinguished a feature of the novel. For in *Dombey and Son* Dickens has no intention of simply writing-off the emergent society, even though his revolutionary plot device allows him to focus on it with a relentless intensity that is quite new in his work (one of the novel's most astonishing characteristics being its feeling of sheer compression in spite of its length). And here we can hardly help but note that *Dombey and Son* is the first of Dickens's novels to be more or less thought through before begun. I think that this implies that the dangerously undisciplined sprawl of *Martin Chuzzlewit* had taught him a salutary lesson. However that may be, there can be no doubt that *Dombey* is the first of his novels to tax him really severely, and that it is therefore the first of the novels to show his genius at something like its full strength. Which is not to say that the novel is without flaws (we can all point to Dickens's failures as a novelist). It is to say that *Dombey and Son* demands of us a degree of engagement and intelligent responsiveness that the earlier works by and large do not require.

It is just because Dickens focuses so powerfully on social realities that his effort at open-mindedness comes under terrific strain. In this context it is worth comparing *Dombey and Son* with the *Chimes*, the Christmas Book for 1844. Like the *Christmas Carol*, the *Chimes* provides an all-out assault on Utilitarianism. It also has a breezy cheerfulness about it, at least in terms of the vision it offers of the future:

> 'The voice of Time,' said the Phantom, 'cries to man, Advance! Time is for his advancement and improvement; for his greater happiness, his better life; his progress onward to that goal within its knowledge and its view, and set there, in the period when Time and He began. Ages of darkness, wickedness, and violence, have come and gone – millions uncountable, have suffered, lived, and died – to point the way before him. Who seeks to turn him back, or stay him on his course, arrests a mighty engine which will strike the meddler dead; and be the fiercer and the wilder, for its momentary check!' (Third Quarter)

Given the context of his story, Dickens's optimism may seem to put him in a very democratic and even socialistic line of thought. For the meddlers whose interference with the engine will serve only to make it fiercer and wilder are presumably those repressive forces which cause Will Fern to proclaim:

> 'There'll be a fire to-night . . . There'll be fires this winter-time, to light the dark nights, East, West, North, and South. When you see the distant sky red, think of me no more; or, if you do, remember what a Hell was lighted up inside of me, and think you see its flames reflected in the clouds.' (Fourth Quarter)

And a few pages later, Trotty is declaring:

> 'I know that our inheritance is held in store for us by Time. I know there is a sea of Time to rise one day, before which all who wrong us or oppress us will be swept away like leaves. I see it, on the flow!' (Fourth Quarter)

I do not find any evidence to suggest that Dickens stands outside Trotty at this point. The vision is both the character's and the writer's. Yet such a vision is surely a form of whistling in the dark, a pious hope for a future which has no stronger claim to probability than lies in Trotty's claim that ' "I know that we must trust and hope, and neither doubt ourselves, nor doubt the good in one another." ' The 'one another' can hardly include those who cause Will Fern to speak as he does; and we have to conclude that in having Trotty state the case for trust Dickens is either preaching a course of conciliation, or that he is turning away from the social actualities to a sort of abstract piety.

To come at the matter a slightly different way, we might remark that although in the *Chimes* Dickens speaks on the side of Progress, he does not regard it as involving a process, except for the moment when Will Fern speaks. I am left with the uncomfortable feeling that although Dickens may make some attempt to see change as problematic, in the end the Chimes ring as hollowly as Tennyson's grooves of change. 'Locksley Hall', it seems to me, has precisely the vatic optimism that the *Chimes* communicates:

> For I dipt into the future, far as human eye could see,
> Saw the vision of the world, and all the wonder that must be . . .
>
> Not in vain the future beacons. Forward, forward let us range,
> Let the great world spin for ever down the ringing grooves of
>   change.

Tennyson's grooves and Dickens's mighty engine come to more or less the same thing; and it hardly needs remarking that in *Dombey and Son* the mighty engine turns out to be the mechanical spirit of the railway age which Dickens now calls 'The Triumphant Monster, Death!' In other words, for all that it may

be open-minded, the novel does not endorse the optimism of the
Chimes. Why and how this should be is what I want now to
investigate.

Perhaps the best way to enter into a detailed discussion of
Dombey and Son is through a consideration of its treatment of
time. For time is crucially important in the novel, as indeed it is
bound to be. *Dombey and Son* is after all about society in transition; it takes for its subject a moment in social change when the
present can be seen as struggling free of the past and in the
process of creating the future. Time, that is, has long perspectives. These are played off against the very limited and entirely
personal notions of time entertained by the various characters
who see time merely as progress, and therefore either on their
side or against them. For the world of the Wooden Midshipman,
time is a destructive agent; for the Dombey world it is fundamentally creative. Yet in putting the matter that way I run the
risk of making the novel seem far too much built on a structure
of naked oppositions, and that is unjust to Dickens's refusal to
allow himself any simplistic antitheses. In *Dombey and Son* both
past and present are highly complex notions, and Dickens goes
out of his way to make sure that there shall be no easy scoring off
the present by a system of appeals to the past. It is obvious how
different this position is from the one adopted or hinted at in
earlier novels. Mrs Skewton, for example, belongs to the past,
and she admires it:

> 'Those darling byegone times, Mr. Carker, with their delicious
> fortresses, and their dear old dungeons, and their delightful places
> of torture, and their romantic vengeances, and their picturesque
> assaults and sieges, and everything that makes life truly charming!
> How dreadfully we have degenerated!' (ch 27)

Mrs Skewton represents qualities which Dickens very clearly
despises, and her efforts to keep up with time while insisting on
her ageless beauty and worth yield not only some of the novel's
funniest moments, but also some of the most alertly imaginative,
since she is marvellously made into the image of a decaying

aristocratic order which finds itself reduced to the necessary absurdity of seeking renewed life through allegiance with a social class whose power and indeed very existence it despises. In inventing Mrs Skewton, Dickens has travelled a long way from the studies of such figures as Mutanhed and Hawk, and although some critics have said that his view of the aristocracy is unfair or inaccurate, I think his presentation of Mrs Skewton is quite simply magnificent. It does not matter at all that she isn't seen in inner detail; Dickens is writing of her as the embodiment of a class that is struggling for survival, and his historical and social sense of what she is seems to me faultless.

Mrs Skewton tries to arrest time by a pretence of ageless vitality, and time as a natural process has its revenge:

> Cleopatra was arrayed in full dress, with the diamonds, short sleeves, rouge, curls, teeth, and other juvenility all complete; but Paralysis was not to be deceived, had known her for the object of its errand, and had struck her at her glass, where she lay like a horrible doll that had tumbled down. (ch 37)

How can anyone possibly complain about that? Dickens's savage contempt is not so much directed against Mrs Skewton as any sort of life-like individual as against her as the embodiment of a class that tries to deny the ineluctable processes of time through which social change occurs. It is of course often said that at such a moment as the one I have quoted here Dickens shows himself to be thoroughly middle-class. Perhaps so, but I do not see why that should count as a criticism. His position was at the least a very good one for understanding the fact and nature of social change, and it enabled him to see what absurdities the class above him was reduced to in its effort to cope with the rise to power of his own class. It also put him in a perfect position to see how absurdly the middle-class could behave in its response to the outer appearance of 'tone' and breeding that the aristocracy and gentry could offer.

Appearance is certainly all Mrs Skewton has to offer and she also offers it in her daughter. Edith is trained to make a financially rewarding marriage so as to guarantee survival for her class (for that is what it comes to). She calls her childhood 'an old age of design', and it answers her mother's need. Dombey buys Edith as a business transaction, because she looks the part of a wife for an aspiring business-man. She is 'fixed' into an identity that denies any possibility of freedom or spontaneity. The effort to preserve a way of life means destroying its chance of growth – i.e. of life. The profundity of that insight should need no defence.

Dickens's severity with Mrs Skewton makes it obvious that he has no intention of indulging a simplistic nostalgia for a past England. Her fake vitality is, in its way, a perfectly fair and acid comment on the hopes of the Young England movement, to say nothing of Ruskin's later yearning for a return to feudalism. And in providing the parallel with Good Mrs Brown and her daughter he tries to seal off any touch of regret for time past. For Mrs Brown is a representative enough figure of the country girl whom enclosure and the lure of factory money brought to the cities throughout the latter half of the eighteenth and the nineteenth centuries. And her seduction by Mr Skewton's brother is an apt metaphor of the brutalizing of class-relations of which she and her daughter are victims. But what of Miss Tox's memories of the past?

> Miss Tox sat upon the window-seat, and thought of her good papa deceased – Mr. Tox, of the Customs Department of the public service; and of her childhood, passed at a sea-port, among a considerable quantity of cold tar, and some rusticity. She fell into a softened remembrance of meadows, in old time, gleaming with buttercups, like so many inverted firmaments of golden stars; and how she had made chains of dandelion-stalks for youthful vowers of eternal constancy, dressed chiefly in nankeen; and how soon those fetters had withered and broken. (ch 29)

We cannot respond to this passage as we do to Mrs Skewton's words about the darling bygone times, and this in spite of Dickens's filtering of Miss Tox's memories through a comic haze. Miss Tox is isolated; her pathetic attempts to keep up with time are doomed to failure because she is incapable of the amount of effort required (Mrs Chick, who pronounces 'this world a world of effort', is in fact about to pronounce Miss Tox's doom). And Miss Tox is a beautifully attentive and sympathetic study of a person whose values and way of life are inevitably defeated by social change. Of course, Dickens's sympathy with her does not necessarily mean he feels sympathy with her values or her past. Yet his childhood had also been spent at a sea-port, and it may just be that in offering his affectionately comic rendering of Miss Tox's memories he is trying to keep at bay any deeply regretful feelings about his own past, not necessarily because they arouse personal feelings of the old unhappy loss of something but because they suggest a set of values that he cannot find it easy to locate in the new world. But I do not want to make much of this. Instead, let me note that his sympathy goes out to Miss Tox just because her effort to keep up is so pathetically inadequate. As Mrs Chick, speaking of Dombey's forthcoming marriage to Edith, tells her husband: ' "I really don't know, as Paul is going to be very grand, and these are people of condition, that [Miss Tox] would have been quite presentable, and might not have compromised myself." ' (ch 29)

Once she has been rejected by the Dombey world, Miss Tox moves over to the other, threatened world of the Wooden Midshipman. But initially she renews contact with the Toodle family. It is when we come to Dickens's presentation of the Toodles and Staggs's Gardens that we see how he tries to play out what we might call a dilemma of preferences. Staggs's Gardens is where the Toodles live, and it is cleared away for the new railroad which gives Toodle his employment:

> There was no such place as Staggs's Gardens. It had vanished from the earth. . . . The miserable waste-ground, where the refuse matter had been heaped of yore, was swallowed up and gone; and in its frowsty stead were tiers of warehouses, crammed with rich goods and costly merchandise . . . Bridges . . . led to villas, gardens, churches, healthy public walks. (ch 15)

Now Dickens seems to be clear that the destruction of the Gardens is a good thing. He never presents the place as other than a mean, miserable 'unhallowed spot', with its 'little rows of houses, with little squalid patches of ground before them'. Yet the Toodles are identified with the Gardens, and throughout the novel they are celebrated for their warmth and decency. Are we then justified in saying that Dickens sees the Gardens as possessing values that will be absent from the world which destroys it? But before I attempt to settle the question let me add that if Toodle is given employment by a world of which Dombey is the chief manifestation, then Dombey also wrecks the oldest Toodle boy, by forcing him into an educational establishment on the grounds that 'it is necessary that the inferior classes should continue to be taught to know their position, and to conduct themselves properly'. (ch 5) And I want also to note that when the Gardens are undergoing the shock of destruction, Dickens remarks that 'the yet unfinished Railroad was in progress; and, from the very core of all this dire disorder, trailed smoothly away, upon its mighty course of civilisation and improvement.' (ch 6) Whether that is meant as ironic I really do not know; but we inevitably reflect that Dombey's schooling of Rob Toodle may be just as much part of civilization and improvement as are the healthy public walks and tiers of warehouses. Yet again, there is the comic genealogy of the Gardens:

> Some were of the opinion that Staggs's Gardens derived its name from a deceased capitalist, one Mr. Staggs, who built it for his delectation. Others, who had a natural taste for the country, held that it dated from those rural times when the antlered herd, under the familiar denomination of Staggses, had rested in its shady precincts. (ch 6)

Does this suggest that the past connected with Staggs's Gardens is of dubious authenticity, let alone worth? At all events, the moment deprives us of the opportunity for simple nostalgia.

But here let me quote again that remark of Hans Meyerhoff which chimes so well with the views held by the inhabitants of Staggs's Gardens about its origins: 'Previous generations *knew* much less about the past than we do, but perhaps *felt* a much greater sense of identity and continuity with it because of the fixity, stability, and relative permanence of their social structure.' With that remark in mind we cannot simply dismiss Staggs's Gardens as worthless, for as a human experience, giving shape and identity to life, the Gardens may be very important. Meyerhoff's remark recalls Wordsworth's famous letter to Fox about the 'statesmen' of the North of England whose 'little tract of land serves as a kind of rallying point for their domestic feelings'. Dickens's regard for the Toodles is very similar to Wordsworth's regard for the statesmen; he takes as seriously the Toodle.' loss of Staggs's Gardens to the railways as Wordsworth takes the loss of the statesmen's small tracts of land to enclosure. Even the name implies a pastoralism which we have seen in earlier novels is always identified with humane values. Staggs's Gardens notionalizes the preservation of the good life within the city, much as Tim Linkinwater's mignonettes and double-wallflowers had been meant to, though there the tone is so jokey and the moment itself so unfocused that it can mean very little in the context of its novel. But the loss of Staggs's Gardens means a great deal within the context of *Dombey and Son*, its vanishing from the face of the earth hints at Dickens's foreboding sense that humane values may have little chance to survive in the world of railway time; and it may be linked with the inverted pastoralism of *Bleak House*, where Lincoln Inn's Fields houses Tulkinghorn and *his* values. It even anticipates Bleeding-Heart Yard, where the pastoral world lingers as a comic and ghostly after-echo: 'To come out into the shop after it was shut, and hear her father sing a song inside this cottage, was a perfect Pastoral to Mrs. Plornish, the Golden Age revived.' (*Little Dorrit*, Bk 2, ch 13). The world of values to which Staggs's Gardens directs our attention is perhaps about to be swallowed up by the voracious present.

Indeed, when we look at what Dickens shows us of this world we begin to sense how the effort of open-mindedness may perhaps become abandoned. All the same, he does not sentimentalize this lingering world of values associated with the past. Captain Cuttle is an innocent, and his friend Bunsby, the 'natural wise man', is a great comic image of flawless stupidity:

'Bunsby!' said the Captain, appealing to him solemnly, 'what do you make of this? There you sit, a man as has had his head broke open from infancy up'ards, and has got a new opinion into it at every seam as has been opened. Now, what do you make o' this?'

'If so be,' returned Bunsby, with unusual promptitude, 'as he's dead, my opinion is he won't come back no more. If so be he's alive, my opinion is he will. Do I say he will? No. Why not? Because the bearings of this observation lays in the application on it.'

'Bunsby!' said Captain Cuttle, who would seem to have estimated the value of his distinguished friend's opinions in proportion to the immensity of the difficulty he experienced in making anything out of them; 'Bunsby,' said the Captain, quite confounded by admiration, 'you carry a weight of mind easy, as would swamp one of my tonnage soon.' (ch 39)

It is a marvellous comic exchange. But it does seem to establish that the values associated with the Midshipman are in the worst possible hands as far as their chances of survival are concerned. Yet it is also true that Dickens's acceptance of Cuttle's values is unqualified. And since he is threatened with exactly the same obliteration as has destroyed Staggs's Gardens we have to reflect that Dickens is sorely afraid of what the destruction will mean in human terms.

Cuttle is without doubt convincingly presented as a good man. And as our knowledge of Dickens's presentation of Tom Pinch confirms, writing about innocent goodness is no easy matter. But we have no difficulty in accepting Cuttle's kindness, charity, fellow-feeling, selflessness, love. Nor can we avoid sensing that his qualities are somehow connected with his being an out-of-date mariner who becomes proprietor of an out-of-date shop which is about to be swept away by the new world. We also sense that the values Dickens celebrates in Cuttle cannot, he thinks, be found in the world which threatens Cuttle.

The reason for the new world's lack of humaneness is intimately linked to its view of time. This view, which is a recognizably modern one, is usefully stated by Meyerhoff when he notes how time came to be seen as a commodity. 'In contrast to the ancient and medieval outlook, time in the modern world has become more and more an instrument serving no other function than to produce goods for consumption and profit.' And it therefore follows that 'The past [is] dead and useless.' For Dombey's world time is money, because it is a commodity like any other, including human nature. To Dombey's house comes a 'Bank director, reputed to be able to buy up anything – human Nature generally, if he should take it into his head to influence the money market in that direction'. (ch 36) But it is the great first chapter which offers so profound a statement about time as commodity.

It begins by showing us time as a natural process. 'On the brow of Dombey, Time and his brother Care had set some marks, as on a tree that was to come down in good time.' But good time is displaced by time which, in a world of effort, is either hurried up or arrested. Mrs Chick is 'a lady rather past the middle age than otherwise, but dressed in a very juvenile way, particularly as to the tightness of her bodice, who [ran up to Mr. Dombey] with a kind of screw in her face expressive of suppressed emotion.' The nurse, Blockitt, is 'a simpering piece of faded gentility', who cannot keep up with time and is therefore used by others much as they like: 'She did not presume to state her name as a fact, but merely offered it as a mild suggestion.' In Dombey's world identities are uncertain and can be changed, as Blockitt's way of stating her name reveals and as Dombey himself proves when he renames Polly Toodle 'Richards'. And Miss Tox is also a victim of time. She has a 'faded air' and in her effort to keep up with the Dombey world transforms herself into the sort of 'fixed' identity whose strange rigidity characterizes that world as a whole (we know too much about reification and role-playing to deny the force of Dickens's insight into her distorted appearance):

> From a long habit of listening admirably to everything that was said in her presence, and looking at the speakers as if she were mentally engaged in taking off impressions of their images upon her soul, never to part with the same but with life, her head had

quite settled on one side. Her hands had contracted a spasmodic habit of raising themselves of their own accord as in involuntary admiration. Her eyes were liable to a similar affection. She had the softest voice that ever was heard; and her nose, stupendously aquiline, had a little knob in the very centre or keystone of the bridge, whence it tended downwards toward her face, as in an invincible determination never to turn up at anything. (ch 1)

It is typical of the leap that Dickens takes from *Martin Chuzzle-wit* to *Dombey and Son* that Miss Tox's decency should be so carefully allowed for, so that we are not surprised when she is abandoned by the Dombey world and goes over to join forces with the characters whom time threatens.

Mrs Dombey does not have Miss Tox's chance to alter allegiances. She is simply hurried out of existence:

> 'Fanny! Fanny!'
> There was no sound in answer but the loud ticking of Mr. Dombey's watch and Dr. Parker Pep's watch, which seemed in the silence to be running a race.
> 'Fanny, my dear,' said Mrs. Chick, with assumed lightness, 'here's Mr. Dombey come to see you . . .'
> No word or sound in answer. Mr. Dombey's watch and Dr. Parker Pep's watch seemed to be racing faster.
> 'Now, really, Fanny my dear,' said the sister-in-law, altering her position, and speaking less confidently, and more earnestly, in spite of herself. 'I shall have to be quite cross with you, if you don't rouse yourself. It's necessary for you to make an effort, and perhaps a very great and painful effort which you are not disposed to make; but this is a world of effort you know, Fanny, and we must never yield, when so much depends on us. Come! Try! I must really scold you if you don't.'
> The race in the ensuing pause was fast and furious. The watches seemed to jostle, and to trip each other up. (ch 1)

Since the Dombey world is essentially characterized by its future hopes and its inevitable readiness to discard the past as 'dead and useless', Mrs Dombey is expendable as soon as she has produced Paul. She does not really belong to the society towards which

Dombey aspires: '"our interesting friend the Countess of Dombey – I *beg* your pardon; Mrs. Dombey."' Dr Parker Pep's confusion points up Mrs Dombey's present uselessness. She has no title and her only relevant achievement is to give birth to a son, for until then the Dombeys had had no issue.

> – 'To speak of; none worth mentioning. There had been a girl some six years before . . . But what was a girl to Dombey and Son!'

This brings us to an interesting problem. What is Dombey? The answer may seem clear. A respectable man of a well-established business. He has 'risen, as his father had before him, in the course of life and death, from Son to Dombey'. But Dickens is not at all precise about what the business actually is. Still, Dombey himself is a figure of hideously perfect rectitude:

> It happened to be an iron-gray autumnal day, with a shrewd east wind blowing – a day in keeping with the proceedings. Mr. Dombey represented in himself the wind, the shade, and the autumn of the christening. He stood in his library to receive the company, as hard and cold as the weather; and when he looked out through the glass room, at the trees in the little garden, their brown and yellow leaves came fluttering down as if he blighted them . . . The stiff and stark fire-irons appeared to claim a nearer relationship than anything else there to Mr. Dombey, with his buttoned coat, his white cravat, his heavy gold watch-chain, and his creaking boots. (ch 5)

An image such as this awakens memories of the Clapham Sect, and Dombey has something about him of the figure of Henry Thornton whom E. M. Forster champions in his biography of *Marianne Thornton*, and for whose kind Sydney Smith had such fine disdain. Like Smith, Dickens despised the self-congratulatory dull piety of the Evangelicals, and he had already attacked Agnew's Sunday Observance Bill in his passionate and bitter *Sunday Under Three Heads*. Clearly it will not do to say that Dombey belongs to the Clapham Sect, but it does make sense to suggest that he has about him that mixture of hard-headed business acumen and cold charity that made the Sect so distinguished a group. His involvement with the Charitable Grinders smacks of the soulless educational ideas of the Evangelicals, his joyless existence strongly echoes their ostentatious renunciation of pleasure, and he shares their deep distrust of sex. As Ford K. Brown points out, for the Evangelicals 'The flesh in itself being evil, it and its attributes, manifestations and operations must be concealed and in no way, or only in the most oblique way, referred to.'[1] Dombey's reticence over sex is surely sketched in at the very beginning of the novel, when he appends 'a term of endearment to Mrs. Dombey's name (though not without some hesitation, as being a man but little used to that form of address), and said, "Mrs. Dombey, my – my dear."' Admittedly, this shows that Dombey cannot manage personal relationships and that in this he embodies what Mill saw as Bentham's error in not recognizing 'the more complex forms' of sympathy. But it also shows that he is afraid of love and presumably sexual relations. That is why he is so quick to send Walter away when he senses that there is some bond between the boy and Florence (it can hardly be that he opposes the idea of her marrying beneath her, since girls have nothing to do with Dombey and Son). It is also why Edith has him so hopelessly at a disadvantage when she refuses to share his bed. At the very least he wants another son, but there is no hope that Edith will produce one. He may say to Carker that '"Mrs Dombey must understand that my will is law"', but faced with Edith he becomes inept simply because she will not submit. And what does Dombey know of seduction?

> He felt his disadvantage and he showed it. Solemn and strange among this wealth of colour and voluptuous glitter, strange and constrained towards its haughty mistress, whose repellent beauty it repeated, and presented all around him . . . he was conscious of embarrassment and awkwardness. (ch 40)

Carker, of course, is a model of lubricity, the seducer of Alice and would-be seducer of Edith. For Carker sex is power, and he images a fuller acceptance of the amoral world he serves than

---

[1] Ford K. Brown, *Fathers of the Victorians*, 1960, p. 437.

does Dombey, who is made almost ridiculous by a frozen rectitude that clings to him as part of his identity.

But here we come to another element in Dombey's make-up. For if his starchy ways recall the upper middle-class Banking firms and City houses which were so closely linked to Evangelical concerns, he also has about him something of the *nouveaux riches*. Dombey might almost be a member of that Working Aristocracy whom Carlyle had so recently been insisting 'must understand that money alone is *not* the representative either of man's success in the world, or of man's duties to man'.[1] But in what sense can Dombey be one of the Working Aristocracy? Not in his actual business-matters; he is neither 'Mill-Owner', 'manufacturer', nor 'Commander of working men', and indeed it feels as though his 'counting house' has much more in common with the business and merchandise which go with an older world. And he has inherited his business from his father. Yet in his social uncertainty Dombey belongs with the *nouveaux riches*. And for all his apparent confidence, Dombey undoubtedly is socially unsure of himself. His friendship with Bagstock illustrates as much, since Bagstock is very clearly *infra dig*. It also shows in his readiness to marry Edith who, with her jewels and Regency Mama, is quite the opposite of what the sober business man expected of his women: 'Young girls should be taught from early days to dress with a decent plainness. Adornment was viewed with suspicion, even the least garish.'[2]

Has Dickens somehow muddled Dombey's identity? We can hardly think so. The truth is that Dombey is a man of no sure identity because he is caught between two; wanting to belong to the new world, but trying repeatedly to do so on his own terms – which are linked to an older way of life. In himself, that is, Dombey provides a great image of society caught at a moment of radically difficult transition, all at sea when it comes to knowing which values, manners, modes of existence should be adopted, got rid of or retained. Dombey wishes to hurry time up,

[1] *Past and Present*, op. cit., p. 177.
[2] *Fathers of the Victorians*, p. 437.

but he, no less than Mrs Dombey, is time's victim. And the identity he tries to create for himself leads to his destruction, because it destroys his son and his second marriage, who are its twin poles: Paul standing for what is retained from an older way of life, Edith for what is new – though only to him, it being one of the novel's typical subtleties that Dombey in hurrying time up should aspire to what ought already to be outworn ("'The family I represent,'" Edith's cousin Feenix laments, "'is now almost extinct.'"). Dombey marries Edith and loses her to Carker, that inevitable and monstrous product of the new world whose only manner of existing, it seems, is in an abject subservience that inevitably brings with it an inhuman resolution to be avenged.

> 'Carker,' returned Mr. Dombey . . . 'you mistake your position in offering advice to me on such a point, and you mistake me (I am surprised to find) in the character of your advice. I have no more to say.'
> 'Perhaps,' said Carker, with an unusual and indefinable taunt in his air, '*you* mistook my position, when you honoured me with the negotiations in which I have been engaged here' – with a motion of his hand towards Mrs. Dombey.
> 'Not at all, Sir, not at all,' returned the other haughtily. 'You were employed – '
> 'Being an inferior person, for the humiliation of Mrs. Dombey. I forgot. Oh, yes, it was expressly understood!' said Carker. 'I beg your pardon.' (ch 47)

We are bound to notice how brilliantly Dickens's awareness of the rapidly increasing complexity of class-consciousness in Victorian England is dramatized in this dialogue. And underneath Carker's fake air of humility there is a bitterness that makes him entirely credible. It is a great pity that Dickens is so determined to turn him into a sort of stage-villain of vulpine sexuality and ingratitude, because the festering sore of Carker's position is all-too believable. He is in fact an image of the modern man whose sense of degraded dependence swells into poisonous hatred of whoever forces him into the posture of dependence. How utterly authentic he sounds, for example, when he denies Edith's charge that he is Dombey's flatterer:

> 'Counsellor, – yes . . . flatterer, – no. A little reservation I fear I must confess to . . . Mr. Dombey is really capable of no more true consideration for you, Madam, than for me . . . Mr. Dombey, in the plenitude of his power, asked me – I had it from his own lips yesterday morning – to be the go-between to you, because he knows I am not agreeable to you, and because he intends that I shall be a punishment for your contumacy. . . . You may imagine how regardless of me, how obtuse to the possibility of my having any individual sentiment or opinion he is, when he tells me I am so employed.' (ch 46)

Dickens's ability to show us Carker's individual sentiment and opinion makes his study of the manager ring true, and even compels us into some sympathetic understanding for him – of the sort we hardly give to his brother. John Carker is meant to be a man of tolerance and forgiveness; but his sympathy with Dombey emerges as nearer to lunacy or mealy-mouthed cant:

> 'It would be a mistake to suppose that it is only you who are tender of his welfare and reputation. There is no one in the House, from yourself down to the lowest, I sincerely believe, who does not participate in that feeling.'
>
> 'You lie!' said the Manager, red with sudden anger. 'You're a hypocrite, John Carker, and you lie. . . . There is not a man employed here, standing between myself and the lowest in place (of whom you are very considerate, and with reason, for he is not far off), who wouldn't be glad to see his master humbled: who does not hate him, secretly: who does not wish him evil rather than good: and who would not turn upon him, if he had the power and boldness. The nearer to his favour, the nearer to his insolence; the closer to him, the farther from him. That's the creed here.' (ch 46)

What makes the manager sympathetic here is exactly his awareness of how in the world to which he belongs people are forced to find a place in society if they are to exist at all, even though this means denying their individuality. And we are more likely to be convinced by Carker's anger than by the crude means Dickens takes to let us know that he is a villain, as for example in his parenthetic insult to his brother. It brings us back to Dombey's determination to educate Rob in the interests of ensuring that 'the inferior classes should continue to be taught to know their position'. And this in its turn reminds us of how vital a role education played in nineteenth-century England in stabilizing class-consciousness, and how Dickens understood as much. Thus Miss Tox enthuses that the nursery school to which Paul is to be sent is 'exclusion itself'. For Paul is not to know the inferior classes. And so when Polly Toodle becomes his wet-nurse Dombey tells her

> 'It is not at all in this bargain that you need become attached to my child, or that my child need become attached to you. I don't expect or desire anything of the kind. Quite the reverse. When you go away from here, you will have concluded what is a mere matter of bargain and sale, hiring and letting; and will stay away. The child will cease to remember you; and you will cease to remember the child.' (ch 2)

No doubt Dickens's own experiences as Maria Beadnell's lover put him in a particularly good position to know about the in-human rottenness of 'unsuitable' attachments; but it would be unworthy to suppose that his really profound insight into a corruption that goes so deep into English social life begins and ends with his own broken love-affair. *Dombey and Son* owes much of its greatness to the sustained power of his awareness that education is created by and feeds the corruption. Under Dr Blimper's cultivation:

> Every description of Greek and Latin vegetables was got off the driest twigs of boys, under the frostiest circumstances. Nature was of no consequence at all. No matter what a young gentleman was intended to bear, Doctor Blimper made him bear to pattern, somehow or other. (ch 11)

I pointed out in my earlier essay that Dickens's imagery here is fairly certainly derived from *Sartor Resartus*, but that *Dombey and Son* is not merely providing an anti-Utilitarian concept of the purposes of education, since 'cultivation' is a word of altogether greater resonance than can be explained in terms of any attack on Utilitarianism. At bottom it connects with the moulding of class-consciousness and therefore class-identity, and the point is made with whiplash accuracy when Mrs Skewton sees Florence and is reminded of the young Edith:

> 'For positively, my dear,' said Mrs. Skewton, 'I do think I see a decided resemblance to what you were then, in our extremely fascinating young friend. And it shows,' said Mrs. Skewton, in a lower voice, which conveyed her opinion that Florence was in a very unfinished state, 'what cultivation will do.'
> 'It does indeed,' was Edith's stern reply. (ch 30)

In a world of effort, parents willingly sacrifice to class-identity what Dickens convincingly shows are the children's true and natural interests.

> 'Ha!' said Doctor Blimper. 'Shall we make a man of him?'
> 'Do you hear, Paul?' added Mr. Dombey; Paul being silent.
> 'Shall we make a man of him?' repeated the Doctor.
> 'I had rather be a child,' replied Paul.
> 'Indeed!' said the Doctor. 'Why?' (ch 11)

As an educationist, Blimper merely serves Dombey's wish to hurry time up and convert Paul into Son and then Dombey. ' "Six years old!" said Mr. Dombey . . . "Dear me, six will be changed to sixteen, before we have time to look about us." ' And it needs to be noted that altogether the novel's analogous patterns work finely in rendering the use of education: Dombey, Mrs Brown, Mrs Skewton, the parents of Briggs, Toots, Tozer: they all destroy their children in an effort to see that they gain a place in the new world and are on the side of time. I know of no more powerful and persuasive writing about the horrors of education as 'cultivation' than Dickens provides in chapters 10, 11, and 13 of *Dombey and Son*. The claim cannot be substantiated by quotation because the effect accumulates over the three chapters, but it is worth saying that the writing is not merely the product of good-hearted feeling but of unequalled intelligence. To come across Dickens at work on the subject of education is to recognize that of all English writers who have had anything to say on the matter, only Blake comes near him in sheer enlightened compassion.

Parent-child relations in the Dombey world are at the mercy of time as commodity, and so it is with all human relationships. It costs Mrs Chick very little to break her friendship with Miss Tox, since she chooses not to remember it. The past is dead and can be exorcised. And since friendships can easily be destroyed they can also easily be created – as witness Mr Dombey and Bagstock and Cousin Feenix. The same holds true for marriages. The unnaturalness of forced relationships is everywhere in Dombey's world; and images of chains and manacles abound. Nor is this a matter of mere surface symbolism. The images testify to and connect with a reality that the novel everywhere makes evident. The language of chains feels proper because it expresses most cogently a truth about the relationships that Dickens presents as typifying the Dombey world.

But what of the Wooden Midshipman and the characters connected with it? Here we are shown a set of natural unforced relationships which testify to that 'natural heart' whose loss in herself Edith laments. In doing so she speaks for the Dombey world as a whole, the world which is also characterized by the Railroad, that plain fact – not symbol – which expresses a general desire to hurry time up. The Railroad alters lives, uproots the past, is both exhilarating and terrifying, irresistibly powerful and man-made. It is the perfect image of time as commodity. And against it is the sea, that image of 'good time' which is intimately associated with the world of the Wooden Midshipman. The sea, it hardly needs saying, testifies to a natural ebb and flow of life, of eternal rhythms, of mutability: it separates and joins, and holds all the disturbing richness of which life is capable. It is, in short, an obvious symbol for a way of life that opposes the new world. As Romantic symbol the sea is 'the Alpha of existence, the symbol of potentiality', possessed of 'perpetual motion', and 'teeming life'.[1] And it is as a Romantic symbol that Dickens uses the sea in *Dombey and Son*.

On the morning of Dombey's wedding

> The steeple-clock, perched above the houses, emerging from beneath another of the countless ripples in the tide of time that regularly roll and break on the eternal shore, is greyly visible, like a stone beacon, recording how the sea flows on. (ch 31)

I think that a passage such as that, whose imagery is frequently echoed in the novel, suggests how Dickens is groping for a meaning which at least partly eludes him. For the 'eternal shore' is too vague to emerge into significance; it is *merely* symbolic. And although we can be reasonably certain that Dickens wants somehow to oppose the unchanging rhythms of life with the unique particularity of Dombey's marriage which is a product of time as commodity, the opposition remains assertive, a matter of language alone and not really bound to any reality that the novel shows. And the same criticism can perhaps be levelled at the final paragraph of chapter 1:

> Thus, clinging fast to that slight spar within her arms, the mother drifted out upon the dark and unknown sea that rolls round all the world.

Yet this passage may have more justification. For in its acceptance of what is 'dark and unknown', it sets up a notion of impalpable mystery that counters the confident aggressiveness of the Dombey world. The novel does not pretend to read the mystery; it merely acknowledges it. Even for Paul, what the waves are always saying may amount as much to a death-wish as to anything else. And we have to accept that the boy's strange fascination with the sea is beautifully just since in its unknowableness it offers a better hope than the world his father is educating him for, about which he knows only too much.

When we come to Mrs Skewton's encounter with the sea, we have to bow to Dickens's greatness:

[1] W. H. Auden, *The Enchafèd Flood*, 1951, p. 28.

She lies and listens to it by the hour; but its speech is dark and gloomy to her, and a dread is on her face, and when her eyes wander over the expanse, they see but a broad stretch of desolation between earth and heaven. (ch 41)

That is how to use symbolism. It so perfectly clinches the reality of Mrs Skewton's wasted life and her dimly terrible perception of how she has destroyed herself and Edith. The 'broad stretch of desolation' quite brilliantly serves to establish a guilty know-ledge of what can never come to full consciousness but neverthe-less hovers in the old woman's mind.

Is the mystery justifiably presented in the reunion of Walter and Florence? Dombey separates them, but the sea brings them together; their enduring love represents a natural relationship honoured by the sea's power and against which the Dombey world is helpless. And here it is perhaps necessary to notice the novel's great formal beauty, quite apart from the resourcefulness of its analogous patterns. It begins with a birth and a death; it ends with an insistent recall of time passing, and of age and youth:

> Buried wine grows older, as the old Madeira did, in its time; and dust and cobwebs thicken on the bottles.
>
> Autumn days are shining, and on the sea-beach there are often a young lady, and a white-haired gentleman. With them, or near them, are two children: boy and girl. And an old dog is generally in their company. (ch 62)

In between, the Dombey world sends away Walter and his Uncle and leaves the Midshipman 'solitary'; and the Dombey world rises to its greatest achievement as the Midshipman world is most threatened and then falls to its lowest ebb as the Midshipman rises towards renewed life. Overall, that is, the novel establishes the rhythms of 'good time', which even the Dombey world must obey.

But is it fair? May it not be that the triumph of good time represents a denial of the strength of the Dombey world which all through is shown to be so irresistible? '"Competition, com-petition,"' Sol Gills tells Walter, '"new invention, new in-vention – alteration, alteration, – the world's gone past me . . . I

have fallen behind the time, and am too old to catch it again.'"
(ch 4) Yet at the end of the novel we are told that 'They do say . . .
that some of Mr. Gill's old investments are coming out wonderfully well; and that instead of being behind the time in these
respects . . . he was in truth, a little before it, and had to wait the
fullness of the time and the design.'" (ch 62) Yes, but whose
design, we are entitled to ask? Isn't this Dickens wrenching
probabilities and even the truth of his novel to fit a resolution
that salvages the people and values he admires? The problem
has a special bearing on the presentation of Walter.

Initially, Dickens intended the boy to be destroyed by the
Dombey world. He wrote to Forster:

> About the boy . . . I think it would be a good thing to disappoint
> all the expectations that chapter [four] seems to raise of his happy
> connection with the story and the heroine, and to show him
> gradually and naturally trailing away, from that love of adventure
> and boyish light-heartedness, into negligence, idleness, dissipation,
> dishonesty and ruin.[1]

It sounds very much as though Dickens is planning for Walter
what Wordsworth had shown as happening to Luke in his great
study of a man whose way of life is destroyed by social forces
he cannot control. But then Dickens changes his mind. Walter
is not destroyed, instead he becomes a good capitalist, 'mounting
up the ladder with the greatest expedition' with the aid of his
uncle's investments which themselves are made good by time –
the time associated with the sea: '"Why, yes, yes – some of my
lost ships, freighted with gold, have come home, truly,"
returns old Sol laughing, "Small craft, Mr. Toots, but serviceable
to my boy."' (ch 62)

I used to think that this optimistic ending was quite improper
and that Dickens allows it to happen only because it is the one
way he can find of importing the values of the 'natural heart'
into a world which he had shown as destroying them. And I
argued in my earlier essay that the novel somehow contradicts

[1] John Forster, *Life of Dickens*, 1893, p. 360.

itself when Walter succeeds, because Dickens has done too good a job of convincing us that the values that Gay and his world embody could never survive in a world governed by what we might call railway-time. But I think now that this criticism may be unfair. For Walter's triumph can be read as a final gesture of open-mindedness, a refusal to settle for an apocalyptic vision, and an attempt to honour a 'design' and 'mystery' that suggest a ceaseless process of change, decay and renewal, by means of which the past may be carried into the future without decisive break or dislocation. I do not think this is cowardice. On the contrary, it is imaginatively courageous, for it allows the novel an open-endedness that is in no way pietistic or vacuous, but alert to historical possibilities.

If we read *Dombey and Son* in this way, the novel's formal rhythms become tactfully mimetic rather than overtly pre-scriptive. Dombey's downfall need not imply a moral nemesis or an escape-route from the emergent society into private love, but the exhaustion of just one phase in the process of change; he himself, that is, has to yield to the time which he has tried to control. That, after all, is what the novel's opening hints at when it speaks of his brow as carrying marks 'as on a tree that was to come down in good time', and which the ending affirms: 'Mr. Dombey is a white-haired gentleman, whose face bears heavy marks of care and suffering.' And for *Dombey and Son* to refuse to confirm its own worst possibilities, given the intensity with which Dickens renders them, is surely a mark of its great-ness.

℁ 5 · *DAVID COPPERFIELD*

After the publication of *Dombey and Son* Dickens allowed some time to elapse before he began another novel. But his mind was turning towards interests that come to the fore in *David Copperfield* some while before he actually started work on it. In the first place, of course, he started an autobiography and quickly broke off – apparently unable to write about the traumatic experiences of his childhood and youth. Much of the autobiographical material is fed into *Copperfield*, and it does not always bear out Dickens's own hope that 'I have done it very ingeniously, and with a very complicated interweaving of fact and fiction'.[1] There is, for example, a lacerating self-pity that strays from autobiography into novel, where it has no place. In a very famous passage of the autobiographical sketch, Dickens notes that:

> It is wonderful to me how I could have been so easily cast away at such an age. It is wonderful to me that, even after my descent into the poor little drudge I had been since we came to London, no one had compassion enough on me – a child of singular abilities, quick, eager, delicate, and soon hurt, bodily or mentally – to suggest that something might have been spared, as certainly it might have been, to place me at any common school. . . . No one made any sign. My father and mother were quite satisfied. They could hardly have been more so if I had been twenty years of age, distinguished at a grammar school, and going to Cambridge.[2]

Compare this with the opening of chapter 11 of *Copperfield*, and it immediately becomes clear that fact has not really been modified into fiction:

[1] *Forster, Life of Dickens* p. 384.
[2] *Forster, op. cit.,* pp. 17–18.

I know enough of the world now, to have almost lost the capacity of being surprised by anything; but it is a matter of some surprise to me, even now, that I can have been so easily thrown away at such an age. A child of excellent abilities, and with strong powers of observation, quick, eager, delicate, and soon hurt bodily or mentally, it seems wonderful to me that nobody should have made any sign on my behalf. But none was made; and I became, at ten years old, a little labouring hind . . .

To be sure, this feeding of autobiographical material into the novel has been often enough noticed, but I mention it again because it does introduce us to the very important point that Dickens keeps the past alive no matter how wounding it has proved. And the point extends to much of his writing at this period. In the last chapter I suggested that one of the concerns of *Dombey and Son* is to probe at the impoverishing consequences for people who deny their own pasts, who try to destroy time's long perspectives. And although in *Dombey* the destruction is more a matter of social than personal concern, it becomes treated in a different way in the Christmas Book for 1848, *The Haunted Man*.

The hero of this story is a famous chemist named Redlaw, who is haunted by the spectre of his miserable past:

> 'Look upon me!' said the Spectre. 'I am he, neglected in my youth, and miserably poor, who strove and suffered, and still strove and suffered, until I hewed out the knowledge from the mine where it was buried, and made rugged steps thereof, for my worn feet to rest and rise on.'
> 'I *am* that man,' returned the chemist.
> 'No mother's self-denying love,' pursued the Phantom, 'no father's counsel, aided *me*. A stranger came into my father's place when I was but a child, and I was easily an alien from my mother's heart. My parents, at the best, were of that sort whose care soon ends, and whose duty is soon done; who cast their offspring loose, early, as birds do theirs; and if they do well, claim the merit; and, if ill, the pity.' (ch 1)

Because of his miserable past Redlaw wants to exorcise it and destroy his memory, and the moral of the tale is that he must learn that to lose 'the intertwined chain of feelings and associations, each in its turn dependent on, and nourished by, the banished recollections', is to lose all that makes life bearable. The story ends with the motto which points its moral, 'Lord, keep my Memory Green'.

As a story, *The Haunted Man* is inconsiderable, but it is inevitably of interest to us, because, like the autobiographical sketch, it indicates that the matter of *David Copperfield* did not suddenly spring unforeknown from the novelist's head. Above all, the story offers a solid clue as to Dickens's crucial enquiry into how a man comes to be what he is, which is given full and massive scope in the novel because the man there is so close to Dickens himself. It was at the time of *Copperfield* that Dickens wrote to Forster to complain about a story he had just been reading, 'It seems to me as if it were written by somebody who lived next door to the people, rather than inside of 'em.'[1] The adoption of a first-person narrative for *David Copperfield* is just one of the ways that Dickens makes sure that he is inside his hero. The method undoubtedly creates a few very awkward moments – as for example the vital scene between Rose Dartle and Emily, which David has to overhear if we are to know about it but which he ought to prevent. But for the most part it seems to me to work well enough.

Still, the great danger of the method is obviously that it will allow the novelist to identify himself quite uncritically with his hero. It would be foolish to pretend that Dickens avoids this danger, but the wonder of the novel is that the lapses are so few and trivial, compared with what is accomplished. If we except a few moments of quite unplaced self-pity and snobbishness, *David Copperfield* comes off magnificently. Partly this is because at its finest it is in no way a restricted study of a special case. For one thing, the voice of the narrator interprets and places remembered incidents in such a way that their particularity is tempered by an almost sad wisdom that can create a human commonplace

[1] Forster, op. cit., p. 391.

out of what might at first glance look strikingly individual. I think, for example, of the incident of Mell's dismissal from Creakle's Academy, and Steerforth's 'Very noble intention to get Mell some money; especially when [Steerforth] told us, as he condescended to do, that what he had done had been expressly for us, and for our cause; and that he had conferred a great boon upon us by unselfishly doing it'. (ch 7) For another thing, there is the novel's dominant rhythm, its steady and irresistible forward movement – as of life. And here it is worth noting the consider- able amount of careful prolepsis: of Emily, as a girl, 'springing forward to her destruction (as it seemed to me)' (ch 3); of Steer- forth's passionate outburst against the guidance he has had; of the look on Annie Strong's face which makes so great an impres- sion on the adolescent David; of the beggar he hears crying 'blind, blind, blind'.

Here we come to one of the most remarkable characteristics of *David Copperfield*, its feeling of inevitability. This is not the inevitability of tragedy, but of temporal rhythms that cumula- tively establish a human life. And because the effect *is* cumulative communicating it through criticism is next to impossible, since the novel is persuasive partly because of its sheer length, and the amount of time we take to read through it. If *Dombey and Son* is remarkable for the wonderful echoing patterns that build up a spatial vision of society caught at a moment of time, *David Copperfield* builds a temporal vision, for successive patterns per- suade us of the ceaseless process of loss and renewal, change and continuity. Such a process is inevitably associated with fictional autobiography. We find it, for example, in the *Prelude*, published – by one of literature's necessary coincidences – in the same year as *David Copperfield*, and I think it possible that Dickens read and made use of Wordsworth's poem. The *Prelude* appeared in July 1850, and the following month Dickens began work on the number to include Dora's death. When Dora dies, David goes to the Alps:

If those awful solitudes had spoken to my heart, I did not know it.

I had found sublimity and wonder in the dread heights and preci-
pices, in the roaring torrents, and the wastes of ice and snow; but
as yet, they had taught me nothing else.

I came, one evening before sunset, down into a valley, where I
was to rest. In the course of my descent to it, by the winding
track along the mountain-side, from which I saw it shining far
below, I think some long-unwonted sense of beauty and tranquillity, some softening influence awakened by its peace, moved
faintly in my breast. . . . In the quiet air, there was a sound of
distant singing – shepherd voices; but, as one bright evening cloud
floated midway along the mountain's side, I could almost believe
it came from there, and was not earthly music. (ch 58)

The Wordsworthian echoes seem to me very strong. And of
course the *Prelude* would be of especial interest to Dickens
because its declared intent to trace 'The Growth of a Poet's
Mind' is so very close to his own subject, which might, I think,
be paraphrased as 'The Growth of a Disciplined Heart'.

But of course it will not do to press the analogies with Wordsworth, if for no other reason than that Dickens's theme is realized
through a great number of people whom David learns properly
to estimate, so that the mature narrator judges them as the growing boy could not. David himself, it should be said, is not the
great example of the disciplined heart, and the novel does not
provide one. Instead, it presents us with several characters who
embody those human qualities which Dickens had celebrated in
the world of the Wooden Midshipman and which figure increasingly in the subsequent novels. And since David is brought to
a just estimation of these characters, it can be said that he is
obviously very close to Dickens. His values are Dickens's and
there is one occasion on which novelist and narrator equally
admit to the troubling complexity of humans who defeat
simplistic moral judgements. Dickens hates Uriah Heep and so
does David. But just once Heep speaks out, and in doing so he
upsets all the calculations on which judgement is based (as Carker
momentarily does, and as Vholes and Merdle do):

But how little you think of the rightful umbleness of a person in my station, Master Copperfield! Father and me was brought up at a foundation school for boys; and mother, she was likewise brought up at a public, sort of charitable, establishment. They taught us all a deal of umbleness – not much else that I know of, from morning to night. We was to be umble to this person, and umble to that; and to pull off our caps here, and to make bows there; and always to know our place, and abase ourselves before our betters. And we had such a lot of betters! Father got the monitor-medal by being umble. So did I. Father got made a sexton by being umble. He had the character, among the gentlefolks, of being such a well-behaved man, that they were determined to bring him in. 'Be umble, Uriah,' says father to me, 'and you'll get on. It was what was always being dinned into you and me at school; it's what goes down best. Be umble,' says father, 'and you'll do.' And really it ain't done bad.

Faced with Heep's sudden truth-telling, David is forced to reflect that

it was the first time that it had ever occurred to me, that this detestable cant of false humility might have originated out of the family. I had seen the harvest, but had never thought of the seed . . . I had never doubted his meanness, his craft and malice; but I fully comprehended now, for the first time, what a base, unrelenting and revengeful spirit, must have been engendered by this early, and this long, suppression. (ch 39)

David's reflection seems to me precisely at one with those which animate so many of Dickens's fictional studies. And there is some justification for saying that as the mature David tries to make sense of his life so Dickens is given the chance to test out and vindicate his own values and attitudes. On the other hand, I do not want to pretend that David is merely a front or mask behind which Dickens can operate. He is too fully realized a character for that. And he becomes convincing through the complex interplay that we trace between the mature David as narrator and the remembered self or selves about whom he writes.

As everybody who reads the novel senses – it is the one thing about it that you cannot miss – David's reality springs from the vivacity of his memories. And although there is not much that needs to be said here about Dickens's achievement in creating David's past, it is fair to remark that I know of nothing in English literature to equal the clarity, immediacy and general rightness of the narrator's early years (and I admit that there are false moments). George Orwell put it best:

> I must have been about nine years old when I first read *David Copperfield*. The mental atmosphere of the opening chapters was so immediately intelligible to me that I vaguely imagined they had been written *by a child* (Orwell's italics).[1]

Orwell himself was clearly influenced by Dickens when he came to write a memoir of his own early years. In *Such, Such Were the Joys*, he remarks that

> it is not easy for me to think of my schooldays without seeming to breathe in a whiff of something cold and evil-smelling – a sort of compound of sweaty stockings, dirty towels, faecal smells blowing along corridors, forks with old food between the prongs . . .[2]

Compare this with David at Salem House, noting that 'there is a strange unwholesome smell upon the room, like mildewed corduroys, sweet apples wanting air, and rotten books' (ch 5), and you see both what Orwell took from Dickens and how Dickens comes off better. Not that Orwell is bad, but he hasn't anything to match the individual rightness and sheer physicality of 'mildewed corduroys'. And the very fact that the narrator lapses into the present tense when describing Salem House, strengthens our awareness of his real and vital connections with his own childhood. It helps us to believe in the identity that has grown and endured through time.

This brings us to a point that perhaps needs to be stressed. *David Copperfield* is about growth, and we do it an injustice if we merely emphasize the wonderful achievements of the childhood scenes. Marvellous though they undoubtedly are, if we concentrate on them alone we shall merely be noting qualities

[1] *A Collection of Essays*. 1954, p. 67.
[2] Ibid., p. 30.

that successive generations of novelists have seized on and out of which they have been able to create a recognizable strain of minor fiction. In other words, it is wrong to judge the novel as falling into two halves, the first of which is splendid, but the second of which is dull stuff. My own very strong feeling is that *David Copperfield* is a great novel precisely because it cannot be divided up into two parts. It shows an unbroken development. Growth and the process of growth are what it is all about. That is why the temporal rhythms are so important. I shall have something to say about them shortly, but I want first to note that David's process of growth has three very natural overlapping stages, parents, schooling and friendship, and marriage, and that David as narrator is always trying to make sense of experiences which he sees have contributed to shape his identity.

Edgar Johnson has written very sensibly about how all of David's parent-figures present different aspects of Dickens's own parents as the novelist saw them, and there is no reason to disagree with any of his remarks. But while Johnson may help us to understand something of the genesis of the Peggottys, of the Micawbers, and of Murdstone, he does not really explain their importance to the novel's success. And in trying to estimate just what that importance is, it is as well to ignore biographical speculation. For in many ways David's early happiness with his mother and Peggotty is the story of Everyman. It is psychologically true. So is David's initial recognition of the intrusive father-figure, who threatens an expulsion from the undivided happiness of mother and child:

> He patted me on the head; but somehow, I didn't like him or his deep voice, and I was jealous that his hand should touch my mother's in touching me – which it did. I put it away, as well as I could.
> 'Oh, Davy!' remonstrated my mother . . .
> 'Let us say "good night," my fine boy,' said the gentleman, when he had bent his head – *I* saw him – over my mother's little glove.
> 'Good night' said I.

'Come! let us be the best friends in the world!' said the gentleman, laughing. 'Shake hands.'

My right hand was in my mother's left, so I gave him the other. 'Why, that's the wrong hand, Davy!' laughed the gentleman.

My mother drew my right hand forward, but I was resolved, for my former reason, not to give it him, and I did not. I gave him the other, and he shook it heartily, and said I was a brave fellow, and went away.

At this moment I see him turn round in the garden, and give us a last look with his ill-omened eyes, before the door was shut. (ch 2)

The narrator's voice breaks in in the last sentence, and it does so in order to emphasize the difference between what the mature man knows to have been culpable in Murdstone – his later harsh treatment of the child – and what the child unfairly but necessarily resents – the sexual attractiveness of the man and woman for each other. Immediately after David's mother has married Murdstone we are told that he 'seemed to be very fond of my mother – I am afraid I liked him none the better for that – and she was very fond of him'. (ch 4) And again the narrator's voice – 'I am afraid' – places the child's misery.

The misery is, of course, acute and follows on the apparently timeless happiness of his Yarmouth holiday:

I never hear the name, or read the name, of Yarmouth, but I am reminded of a certain Sunday morning on the beach, the bells ringing for church, little Em'ly leaning on my shoulder, Ham lazily dropping stones into the water, and the sun, away at sea, just breaking through the heavy mist, and showing us the ships, like their own shadows. (ch 3)

One of the chief ways in which *David Copperfield* builds up its slow, steady sense of growth is through a series of expulsions and severences; and David's first expulsion is from the 'timeless' idyll of Yarmouth. He returns from his holiday to the news of his mother's remarriage and the discovery of those shades of the prison house that begin to grow about him, shutting out the sight of the children who sported upon the shore. With the introduction of the Murdstones David is confronted by a new world that 'brought a cold blast of air into the house which blew away the old familiar feeling like a feather'. (ch 8) And there is no going back:

> I was in the carrier's cart when I heard her calling to me. I looked out, and she stood at the garden gate alone, holding her baby up in her arms for me to see...
> So I lost her. So I saw her afterwards, in my sleep at school – a silent presence at my bed – looking at me with the same intent face – holding up her baby in her arms. (ch 8)

'So I lost her.' It is perfectly reasonable to see in the image of mother and baby the proof that David has journeyed away from the old relationship and that there can be no return to it. He is expelled from the safe world of his mother's love and under the Murdstones becomes an 'outcast, bewildered and depressed'. I find it impossible to avoid linking David's first years with the passage about the discipline of love in the second book of the *Prelude*, not because Dickens could have read it when he was at work on this part of the novel, but because he and Wordsworth share the same deeply pondered insight into early childhood.

Miss Murdstone is the next mother. She is the mother-figure who occurs again in Mrs Clennam and Mrs Gargery, the stern repudiator of warmth and familiarity. As most critics notice, Miss Murdstone is to all intents and purposes Murdstone's wife. Certainly she becomes mistress of the house, possessor of the household keys and jointly responsible for David's education. The Murdstones do not operate by love:

> Firmness, I may observe, was the grand quality on which both Mr. and Miss Murdstone took their stand. However I might have expressed my comprehension of it at that time, if I had been called upon, I nevertheless did clearly comprehend in my own way, that it was another name for tyranny; and for a certain gloomy, arrogant, devil's humour, that was in them both. (ch 4)

Yet the very fact that the narrator finds it possible to speak of the Murdstone firmness with such scornful detachment, is evidence of his having survived it and being therefore able to judge it objectively. He even goes so far as to provide a glimpse of Murdstone that helps explain the man's firmness in a way that further emphasizes his own mature sanity. When the boy David has run away to his aunt Betsey Trotwood, the Murdstones come after him. Betsey tells Murdstone that it was clear to her that David's mother would marry again:

> 'but I did hope it wouldn't have been as bad as it has turned out. That was the time, Mr. Murdstone, when she gave birth to her boy here,' said my aunt; 'to the poor child you sometimes tormented her through afterwards, which is a disagreeable remembrance and makes the sight of him odious now. Aye, aye! you needn't wince!' said my aunt. 'I know it's true without that.'
>
> He had stood by the door, all this while, observant of her with a smile upon his face, though his black eyebrows were heavily contracted. I remarked now, that, though the smile was on his face still, his colour had gone in a moment, and he seemed to breathe as if he had been running. (ch 14)

To recover that moment from the past is to do Murdstone a sort of justice. It prevents him from being an inexplicable tyrant. And I think we need to note that when on later occasions in the novel the Murdstones are reintroduced, it is not as part of a mechanical way of telling us more about all the novel's characters, but so that we can see David's ability to cope with them. Childhood terror shrinks into at worst contempt. Thus, when Miss Murdstone turns up as Dora's 'confidential friend', David finds it possible to agree to her suggestion that they meet 'as distant acquaintances.'(ch 26) Much later, hearing that Murdstone has remarried, he speaks with amused scorn of the Murdstone behaviour. Mr Chillip says:

> 'Strong phrenological development of the organ of firmness, in Mr. Murdstone and his sister, sir.'
>
> I replied with such an expressive look, that Mr. Chillip [exclaimed] 'Ah, dear me! We remember old times, Mr. Copperfield.'
>
> 'And the brother and sister are pursuing their old course, are they?' I said.

'Well, sir,' replied Mr. Chillip, 'a medical man, being so much in families, ought to have neither eyes nor ears for anything but his profession. Still, I must say, they are very severe, sir: both as to this life and the next.'

'The next will be regulated without much reference to them, I dare say,' I returned: 'what are they doing as to this.' (ch 59)

When we consider how intensely Dickens has communicated the horror of David's childhood years under the Murdstones, Chillip's remark about remembering the old times and David's cool dismissal of Murdstone firmness serves as extremely satisfying evidence of his attained growth, his ability to survive their baleful effect on him. And I think we feel this to be true even though we may have ruefully to reflect that Dickens is forced to be quite blatant about his re-introductions of the Murdstones.

In contrast with the Murdstones, the narrator always recalls the Micawbers with an amused tolerance:

At last Mr. Micawber's difficulties came to a crisis, and he was arrested early one morning, and carried over to the King's Bench Prison in the Borough. He told me, as he went out of the house, that the God of day had now gone down upon him – and I really thought his heart was broken and mine too. But I heard, afterwards, that he was seen to play a lively game at skittles, before noon. (ch 11)

The Micawbers are, of course, clearly modelled on aspects of Dickens's own parents. Mrs Micawber's plans for a 'Boarding Establishment for Young Ladies' directly echoes an absurd plan Mrs Dickens had dreamed up in order to make money; and Mr Micawber's feckless charm and orundity of speech come straight from the novelist's father. But the Micawbers are important to David's development because they are totally unable to offer him any help or comfort over his life at Murdstone and Grinby's warehouse. If anything, it is he who offers them help. For while he recalls that 'I had no advice, no counsel, no encouragement, no consolation, no assistance, no support, of any kind, from anyone, that I can call to mind', he also recalls being of use to the Micawbers in pawning their goods and generally looking after their household affairs, to the point where he almost takes charge of them. David, that is, learns a tough independence through being forced to reverse the normal parent-child relationship, and it is worth noting how often such a reversal crops up in the later novels. It is one of Dickens's obsessive themes. Yet David's attitude to the Micawbers, clear-sighted though his knowledge of them is, never degenerates into bitterness. When in adult life he encounters them again, he can say of Mrs Micawber that she is 'a little more slatternly than she used to be, or so she seemed now to my unaccustomed eyes, but still with some preparation of herself for company, and with a pair of brown gloves on' (ch 27); and the observation is affectionate rather than malicious. It is one more proof of his achieved maturity.

Peggotty and Betsey Trotwood are, it hardly needs saying, images of the good surrogate parents, and they are characterized by the selfless devotion and warmth that always calls out Dickens's fullest praise. His success with them is so obvious that it does not need comment. But I do need to note that they, too, represent moments and elements in David's life that he must learn to grow away from. And he experiences a quasi-expulsion from both of them, marked by the destruction of their houses.

Houses, indeed, provide one of the chief means of the novel's focusing on time passing. There is, for example, the leave-taking of Dr Strong's house:

> But morning brought with it my parting from the old house, which Agnes had filled with her influence; and that occupied my mind sufficiently. I should be there again soon, no doubt; I might sleep again – perhaps often – in my old room; but the days of my inhabiting there were gone, and the old time was past. (ch 19)

And later comes a glimpse of David's first home:

> There were great changes in my old house. The ragged nests, so long deserted by the rooks, were gone; and the trees were lopped and topped out of their remembered shapes. The garden had run wild, and half the windows of the house were shut up. (ch 22)

Such moments as these provide, very beautifully, for the natural rhythms of time passing. The break-up of Peggotty's and Betsey's houses is far less natural. Peggotty's house is destroyed as a result of Steerforth's abduction of Emily and the incident creates a sharp sense of an expulsion. David's own early paradisal innocence is finally destroyed by the sophisticated friend he so much admires:

> Everything was gone, down to the mirror with the oyster-shell frame. I thought of myself, lying here, when that first great change was being wrought at home. I thought of the blue-eyed child who had enchanted me. I thought of Steerforth: and a foolish fearful fancy came upon me of his being near at hand, and liable to be met at any turn. (ch 51)

Psychologically considered, David's 'fancy' is exactly right; for it establishes his own nearly guilty sense of how finally wrecked his 'safe' childhood paradise is, and of how hopelessly vulnerable it has proved against the intrusions of Steerforth and his world. When Betsey's house also goes, David's last childhood refuge is lost.

But Peggotty and Betsey are not just good parents. They are also examples of the 'disciplined heart', able to cope with and survive personal disaster. In his time of distress, Peggotty remains as 'grave and steady as the sea itself', and his worth communicates itself to Mrs Gummidge who becomes 'so forgetful of herself, and so regardful of the sorrow about her, that I held her in a sort of veneration'. (ch 32) And Betsey meets her loss by saying that ' "We must meet reverses boldly, and not suffer them to frighten us, my dear. We must learn to act the play out. We must live misfortune down, Trot." ' (ch 34) Mere words? Not really. For Betsey provides a constant image of that discipline towards which David must try to grow and which as narrator he learns to estimate at its true worth, whether he achieves it himself or not.

Betsey's disciplined heart is to be contrasted with Murdstone's parody of discipline and Wickfield and Mrs Steerforth, two

parents of undisciplined hearts. Wickfield himself admits that
' "Weak indulgence has ruined me. Indulgence in remembrance,
and indulgence in forgetfulness" '. (ch 39) Wickfield's disease is, I
think, too stridently insisted on, yet Dickens's basic insight into
him is surely very fine. The morbidity of emotion to which he
becomes a prisoner and from which through drink he seeks release – or the excuse of further indulgence – makes him recognizably human. And it may be worth noting that his house
is also destroyed. On a visit there David finds

> Uriah in possession of a new, plaster-smelling office, built out in
> the garden . . . He took me into Mr. Wickfield's room, which was
> the shadow of its former self – having been divested of a variety of
> conveniences, for the accommodation of the new partner. (ch 39)

As for Mrs Steerforth, her own son says that ' "I wish with all
my soul that I had been better guided! . . . I wish with all my
soul that I could guide myself better." ' (ch 22) That Steerforth
can admit his failure reveals both how firmly Dickens repudiates
any deterministic notion of growth and also how prepared he is
to honour Steerforth's candour. All the same, Mrs Steerfort his
culpable, as Rosa Dartle brings home to her when they hear of his
death. ' "Mourn for your nurture of him, mourn for your corruption of him." ' The speech is in that shrill vein of melo-
dramatics which so often accompanies accusation in Dickens's
novels and which we rightly dislike. Yet what lies beneath Rosa's
words has a proper relevance to the theme of untrammelled or
warped growth, disciplined and undisciplined hearts. And there
can be no doubt that Mrs Steerforth's outburst to Peggotty after
her son's elopement with Emily has the unmistakable accent of
authenticity. This is what possessive love is really like:

> 'My son, who has been the object of my life, to whom its every
> thought has been devoted, whom I have gratified from a child in
> every wish, from whom I have had no separate existence since his
> birth, – to take up in a moment with a miserable girl, and avoid me!
> To repay my confidence with systematic deception, for her sake,
> and quit me for her! To set this wretched fancy, against his

mother's claims upon his duty, love, respect, gratitude – claims that every day and hour of his life should have strengthened into ties that nothing could be proof against.' (ch 32)

What we might call the moral patterning of the book in regard to the theme of child-parent relationships and the growth of the disciplined heart has about it a sort of effortless relevance that by and large denies us any chance to think of it as obtrusive or having designs upon us. David and the Murdstones, David and Betsey, Mr Peggotty and Emily, Wickfield and Agnes, Mrs Steerforth and James, even Uriah and Mrs Heep (for there is a parodic discipline involved in learning umility): these links and distinctions play an important part in making us feel that the novel is almost inexhaustible comprehensive.

Schooling also relates to the growth of the disciplined heart. But here the matter is far simpler. Dickens is very good on David's initial awe of school, and he is predictably brilliant on the ignorant bully Creakle, whom we can usefully compare with Squeers to see how much the novelist has gained in sense of over-all control of tone between *Nicholas Nickleby* and *David Copperfield*:

> 'I have the happiness of knowing your father-in-law,' whispered Mr. Creakle, taking me by the ear; 'and a worthy man he is, and a man of strong character. He knows me, and I know him. Do *you* know me? Hey?' said Mr. Creakle, pinching my ear with ferocious playfulness. (ch 6)

Creakle is good because he is never parodied, and in general the chapters devoted to David's stay at Salem House seem to me an unqualified success.

Unfortunately, the same cannot be said for Dr Strong's Academy. We are told that 'Doctor Strong's was an excellent school; as different from Mr Creakle's as good is from evil'. (ch 16) We can hardly object to a recommendation for a humane system of education, but we are forced to admit that vague recommendation more or less exhausts what Dickens has to offer us in his writing about the school. Still, I do not think this is a

very important matter, for the real schooling that David under-
goes at both Creakle's and Dr Strong's is in the experience of
personal relationships. And if I am to show how magnificently
this theme develops I must say something about the growth of
David's friendship with Steerforth and Traddles, those paradigms
of the undisciplined and disciplined hearts. But to call them paradigms is grotesquely unfair, since they are in no way obtrusively
part of a pattern. They are marvellously fleshed out; and their
being opposites is beautifully and naturally allowed for.

Traddles is the simpler study, and initially perhaps he recalls
Tom Pinch in his selflessness and keen sense of duty. But whereas
Pinch was a gross and sentimental moral abstraction, Traddles is
totally convincing and attractive. Partly this is because in him
character is action:

> He was very honourable, Traddles was, and held it as a solemn
> duty in the boys to stand by one another. He suffered for this on
> several occasions; and particularly once, when Steerforth laughed
> in church, and the Beadle thought it was Traddles, and took him
> out . . . But he had his reward. Steerforth said there was nothing
> of the sneak in Traddles, and we all felt that to be the highest
> praise. (ch 7)

The narrator here places David's innocent condescension to
Traddles, as he later places a condescension that is less innocent,
when David compares Traddles' fiancée, who neither sings nor
paints, with his own, who does both:

> I promised Traddles that he should hear Dora sing, and see some
> of her flower-painting. He said he should like it very much, and
> we went home arm in arm in great good humour and delight.
> I encouraged him to talk about Sophy, on the way; which he did
> with a loving reliance on her that I very much admired. I com-
> pared her in my mind with Dora, with considerable inward
> satisfaction; but I candidly admitted to myself that she seemed to
> be an excellent kind of girl for Traddles, too. (ch 41)

It is lightly done, but we can hardly miss the improper condescension, and in general Traddles emerges as an attractive

character because his qualities are refracted through the narrator's wry recognition of his own past blindness.

But Steerforth is much more attractive to the young David. He is also one of the novel's finest achievements. He belongs to a line of characters which begins with Martin Chuzzlewit and runs through Gowan, Pip and Eugene Wrayburn; and I do not think it wildly speculative to feel that he represents a side of masculinity to which Dickens himself was dangerously attracted (just as Traddles – and Herbert Pocket for that matter – may be said to image the sort of normality that was so different from Dickens's near-demonic life and which it might be natural to think that he sometimes yearned for). When David and Steerforth visit the Peggotty's, David is full of praises for his friend:

> There was no noise, no effort, no consciousness, in anything he did; but in everything an indescribable lightness, a seeming impossibility of doing anything else, or doing anything better, which was so graceful, so natural, and agreeable, that it overcomes me, even now, in the remembrance. (ch 21)

So much of Dickens is present in Steerforth: his dandiacal streak, his wanting to be taken for a gentleman, his desire for an unfailing ease of social accomplishment. But in the study of Steerforth these things can be placed. And that is very important, for they are by no means always placed in the study of David. Indeed, I think that Dickens needs Steerforth if he is to objectify and cope with an element of snobbishness in the young David which is never tempered by the narrator and which undoubtedly has in it a good deal of Dickens himself. For example, David recalls that at Murdstone and Grinby's warehouse, he suffered 'in secret,' because his conduct and manners were different enough from the other boys 'to place a space between us'. (ch 11) Later, at Dr Strong's school the head boy shows David to his place and presents him to the masters 'in a gentlemanly way that would have put me at my ease, if anything could.' Yet

> my mind ran upon what [the boys] would think, if they knew of my familiar acquaintance with the King's Bench Prison? Was

there anything about me that would reveal my proceedings in
connexion with the Micawber family – all those pawnings, and
sellings, and suppers – in spite of myself? Suppose some of the boys
had seen me coming through Canterbury, wayworn and ragged,
and should find me out? What would they say, who made so light
of money, if they could know how I had scraped my halfpence
together, for the purchase of my daily saveloy and beer, or my
slices of pudding? How would it affect them, who were so innocent
of London life, and London streets, to discover how knowing I was
(and was ashamed to be) in some of the meanest phases of both?
(ch 16)

It is of course utterly natural that the boy should feel such acute
distress. But the narrator is clearly quite incapable of distancing
himself from his own earlier attitudes, for there is no interposed
mature voice to counter the young David's feelings of shame
and inferiority. And without doubt this is because the material
was so close to Dickens's own childhood experiences that he
simply could not attain to a balanced or mature view of them.
As a result we have an unplaced snobbishness which he can cope
with only as he projects it onto Steerforth. It is a flaw in the
novel, and one that arises out of Dickens's own deep split between his desire for a secure middle-class identity and his contempt for such a desire. Yet without the flaw we would not have
Steerforth.

Steerforth is an example of the ruinous effect of great expectations. They foster in him a shiftless dilettantism and an undisciplined life. But Steerforth's power and vitality are totally convincing. Inevitably he is the boy whom David admires; his grace,
insouciance, daring, easy air of superiority, are all marvellously
communicated through David's eyes. And in the great scene of
Mell's dismissal, Dickens manages quite remarkably not to abandon all sympathy for Steerforth. The scene is far too long to
quote in its entirety, but I want to note the snatch of dialogue
between Steerforth and Traddles. Traddles says that Mell has
been ill-used:

'Who has ill-used him, you girl?' said Steerforth.

'Why, you have,' returned Traddles.

'What have I done?' said Steerforth.

'What have you done?' retorted Traddles. 'Hurt his feelings, and lost him his situation.'

'His feelings?' repeated Steerforth disdainfully. 'His feelings will soon get the better of it, I'll be bound. His feelings are not like yours, Miss Traddles. As to his situation – which was a precious one, wasn't it? – do you suppose I am not going to write home, and take care that he gets some money? Polly?'

We thought this intention very noble in Steerforth, whose mother was a widow, and rich, and would do almost anything, it was said, that he asked her. (ch 7)

No need to underline how finely Dickens brings out Steerforth's sense of guilt here, nor how David is still bound to feel committed to him. And the commitment survives other possible shocks, simply because Steerforth's real attractions seem to outshine his selfishness and indifference to others. There is his reply to Rosa Dartle's question about how the Peggottys are different:

'They are not to be expected to be as sensitive as we are. Their delicacy is not to be shocked, or hurt easily. They are wonderfully virtuous, I dare say – some people contend for that, at least; and I am sure I don't want to contradict them – but they have not very fine natures, and they may be thankful that, like their coarse rough skins, they are not easily wounded.' (ch 20)

It is natural that David should think Steerforth 'in jest' here – as indeed he partly is, at least to the extent that he does not take seriously what he says. That of course is just the trouble and it amounts to a severe criticism of him. But against it has to be placed his actual conduct when confronted by the Peggotty family. He goes into Barkis's room

like light and air, brightening it and refreshing it as if he were healthy weather . . . and his consciousness of success in his determination to please inspired him with a new delicacy of perception, and made it, subtle as it was, more easy for him. (ch 21)

And yet against that has to be set the callousness that emerges in his talk with David as they come away from the Peggottys:

> 'A most engaging little Beauty!' said Steerforth, taking my arm. 'Well! It's a quaint place, and they are quaint company, and it's quite a new sensation to mix with them.'
> 'How fortunate we are, too,' I returned, 'to have arrived to witness their happiness in that intended marriage! I never saw people so happy ...'
> 'That's a rather chuckle-headed fellow for the girl; isn't he?' said Steerforth.
> He had been so hearty with him, and with them all, that I felt a shock in this unexpected and cold reply. But turning quickly upon him, and seeing a laugh in his eyes, I [was] much relieved. (ch 21)

Chapter 21 is particularly important in any discussion of Steerforth, because it is here that Dickens most subtly establishes the man's nature. And it is done through a beautiful combination of sympathy, severity, accuracy and imaginative intelligence. How finely, for example, the semi-colon before Steerforth's 'isn't he?' catches his hesitant wish to play down the brutal force of the remark about Ham and also to test out David's own allegiances. It might even be possible to say that at such a moment Steerforth is almost looking for the guidance that David so often expects from him.

But for all Dickens's restrained handling of Steerforth, he does judge him severely. Rosa Dartle bears the mark of his casual and intermittent brutality. She also testifies to Steerforth's hold over women. Indeed her passionate identification with Steerforth feels very nearly to echo another heroine in a very different kind of Victorian novel:

> 'Look here!' ... striking the scar again, with a relentless hand. 'When he grew into the better understanding of what he had done, he saw it, and repented of it! I could sing to him, and talk to him, and show the ardour that I felt in all he did, and attain with labour to such knowledge as most interested him; and I attracted him. When he was freshest and truest, he loved *me*. Yes, he did! Many

a time, when you were put off with a slight word he has taken Me to his heart!' (ch 56)

One almost waits for her to cry, 'I *am* Steerforth.' Yet perhaps that is not really fair. For in spite of the undoubted element of destroyed and destructive passion in Steerforth and Rosa's relationship, Dickens's interests are on the whole taking him in a different direction, as Rosa's subsequent words make clear.

'I descended – as I might have known I should, but that he fascinated me with his boyish courtship – into a doll, a trifle for the occupation of an idle hour, to be dropped, and taken up, and trifled with, as the inconstant humour took him.'

The word 'doll' inevitably recalls us to David's worry over the fact that Dora 'seemed by one consent to be regarded like a pretty toy or plaything'. (ch 41) And the echo makes us realize that as with the other elements in David's growth, so his education in marriage is part of a complex pattern that takes up Rosa and Steerforth, Emily and Steerforth, Annie and Dr Strong, Annie and Jack Maldon, Traddles and Sophy; and also Murdstone and Clara, and Betsey Trotwood and her imprudent marriage; and even the Beauty, Sophy's sister, and *her* imprudent marriage to a vagabond, 'there being a certain dash and glare about him that caught her', as Traddles explains.

The essence of David's education is contained in Annie's cry, ' "There can be no disparity in marriage like unsuitability of mind and purpose" '. (ch 45) Her remark voices an idea that had already been treated of in Victorian literature and which by 1850 had become almost familiar. For what Annie says and what she does provide one version of the debate about the role of woman in marriage and social life. Her words call to mind those uttered by the Prince in Tennyson's *Princess*:

> either sex alone
> Is half itself, and in true marriage lies
> Nor equal, nor unequal: each fulfils
> Defect in each, and always thought in thought,

> Purpose in purpose, will in will they grow,
> The single pure and perfect animal . . .[1]

Dickens had read his Tennyson, and although I do not suppose
that Annie's words are intended as a direct echo of the Prince's,
there is no doubt that they state a view of marriage which finds a
ready parallel in the theme of Tennyson's poem. But there is a
difference, since Tennyson cannot make up his mind how serious
he wants to be about women's claims for equality, whereas
Dickens is in deadly earnest in rejecting the notion that a woman
should be 'a trifle for the occupation of an idle hour'. On the
other hand, it has to be said that Dickens is far from convincing
in the image he provides of a marriage of true minds. Dr Strong
is a purely embarrassing cliché of the learned man, absent-
minded, naive in worldly matters, and the possessor of books that
are gratingly referred to as 'sacred favourites'. To top it off, he is
at work upon a Greek Dictionary which 'might be done in one
thousand six hundred and forty-nine years, counting from the
Doctor's last, or sixty-second, birthday'. Annie's devotion to
him, we are given to understand, stems from more than sexual
attraction. That indeed seems in very short supply. She speaks
of him as a 'friend', and calls herself his 'pupil, and almost your
child'; and she begs him not to think or speak ' "of any disparity
between us, for there is none, except in all my many imperfec-
tions. Every succeeding year I have known this better, as I have
esteemed you more and more." ' (ch 45) Esteem does not have
the force here that it has, say, in Crabbe:

> Love will expire. The gay, the happy dream,
> Will turn to scorn, indifference, or esteem.[2]

For Crabbe the word implies a sure and rational perception of
worth, for Annie it is tied to a principle of self-abasement. She is
not worthy of her husband's intellect, and in view of what we see
of that it is tempting to believe that George Eliot's great study of
Dorothea's mistaken esteem for Casaubon had a possible starting

[1] *The Princess: a Medley*, 1847, p. 173.
[2] Crabbe, *Tales*, 1812, p. 63.

point in her reading of *David Copperfield*. At all events it is a crushing answer to Dickens's sentimentality.

Because Dickens does not do very well with true marriage the temptation Jack Maldon presents to Annie's undisciplined heart emerges as too obvious and crude a contrast with Dr Strong's disinterested love. Annie says of herself and Jack that ' "We had been lovers once. If circumstances had not happened otherwise, I might have come to persuade myself that I really loved him, and might have married him, and been most wretched." ' (ch 45) Jack appeals to the least worthy side of Annie's character. His casual flirtation is part of his trivial view of life:

> 'Is there any news today?' inquired the Doctor.
> 'Nothing at all, sir,' replied Mr. Maldon. 'There's an account about the people being hungry and discontented down in the North, but they are always being hungry and discontented somewhere.' (ch 36)

I think it something of a pity that Dickens's study of Maldon's bored detachment and impudent familiarity should so often push towards parody. Compared, shall we say, with James's Captain Sholto, Maldon is insufficiently rendered. He is, however, interestingly similar to the Hobbes of Clough's *Bothie of Tober-Na-Vuolich*. Like the *Princess*, Clough's poem is about woman's role in marriage and social life, and Hobbes is an intellectual dandy, 'contemplative, corpulent, witty', who calls Philip, the poem's hero, a 'Pugin of women' who shall teach them

> How even churning and washing, the dairy, scullery duties,
> Wait but a touch to redeem and convert them to charms and attractions,
> Scrubbing requires for true grace but frank and artistical handling,
> And the removal of slops to be ornamentally treated.[1]

Hobbes is of course a much wittier and more intelligent man than Maldon, but he is crippled by exactly the same vulgarity of regard for women. And perhaps the worst feature of Steerforth's

[1] Clough, *Poems*, 1910, p. 99.

tragedy is that he too is guilty of this vulgarity. When he calls Emily 'A most engaging Little Beauty' the diminutive expresses his disregard for the girl's actual condition. To him she appears only as a doll, not a person for whom he must sacrifice the class identity that Eugene Wrayburn eventually surrenders and that Philip willingly sloughs off:

They are married and gone to New Zealand,
Five hundred pounds in pocket, with books, and two or three pictures,
Tool-box, plough and the rest, they rounded the sphere to New
    Zealand.
There he hewed, and dug; subdued the earth and his spirit;
There he built him a home; there Elspie bare him his children[1]

Steerforth's vulgarity is at bottom more terrible and crippling than Maldon's, because he is potentially a much finer person, but as an expression of class-snobbishness it radically affects all his relationships. And again we may draw a parallel with the *Bothie*, and Philip's reproof to his tutor Adam, who argues that inequality is a fact of creation and that the one thing necessary is for each man to remain true to his station. Philip says:

Alas! the noted phrase of the prayer-book,
Doing our duty in that state of life to which God has called us,
Seems to me always to mean, when the little rich boys say it,
Standing in velvet frock by mama's brocaded flounces,
Eying her gold-fastened book and the watch and chain at her bosom,
Seems to me always to mean, Eat, drink, and never mind others.[2]

It is Steerforth's condition exactly, and the one his mother has laboured to create.

I do not know whether Dickens had read the *Bothie*. Probably he had not. Yet Clough's splendid poem is concerned with much that is important in *David Copperfield* and in particular it throws interesting light on Dickens's exploration of the role of women. When Mrs Steerforth tells Peggotty that her son cannot marry Emily, we may hear in Dickens's handling of the speech the

[1] *Poems*, p. 162.
[2] Ibid., p. 102.

same sense of outrage as prompted elements in Clough's poem:

> 'It is impossible. He would disgrace himself. You cannot fail to know that she is far below him. . . . Such a marriage would irretrievably blight my son's career, and ruin his prospects. Nothing is more certain than that it never can take place and never will.' (ch 32)

It is an essential part of David's education that he should be exposed to the inequities of class-distinctions and that he should see in Steerforth someone who co-operates with them and is therefore corrupted by them. And I think it is better to take the Steerforth-Emily relationship as part of such a context rather than to see it as merely a crude melodrama about fallen woman, even if that is what the case of Martha reduces itself to (and we are bound to reflect that even her tragedy is part of the social rottenness which has created it). Steerforth and Emily belong to a pattern that is further elaborated in the Heeps and their humility, Littimer, who has 'a character to maintain', and of course the scabrously funny Waterbrook dinner-party:

> 'I confess I am of Mrs. Waterbrook's opinion,' said Mr. Waterbrook, with his wine-glass at his eye. 'Other things are all very well in their way, but give me Blood!'
> 'Oh! There is nothing,' observed Hamlet's aunt, 'so satisfactory to one! There is nothing that is so much one's *beau-ideal* of – of all that sort of thing, speaking generally. There are some low minds (not many, I am happy to believe, but there are *some*) that would prefer to do what *I* should call bow down before Idols! . . . Before service, intellect, and so on. But these are intangible points. Blood is not so. We see Blood in a nose, and we know it. We meet with it in a chin, and we say, "There it is! That's Blood!" It is an actual matter of fact. We point it out. It admits of no doubt.'
> The simpering fellow with the weak legs . . . stated the question more decisively yet, I thought.
> 'Oh, you know, deuce take it,' said this gentleman, looking round the board with an imbecile smile, 'we can't forgo Blood, you know. We must have Blood, you know. Some young fellows, you know, may be a little behind their station perhaps, in point of

education and behaviour, and may go a little wrong, you know,
and get themselves and other people into a variety of fixes – and
all that – but, deuce take it, it's delightful to reflect that they've got
Blood in 'em!' (ch 25)

When Dickens writes like this you realize just how sane and
bracing a force he can be against the social absurdities of Victorian
England which find out such otherwise intelligent people as
Ruskin and Disraeli, for example. And it is by the hard clear light
of his values that Steerforth is judged. Dickens may have his
faults but they do not include the faults of class-snobbishness.

Or do they? For we are bound to be uncomfortably aware of
David's quite unplaced feeling of innate superiority to the Peggottys (we have only to compare the handling of Pip and Joe's
relationship to realize how indulgent Dickens is towards David).
It is as though Dickens can focus on the absurdities of class only
when he is looking upwards. Even David's praise of Ham for
having the 'soul of a gentleman' seems less genuine commenda-
tion than a certificate of worthiness. I do not think we can
reasonably deny that David has about him residual elements of
the snobbishness that make Nicholas Nickleby so unpleasant a
hero; and that is why, I think, Dickens was in such great need of
Steerforth. For Steerforth can be objectively judged and David is
his chief judge. To be sure, this is a hedging of the issue, but we
have to accept that Dickens found it desperately difficult to condemn the values of his hero (which are in some ways his own)
unless they could be pinned on to somebody else. And Steerforth
provides the terrible warning of the damaging effect of values to
which David – and Dickens – are attracted. Steerforth's life is,
after all, one of tragic waste and the fact is emphasized not just
by his name but by his being finally shipwrecked on the Yarmouth beach where he had first met Emily:

And on that part of [the shore] where she and I had looked for
shells, two children – on that part of it where some lighter fragments of the old boat, blown down last night, had been scattered
by the wind – among the ruins of the home he had wronged – I

saw him lying with his head upon his arm, as I had often see him lie at school. (ch 55)

Too obvious, too overtly symbolic, having too apparent a moral design upon us? I can only report that I find the episode almost unbearably moving because it completes one of the novel's major rhythms, brings to its close a great slow tidal pull of narrative through time and the establishing of David's identity out of lost worlds and attained insights.

In clear contrast to Steerforth's ruined life we have to set the successful life of Traddles. And his success has little to do with becoming a judge, which is merely a sop to facile expectations. It has nothing to do with Traddles' essential achievement. For that comes from the discipline of commitment which gives him a sureness of identity, of possession of himself, which Steerforth can never match. Traddles's commitment is total: to work, to personal relationships, to marriage. His marriage to Sophy is a triumph of loyal devotion over all discouragements, and as such it fits the pattern of marriages that *David Copperfield* creates. In some ways, indeed, I think it is meant to be a sort of ideal. The trouble is that it does not seem very different from the point of view offered by the rumbustiously benighted King in the *Princess*:

> Man for the field and woman for the hearth:
> Man for the sword and for the needle she:
> Man with the head and woman with the heart:
> Man to command and woman to obey;
> All else confusion . . .
> Besides, the woman wed is not as we,
> But suffers change of frame. A lusty brace
> Of twins may weed her of her folly. Boy,
> The bearing and the training of a child
> Is woman's wisdom.[1]

When David visits Sophy and Traddles shortly after their marriage, he finds

a loving, cheerful, fireside quality in Sophy's bright looks . . .

[1] *The Princess*, p. 130.

which assured me that my friend had chosen well. . . . Mrs. Traddles, with perfect pleasure and composure beaming from her household eyes, having made the tea, then quietly made the toast as she sat in a corner by the fire. (ch 59)

Sophy for the hearth and with the heart (oh, that quiet making of toast. How would you make toast noisily?). Still, it has to be said that there is nothing in what we see of the couple to suggest that Traddles commands and Sophy obeys. If anything, their marriage is characterized by a mutual 'self-forgetfulness' and that makes it a good deal more enlightened than anything Tennyson's 'hard old king' recommends, or than is imaged in Murdstone's idea that marriage provides the ideal context for a display of firmness. At best, then, the Traddles marriage provides an image of what I think Dickens saw as typifying a normality from which he himself was bound to be excluded, not just because Kate lacked Sophy's sort of practical gifts, but because he himself was so different from the person he shows Traddles to be.

There is, of course, something of Dickens's own marriage in David and Dora's. And David's marriage is clearly one without a basis for success because Dora is in no position to help her husband.

> If she be small, slight-natured, miserable,
> How shall men grow?[1]

The rhetorical question of the *Princess* is given its answer in *David Copperfield* through what Betsey says of David's child-wife.

'You have chosen a very pretty and affectionate creature. It will be your duty, and it will be your pleasure too – of course I know that; I am not delivering a lecture – to estimate her (as you chose her) by the qualities she has, and not by the qualities she may not have. The latter you must develop in her, if you can. And if you cannot, child,' here my Aunt rubbed her nose, 'you must just accustom yourself to do without 'em'. (ch 44)

David tries to accustom himself. He notes that it remained 'for me to adapt myself to Dora; to share with her what I could, and

[1] *The Princess*, p. 171.

be happy; to bear on my own shoulders what I must, and be happy still'. (ch 48) It would be foolish to pretend that the exploration of David and Dora's failing marriage has anything like the scope and intensity of the study of Lydgate and Rosamund's, but it is all the same finely attentive to the disasters that spring from 'the first mistaken impulse of an undisciplined heart', and few things in the novel are finer than the chapters dealing with David's early love for Dora, which have about them an easy ebullience that is unique to Dickens. Equally fine is the growing sense of separateness between the two:

> I had a great deal of work to do, and had many anxieties, but [I kept] them to myself. I am far from sure, now, that it was right to do this, but I did it for my child-wife's sake . . . The old unhappy loss or want of something had, I am conscious, some place in my heart; but not to the embitterment of my life. When I walked alone in the fine weather, and thought of the summer days when all the air had been filled with my boyish enchantment, I did miss something of the realisation of my dreams; but I thought it was a softened glory of the Past, which nothing could have thrown upon the present time. I did feel, sometimes, for a little while, that I could have wished my wife had been my counsellor; had had more character and purpose, to sustain me and improve me by; had been endowed with power to fill up the void which somewhere seemed to be about me; but I felt as if this were an unearthly consummation of my happiness, that never had been meant to be, and never could have been. (ch 44)

This passage is of course directly relevant to Dickens's own marriage. And may be that accounts for how oddly the apparently stoical moral jars against the tone of acute melancholia which the passage releases. I hear Tennyson and Wordsworth just beneath the surface of Dickens's prose: the passage has so much to do with 'thinking of the days that are no more' and feeling regret for something that is gone, the glory and the dream. And surely David's old unhappy loss or want of something has a direct connection with the famous lyric of the *Princess* that speaks of the tears that are

deep as love,
Deep as first love, and wild with all regret.[1]

But if Wordsworth and Tennyson are available to Dickens in his rendering of David's condition, I do not think that their shadowy presence means that the author is betraying himself, no matter how close the mood may be to his own. For David's brooding becomes a tactful record of a psychological state, whereby what is in part the inevitable sadness that accompanies an awareness of time passing is blended with great subtlety into a more specific regret for a decision which is not yet truly recognized as imprudent. The passage meticulously catches a moment in the growth of David's disciplined heart, his gradual coming to accept both the loss of the paradise world of childhood and young love, and the need to take personal responsibility for his own life and the lives of others with whom he is involved.

But what then of Dora? How justifiable is it that she should die as soon as David has learnt fully to recognize his mistake? In one fine and considerate scene, Dickens shows us Dora's case in a manner that shames David's and our easy judgement of her:

'Oh, what a weary boy!' said Dora, one night, when I met her eyes as I was shutting up my desk.

'What a weary girl!' said I. 'That's more to the purpose. You must go to bed another time, my love. It's far too late for you.'

'No, don't send me to bed!' pleaded Dora, coming to my side. 'Pray, don't do that!'

'Dora!'

To my amazement she was sobbing on my neck.

'Not well, my dear! not happy!'

'Yes! quite well, and very happy!' said Dora. 'But say you'll let me stop, and see you write.' (ch 44)

It is typical of *David Copperfield*'s greatness that Dickens should allow for this moment of insight into Dora's sense of isolation, her acute feeling of being separated from her husband. A moment such as this makes it impossible for us to call her 'small, slight-

[1] *The Princess*, p. 77.

natured, miserable' without being uncomfortably aware that
although the epithets fit they do not alter the fact that she has
undeniable claims on David which in the end he cannot meet.
And here I think we reach a point where autobiography has to
be admitted. The pathos of Dora's loneliness is manifestly connected with Dickens's exacerbated feeling of guilt about his
own marriage and his wish that it could be undone as David's so
conveniently is. For of course Dora is too easily disposed of. And
Dickens knew this himself. That is why her death is made part of
a quite amazing *tour de force*. Surrounding it is a multiple narrative, one of whose main achievements is to divert our attention
away from Dora herself. In the space of fifty pages we are given
the unmasking of Heep, the unravelling of Peggotty's affairs,
Ham's death, the Micawbers' decision to go to Australia, Dora's
death and Steerforth's death. Dickens marvellously controls the
pace of the narrative here so that we are confronted by a thick
flurry of affairs of which Steerforth's death emerges as most
important, since it comes as the culmination of events, is the most
extensively treated, most tightly written, becomes the fitting
token of David's final recognition and abandonment of his undisciplined heart, and therefore usurps the significance of Dora's
death.

But Steerforth and Dora's deaths are linked together. They
form part of the novel's total scheme, its study of lives that do
not come to what was planned. David mourns

> for my child-wife, taken from her blooming world, so young. I
> mourned for him who might have won the love and admiration of
> thousands, as he had won mine long ago. I mourned for the broken
> heart that had found rest in the stormy sea; and for the wandering
> remnants of the simple home, where I had heard the night-wind
> blowing, when I was a child. (ch 58)

In spite of the affectations of that prose and its slide towards
blank verse, I think we reach here towards a note that sounds far
more clearly and finely in *Little Dorrit* and *Great Expectations*. It
is so like Forster's remark that in Schumann one hears 'the sadness

of the incomplete – the sadness that is often Life'. Dickens's melancholic perception of the broken rhythms of life is, to be sure, rather too literary at this point in *David Copperfield*; for with Dora's death David can find a way out of the sombre reflections that go with an awareness of his own abandoned youth. The melancholy becomes something of an indulgence. But not entirely. Nothing can undo the sadness of Steerforth's end nor affect the legitimacy of regret for lost innocence.

There can however be the pretence of fresh beginnings. And in *David Copperfield* that means Agnes. Agnes is the prize for the disciplined heart, the woman for whom Dora must die. She is 'hopeful, earnest, and cheerful', and she says that ' "I hope that real love and truth are stronger in the end than any evil or misfortune in the world" '. (ch 35) We are meant to praise her for speaking those words, whether they are true or not. She is herself an example of courage and resilience, able to ride out the evil of Heep and the misfortune of her father's disease, and able too to make men grow by 'ever pointing upward . . . ever leading [them] to something better; ever directing [them] to higher things!' (ch 60) She is also a bit of a bore, even if not actually unbearable. For unlike most of the characters in *David Copperfield* Agnes fits too snugly into a symbolic or exemplary role, of duty and aspiration; and she is too patently bred out of Dickens's desire to show that woman is more than 'for the hearth'. It hardly needs saying that she is also a product of Dickens's own search for that marriage of 'interest, sympathy, confidence, sentiment, tender union', which, he told Miss Coutts, he did not share with his wife.[1]

It may even be that for Dickens himself Agnes represents an impossible ideal. For although we are asked to see in her the ability to guide David 'ever upward', it is difficult to see in what very real sense this is to be accomplished. David is a writer and the solitary nature of his work is not altered by a marriage of true minds. Even before Dora's death he has, he says, been 'devoting myself to [writing] with my strongest earnestness, and

[1] *Johnson*, Vol. II, p. 905.

bestow[ing] upon it every energy of my soul'. (ch 61) The words are true of Dickens, and they remind us that his creativity was not impaired by his own domestic misery. On the contrary, his greatest work was produced at a time when his misery had become greatest. Which is not to equate suffering and creativity, far less to offer Dickens the lesson of the master. It is merely to say that the invention of Agnes is a concession to ideals of aspiration which at his deepest and truest Dickens did not really need.

Yet Agnes has a more relevant part to play. For like Traddles she is distinguished not only by cheerfulness but by 'earnestness'. And earnestness does not mean here what is so frequently comes to mean in high Victorian England. Unlike Ruskin and Carlyle, for example, Dickens uses the word to define a fierceness of commitment to work and personal relationships. And in view of the fact that Dickens comes unswervingly to praise this commitment it is a matter of amazement to me that Orwell should have thought he had 'no ideal of *work*' (Orwell's italics). Orwell does, it is true, make a doubtful exception of *David Copperfield*, but even here he feels that it is only David himself who expresses any degree of commitment. For the rest, there is 'nothing [Dickens] admires except common decency . . . Really there is no objective except to marry the heroine, settle down, live solvently and be kind'. And Orwell adds that most of Dickens's books end in a sort of 'radiant idleness'.[1] He could hardly be more wrong (and that subsequent critics have hardly ever taken him up on this point does not make him less so). Dickens's highest praise is always extended to those who have the courage to endure, to remain true to commitment, to personal relationships and work. Traddles's earnest and selfless devotion to his wife and her sisters is exactly matched by his devotion to his studies, Peggotty is loved as a man of unremitting industry, when Miss Mowcher is reintroduced to make amends for the earlier slight David notes that her face is 'so earnest' that there can be no question of her worth; and even Mrs Gummidge becomes a figure of approbation when she vows ' "I can dig, Dan'l. I can work. I can live

[1] *A Collection of Essays*, pp. 93–4.

hard." ' (ch 51) Of course, it could be objected against this that for the most part the praise of work is not accompanied by any deep insight into what it actually is or implies. Certainly there is nothing in *David Copperfield* to match the studies of, for example, Pancks or Jaggers. But then why should there be? The growth of the disciplined heart has to do with commitment but not necessarily with the potential agonies of work as Dickens later investigates them. Besides, in the example of David himself we come face to face with a very deep understanding of how industry identifies the quality of work.

David speaks of a

> patient and continuous energy which then began to be matured within me, and which I know to be the strong part of my character, if it have any strength at all.

And in what is plain testimony to his recognition of the necessary discipline of work he remarks that 'whatever I have devoted myself to, I have devoted myself to completely . . . in great aims and in small, I have always been thoroughly in earnest'. (ch 42) It would be vulgar to suppose that David's words offer us anything like a Smilesian recipe for success in life. They cut much deeper than that, for the root of the matter is Dickens's profound understanding of how a mature identity comes to be created; and we have only to place David's earnestness against the great expectations of Steerforth, Maldon and Micawber to recognize how earnestness becomes a valid test of growth.

It is when we consider how constantly we are invited to place characters against each other in this novel that we see how marvellously the narratives of *David Copperfield* serve its meaning rather than revealing themselves as the randomly multiplying tangles that Orwell and others have complained of. The complaint is heard less often nowadays, yet I do not know that there has been the proper praise for the wonderful imaginative intelligence that could create so natural and inevitable a study as *David Copperfield*, while yet seeing to it that everything is relevant.

It might be objected that I overstate the case. What of the

novel's many coincidences? In what sense can they be regarded as natural and inevitable? Sooner or later, everybody is re-introduced, and the novel ends by telling us what happened to the ones who are still alive. I think the ending needs neither praise nor defence. It is simply how Dickens chose to complete his novels, partly out of deference to his readers' concern with the characters he had created and partly out of his own concern for them. But the coincidental reappearance of characters may seem a rather more ticklish problem. I cannot myself, however, really feel that it is one. For the characters who return are used to measure David's growth; they establish the various ways by which he and we come to accept the facts of change, of the shift-ing perspectives of childhood, youth and maturity, of loss and renewal and the great natural rhythms which the novel estab-lishes.

This brings us back to a point I made at the beginning of this chapter. I said that David is not treated as a special case; and I implied that the air of inevitability which the novel's rhythms create provides a way of seeing him as everyman. It is something of an overstatement. For there is also the 'ragged way-worn boy, forsaken and neglected' who mostly grows beyond self-pity to gratitude and love for the people who aid his growth, and sad forbearance towards those whose growth is warped or destroyed. Yet that this should be so is proof of the novel's central strength, its humaneness. Not perhaps entirely about everyman, but certainly for him.

✤ 6 · BLEAK HOUSE

As the writing of *David Copperfield* neared completion, Dickens began to plan another project, his weekly magazine, *Household Words*. He knew exactly what he wanted of it. As Johnson points out, the magazine was to entertain but also function as 'the instrument of serious social purpose'. And in his Preliminary Word to the first number, Dickens announced that 'Not harsh efficiency, not the clanking of an economic machine, were the goal of society, but the loving union of multitudes of human lives in generous feeling and noble purpose.'[1] Dickens's aim was to confront his enormous audience with those ills of contemporary society which he saw all about him and which ate into his mind. He did not intend to widen his popularity by offering his readers an escape from their world; on the contrary, he was prepared to risk his appeal in the interest of hammering away at their consciences and forcing them to look at the world in which they lived. *Household Words*, he said

consistently opposes racial, national, religious, and class prejudices. It crusades against illiteracy, and in favour of government aid for public education and free elementary and industrial schools for the poor. It crusades for proper sewage disposal, cheap and unlimited water supply, and the regulation of industries vital to health. It demands the replacement of slums by decent housing for the poor, pleads for the establishment of playgrounds for children, and advocates systematic municipal planning. . . . It insists that industrialists must not be allowed to mutilate and kill their labourers in order to save the cost of preventing accidents. It scandalously affirms that working men have the right to organize into unions,

[1] *Johnson*, Vol. II, p. 703.

and calls upon the working class to use its power to turn 'the Indifferents and Incapables' out of Downing Street and Westminster and force the government to remedy the ills from which poor men suffer.[1]

It is obvious from such a declaration of intent that *Household Words* is taking on itself the task of becoming the conscience of Victorian England, and since all its articles were anonymous but Dickens was announced as editor, it is above all he who becomes the voice of that conscience.

Moral vanity? Hardly. It is more an honourable determination that the artist shall use his abilities to confront the age as best he can. But how can he do that *qua* artist? May it not be that the abilities of the polemicist and of the artist are very different and that by confusing roles Dickens sinks into a sort of propagandizing which, if it displays a good heart, is bound to hurt the integrity of his fiction? Such a charge is not uncommon, yet it seems to me quite without foundation. For the plain fact is that both as editor of *Household Words* and as novelist, Dickens is *the* spokesman for the conscience of his age. From *Bleak House* onwards, the great novels have about them a fierce integrity of purpose which makes them central statements and judgements of Victorian England. They are written out of Dickens's deep and unswerving sense of responsibility, both to his art and to his audience. If my books are of no worth, David Copperfield says, 'I shall have written to poor purpose', and by worth he does not mean entertainment value. For Dickens's purpose is quite unashamedly to force his readers into an unprotected awareness of the age in which they live, to present them with issues which, as they read, will more and more impinge upon their consciousnesses. Fiction is not to be an escape or a refuge.

Still, such an ambition is not dissimilar from that which prompts the sort of naïve didacticism often found in Victorian fiction. But of course Dickens does not use the novel as a means to put across some 'message' or as a platform for preaching. There is a world of difference between *Bleak House* and *Hard*

[1] *Johnson*, Vol. II, p. 714.

Cash or *Jessie Phillips*, for example. The point is not that Dickens's novel dogmatizes, but that it shocks. And Dickens would, I think, have approved of Kafka's famous remark to Oskar Pollak that

> the books we need are the kind that act upon us like a misfortune, that make us suffer like the death of someone we love more than ourselves, that make us feel as though we were on the verge of suicide, or lost in a forest remote from all human habitation – a book should serve as the axe for the frozen sea within us.

In the end the words are perhaps too strident for Dickens, but their basic meaning is surely relevant to *Bleak House*, for whatever else we may think about that novel, it seems to me by far the most upsetting of all his works. Such a statement may lead me into difficult territory. I realize that the affective fallacy could be wheeled up to dispossess me of the critical relevance that I find in *Bleak House*'s power to disturb. Still, I see no way round accepting that Dickens wanted to upset his readers and that he succeeded. And I am sufficiently convinced of this to disbelieve those readers who claim not to be radically upset by such moments as Jo's death, the discovery of Charley and her brothers and sisters, the slum graveyard, Skimpole's ridding himself of Jo, and countless other incidents. Again and again, *Bleak House* destroys our comfortable notion of art as a refuge, an enclosed world answering to its own laws and prescriptions; it turns outward to the real world and in so doing banishes for ever the idyllic world of the *Pickwick Papers*.

The art that consoles a rotten society has no worthy purpose. Hence Dickens's hatred of Skimpole. Sir Leicester Dedlock approves of Skimpole as an artist, and he is even more approving when Skimpole calls himself 'a perfectly idle man. A mere amateur'. (ch 43) And Dickens has a wonderfully witty contempt for Sir Leicester 'condescendingly perusing the backs of his books, or honouring the fine arts with a glance of approbation'. (ch 29) In a great letter to Forster, written shortly after he had finished *Bleak House*, Dickens said that 'mere forms and conventionalities usurp, in English art, as in English government and social relations, the place of living force and truth.' And telling Forster of paintings by Englishmen that he had recently seen in Paris, he added, 'There is a horrid respectability about most of the best of them – a little, finite, systematic routine in them, strangely expressive of the state of England itself.'[1] It is not a criticism that can be applied to *Bleak House*.

And yet though Dickens is now quite certain what the purpose of art must be, he is far from dreaming that it is capable of breaking open the frozen seas within all men. He knows only too well that the artist must accept the misappropriation of his purpose. In a brilliant and vicious scene, Skimpole recommends turning Jo out, and then sings a ballad about a peasant boy '"Thrown on the wide world, doom'd to wander and roam,/ Bereft of his parents, bereft of a home', a song 'that always made him cry, he told us'. (ch 31) There is a vibrancy and power about Dickens's hatred of Skimpole that seems to me to mark something new in the novels, an absolute determination to reject any notion that art is sufficient unto itself. The point may be difficult to grasp in the abstract, but *Bleak House* everywhere affirms it. The novel's narrator is determined that his audience shall not rest in the consolations of art:

> 'Jo, my poor fellow!'
> 'I hear you, sir, in the dark, but I'm a-gropin – a-gropin – let me catch hold of your hand.'
> 'Jo, can you hear what I say?'
> 'I'll say any think as you say, sir, fur I knows it's good.'
> 'OUR FATHER'
> 'Our Father! – yes, that's wery good, sir.'
> 'WHICH ART IN HEAVEN.'
> 'Art in Heaven – is the light a-comin, sir?'
> 'It is close at hand. HALLOWED BE THY NAME!'
> 'Hallowed be – thy –'
> The light is come upon the dark benighted way. Dead!
> Dead, your majesty. Dead, my lords and gentlemen. Dead, Right Reverends and Wrong Reverends of every order. Dead,

[1] Forster, p. 478.

men and women, born with Heavenly compassion in your hearts. And dying thus around us every day. (ch 47)

Until the last paragraph that death-scene might be described as one of mere pathos; and we could take the use of the Lord's prayer as Dickens's way of stilling any unease about Jo's be-nighted way – at the end, he was led by a kindly light. But in turning on his audience, Dickens deliberately and savagely disrupts this response. For what in effect the last sentences say is, this is a real person who is really dead and I refuse to let any of you evade the fact. When Dickens says 'Your Majesty', he actually *is* addressing Queen Victoria, and when he spins on the 'men and women' he is confronting his safe, respectable audience with a sudden blast of anger over a fact that proves the failure of a society towards its mutual responsibilities. It works because the audience does after all know exactly what Dickens is talking about. 'In *Bleak House*, I have purposely dwelt upon the romantic side of familiar things,' he said in his prefatory note, and in the case of Jo – and so much else in the novel – the romantic and the familiar blend together to defeat disjunctions. We are told in the Preface that Gridley's suit 'is in no essential altered from one of actual occurrence, made public by a disinterested person who was professionally acquainted with the whole of the monstrous wrong from beginning to end'. And much of *Bleak House* was, we know, built up from newspaper reports. But what we know by patient research, Dickens's audience knew at first hand. They knew, for example, that Jo was not just a fictional character but the boy George Ruby, whose appearance at the Guildhall in 1850 to give evidence in a case of assault was reported in detail in the *Household Narrative*.[1] Besides, when Jo finds the first two words of the Lord's prayer 'very good', Dickens's readers would almost certainly recall how, in a Blue-Book report for 1842, Richard Horne had recorded the tale of apprentices in Stafford-shire who went to sleep at night comforting themselves by mouthing 'Our Father', which they thought was an entire

[1] See H. House, *The Dickens World*, 1942, pp. 32–3.

prayer and could be regarded as a sort of magic incantation against the evils of their next day's work.

In forcing his readers to recognize that the fictional world of *Bleak House* turns out to be about the real one, Dickens forces them to the acknowledgement of a world they wish to deny. 'Our novelists,' Clough said, by way of criticizing Victorian poets, 'give us a real house to live in.' And in large part *Bleak House* is upsetting precisely because of its use of actualities. For the novel is about England as a society which is failing of mutuality, and it brings out the absence of 'the loving union of multitudes of human lives in generous feeling and noble purpose.' Or, to give it the word Carlyle chose, it is about the collapse of brotherhood.

> One of Dr. Alison's Scotch facts struck us very much. A poor Irish widow, her husband having died in one of the Lanes of Edinburgh, went forth with her children, bare of all resource, to solicit help from the Charitable Establishments of that City. At this Charitable Establishment and then at that she was refused; referred from one to another, helped by none; – till she had exhausted them all; till her strength and heart failed her; she sank down in a typhus-fever; died, and infected her Lane with fever, so that 'seventeen other persons' died of fever there in consequence. The Humane Physician asks there-upon, as with a heart too full for speaking. Would it not have been *economy* to help this poor Widow? She took typhus-fever and killed seventeen of you! – Very curious. The forlorn Irish Widow applies to her fellow creatures, as if saying, 'Behold I am sinking, bare of help: ye must help me! I am your sister, bone of your bone; one God made us: ye must help me!' They answer, 'No, impossible; thou art no sister of ours.' But she proves her sisterhood; her typhus-fever kills *them*: they actually were her brothers, though denying it! Had human creature ever to go lower for proof?[1]

I imagine there is no need to emphasize how nearly this anticipates the treatment of Tom-all-Alone's and Jo's illness. And as Dickens's audience is repeatedly offered what look to be fictions that turn out to be facts, so the characters in the novel themselves mime their readers' efforts to escape reality only to find

[1] *Past and Present*, Centenary Edn., p. 143.

it thrust at them. For many of the characters practise escape-routes that lead them inexorably back to face what they wish to escape from; the novel is unremitting in its methods of denying the denials of brotherhood.

Carlyle's statements about brotherhood are meant to be definitive of mid-Victorian England. *Bleak House* is no less definitive. Its scale is dizzying. For it is about England, no less, and it composes a visionary judgement about a whole society seen – or so it feels – in all its randomness, a mighty maze utterly without a plan. One of the most brilliant tricks of a novel which is surely the most brilliant in the language is to set the omniscient narrative in the continuous present, so that we have a sense of events being recorded as they happen rather than as they have been assimilated and understood (nobody could take seriously Dickens's casual pretence that the novel is set in the late 1830s). And the fact that in the end the multiple narratives form a pattern, gives a final authority to the concept of brotherhood; we are brought to accept the inevitability of what had appeared to be only contingent. Esther's narrative complements this trick, since it has to do with what seem to be entirely different matters and yet all the while is moving closer to the other narra-tive, until there is a total fusion of the two in the girl's reunion with the mother who has denied her. To put it rather differently, the novel realizes a moral pattern whilst miming the collapse of a social framework. And in this sense it bears an uncanny resem-blance to Blake's *London*. I have quoted the poem before, but it is worth having before us once again, especially the lines where Blake records:

> How the Chimney-sweeper's cry
> Every black'ning Church appalls;
> And the hapless Soldier's sigh
> Runs in blood down Palace walls.

> But most thro' midnight streets I hear
> How the youthful Harlot's curse
> Blasts the new born Infant's tear,
> And blights with plagues the Marriage hearse.

The collapse of a communal society into class-interests destroys the very class which means to protect itself, as well as all those whose interests it chooses to ignore. Blake and Dickens share the profound insight into what was happening to the England they lived in, and for the rest of this chapter I shall try to argue out what I take Dickens's insight to have been and how he realizes it in his novel. But before I do that I think it necessary to admit that I am acutely aware that *Bleak House* is too great and rich a novel for my account of it to be more than partial. The best I can hope to do is to draw attention to what I see as being important in shaping its greatness.

We can begin conveniently enough with a remark of Sir Leicester Dedlock's. '"The floodgates of society are burst open, and the waters have – a – obliterated the landmarks of the framework of the cohesion by which things are held together."' (ch 40) Sir Leicester is haunted by his apocalyptic imagination, and although his fears are comically treated, the novel as a whole takes seriously the collapse which he envisages. Those famous opening paragraphs are surely not just a way of establishing the fog of Chancery. They emblematize England itself as existing in the sort of limbo world reminiscent of Dante's vision of a place 'pierc'd by no star' (I quote Cary's version, which Dickens would have read):

> Fog everywhere. Fog up the river, where it flows among the green aits and meadows; fog down the river, where it rolls defiled among the tiers of shipping, and the waterside pollutions of a great (and dirty) city. Fog on the Essex marshes, fog on the Kentish heights . . . Chance people on the bridges peeping over the parapets into a nether sky of fog, with fog all around them, as if they were up in a balloon, and hanging in the misty clouds.

A featureless world in which nothing has significance or point. And so with the rain of Chesney Wold:

> The waters are out in Lincolnshire. An arch of the bridge in the park has been sapped and sopped away. The adjacent low-lying ground, for half a mile in breadth, is a stagnant river, with melancholy trees for islands in it, and a surface punctured all over, all day

long, with falling rain. My Lady Dedlock's 'place' has been extremely dreary. (ch 2)

'Sapped and sopped.' How those words catch the physical
sensations they describe. The prose is so finely judged here that
the temptation is simply to go on quoting, and indeed there is
every reason to do so, for we begin to sense some reason for the
apocalyptic rain:

> The weather, for many a day and night, has been so wet that the
> trees seem wet through, and the soft loppings and prunings of the
> woodman's axe can make no crash or crackle as they fall. The deer,
> looking soaked, leave quagmires, where they pass. The shot of a
> rifle loses its sharpness in the moist air, and its smoke moves in a
> tardy little cloud towards the green rise, coppice-topped, that
> makes a background for the falling rain. The view from my Lady's
> own windows is alternately a lead-coloured view and a view in
> Indian ink. The vases on the terrace in the foreground catch the
> rain all day; and the heavy drops fall drip, drip, drip, upon the
> broad flagged pavement, called, from old time, the Ghost's Walk,
> all night. On Sundays, the little church in the park is mouldy; and
> the oaken pulpit breaks out into a cold sweat; and there is a general
> smell and taste as of the ancient Dedlocks in their graves. My Lady
> Dedlock (who is childless), looking out in the early twilight from
> her boudoir at a keeper's lodge, and seeing the light of a fire upon
> the latticed panes, and smoke rising from the chimney, and a child,
> chased by a woman, running out into the rain to meet the shining
> figure of a wrapped-up man coming through the gate, has been
> put quite out of temper. My Lady Dedlock says that she has been
> 'bored to death' (ch 2)

There is no mistaking the wonderful rightness of this prose, its
ability to render the scene in terms of local detail (those 'soft
loppings' sound exactly right) and in terms of the drifting weary
cadences that have scarcely sufficient energy to complete themselves and marvellously catch and mock a note of civilized
langour and, more profoundly, establish a terrible ennui. 'And
the heavy drops fall drip, drip, drip, upon the broad flagged pavement, called, from old time, the Ghost's Walk, all night.' The

pauses become heavier, the effort of starting again greater, and the last phrase only just makes it. Only once is this note of deep lassitude disturbed, when the diction and syntax become suddenly energized by the intrusive little scene of the child, woman, and man, which, it is indirectly suggested, has put Lady Dedlock 'quite out of temper'. To be blunt, Lady Dedlock's childlessness is, she knows, a denial of the life that briefly flares up in the fire, the shining figure and the running child. The order with which she chooses to identify herself is dying of an inner pointlessness; there is no function for it to fulfil since it has no sense of what the true 'framework' of society is. Whatever life there is in England, the Dedlocks do not participate in it. At best they are spectators.

Dickens's judgement is an historical one and he has no interest in Sir Leicester except in so far as the Baronet symbolizes an order that is very nearly past. 'His family is as old as the hills, and infinitely more respectable. He has a general opinion that the world might get on without hills, but would be done up without Dedlocks.' Nor does this mean that the class Sir Leicester represents is in fact dying out. Not fact but function, is Dickens's concern; the inner life not the outer show. Sir Leicester has no true function left to fulfil:

> He is a gentleman of strict conscience, disdainful of all littleness and meanness, and ready, on the shortest notice, to die any death you may please to mention rather than give occasion for the least impeachment of his integrity. He is an honourable, obstinate, truthful, high-spirited, intensely prejudiced, perfectly unreasonable man. (ch 2)

Throughout the novel, Sir Leicester is treated with this courteous ruthlessness; and the narrator's poised and comprehensive knowledge give him an authority we do not feel ourselves in a position to challenge. By being even more civilized than Sir Leicester, he defeats him at his own game.

Sir Leicester's game is, of course, assuming that he embodies the natural right of government. I do not think we need at this point enter into a discussion of the view that government is the natural right of individuals who can be identified through class and family; it is enough to note how deeply such a view was rooted in Victorian England, and that, as I hinted in the previous chapter, appeals to the unquestionable authority of 'Blood' were made by such otherwise very different people as Ruskin and Disraeli. Once we grasp this fact we shall see that Dickens's satire against Sir Leicester's concern for the country is no trivial matter; it confronts some of the most deeply held convictions of the age. And as a whole the novel demonstrates that England's 'governors' have barely the glimmering of an idea about what England actually is. Dickens's pointing to this is more than his making a Disraelian formulation of two nations; for *Bleak House* demonstrates that there are multitudes of people living in profound ignorance of each other, so that the dream of government can be no more than a solipsistic game:

> England has been in a dreadful state for some weeks. Lord Coodle would go out, and Sir Thomas Doodle wouldn't come in, and there being nobody in Great Britain (to speak of) except Coodle and Doodle, there has been no government. (ch 40)

Funny though the passage undoubtedly is, it has an intensity to it that does not just spring from Dickens's contemptuous recognition of one politician's being just like another, but more savagely from his awareness of the sheer pointlessness of a system of government that makes no contact with the 'old ship' it is supposed to be steering. That parenthetic 'to speak of' means that for the governors most people are unimportant if not downright unspeakable. And so much else in the novel testifies to this. When Mrs Pardiggle tries to take the brickmakers and their families into religious custody, Esther reflects that 'between us and these people was an iron barrier, which could not be removed by our new friend'. (ch 8) The barrier is a perfectly fair way of indicating the atomistic society which Dickens concerns himself with. That is why the omniscient narrator is so necessary, for he is the only person who can surmount the barriers; it is he who provides what feels to be the comprehensive vision of

England and who can speak about and for all the characters in the novel. And it is the narrator who can show something of how the barriers came to be fixed into place.

Partly, of course, they are created through the solipsistic absurdities of government, partly through wilful ignorance. But the terrible schismatic nature of society has also been fostered by what ought to be socially responsible forces which in fact reveal themselves as either inadequate or as agents of class-concerns. Whatever the reason, they contribute to the creation of a radically unjust society. And here we come upon the importance of Chancery in *Bleak House*. As a prestigious institution which destroys people's lives, Chancery is an apt instance of the mindless futility of law in all its aspects. For law has become a letter; justice means a blind adherence to formulae. Hence the great scene of Jo's being moved on:

> 'This boy,' says the constable, 'although he's repeatedly told to, won't move on –'
>
> 'I'm always a-moving on, sir,' cries the boy, wiping away his grimy tears with his arm. 'I've always been a-moving and a-moving on, ever since I was born. Where can I possibly move to, sir, more nor I do move!'
>
> 'He won't move on,' says the constable, calmly, with a slight professional hitch of his neck, involving its better settlement in his stiff stock, 'although he has been repeatedly cautioned, and therefore I am obliged to take him into custody. He's as obstinate a young gonoph as I know. He WON'T move on.'
>
> 'Oh my eye! Where can I move to!' cries the boy, clutching quite desperately at his hair, and beating his bare feet upon the floor of Mr. Snagsby's passage.
>
> 'Don't you come none of that, or I shall make blessed short work of you!' says the constable, giving him a passionless shake. 'My instructions are, that you are to move on. I have told you so five hundred time.'
>
> 'But where?' cries the boy.
>
> 'Well! Really, constable, you know,' says Mr. Snagsby wistfully, and coughing behind his hand his cough of great perplexity and doubt; 'really that does seem a question. Where, you know?'

'My instructions don't go to that,' replies the constable. 'My instructions are that this boy is to move on.' (ch 19)

The scene offers us a glimpse of a world about which the Doodles, Coodles and Dedlocks are in as profound ignorance as Jo is of them. But that is not its main purpose nor what makes for its real strength. Its greatness and centrality lie in how much it typifies about the society that Dickens explores in *Bleak House*. Casual though it may seem, it has the sort of relevance and just-ness that I have suggested Dickens repeatedly manages to find for all his best work. It is intensely dramatic in its rendering of the novel's central issues. It also has about it something of the repor-ter's desire to make his readers acknowledge the unfamiliar; but beyond that it characterizes law as a dreadful madness. Coming across this scene we remember the Dodger's contemptuous remark that 'This ain't the shop for justice'. But the matter is more profound now; the policeman's passionless impartiality is a revealing parody of the prized impartiality of the law. It simply has no reference to the human beings it is supposed to serve. The policeman does not feel any personal dislike for Jo; he is merely doing his duty. But doing your duty in this society is an offence against decency and men's interests. And as we shall see, much of the horror of the social situation that Dickens presents in *Bleak House* is caused by people doing their duty.

Duty is the great Victorian recommendation for personal salvation – material and moral. 'Wellington's watchword, like Nelson's, was "Duty",' Smiles said, by way of proving its worth;[1] and Dickens himself praised it. But the duty he had in mind was duty to oneself and others, not duty to a society whose essential rottenness is perpetuated by appeals to duty. 'No one can be a great thinker,' Mill said, 'who does not recognize that as a thinker it is his first duty to follow his intellect to whatever conclusions it may lead.'[2] Dickens's intellect led him to the in-escapable conclusion that the appeal to duty was often totally fraudulent. What he has to say about it has much in common

1 *Self-Help*, 1908 edn., p. 270.
2 *On Liberty*, ed. Lindsay, 1950, p. 125.

with Blake's bitter joke that 'If all do their duty they need not fear harm.' And it is here that much of the importance of Bucket lies.

Bucket is a guardian of the law, and at the end of the novel he is presented in a manner similar to Nadgett, as a kind and considerate man. But this is a simplifying and sentimentalizing of his earlier image. At the very least it is severely challenged by the fact that in the bulk of *Bleak House* Bucket emerges as a man whose unpleasantness and human inadequacies are intimately bound into his social role. He is incurious and complacent. Faced with the brickmaker's wife and her baby, he says '"you train him respectable, and he'll be a comfort to you, and look after you in your old age, you know"'. (ch 22) He does not mean to speak ironically, and that the brickmakers are well beyond the pale of respectability is not a matter Bucket cares to enquire into. Enquiries for him are a matter of mechanical routine, and if they cause human distress – as they do, for example, to George Rouncewell and to Jo – well, that is merely in the line of duty. Bucket is like Tulkinghorn. He takes possession of people in a way that denies any deep sense of human responsibility, of duty in the sense which Dickens praised and which George Eliot found 'peremptory and absolute'. There is something really terrifying about Bucket's asking his wife to keep watch on Hortense night and day, and persuading her to say:

'She shall do nothing without my knowledge, she shall be my prisoner without suspecting it, she shall no more escape from me than from death, and her life shall be my life, and her soul my soul, till I have got her, if she did this murder'. (ch 54)

Bucket is not a villain. It is simply that in doing the state some service he becomes vicious and corrupt. No matter how much Dickens may try at the end of the novel to show that there can be wise guardians of the law, he himself has shown such a hope to be impossible.

Law is the product of a system that destroys any idea of a unified people. So is religion. And again, Dickens's satire is directed not against local issues but at a deep failure of responsibility. His attack on dandyism in religion is not an echo of Carlyle; it is dictated by the insight implicit in Blake's perception of how 'the chimney- sweeper's cry/Every black'ning Church appalls':

> There *are*, at Chesney Wold this January week, some ladies and gentlemen of the newest fashion, who have set up a Dandyism – in Religion, for instance. Who, in mere lackadaisical want of emotion, have agreed upon a little dandy talk about the Vulgar wanting faith in things in general; meaning, in the things that have been tried and found wanting, as though a low fellow should un-accountably lose faith in a bad shilling, after finding it out! Who would make the Vulgar very picturesque and faithful, by putting back the hands of the Clock of Time, and cancelling a few hundred years of history. (ch 12)

It is a compressed passage, but Dickens has in mind, I think, both Puseyism and the Young England movement, or at least such elements of the two as combined to form the aggressive High Anglican conservatism that is so marked a feature of mid-Victorian religious thought. His point is that such a movement has forfeited any right to serious regard since it is exclusively a class-concern; its claim to be a responsible social body is absurd. Nor is the attack limited to what was happening in the late 1830s and 1840s. Although both Puseyism and Young England, as such, ceased to have any ostensible influence after 1845, movements of their sort do not simply die overnight, and in fact the mixture of nostalgia and class-arrogance they represent continued to be of importance until much later in the century.

When Dickens speaks of the dandy talk 'about the Vulgar wanting faith in things in general' he has in mind the general failure of Anglicanism to recommend itself to the working-class. He could have known of this from the Religious Census of 1851, which recorded how low a proportion of the working-class professed any religion, but it is more likely that he wisely sensed what scholars of the period have recently been discovering – the radical estrangement of the working-class from religion during the first half of the nineteenth century. The point is repeatedly made by E. P. Thompson, in his *Making of the English Working Class*, and Henry Pelling, writing about E. R. Wickham's *Church and People in an Industrial City*, accepts Wickham's evidence that in Sheffield the working-class did not merely find it difficult to go to church or chapel, it was downright unwilling to go.[1] Sheffield's example is typical. Some years after *Bleak House* was written, John Morley noted that that Anglican church was 'not the church of a nation, but the church of a class; not the benign counsellor and helpful protectress of the poor, but the mean serving-maid of the rich'.[2] Dickens's references to Dandyism in religion, brief though they are, throw a harsh light on the church of a class. That is why the sentences which close chapter 19 are so crucial:

> And there [Jo] sits, munching and gnawing, and looking up at the great Cross on the summit of St. Paul's Cathedral, glittering above a red and violet-tinted cloud of smoke. From the boy's face one might suppose that sacred emblem to be, in his eyes, the crowning confusion of the great, confused city; so golden, so high up, so far out of his reach.

As an alternative there is Chadbandism. Dickens's attack here is simpler, of course. He sets himself against the ignorance and plain hypocrisy of those nonconformists whom he sees as battening and fattening on the working-class, because as Sydney Smith had earlier recognized, 'It is impossible not to observe how directly all the doctrines of the Methodists is calculated to gain power among the poor and ignorant.'[3] Chadbandism is created by class-distinctions. The horror is, that it should find an audience for its absurd cant. '"You are a human boy, my young friend. A human boy. O glorious to be a human boy!"' (ch 19) We fail to do Dickens justice if we see in Chadband the sort of fool whom he presents in the Reverends Stinger and Howler. They are merely canting individuals, but Chadband is securely placed in

1 See article in *Past and Present*, 27, April 1964, pp. 128–33.
2 *The Fortnightly Review*, N.S. XV, p. 314.
3 *Sydney Smith's Works*, I vol., 1869 edn., p. 111.

the social context which produces him and, worse, needs him. Chadbandism aims to provide for its audience a refuge from the truths that the narrator forces on our attention. Why is Jo un-happy? Because, Chadband says to him, '"You are in a state of darkness, because you are in a state of obscurity, because you are in a state of sinfulness, because you are in a state of bondage."' That Chadband is obviously despicable is not calculated to put Dickens's first audience any more at its ease. It pulls from under its feet the possibility that since virtue is always rewarded by success, Jo's sufferings are in some way deserved. It makes uncomfortably obvious the cant that often passes for moral truth.

And to the failures of law and religion are added those of education. As I have suggested, *Dombey and Son* had shown edu-cation to be a perfect agent for the creating of class-consciousness, and in *Bleak House* Dickens takes up the matter again. There is, for example, the truly marvellous moment when we see Krook teaching himself to read and write:

> 'And how do you get on?'
> 'Slow. Bad.' returned the old man, impatiently. 'It's hard at my time of life.'
> 'It would be easier to be taught by some one,' said my guardian.
> 'Aye, but they might teach me wrong!' returned the old man, with a wonderfully suspicious flash in his eye. 'I don't know what I may have lost, by not being learned afore. I wouldn't like to lose anything by being learned wrong now.'
> 'Wrong?' said my guardian, with his good-humoured smile. 'Who do you suppose would teach you wrong?'
> 'I don't know, Mr. Jarndyce of Bleak House!' replied the old man . . . I don't suppose as anybody would – but I'd rather trust my own self than another!' (ch 14)

This scrap of dialogue goes right to the heart of Dickens's con-cern with education in *Bleak House*. Education may and probably does teach wrong; it imposes a way of seeing; and in suggesting as much, Dickens denies all the liberal suggestions about educa-tion as a process of disinterested enlightenment.

It is not unusual for critics to suggest that Dickens's animus against gentlemanly education springs from his envy at having been himself denied it. But this is hardly borne out by the authority with which he identifies what is wrong with Rick (and what he has to say of Rick is repeated and enlarged on in his studies of Gowan, Pip and Eugene). Apart from not wanting to go into the church, Rick is not very sure what he would like to do in life. Articled clerk, perhaps? Or surgeon? Watching his being taken up with the newest idea, Esther wonders whether the Latin Verses he had made for eight years at public school 'often ended in this, or whether Richard was a solitary case'. (ch 13) Dickens is not being philistinic here. He knows the worth of education, is appalled that Jo should know nothing, and that the house of Smallweed 'has strengthened itself in its practical character, has discarded all amusements, discountenanced all story-books, fairy tales, fictions, and fables, and banished all levities whatsoever', so that it produces no children but only 'complete little men and women'. (ch 21) But he also knows that the radical disaster of education is that it defines class-consciousness and destroys individual worth; Rick's being a gentleman is connected with his lack of commitment, and the great expectations he entertains are inevitably a product of the education he has received.

Education is the badge of class or 'station', as the iron-master calls it. He tells Sir Leicester that if Rosa is to marry his son, then she must be better educated:

> 'Are you aware, sir, that this young woman whom my Lady – my Lady – has placed near her person, was brought up at the village school outside the gates?'
> 'Sir Leicester, I am quite aware of it. A very good school it is, and handsomely supported by this family.'
> 'Then, Mr. Rouncewell, the application of what you have said is, to me, incomprehensible.'
> 'Will it be more comprehensible, Sir Leicester, if I say,' the iron-master is reddening a little, 'that I do not regard the village school as teaching everything desirable to be known by my son's wife?' (ch 28)

It is Sir Leicester who is the philistine here. He detects in Rounce-well's remarks one more piece of evidence that people are wanting to educate other 'people out of *their* stations, and so [are] obliterating the landmarks, and opening the floodgates, and all the rest of it'. In other words, for him far more than for Rouncewell, education is a way of creating or confirming class-consciousness. Rouncewell's request has a proper reasonableness about it. There is no reason to suppose that the education that the village school has to offer is much good. Even so, we are meant to feel, I think, that what he plans for Rosa may have perhaps less to do with consideration for her than for her future social position.

And here we may justifiably consider Esther's attempts to teach Charley to write:

> Writing was a trying business to Charley, who seemed to have no natural power over a pen, but in whose hand every pen appeared to become perversely animated, and to go wrong and crooked, and to stop, and splash, and sidle into corners, like a saddle-donkey. It was very odd, to see what old letters Charley's young hand had made; they, so wrinkled, and shrivelled, and tottering; it, so plump and round. Yet Charley was uncommonly expert at other things, and had as nimble little fingers as I ever watched. (ch 31)

Inevitably, this mention of Charley's hand and fingers carries us back to our first view of her, when Esther and Jarndyce go to Bell Yard and discover Neckett's children:

> We were looking at one another, and at these two children, when there came into the room a very little girl, childish in figure, but shrewd and older-looking in the face – pretty-faced too – wearing a womanly sort of bonnet much too large for her, and drying her bare arms on a womanly sort of apron. Her fingers were white and wrinkled with washing . . . (ch 15)

Without doubt the scene that follows this description provides the greatest and most deeply moving image of human commit-ment and selfless duty in the entire novel. The result is that when we come to Esther's condescending remarks about Charley's

poor handwriting we are bound to sense their appalling trivi-
ality. How far Dickens consciously intended our response I do
not know. But I do not see how we can avoid recognizing in
Esther's interest in Charley's education the same sort of impure
concern as conditions the iron-master's interest in Rosa's. If
there is a difference between the two it lies in the fact that Rouncewell thinks he can lift Rosa from one side of the iron-barrier to
the other, whereas Esther thinks that Charley, for all her worth,
is permanently stuck on the far side. Charley's inability to write
is proof of her inferiority. Admittedly, Esther doesn't put it that
way, but it is what her condescension comes to. She is as much
trapped inside class-consciousness as anyone in the novel. Nor
need that be a severe criticism of her. It merely testifies to
Dickens's willingness to expose his characters as creatures of
their society. And again, the question of whether he consciously
intended to do so does not matter; the fact is that he does it, and
even if it is said that he is identified with Esther's condescension
it cannot alter the fact that the earlier view of Charley which he
provides makes its own criticism of Esther's later attitude.

Law, religion, education. They do not create and minister to
the just society. On the contrary, they are products of an unjust
society. Responsibility is in the hands of individuals and therefore futile; Jarndyce's powerlessness is in sharp contrast to the
efficacy of the Cheerybles, because the very comprehensiveness
of *Bleak House* requires a social mimesis that automatically rules
out benevolence as a factor conditioning what society is. At best,
Jarndyce is a recommendation. He is certainly different from
those parodies of individual responsibility, Mrs Jelleby and Mrs
Pardiggle.

The unjust society creates the hell of Tom-all-Alone's, of Jo,
Krook, Nemo, the brickmakers, of all those untouchables who
are denied identity and can be known only to the narrator.
Consider, for example, the description of Nemo's death which,
long as it is, has to be quoted in its entirety. Mr Tulkinghorn
accidentally extinguishes his candle going into the law-writer's
room. But we are forced to see:

The air of the room is almost bad enough to have extinguished it, if he had not. It is a small room, nearly black with soot, and grease, and dirt. In the rusty skeleton of a grate, pinched at the middle as if Poverty had gripped it, a red coke fire burns low. In the corner by the chimney, stands a deal table and a broken desk; a wilderness marked with a rain of ink. In another corner, a ragged old portmanteau on one of the two chairs, serves for cabinet or wardrobe; no larger one is needed, for it collapses like the cheeks of a starved man. The floor is bare; except that one old mat, trodden to shreds of rope-yarn, lies perishing upon the hearth. No curtain veils the darkness of the night, but the discoloured shutters are drawn together; and through the two gaunt holes pierced in them, famine might be staring in [at] the Banshee of the man upon the bed.

For, on a low bed opposite the fire, a confusion of dirty patch-work, lean-ribbed ticking, and coarse sacking, the lawyer, hesitating just within the doorway, sees a man. He lies there, dressed in shirt and trousers, with bare feet. He has a yellow look in the spectral darkness of a candle that has guttered down, until the whole length of its wick (still burning) has doubled over, and left a tower of winding-sheet above it. His hair is ragged, mingling with his whiskers and his beard – the latter, ragged too, and grown, like the scum and mist around him, in neglect. . . .

'Hallo, my friend!' [the lawyer] cries, and strikes his iron candlestick against the door.

He thinks he has wakened his friend. He lies a little turned away, but his eyes are surely open.

'Hallo, my friend,' he cries again. 'Hallo! Hallo!'

As he rattles the door, the candle which has drooped so long, goes out, and leaves him in the dark; with the gaunt eyes of the shutters staring down upon the bed. (ch 10)

It is an amazing passage. And what above all else stands out is the total resourcefulness of Dickens's attending to the dehumanized figure of a man so subdued to his hideous environment that he and it and his candle are fused to the point of his losing all identity. This is the real dark underworld of hopeless poverty, and the language forces us to recognize all that it implies.

But it is Jo rather than Nemo who becomes the crucial figure in Dickens's journey into hell. Jo's prototype appears in the *Christmas Carol*, where the Spirit of Christmas Present forces Scrooge to see the work of Man:

yellow, meagre, ragged, scowling, wolvish . . . No change, no degradation, no perversion of humanity, in any grade, through all the mysteries of wonderful creation, has monsters half so horrible and dread.

'"This boy is Ignorance,"' the Spirit warns Scrooge. '"This girl is Want. Beware them both, all their degree, but most of all beware this boy, for on his brow I see written that which is Doom, unless the writing be erased."' (stave 3) He also appears in the *Haunted Man* as a 'baby savage, a young monster, a child who had never been a child, a creature who might live to take the outward form of man, but who, within, would live and perish a mere beast'. (ch 1) Both stories present the children as images of the inhuman horror that mid-Victorian England produced, and in both cases their appearance is accompanied by an apocalyptic note of warning. The warning is, I think, fairly direct and simple, perhaps induced by the panicky mood of the 1840s, and directed towards the possibility of violent civil conflict. But in *Bleak House* the matter is altogether more subtle.

In the great scene where Lady Dedlock makes Jo lead her to her lover's grave we are witness to one of the many denials of shared humanity which the novel presents. He is not to touch her, not to come near her, not to speak to her. The scene has a naked strength that both makes it immediately powerful and also serves a wider purpose of emblematizing a general condition that Dickens wants to shock us into an awareness of. Lady Dedlock cannot deny Jo. They are linked not just through her lover who is Jo's friend, but because she has to come to his world, as she finally returns to it in order to die. Her effort to escape, to keep clear, is metaphoric of a general condition which produces such perversions of the human as to make further attempts to keep clear all too understandable. Even the humane physician finds it difficult to acknowledge Jo. Woodcourt has to make 'a strong effort to overcome his repugnance' before he can go near the boy, and he 'constrains himself to touch him'.

It is well worth contrasting Dickens's presentation of Jo with what Ruskin had to say in 1853 about the painting of

> those two ragged and vicious vagrants that Murillo has gathered out of the streets. You smile at first, because they are eating so naturally and their roguery is so complete. But is there anything else than roguery there, or was it well for the painter to give his time to the painting of those repulsive and wicked children? Do you feel moved with any charity towards children as you look at them? Are we the least bit more likely to take any interest in ragged schools, or to help the next pauper child that comes in our way, because the painter has shown us a cunning beggar eating greedily.[1]

Although Dickens could hardly have been aware of the existence of Ruskin's remarks when he was at work on *Bleak House*, his way of treating Jo fully meets Ruskin's point. For Jo *is* repulsive, the fact cannot and must not be ignored or softened, or it will demean the shock that comes from realizing that he is the inevitable product of a diseased society. Jo is a brutal and irreducible fact, as Dickens's audience had to know, and his infection is part of a general disease. The famous visionary passage about Tom-all-Alone's revenge – 'It shall pollute this very night, the choice stream (in which chemists on analysis would find the genuine nobility) of a Norman house, and his Grace shall not be able to say Nay to the infamous alliance' – does not merely substitute typhoid for Blake's syphilis as emblem of retributive justice; it points up the fact that what is rotten in the state cannot be avoided by any amount of travel or denial or ignorance. For the innocent suffer, as Esther's pock-marked face makes plain, and what may at first seem a randomness of suffering yields on closer inspection to the awareness of a formidable disease that takes root at all levels. Hence the echoic pattern of *Bleak House*, far grander and more comprehensive than *Dombey and Son*. And it is worth noting here how far Dickens has moved from *Oliver*

[1] *Stones of Venice, Works*, Vol. X, pp. 228–9.

Twist. In the early novel Fagin's black underground world made ominous but infrequent irruptions into the daylight world of the good, respectable society. Now, the corruption is everywhere.

Among children, for example. It is impossible to miss the number of diseased or maimed children in *Bleak House*. Quite apart from Jo, we have the Snagsby's epileptic maid Guster, Jenny's baby who dies and joins the 'five dirty and unwholesome children . . . all dead infants' of the brickmaker's family, Caddy's deaf and dumb child, the Smallweed family, which gives birth to men and women rather than children, and who 'bear a likeness to old monkeys with something depressing on their minds'; (ch 21) and of course Esther herself, born into the knowledge which her godmother gives her, that her life has a shadow on it and that she is set apart. We may add to the list the childlessness of Sir Leicester Dedlock, whose sterility provides one version of the diseases that threaten the future health of England. And we shall see the pattern beginning to thicken still more if we consider the number of unnatural parent-child relationships in the novel. It is hardly necessary to list all these, they are so many and so obvious; it is enough to suggest how they add to the picture of a radical corruption of human values.

Underlying all the corruptions are, I think, the desire and often the need for money, and considerations of class; and on one or both of these motives most of the characters in the novel base their conduct. At one extreme are the dilettantism and expectations that Rick nurtures to his destruction, which Skimpole shares, and which Jobling, who trusts to all things coming round, parodies: '"What I may think after dinner . . . is one thing, my dear Guppy, and what I may think before dinner is another thing. Still, even after dinner, I ask myself the question, What am I to do? How am I to live?"' (ch 20) At another is the rapacious selfishness which springs from a cynical understanding of the notion Jarndyce voices when he says that the universe makes a rather indifferent parent. Hence the Smallweeds and Skimpole, who imply that they are villains on necessity; and who are among the least human characters in the novel. Skimpole is introduced speaking of himself as if he were not at all his own affair, as if Skimpole were a third person, as if he knew that Skimpole had his singularities but still had his claims too, which were the general business of the community and must not be slighted. (ch 6)

This masterly touch of having Skimpole speak of himself in the third person – it had been used before for Pecksniff – does not merely establish the man's ruthless irresponsibility, it also points up what we are meant to see as his inhumanity, since for Dickens human worth is determined by an awareness of others that goes with self-awareness.

The Smallweeds are equally inhuman. '"Lord!"' Bucket says of them, '"there ain't one of the family that wouldn't sell the other for a pound or two, except the old lady – and she's only out of it because she's too weak in her mind to drive a bargain."' (ch 62) The savagery with which Dickens handles the Smallweeds and Skimpole is reminiscent of Jonson. At least, if it is comic it is comic in Jonson's way. The imagery suggests as much. The Small-weeds are likened to broken puppets, the grandfather is compared to a 'mere clothes-bag with a black skull-cap on the top of it', they are referred to as parrots, monkeys, and they rummage among Krook's papers for all the world as if they are dung beetles. The imagery which surrounds the Smallweeds is not superficial or merely fanciful, because it so powerfully affirms their non-humanity. And I imagine that most readers note how much animal imagery there is in *Bleak House*.

There is a point to such imagery which extends beyond whatever Dickens may want to show about the de-humanizing aspects of the world in which the characters of *Bleak House* move. Or rather, in showing these aspects he proposes a sort of inverted evolution. Everything tends downward to the condition of that rudimentary slime in which Tom-all-Alone's exists, with its ruined shelters which breed 'a crowd of foul existence that crawls in and out of gaps in walls and boards; and coils itself to sleep, in maggot numbers, where the rain drips in'. (ch 16) Tom-all-Alone's is a terrible negation of that hope of the 'one far-off divine event,/To which the whole creation moves', which

Tennyson had recently been promising. It is the opposite of the Crystal Palace, with its dream of unlimited progress and belief that 'violence is not heard in our land, wasting nor destruction within its borders', as the Archbishop of Canterbury had claimed in his opening prayer to the Great Exhibition of 1851. For the slime of Tom-all-Alone's takes us back to the beginning of the novel and the vision of

> as much mud in the streets, as if the waters had but newly retired from the face of the earth, and it would not be wonderful to meet a Megalosaurus, forty feet long or so, waddling like an elephantine lizard up Holburn Hill.

It reminds us of the brickmakers's houses at St Albans:

> a cluster of wretched hovels in a brickfield, with pigsties close to the broken windows, and miserable little gardens before the doors, growing nothing but stagnant pools. Here and there, an old tub was put to catch the droppings of rain-water from the roof, or they were banked up with mud into a little pond like a large dirt-pie. (ch 8)

It transfers to the figure of Jo, who knows 'it's hard to keep the mud off the crossings in dirty weather' (ch 16) – as though, irony of ironies, he is the last feeble hope standing between man and the encroaching devastation of the non-human world. And it makes us aware that the rain at Chesney Wold is part of an apocalyptic vision that has nothing to do with predicting an actual moment of social revolution, such as Tom's 'revenge' might lead us consider, and everything to do with Dickens's horrified awareness of a society that looks to be in the process of destroying itself humanly. The imagery of animals, mud, slime and rain is part of a vision that seems to me far more subtle and terrific than the Jeremiad gloom that envelopes other Victorian prophet-figures.

It is moreover firmly rooted in social actualities. For Dickens does not merely satirize those views of progress that we find in the mid-Victorian thinkers who look even to Lyell and Chambers for confirmation of their optimistic reading of the human situation; by his attention to the salient facts of class-consciousness he shows that such views are bound to be absurdly inadequate. I think we are so used to accepting Dickens as the critic of class-pretension that we tend to underestimate the unerring rightness of his perception that in Victorian England the claims of class usurp or corrupt more general human claims. Yet his is after all the properly acerbic voice we need to attend to if we are to understand just how deep the usurpation and corruption go. Admittedly this can lead him into the sort of discursive attack we find him putting, very improbably, into the mouths of Esther and Miss Flite:

> I said it was not the custom in England to confer titles on men distinguished by peaceful services, however good and great; unless occasionally, when they consisted of the accumulation of some very large amount of money.
> 'Why, good gracious,' said Miss Flite, 'how can you say that? Surely you know, my dear, that all the greatest ornaments of England in knowledge, imagination, active humanity and improvement of every sort, are added to its nobility!' (ch 35)

But typically, *Bleak House* unremittingly explores the horror of class-consciousness. As in Lady Dedlock, for example, about whom Dickens remarks that 'in truth she is not a hard lady naturally', but in pursuing her social ambition she has become 'so long accustomed to suppress emotion, and keep down reality; so long schooled, for her own purpose, in that destructive school which shuts up the natural feelings of the heart' (ch 55) that she has been forced into the terrible error of denying love and the truest personal relationships in the pursuit of money and title. And wherever we turn in the novel, we find others making similar mistakes.

Mrs Woodcourt, for example. She remarks that wherever her son Allan goes he will remember his pedigree and on no account form an alliance beneath him. Mrs Woodcourt is not presented unsympathetically. She is a far cry from the Waterbrooks. But in showing her class-snobbishness, Dickens is forcing his audience to attend to an absurdity that is positively cancerous in its effect on people. It leads Mrs Woodcourt to try and destroy her son's love affair with Esther. '"My son's choice of wife is limited"' by his high connections, she tells Esther. '"But the matrimonial choice of the Royal family is limited in much the same manner."' (ch 30) When Woodcourt eventually marries Esther, Jarndyce voices Dickens's own attitude in placing her true worth against the matter of pedigree, but it is in the nature of the novel that we should be aware that such worth carries little weight. Thus Guppy's proposals provide a parodic counterpart to Esther's relationship with Woodcourt. He first of all proposes because he thinks the girl is somehow connected with Lady Dedlock, so that marriage to her would open his way to good connections. Later, after her illness, he asks her to forget his proposal (Dickens has him do this in order to offset Allan's being indifferent to Esther's disfigurement since it hasn't altered her nature). Later still, Guppy proposes marriage for the second time, since the secret of Esther's birth is now out and he can expect that she will help him in his profession. As an extra inducement, he throws in the information that his friend Jobling 'is naturally aristocratic by taste'.

Rosa's love-affair with the iron-master's son provides a variation on the theme. Lady Dedlock adopts her as a surrogate daughter, but is forced to renounce her, partly so that the girl will not share in her mistress's impending fate, and partly because Rosa 'is so far insensible to her many advantages and her good fortune, that she is in love'. (ch 48) Rouncewell wants her educated to be 'worthy of any station', and this means that he does not see class-relationships and identities as fixed, but as fluid and alterable. Rouncewell is, indeed, the nearest approach to Dickens's ideal of non-servile equality that the novel has to offer. When he meets Sir Leicester, he has 'a perfectly natural and easy air, and is not in the least embarrassed by the great presence into which he comes'. (ch 28) He is, of course, conditioned by class. Rosa has to be fit 'for any station'. But given the social realities that is merely good sense. And 'any station' can mean low as well as high. Rouncewell wants her to be well educated rather than given the education that might be regarded as fit or sufficient for a servant-girl. His attitude may be conditioned by class-consciousness, but it is very different from the typical obsequiousness of the middle-class which Dickens contemptuously refers to as 'nothing but a poor fringe on the mantle of the upper',[1] and which in *Bleak House* is represented by the Bayham Badgers and Turveydrop. '"Alas, my country! – has degenerated very much, and is degenerating every day. She has not many gentlemen left. We are few. I see nothing to succeed us, but a race of weavers."' (ch 14) In his absurd respect for the past, and his superannuated manner, Turveydrop is a version of Sir Leicester Dedlock who, no matter how much personally better than the master of Deportment, is every bit as much prevented from recognizing individual worth because he sees only a complex but rigid pattern of class-relationships as having any relevance to human affairs. He 'supposes all his dependants to be utterly bereft of individual characters, intentions or opinions, and is persuaded that he is born to supersede the necessity of their having any'. (ch 7)

It is clear enough that Dickens's intense satiric study of class is not a static one. It does not content itself with miming appearances. Instead, it enquires into how class-relationships become a vitally corrupting process. That is why the novel pays so much attention to friendship, to love and, in a deceptively simple manner, to duty. For Dickens is terribly troubled by all appeals to duty. I have already shown something of this in what I have had to say of Bucket, but I need to take up the matter again since it runs right through *Bleak House*. Here, then, is a man doing his duty:

'As to sparing the girl, of what importance or value is she? Spare! Lady Dedlock, here is a family name compromised. One might have supposed that the course was straight on – over everything, neither to the right nor to the left, regardless of all considerations in the way, sparing nothing, treading everything underfoot.'

She has been looking at the table. She lifts up her eyes, and looks at him. There is a stern expression on her face, and a part of

1 See *Johnson*, Vol. II, p. 858.

her lower lip is compressed under her teeth. 'This woman understands me,' Mr. Tulkinghorn thinks, as she lets her glance fall
again. '*She* cannot be spared. Why should she spare others?' (ch 48)

Dickens's way with Tulkinghorn has often been criticized on the
grounds that he provides no motive for the lawyer's behaviour.
But surely what Tulkinghorn does is sufficient explanation of his
motive for doing it? He is the perfect emblem of impersonal
devotion to family and lineage (his name suggestive of some
heraldic piece of medieval weaponry) and devastatingly vicious
because his devotion is so unswerving. Lady Dedlock sums him
up when she calls him 'mechanically faithful without attachment',
and in one brilliant image Dickens describes Tulkinghorn's
quarters in Lincoln's Inn Fields in what had formerly been a house
of state and where now 'in those shrunken fragments of its
greatness, lawyers lie like maggots in nuts'. (ch 10) Tulkinghorn,
too, is part of the non-human world in which the novel deals.
'Indifferent to everything but his calling', he goes on his business
consideration of matters 'like a machine', and is seen as 'a dingy
London bird among the birds at roost in these pleasant fields [of
Lincoln's Inn], where the sheep are all made into parchment, the
goats into wigs, and the pasture into chaff'. (ch 42) It is a marvellously witty rendering of Tulkinghorn's involvement with a
way of life that is the opposite of the naturally good which, as we
have seen in previous chapters, Dickens so frequently identifies
through pastoral imagery.

More hideous even than Tulkinghorn, is Vholes, whose name
is a broad hint of his non-humanness. He is

> a sallow man with pinched lips that look as if they were cold, a red
> eruption here and there upon his face, tall and thin, about fifty
> years of age, high-shouldered, and stooping. Dressed in black,
> black-gloved, and buttoned to the chin, there was nothing so
> remarkable in him as a lifeless manner, and a slow fixed way he
> had of looking at Richard. (ch 37)

A little later, Esther explains Vholes's look as that of someone
'looking at his prey'. Yet if we simply call Vholes an unnatural

predator and leave it there we do not give proper credit to the novel's extremely discomforting presentation of the man. Not that it is always that. On occasions, Dickens settles into a righteous indignation over the attorney's way of feeding off his clients; and there is also an abrupt dismissiveness about his writing of Vholes tapping his desk so that it sounds 'as hollow as a coffin', and in the remark that Vholes's spots indicate 'an unclean spirit within him that will neither come out nor speak out'. I think that Dickens falls back on such language because it is a way of trying to get rid of Vholes as a problem. Yet a problem is what he remains. Consider his conversation with Esther:

> 'Mr. Carstone has laid down the principle of watching his own interests,' said Mr. Vholes, 'and when a client lays down his own principle, and it is not immoral, it devolves upon me to carry it out. I wish in business to be exact and open. I am a widower with three daughters – Emma, Jane, and Caroline – and my desire is so to discharge the duties of life as to leave them with a good name.' (ch 37)

For all the effort to dispose of Vholes, Dickens cannot do it. Vholes, after all, is doing his duty in order to live and in order to serve his family. Yet he can do this only by serving as corrupt a system as Tulkinghorn serves. And no matter how Dickens may try to pin Vholes down as a villain, he is too great to be satisfied with so easy a solution. Chapter 38 shows how he nags away at the problem:

> Mr. Vholes is a very respectable man. He has not a large business, but he is a very respectable man. He is allowed by the greater attorneys who have made good fortunes, or are making them, to be a most respectable man. He never misses a chance in his practice; which is a mark of respectability. He never takes any pleasure; which is another mark of respectability. He is reserved and serious; which is another mark of respectability. His digestion is impaired, which is highly respectable. And he is making hay of the grass which is flesh, for his three daughters. And his father is dependent on him in the Vale of Taunton.

That prose is not going anywhere. You can almost feel Dickens circling round in a sort of intense frustration, looking for the weak spot whereby he can hit Vholes hard, and having to give the matter up. The attack on the attorney's respectability feels so trivial, so nearly irrelevant. So Dickens tries again. Assume that Vholes's business were to be wiped away by an improvement in the legal system. Many would protest:

> Take a few more steps in this direction, say they, and what is to become of Vholes's father? Is he to perish? And of Vholes's daughters? Are they to be shirt-makers or governesses? As though, Mr. Vholes and his relations being minor cannibal chiefs, and it being proposed to abolish cannibalism, indignant champions were to put the case thus: Make man-eating unlawful, and you starve the Vholeses!

But the analogy is brutally simplistic. It ignores the fact that Vholes's hideous life is one created by the system that Conversation Kenge so lovingly praises, and that Vholes himself is trapped by it. Of course, his respectability, predatoriness and lifelessness are the tokens of a diseased society, of course what he stands for may justly be regarded as a negation of all that we would want to regard as humane; but the awkward fact remains that Vholes is not a free agent, and that he is doing his duty. Accordingly, Dickens tries once more:

> In a word, Mr. Vholes, with his three daughters and his father in the Vale of Taunton, is continually doing duty, like a piece of timber, to shore up some decayed foundation that has become a pitfall and a nuisance. And with a great many people in a great many instances, the question is never one of change from Wrong to Right (which is quite an extraneous consideration), but is always one of injury or advantage to that eminently respectable legion, Vholes.

And there, he gets it. For now he has come clean and admitted that Vholes is a passive agent, and because of this he can set the dilemma out more fairly. Vholes's passivity can rightly hint at his culpable indifference to protesting against an evil system; he stands for all those colourless and unimaginative men for whom acceptance is easier than challenge and who live in a perpetual limbo of unresisting deference. He belongs to that crowd of 'ordinary decent folk' whom Auden remarks 'neither moved nor spoke' as evil is done to others. Yet at the same time Dickens has seen his way to admitting that society has conditioned Vholes into being passive, or rather it has created the opportunities for a man like Vholes to do his duty by his dependents and so seem to be behaving decently, while in fact it has destroyed him humanly. It is a profoundly discomforting insight.

And what of Neckett? For he also does his duty, serving a corrupt system in order to provide for his children. Jarndyce puts the point – almost:

> 'If we make men necessary by our faults and follies, we must not revenge ourselves upon them. There was no harm in his trade. He maintained his children.' (ch 15)

It nearly persuades us that there is no harm in Neckett's trade *because* it allows him to maintain his children. Yet the harm cannot be wished away by talk about faults and follies. For even though Jarndyce has Skimpole particularly in mind, Neckett is the low and mechanical servant of a ruthless system. Jarndyce asks a boy who had known Neckett whether the man was industrious:

> 'Was Neckett?' said the boy. 'Yes, wery much so. He was never tired of watching. He'd set upon a post at a street corner, eight or ten hours at a stretch, if he undertook to do it.'
> 'He might have done worse,' I heard my guardian soliloquize. He might have undertaken to do it, and not done it.'

But would that have been worse? And if it would, then what is wrong with Vholes's fulfilling *his* occupation? When Mrs Blinder says that Neckett ' "did what he had to do . . . and it's something in this world even to do that" ' we can hardly avoid feeling that exactly the same claim could be made on behalf of Vholes. And if on his behalf then why not on behalf of the policeman who moves Jo on? For all these people are trapped in the web of a corrupt system, and if they can be accused of complicity in it they can also be defended on the grounds that they do what they have to do out of economic necessity or duty to others. This is what the system does to individuals. And at its worst it enforces loyalty even on those whom it most obviously destroys; Jo after all does his duty in sweeping the crossing, day in, day out. Even he is a victim of a concept which so frequently turns into the cant of Mrs Jelleby, for whom 'public duties' are her 'favourite child'.

And yet the alternative is worse. The dream of breaking out of bondage to the system depends on an escapist notion of great expectations, a purely economic dream of freedom which destroys Gridley, Miss Flite, Rick, Lady Dedlock, and comes near to destroying George. All of them try to escape, none can; and I think myself that this is not intrusive moralizing on Dickens's part. He is not saying that freedom cannot be bought. Lady Dedlock buys it. But the cost in human terms is too high:

> Weariness of soul lies before her, as it lies behind – her Ariel has put a girdle of it round the whole earth, and it cannot be unclasped – but the imperfect remedy is always to fly, from the last place where it has been experienced. (ch 12)

In the presentation of Lady Dedlock we have a relentless yet compassionate study of a person who damages herself terribly in trying to find freedom, for the search inevitably requires an attempt to escape from human commitment and produces an impoverishment of life. There is nothing shrill or pietistic about this; in his exploration of the society in which people find themselves, Dickens makes us aware of the pressures that can cause individuals to seek freedom. But he is no less aware of the cost; and Rick, Gridley and Miss Flite are all images of human beings for whom relationships have become unreal or warped as a result of their pursuit of that dream of freedom which feeds so destructively on them. George too is tainted by it. He runs away to enlist ' "Making believe that I cared for nobody, no not I, and that nobody cared for me" '. (ch 55) But for all that he is committed to others, and it saves him.

And this brings us back once more to Dickens's study of the nature of duty. Some words of Kant will help in defining his position:

> Duty's title to respect has nothing to do with happiness. It has its own peculiar law and its own peculiar tribunal. And no matter how one might wish to shake up duty and pleasure together in order to offer them as a medical compound, as it were, to an ailing spirit, they will presently sort themselves out of their own accord, and if not, duty will not function. Even if in this way physical life gained a certain strength, the moral life would inevitably decline.[1]

What Kant says is as prescriptive and absolute as Esther's self-admonishment 'Duty, my dear!' Yet although Esther's constant self-reminders hardly amount to the austere moral life Kant had in mind, *Bleak House* by and large offers convincing images of the moral life. And I think that they convince just because Dickens is so acutely aware of the problems and dilemmas of duty, to say nothing of the terrible pressures that it can exert. In a way what Kant says of the moral life could be merely tautologous: it means doing one's duty. But if Vholes is a case in point, then the moral life has little to recommend it. Charley, however, is a very different case. The scene where we break in on that unexpected world of the children for whom she cares is without doubt immensely moving, but in its presentation of the girl's marvellous goodness it is also immensely exhilarating. Without fuss or special pleading, Dickens offers us an example of the moral life as an enriching and deeply humanizing process.

I realize that in using such terms I sound morally strident, but then Dickens, in common with all the greatest artists, has the ability to uncover those central truths about life for which there are only the obvious words. Certainly, when he provides the scene of Charley's caring for the children we come to realize how wide of the mark George Eliot's criticism of him is:

[1] *Works*, Vol. 5, p. 97.

But for the precious salt of his humour, which compels him to reproduce external traits that serve, in some degree, as a corrective to his frequently false psychology, his preternaturally virtuous poor children and artisans . . . would be as noxious as Eugène Sue's idealized *proletaires* in encouraging the miserable fallacy that high morality and refined sentiment can grow out of harsh social relations, ignorance and want; or that the working-classes are in a condition to enter at once into a millenial state of *altruism*, wherein everyone is caring for everyone else, and no one for himself.[1]

Great novelist though George Eliot is, that passage seems to me chiefly remarkable for its way of exposing her own limitations. For what she has to say about the working-class stems from a liberal attitude far more rigid and absolute than Dickens's recognition that human worth not only can grow out of harsh social relations, ignorance and want, but indeed very probably will. Which is not to say that it always will: Krook and the Smallweeds are sufficient evidence of Dickens's refusal to generalize. And if it comes to that, Charley is not 'preternaturally virtuous'. She is simply a good person. But that of course is the great triumph of Dickens's art. He confronts his audience with an image of goodness that is in no sense sentimentalized but is in every way utterly convincing.

There are other such images in *Bleak House*. Phil Squod, the Bagnets, Woodcourt, Snagsby, Caddy and young Turveydrop are all examples of the moral life. They all manage to 'survive under . . . discouragement', as Esther says of Caddy. And the very fact that they do so is sufficient to act as refutation against any idea that Dickens's view of mid-Victorian society is one of unrelieved gloom or pessimism. These people are opposed to Mrs Jelleby who sweeps 'the horizon in search of duties' rather than performing 'her own natural duties and obligations'. But here we come up against what might be a problem. For as we have already seen, natural duties cannot always be isolated from duties that seem decidedly unnatural. And besides, isn't the attack on

[1] *Essays of George Eliot*, ed. Pinney, 1963, pp. 271–2.

Mrs Jelleby suspiciously like a short-tempered reproof to any idealism? 'His whole "message",' Orwell said, 'is one that at first glance looks like an enormous platitude: If men would behave decently the world would be decent.' *Bleak House* may seem to support Orwell's contention. When Turveydrop tells his son that ' "Your qualities are not shining, my dear child, but they are steady and useful" ' (ch 23) he is unwittingly putting the case for decency. On the other hand, I do not think we can say that this amounts to a message, if only because in *Bleak House* Dickens is far less concerned with what ought to be than with what is. But of course what Orwell really means is that Dickens is not against the social system as such, he merely wants it to work well enough to give everybody a chance of living decently. 'Hence that recurrent Dickens figure, The Good Rich Man.' Jarndyce versus Mrs Pardiggle. Practical benevolence against a contemptuously dismissive presentation of idealism. But it is the wrong opposition. Certainly Dickens is contemptuous of Mrs Jelleby and of Mrs Pardiggle, but only because their notions of improving people are so absurdly inadequate, their ideals so ludicrously beside the point:

> Jo is brought in. He is not one of Mrs. Pardiggle's Tockahoopo Indians; he is not one of Mrs. Jelleby's lambs; being wholly unconnected with Borrioboola-Gha; he is not softened by distance and unfamiliarity; he is not a genuine foreign-grown savage; he is the ordinary home-made article. Dirty, ugly, disagreeable to all the senses, in body a common creature of the common streets, only in soul a heathen. Homely filth begrimes him, homely parasites devour him, homely sores are in him, homely rags are on him: native ignorance, the growth of English soil and climate, sinks his immortal nature lower than the beasts that perish. (ch 47)

Jarndyce is a better man than the two women, because he cares about the home-made article. But as I have already suggested, Dickens shows him to be all but impotent. The Good Rich Man is simply not effective.

We might try to deduce from this that Dickens all but despairs of the society he confronts, and that he keeps alive hope only because there are some people who behave decently. But this would be to misunderstand the nature of *Bleak House*. There is a widespread temptation among critics to feel that Dickens presents society as a rigid mould that can be neither shattered nor altered. Yet actually *Bleak House* is much concerned with the nature of social change. This may seem obvious enough when we consider the figure of Sir Leicester Dedlock, but then his fears of the floodgates and Watt Tylerism might seem to be supported by the horrors of the society with which Dickens presents us and which I have spent some time analysing. Yet the deluge that Sir Leicester prophesies may turn out to be a cleansing flood. At least it will sweep away the absurdities and corruptions of the past. And to say this suggests that the novel is open-minded, rather than condemnatory

But here we have to consider Dickens's use of pastoralism:

> As he comes into the iron country further north, such fresh green woods as those of Chesney Wold are left behind; and coal-pits and ashes, high chimneys and red bricks, blighted verdure, scorching fires, and a heavy never-lightening cloud of smoke become the features of the scenery. (ch 63)

Odd that the woods of Chesney Wold are made into a sort of pastoral ideal here, when they are customarily associated with rain, mould and decay. Should we feel that at this moment Dickens is beginning to idealize the past? Better the Dedlocks even, than a society of iron masters! Certainly, the countryside that George encounters on his journey to see his brother is very different from the one he has earlier spoken about to Phil Squod:

> 'The country,' says Mr. George . . . 'why, I suppose you never clapped your eyes on the country, Phil?'
> 'I see the marshes once,' said Phil . . .
> 'What marshes?'
> '*The* marshes, commander,' returns Phil.
> 'Where are they?'
> 'I don't know where they are,' says Phil; 'but I see 'em, guv'nor. They was flat. And misty' . . .

'I was born in the country, Phil.'

'Was you indeed, commander?'

'Yes. And bred there. . . . There's not a bird's note that I don't know,' says Mr. George. 'Not many an English leaf or berry that I couldn't name. Not many a tree that I couldn't climb yet, if I was put to it. I was a real country boy, once. My good mother lived in the country.'

'She must have been a fine old lady, guv'nor,' Phil observes. (ch 26)

George's memory of the country may be compared with Miss Tox's nostalgia for her childhood; for both a vast gap has opened up between past and present, and in George's case the gap is emphasized by Phil Squod, for whom the country is so unimaginably distant that he necessarily thinks of George's mother as belonging to a past world. Phil indeed is an image of that cockneyism of which Ruskin and others were beginning to complain in the 1850s. He is the townsman so cut off from nature that – according to Ruskin at least – he must be a crippled being:

> For one man who is fitted for the study of words, fifty are fitted for the study of things, and were intended to have a perpetual, simple, and religious delight in watching the processes, or admiring the creatures, of the natural universe. Deprived of this source of pleasure, nothing is left to them but ambition or dissipation.[1]

But Phil Squod is a responsible and good man, and certainly no image of ambition or dissipation. His work-chapped hands provide the immediate token of his worth. Yet I think we are meant to contrast his physical appearance with George's, not in order to make any obvious criticism of Phil, but to understand that his deprivations are important.

And going with Phil's stunted appearance we must notice the encroachment of town upon country. There is the iron-country itself, there is the approach to St Alban's, all mud and muck, and there is that parodic pastoralism of Lincoln Inn's Fields, which I have already noted, where 'the sheep are all made into parch-

[1] Ruskin, *The Stones of Venice, Works*, Vol. X, p. 259.

ment, the goats into wigs, and the pasture into chaff'. Such images and moments as these suggest a deep fear on Dickens's part, that important values are perhaps being lost in the process of social change.

Yet he tries to dispel such fears. Or rather, he finds himself an opportunity to mock any simple belief that the values he cherishes are linked to the past and can be rendered only through pastoral imagery. If I had my way, Skimpole tells Esther, ' "there should be no brambles of sordid realities in such a path as that. It should be strewn with roses; it should lie through bowers, where there is no spring, autumn, or winter, but perpetual summer." ' (ch 6) It is very Leigh-Huntish, and it also constitutes an absurd effort to deny the realities of life in favour of a dream-pastoralism. Dickens, we may say, turns his back on any such dream. But then how to explain the description of Esther's going to see her new house on 'a most beautiful summer morning'?

> We went on by a pretty little orchard, where the cherries were nestling among the green leaves, and the shadows were sporting on the grass . . . such a lovely place, so tranquil and so beautiful, with such a rich and smiling country spread around it, with water sparkling away into the distance, here all overhung with summer-growth, there turning a humming-mill; at its nearest point glancing through a meadow by the cheerful town, where cricket-players were assembling in bright groups, and a flag was flying from a white tent that rippled in the sweet west wind. (ch 64)

This is Skimpole-land with a vengeance. And it does seem to me that at this point Dickens is offering Esther an individual way out of the world that for most of the novel he has shown to be inescapable. This landscape is not only a dream landscape, it is linked to a past which is rapidly being obliterated. And in offering Esther the escape he does, we may feel that Dickens's open-mindedness is faltering badly, or that in the end he simply cannot see much hope in what is happening to England.

But against this we have to set his admiration for the iron-master, whom he clearly shows to be preferable to Sir Leicester. Dickens is unequivocal in his celebration of Rouncewell's hard work, resilience, kindness and tough-minded independence. Rouncewell is a very different kind of man from Bounderby of *Hard Times*, and it is perhaps important that *Hard Times* has none of *Bleak House's* open-mindedness. It is not just that Bounderby is a bullying villain, but that the system he serves is seen as a fixity rather than a process so that any attempt to change it is doomed to failure or, in the case of Slackbridge, the union man, is merely a cynical excuse for devilish irresponsibility.[1] This may show that in *Bleak House* Dickens is only just keeping control of fears that take control of him in his next novel. But it is also possible to say that *Bleak House* is a great novel just because it refuses to submit to such fears, even if it finds a place for them. It is a difficult matter to decide about, but I think that in *Bleak House*, Dickens's awareness of the nature of change is extremely complex, so that even the rape of the countryside has to be balanced against our final vision of Chesney Wold:

> a vast blank of over-grown house looking out upon trees, sighing, wringing their hands, bowing their heads, and casting their tears upon the window-panes in monotonous depression. (ch 66)

It is a deeply ambiguous image. Nature mourns the passing of the Dedlocks, of what might therefore seem to be the death of a natural order. Yet nature itself is dispossessed of all vitality. It is as though Dickens feels it necessary to provide this image as a corrective against the suggestions of health and life released in his other pastoral images.

Dickens's complex use of nature is crucial to his rendering of social change. So, too, is his use of the young. Many of them carry in their bones inherited ills. The destruction of youth and beauty of which we hear so much in *Bleak House* does not merely belong to the novel's rhetoric, it is fundamental to the imaging of the difficult and often disastrous process of change, of the corruptions of the past which linger into the present and condition the future. Yet for all the horror implicit in Caddy's mute

[1] I have written about this in my essay 'Mrs. Gaskell and Brotherhood', in *Tradition and Tolerance in Nineteenth Century Fiction*.

child and the deaths of Jo and Rick, Dickens's vision is not one of total gloom. For against disease and death are the positive images of the moral life which can make themselves out of such horror. And it is part of the complex greatness of *Bleak House* that it should allow us to understand that change comes about through or is potential in such people as Charley, Phil and Snagsby, frail though they may seem in comparison with the forces set against them. The novel does not have to intrude a message or an ideal. On the contrary, in spite of Esther's way out – and even she carries the mark of society's ills – *Bleak House* denies the possibility of freedom, either from history, society or the self. But in forcing us to accept this, Dickens also forces us to accept the truth that human beings are not inevitably crushed by the social forces they encounter and that despair is therefore ill-judged or an improper and Dedlock-like declaration of preferences.

🦁 7 · *LITTLE DORRIT*

It would not be difficult to make *Little Dorrit* sound very like *Bleak House*. If we say that both novels are about society as a prison from which nobody can escape and by which everyone is tainted we say what is, after all, perfectly true. And it is just as true of *Our Mutual Friend*. All three novels are critiques of Victorian society. But as Edmund Wilson wisely pointed out, it simply will not do to make believe that Dickens goes on from novel to novel saying more or less the same thing. On the contrary:

> It may be said that Dickens never really repeats himself: his thought makes a consistent progress, and his art, through the whole thirty-five years of his career, keeps going on to new materials and new effects.[1]

These words have an immediate bearing on my present concern. For I want to begin this chapter by pointing out how very different *Little Dorrit* is from *Bleak House*, and attempting to indicate its especial or distinctive quality.

There is a great passage describing Arthur Clennam's walk to his mother's 'grim home':

> It always affected his imagination as wrathful, mysterious, and sad; and his imagination was sufficiently impressible to see the whole neighbourhood under some dark tinge of its dark shadow. As he went along, upon a dreary night, the dim streets by which he went, seemed all depositories of oppressive secrets. The deserted counting-houses, with the secrets of books and papers locked up in chests and safes; the banking-houses, with their secrets of strong

[1] *The Wound and The Bow*, 1961, p. 66.

rooms and wells, the keys of which were in a very few secret pockets and a very few secret breasts; the secrets of all the dispersed grinders in the vast mill, among whom there were doubtless plunderers, forgers and trust betrayers of many sorts, whom the light of day that dawned might reveal; he could have fancied that these things, in hiding, imparted a heaviness to the air. The shadow thickening and thickening as he approached its source, he thought of the secrets of the lonely church-vaults, where the people who had hoarded and secreted in iron coffers were in their turn similarly hoarded, not yet at rest from doing harm; and then of the secrets of the river, as it rolled its turbid tide between the frowning wildernesses of secrets, extending, thick and dense, for many miles, and warding off the free air and the free country swept by winds and wings of birds. (Bk 2, ch 10)

It is an extremely inclusive passage, and since everything in *Little Dorrit* has relevance to the theme of secrecy, passages such as this seem to be attempts to sum up or define the nature of the experience that the novel as a whole offers. But I think there is more to it than just that. For *Little Dorrit* has, very importantly, a generalizing, almost abstractive air about it. It is not mimetic in anything like the same way as *Bleak House*: prose, form, plot, characters, all seem endlessly to testify to general truths about the human condition, to have about them a sort of mythic completeness of statement. I do not mean that the novel is symbolist in any trite way. Dickens never loses sight of the fact that the human condition cannot be divorced from the social context. But granted that much, *Little Dorrit* has about it the appearance of trying to explore and utter what I have reluctantly to call archetypal truths.

In an effort to pin this utterance down, we have to consider the novel's attitude to freedom. And here we notice something odd, that *Little Dorrit* is the only novel Dickens wrote that has nothing whatsoever to do with the countryside. The nearest we get to it is Twickenham, and the 'freedom' that Twickenham seems to offer turns out to be delusive. But Twickenham apart, nature in *Little Dorrit* has become mythic; it operates in terms of such ballad-like phrases as 'the free air and the free country swept by winds and wings of birds'. And as in previous novels nature had been linked to freedom, now it exists only as a mode of giving utterance to a human yearning, a passionate desire for an escape from the prison. For there can be no doubt that *Little Dorrit* voices such desire, and in an especially poignant manner, because it cannot be realized. The novel is a deeply pondered statement about the human condition, and it has a heavy, almost oppressive brooding quality. It is not a pessimistic novel, but it is certainly a very sombre one. And much of its characteristic quality comes from the near folk-tale element of its plot, which is made out of sets of apparent contingencies and accidents that reveal themselves as part of an inexorable pattern. ' "In our course through life we shall meet the people who are coming to meet *us*, from many strange places and by many strange roads," ' Miss Wade says, ' "and what it is set to us to do to them, and what it is set to them to do to us, will all be done." ' (Bk 1, ch 2) Her words sound like the opening of an old folk-tale. Yet they do not have to do with any crude determinism on Dickens's part. It is more that she voices what the novel shows in so many other ways, that there can be no reversal of the doom of man, no fulfilling the dream of freedom. And although Miss Wade does not – how could she? – specify what is set for people to do, her words reach out to that deep theme the novel communicates, of the impossibility of escape from commitment in the darkest and most difficult sense: that the effort to find freedom in escape exacts a terrible cost in human terms, does irreparable psychic damage.

This again brings *Little Dorrit* back to *Bleak House*. And again there is a profound difference. It can partly be indicated by noting Dickens's choice of names. In *Bleak House*, names have a social resonance: Krook, Tulkinghorn, Nemo, Dedlock. Or they may be clever ways of fixing types: Miss Flite, Smallweed, Weevle. But in *Little Dorrit* the names are more mysteriously allusive. Clennam (clean, clam, clem), Casby (Caspar, Casbah), Merdle (merd, medal), Gowan (meaning daisy, often taken to mean lily), Meagles (meek, eagle), Plornish (poor, plenish),

Rigaud (the name of a seventeenth-century dancing-master of Marseilles). Other names are undoubtedly more limited in their resonance, as for instance Maggy and Chivery; and some belong to the simpler satiric side of the novel, above all the Barnacles. But Dorrit is more important. In its echo of Doric lie not just hints of the rusticity and uncouthness which prevent William Dorrit from being quite the gentleman he wishes to be, there is also a suggestion of pastoralism which we might expect Dickens automatically to associate with positive values. And as we shall see, at one very crucial point of the novel Amy Dorrit is indeed directly connected with pastoral imagery.

I do not want to make much of the names in the novel. But they do reinforce the feeling of its archetypal quality. And this feeling gains added sustenance from the novel's title. Dickens of course had originally planned to call his work *Nobody's Fault* and there seems to be widespread agreement that his change of mind is regrettable. But is it? At the very least his decision to call the book *Little Dorrit* suggests that he did not want his novel to be regarded primarily as a social satire, and it also implies that he is more concerned to direct our attention towards the qualities of his heroine. This should not be taken to mean that *Little Dorrit* can somehow be abstracted from the social considerations it so obviously deals in. To try and make it a symbolic statement about eternal human verities without reference to its view of society would be an absurdly procrustean exercise. It does, however, mean that we have to be very cautious in claiming, as Lionel Trilling does, that *Little Dorrit* 'is *more* about society than any other of the novels, that it is about society in its very essence'.[1] I do not see that *Bleak House* or *Our Mutual Friend* are any less about society than *Little Dorrit*. It is rather that all the novels see society from different angles and have other concerns besides.

One of *Little Dorrit's* concerns is with the impossible dream of freedom. And Dickens's treatment of the dream is very brilliant.

---

[1] 'Little Dorrit' in *The Dickens Critics* ed. Ford and Lane, 1961, p. 280. The essay first appeared as his Introduction to the Oxford *Little Dorrit* 1953, and was reprinted in *The Opposing Self*, 1955.

The novel opens with an evocation of a terrible elemental world, too awful almost for human beings to bear:

> The universal stare made the eyes ache. Towards the distant line of Italian coast, indeed, it was a little relieved by light clouds of mist, slowly rising from the evaporation of the sea, but it softened nowhere else. Far away the staring roads, deep in dust, stared from the hill-side, stared from the hollow, stared from the interminable plain. Far away the dusty vines overhanging wayside cottages, and the monotonous wayside avenues of parched trees without shade, drooped beneath the stare of earth and sky. . . . Everything that lived or grew, was oppressed by the glare; except the lizard, passing swiftly over the rough stone walls, and the cicala, chirping his hot dry chirp, like a rattle. The very dust was scorched brown, and something quivered in the atmosphere as if the air itself were panting.

I do not think Dickens himself entirely knows what the language of this passage is trying for. It is so strange, its significance so difficult to grasp. But it also seems to me quite certain that essentially the description struggles to glimpse or notionalize a non-human universe, drained of life and of value. It cannot escape our notice that this pitiless state of the sun is contrasted with the dark shadow of Mrs Clennam's house that throws a condition of secrecy over society. Much closer to hand, however, is the prison in which Rigaud and John Baptist lie. It puts a 'prison taint on everything there. The imprisoned air, the imprisoned light, the imprisoned damps, the imprisoned men, were all deteriorated by confinement'. And of course everyone in *Little Dorrit* is tainted by the prison. It is the condition of being human. To escape the prison is to come into that world of pitiless sun.

But putting the matter this way rather invites a pessimistic reading of the novel. The imagined alternatives seem so appalling (there is, of course, no *real* alternative to the prison). And there can be no doubt that the deep sombreness of *Little Dorrit* makes it sharply different from *Bleak House*. For in *Bleak House*, Dickens's disgust has an exhilarating sanity about it. In spite of the horrific studies it presents, it is the most exuberant of all his novels, because of the envigorating range of his own powers; anger, contempt, eloquent rage, mimicry, comic scorn and praise, effortless championing of the right and putting down of the wrong. It is a colossal stylistic *tour de force*, and it leaves us in no doubt that Dickens feels himself to be in intellectual and imaginative control of the world he renders, and able to use his art to challenge its horrors. But *Little Dorrit* does not provide the same certainties. There is, for example, an almost weary contempt about his writing of Edmund Sparkler's promotion that is in marked contrast to his treatment of the Coodles and the Doodles. He had defied them to do their worst. But he fears that Sparkler will.

More deeply, however, there is the matter of Dickens's involvement in Clennam:

> When he got to his lodgings, he sat down before the dying fire, as he had stood at the window of his old room looking out upon the blackened forest of chimneys, and turned his gaze upon the gloomy vista by which he had come to that stage in his existence. So long, so bare, so blank. No childhood; no youth, except for one remembrance; that one remembrance proved, only that day, to be a piece of folly.

At this point Clennam has just returned from his meeting with Flora and we do not need to know of Dickens's reunion with Maria Beadnell to sense that this passage comes from something very close to the novelist himself. Nor is this improper. But there is no doubt that the note is entirely new in Dickens's novels. There is no self-pity about it; indeed, Dickens goes out of his way to show that Arthur cannot be judged guilty of 'whimpering weakness . . . A disappointed mind he had, but a mind too firm and healthy for such unwholesome air'. It is not special pleading. Arthur has none of David Copperfield's indulgent feeding on his own past miseries. On the other hand, the sombreness of Arthur's mind has much to do with his feeling of the utter pointlessness of his life:

Therefore, he sat before his dying fire, sorrowful to think upon the way by which he had come to that night, yet not strewing poison on the way by which other men had come to it.

I would not defend that prose. It seems to me merely inert, and the recommendation of Arthur's magnanimity is not supported by anything like an adequate image. Yet as we go deeper into his actual thoughts the language begins to gain in authenticity of rhythm and phrase and marvellously survives what might at first sight look to be a cliché of the sinking fire, but which on reflection is surely beautifully and naturally apt (it is a part of Dickens greatness that when he is writing well he can revitalize cliché by the intensity and resourcefulness of his prose):

> He looked at the fire from which the blaze departed, from which the after-glow subsided, in which the ashes turned grey, from which they dropped to dust, and thought 'How soon I too shall pass through such changes, and be gone!'
>
> To review his life was like descending a green tree in fruit and flower, and seeing all the branches wither and drop off one by one, as he came down towards them.
>
> 'From the unhappy suppression of my youngest days, through the rigid and unloving home that followed them, through my departure, my long exile, my return, my mother's welcome, my intercourse with her since, down to the afternoon of this day with poor Flora,' said Arthur Clennam, 'what have I found!'
>
> His door softly opened, and these words startled him, and came as if they were an answer:
>
> 'Little Dorrit.' (Bk 1, ch 13)

The downward dark is arrested only in the very last words, and though it would be unforgivably crude to claim that Little Dorrit represents the woman that neither Kate nor Maria Beadnell had proved themselves to be for Dickens, we can justifiably suggest that the brooding introspective quality of the novel that is so strongly focused in Arthur and which makes it so strikingly different from *Bleak House* comes from the crises in Dickens's own life, over his marriage, children, his work and the state of his country. But this does not imply that *Little Dorrit* suffers from

its author's personal situation. On the contrary, I think it is without doubt Dickens's greatest novel and far and away the greatest
novel in the language. And much of its greatness depends on the
depth and richness of the artist's sanity in coping with the crises
that the novel expresses.

Amy Dorrit is the figure around whom the novel's assertions
are built and I think Dickens's ability to invent her is a vindication of his art and throws a perhaps unexpected light on what
might otherwise seem his evasive reply to Maria Beadnell's
request that they meet again. Dickens wrote to refuse her. 'Whoever is devoted to an Art,' he said, 'must be content to deliver
himself wholly up to it, and to find his recompense in it.'[1] I do
not think this remark can be fitted into a Romantic Image.
What Dickens means is that art allows the artist to triumph over
his own condition, to 'rise into the light, seeing it shine on others
and hailing it'. We are unaccustomed to and embarrassed by such
fervency of language; and on the whole critics prefer to see *Little
Dorrit* as a merely gloomy or pessimistic novel about society as
an intolerable prison. It is my very strong feeling that the novel
ends by making pessimism seem sentimental, and nobody should
think that this means that it evades its own themes, or that in
Amy Dorrit Dickens is creating an image of Christian salvation
or divine grace because this is the only way out of the mess that
he can see. Amy Dorrit was born in the Marshalsea and not in
Heaven, and if she symbolizes anything it is the power of the
human to cope with the worst that society is and does. That may
make her sound like Charley, but the difference is that in Amy
the general implications are richer.

I do not however think the implications lead in the direction
to which Lionel Trilling points when he says that 'the whole
energy of the imagination of *Little Dorrit* is directed towards the
transcending of the personal will, to the search for the Will in
which there shall be peace'.[2] Trilling's essay makes some very
valuable points about the novel, but this does not seem to me to

[1] Johnson, Vol. II, p. 837.
[2] *Trilling*, op. cit., p. 293.

be one of them. It is true that Dickens is liable to use language that has clear Biblical and Christian echoes, and the novel undoubtedly has about it the sort of intensity of affirmation – and for that matter condemnation – that could be called religious. But I am not at all persuaded that Dickens's search is, as Trilling claims, for a general 'moral idea which tends to find its full development in a religious experience'; it is for what can be affirmed about the human condition. But search it certainly is, and I think it fair to say that Dickens probably feared it would turn up different answers from the ones we are presented with. There is no trace of a thesis about *Little Dorrit*. One of its most remarkable features is the degree to which it seems both random *and* well-ordered. There is no explaining that except by the mystery of genius. Unless, that is, we apply to Dickens the words that Arthur Clennam uses of Daniel Doyce. 'He never said, I discovered this adaptation or invented that combination; but showed the whole thing as if the Divine Artificer had made it, and he had happened to find it.' Trilling quotes this as vindication of his claim that *Little Dorrit* is a search for the Will in which there shall be peace. To my mind, it is much more a vindication of Dickens's discovery that his art offered the 'recompense' of which he spoke to Maria Beadnell.

Because *Little Dorrit* is so deeply committed to its search, it explores more lives more deeply than any other of Dickens's novels. To quote Trilling once more:

> We do not have the great population of characters from whom shines the freshness of their autonomous life. Mr. Pancks and Mrs. Plornish and Flora Finching and Flintwinch are interesting and amusing, but they seem to be the fruit of conscious intention rather than of free creation.

I am not sure I entirely agree with this, if only because it seems to accept rather too easily that characters in novels other than *Little Dorrit* do have autonomous lives, whereas I think that Captain Cuttle, shall we say, is as much the fruit of conscious intention as is Mr Pancks. But Trilling is right to imply that

Dickens wants to do more with the characters of *Little Dorrit* than we are used to from the other novels. He explores the qualities and possibilities of their lives with an extraordinary intensity and care (it is relevant to mention here how hard he worked on his manuscript, how much he revised, edited, cut). And if *Little Dorrit* manages finally to be something of an affirmation, it has to be said that the novel ends by severely qualifying what affirmation there is. It acknowledges the social pressures which surround and threaten the individual. Amy and Clennam go down into the roaring streets:

> inseparable and blessed; and the noisy and the eager, and the arrogant and the froward and the vain, fretted, and chafed, and made their usual uproar.

On the other hand, though I have no wish to push beyond limits the resonances of Dickens's prose, I think it proper to note how the bridal pair pause for a moment above the crowd, 'on the steps of the portico, looking at the fresh perspective of the street in the autumn morning sun's bright rays, and then went down'. The sun at this final juncture does not have the pitiless stare of the Marseilles sun, and it is possible to feel that momentarily Dickens's prose hints at those larger human possibilities that Amy and Clennam's 'inseparable' union suggests. There is a sustenance implicit in the 'fresh perspectives' that aids their going down into the roaring streets, their return to the human condition. It is, of course, difficult to set this down without making it seem either trite or merely whimsical, yet it provides further evidence of the novel's unique quality that I have been trying to put my finger on.

Whatever this quality may be, I have said that we do not find it in *Bleak House*. And here I have to admit that I have used *Bleak House* as the point of comparison in what may seem a misleading manner. For although it, too, is about society as a prison it is not *Little Dorrit*'s immediate predecessor. *Hard Times* comes after *Bleak House* and it might be more just to compare the later novel with *Little Dorrit*. The trouble is, that *Hard Times* seems to me an unsuccessful novel, and for fairly obvious reasons. It has a bleakly deterministic view of the hopelessness of the human situation, and I think it is a sort of thesis-novel. Dickens marks out his enemies, Gradgrind and Bounderby, and he makes of them mere cyphers, predictable, hateful and easily condemned. But between them they represent a way of life which is meant to be powerful enough to squeeze out all hope for human decency. At the end of the novel, the circus-owner Sleary remarks to Gradgrind that

> 'people mutht be amused. They can't be alwayth a learning, nor yet they can't be always a working, they ain't made for it. You *mutht* have us, Thquire.'

Slearly undoubtedly is seen as embodying the novel's positive values; but his remark is feebly prescriptive. The chance of 'fun' is infinitely remote from the lives of the Coketowners. And in terms of what the novel proposes, it follows that the people of Coketown are as good as dead.

Now *Hard Times* is in the grip of an idea. Dr Leavis speaks of its 'peculiarly insistent moral intention', and although the phrase is perfectly just I do not think it suggests much that is praiseworthy. On the contrary, it is the insistence that strangles the life of *Hard Times* and is responsible for the simplistic presentation of issues and characters (always excepting the marvellous handling of Mrs Sparsit and of Louisa's relationship with Harthouse). It will hardly do to explain away the simplicities of *Hard Times* by calling it a moral fable, because the complexity of the issues that Dickens takes up cannot be reduced to the formulae that he presents. And Dickens quickly came to realize this himself. One of the most striking features of *Household Words* is how it champions the very attitudes that are either rejected or deplored in *Hard Times*. For example, when Henry Morley sent Dickens an article on the Manchester Strike, Dickens would not accept it until Morley had cut out his remark that the strikers were '*of course*, entirely and painfully in the wrong'. What else could the men do, Dickens wanted to know, if they could not obtain a peaceful hearing? It is a reasonable point. On the other hand, Morley might well have replied that in *Hard Times* Dickens himself had been entirely contemptuous of Slackbridge, the man who tries to bring the men out on what would seem to be a perfectly justifiable strike.

But the great answer to *Hard Times* is *Little Dorrit*. For *Little Dorrit* has none of the earlier novel's thinness or reductiveness. It is inexhaustibly rich in its enquiry into the sort of lives that *Hard Times* had simply dismissed, and far from dealing in the mere blacks and whites that are present in the fable, it has a complexity and range which its own elements of fable enrich rather than prohibit.

At first glance the material of *Little Dorrit* looks familiar enough. And this extends beyond what the novel is 'about' to the characters. Mrs Clennam looks back to Mrs Snagsby, and her world of hideous Sundays reminds us of Dickens's early essay on *Sunday Under Three Heads*. Gowan recalls a whole line of dilettantes which begins with Martin Chuzzlewit. Casby is like Pecksniff, the ways of Circumlocution echo the ways of Chancery, Rigaud is reminiscent of Tigg, the Plornishes are similar to the Toodles, Pancks to Newman Noggs, Merdle to Dombey, Dorrit to Micawber and even Miss Wade in some respects looks back to Rosa Dartle. Only Arthur, it seems, is really new. But of course it won't do. For the characters of *Little Dorrit* are only initially 'like' the characters of earlier novels. They are profoundly different because they are studied with a brooding intensity for which the invention of Arthur is a fit token. And as with characters so with themes. Class-snobbishness, dilettantism, money-lust, the dark horror of nonconformist religion, irresponsible government; and on the other side, work, good fellowship, love, duty, the family: all these familiar themes are explored in ways that make them utterly unfamiliar.

Little Dorrit uses the parodic echoic structure that Dickens had first discovered for himself in *Dombey and Son* and which he had enlarged on in *Bleak House*. And in *Little Dorrit* the echoes and parodies are of the prison. So much is obvious. It also takes us into mere cliché. What is far from cliché is the nature of *Little Dorrit*'s concern with prisons. And I think that this concern can be expressed as an attempt to discover whether society is entirely responsible for the many and different kinds of prisons which it creates or which at least seem to owe their existence to its existence, or whether some of them represent categories of experience that make up the human condition as such.

We start with the obvious prisons, of Marseilles and the Marshalsea. Wicked creations of an unjust society, we may say, fit symbols of the inequities they were built to preserve. Certainly, Dickens shows how absurd and wicked are the imprisonments of John Baptist and Plornish. But then what of Rigaud? It is with Rigaud in mind that Dickens has the French landlady say:

> 'And I tell you this, my friend, that there are people (men and women both, unfortunately) who have no good in them – none. That there are people whom it is necessary to detest without compromise. That there are people who must be dealt with as enemies of the human race. That there are people who have no human heart, and who must be crushed like savage beasts and cleared out of the way. (Bk 1, ch 11)

The difficulty is to decide how well these words apply to Rigaud. ' "Society sells itself and sells me: and I sell Society," ' he tells Clennam. If we take up the clue his name affords, we might see him dancing to the tune society calls. A more evil version of Mr Sludge, perhaps. Dickens of course hates Rigaud. He describes him waiting to be fed, 'with much of the expression of a wild beast in similar expectation'. (Bk 1, ch 1) And Trilling is certainly right to remark that for Dickens 'Because Blandois exists, prisons are necessary'. But we have still to accept that Rigaud exists because a society based on appearances exists, and that such a society deserves its villains. Not that this exonerates Rigaud. But it does suggest that the enemies of the human race are more difficult to pin down than the landlady's words imply. And the real horror is that it is often among good people that the enemies find the conditions in which to flourish.

There is, for example, Mr Rugg, mild, propitiatory, genuinely anxious to help and to please. It is he who warns Clennam of the writs out against him, after the loss of Doyce's money:

'Now, I find there's a little one out – a mere Palace Court injunction – and I have reason to believe that a caption may be made upon that. I wouldn't be taken upon that.'

'Why not?' asked Clennam.

'I'd be taken as a full-grown one, sir,' said Mr. Rugg. 'It's as well to keep up appearances. As your professional advisor, I should prefer your being taken on a writ from one of the Superior Courts, if you have no objection to do me that favour. It looks better.' (Bk 2, ch 26)

Mr Rugg is a very different sort of person from Mrs General, whose professional task in life is to form surfaces. Yet he shares with her and with many other characters of the novel that desire to keep up appearances by means of which Rigaud can find scope for existing.

But if *Little Dorrit* were merely concerned to highlight the absurdities and disasters of appearance it would be satire and nothing more. And it is so much more. For it becomes great as it enquires beneath the surface, into what happens to people who struggle for appearance. William Dorrit is certainly the occasion for satire, but that is not what makes Dickens's study of him so great. Dorrit is also a very disturbing character, as in the scene where Plornish offers him some halfpence:

The father of the Marshalsea had never been offered tribute in copper yet. His children often had, and with his perfect acquiescence it had gone into the common purse, to buy meat that he had eaten, and drink that he had drunk; but fustian splashed with white lime, bestowing halfpence on him, front to front, was new.

'How dare you!' he said to the man, and feebly burst into tears.

The plasterer turned him towards the wall, that his face might not be seen; and the action was so delicate, and the man was so penetrated with repentance, and asked pardon so honestly, that he could make him no less acknowledgement than, 'I know you meant it kindly. Say no more.' (Bk 1, ch 6)

In any illustration of *Little Dorrit*'s greatness that passage is a very good one from which to start. We notice in it Dickens's sure placing of self-deception, his ability to pin down without making coarse the fact of vanity and its accompanying self-pity, his recognition that the vice of appearance works at all levels of society – for Plornish's 'fustian' is as much an affront to Dorrit as is Clennam's appearance inside Lord Decimus Barnacle's house – his confident knowledge of the ways in which habits of deference and condescension are built into all social relationships. And having taken due note of all these things, we have then to go on to what is far more important, Dickens's refusal to make a simple or single judgement about Dorrit. He earns the right to judge him because he has such a full and compassionate under-standing of him. And it is remarkable but true, that although Dorrit is presented to us in all his faults of selfishness, weakness, vanity, self-deception, yet he never entirely forfeits our sym-pathy. Compassion is a word that is over-used and consequently degraded in critical discussion, but no other will do justice to Dickens's treatment of Dorrit. It took a brilliant artist to produce the scene where Dorrit condescends to Nandy. ' "We don't call this a shilling, Nandy, you know!" he said, putting one in his hand, "We call it tobacco." ' But it took a great one to write the following dialogue, where Dorrit tries to apologize to Amy for her life in the Marshalsea:

'My love, you have had a life of hardship here. No companions, no recreations, many cares I am afraid.'

'Don't think of that, dear. I never do.'

'You know my position here, Amy. I have not been able to do much for you; but all I have been able to do, I have done.'

'Yes, my dear father,' she rejoined, kissing him. 'I know, I know.'

'I am in the twenty-third year of my life here,' he said, with a catch in his breath that was not so much a sob as an irrepressible sound of self-approval, the momentary outburst of a noble consciousness. 'It is all I could do for my children – I have done it. Amy, my love, you are by far the best loved of the three; I have had you principally in my mind – whatever I have done for your

sake, my dear child, I have done freely and without murmuring.'
(Bk 1, ch 19)

Given this, there is no need for Dickens to add that 'Only the
wisdom that holds the clue to all hearts and all mysteries, can
surely know to what extent a man, especially a man brought
down as this one had been, can impose upon himself.' For he
himself has shown that he knows the extent: he demonstrates
it in the beautiful and attentive way he tracks the working of
Dorrit's mind from genuine concern for Amy through the
gathering excuse that begins to ward off acknowledgement of
guilt, to the final justification and retreat into self-pity. A scene
such as this testifies to Dickens's awareness of how the prison of
appearances shuts out self-knowledge and bars all true communication.

Dorrit's final collapse is the awful revenge of a mind that
eventually breaks out of its own prison and destroys its gaoler in
the process. And the scene where this is shown to happen as
Dorrit welcomes his guests in Italy to the Marshalsea seems to me
quite simply beyond criticism. I will only say that it is one more
example of that apt dramatization of a theme which I have repeatedly suggested is part of Dickens's greatness. I do, however,
think it worth noting Dorrit's pallid efforts at communication
after his breakdown. At the very last he becomes concerned for
the well-being of others. He manages to explain that he wants
Amy to raise money on his 'pompous gold watch that made as
great a to-do about its going, as if nothing else went but itself
and Time':

In another day or two he sent off his sleeve-buttons and finger-
rings. He had an amazing satisfaction in entrusting her with these
errands, and appeared to consider it equivalent to making the most
methodical and provident arrangements. After his trinkets, or such
of them as he had been able to see about him, were gone, his
clothes engaged his attention; and it is as likely as not that he was
kept alive for some days by the satisfaction of sending them, piece
by piece, to an imaginary pawnbroker. (Bk 2, ch 19)

Naked, unaccommodated man. More, a man instinctively trying to atone for his past by stripping away appearances in an effort to become responsible to and for others, and making one final effort to establish a form of communication with his daughter. Altogether, a man trying to break out of the prison of self.

And what is true of Dorrit is true of others. Merdle, for example. 'Mr Merdle was immensely rich; a man of prodigious enterprise; a Midas without ears, who turned all he touched into gold. He was in everything good, from banking to building.' (Bk 1, ch 21) We know where we are with this, especially when we read of Merdle's anxious desire 'to hide his hands'. Merdle is a man who is socially ill at ease and also aware of the dirty means by which he has gained wealth. He is constantly pushing his hands into their opposite coat-sleeves as though he is taking himself into custody. He is a dull, mindless tool of society, guaranteeing his wife's appearance by hanging jewels on her bosom, providing money, talk and dinner for others. He hardly ever speaks, and is most often seen alone in the pointlessness of his wealth, looking 'out of nine windows in succession, and appear [ing] to see nine wastes of space'. (Bk 1, ch 33) When he is dead, he is found to have had 'coarse, mean, common features', and to be a 'low, ignorant fellow'. And the full extent of his pointless existence becomes plain with the Butler's wish to give a month's notice since ' "Mr Merdle never was the gentleman, and no ungentlemanly act on Mr Merdle's part would surprise me." ' (Bk 2, ch 25) These details compose what seems to be a firm enough study in the social malaise of financial gain for the sake of respectability. It is an old Dickensian theme and inevitably it provides him with some fine satire on society's equation of money and virtue – Merdle's being in 'everything good' is an obvious but strong idea – and on the socially desirable anonymities who in eating with Merdle confer respectability on him: Horse-Guards, Treasury, Bar, Bishop, and so on.

Yet we have not done with Merdle when we have registered his presence in the satiric study of society that *Little Dorrit* offers us. For Dickens also explores in him the consequences of the prison of self into which he has shut himself, because of the prison of appearance which he has chosen to build for himself. There is nothing satiric about the scene where Merdle goes to see Fanny and Edmund Sparkler, just prior to committing suicide:

'I thought I'd give you a call,' he said. 'I am rather particularly occupied just now; and, as I happened to be out for a stroll, I thought I'd give you a call.' ...

At this period of his visit, Mr. Merdle took the chair which Edmund Sparkler had offered him, and which he had hitherto been pushing slowly about before him, like a dull man with a pair of skates on for the first time, who could not make up his mind to start. He now put his hat upon another chair beside him, and, looking down into it as if it were twenty feet deep, said again: 'You see I thought I'd give you a call.'

'Flattering to us,' said Fanny, 'for you are not a calling man.'

'No – no,' returned Mr. Merdle, who was by this time taking himself into custody under both coat-sleeves. 'No, I'm not a calling man.' (Bk. 2, ch 24)

The scene goes on for much longer and I realize that quotation cannot communicate its power and awful truth. Yet even as little as I have quoted gives, I think, a fair indication of Dickens's concern with Merdle's last pathetic attempts to communicate with his daughter-in-law and so break out of his prison of self. There is nothing sentimental about the scene. Merdle remains stupid, dull, shut into himself, even grotesquely comic. Yet he also becomes an object of compassion, for the appalling facts of his loneliness and wasted life are forced on our attention. And they are nowhere more apparent than in our final view of him, absurdly distorted through Fanny's tears of bored vexation, which 'had the effect of making the famous Mr Merdle, in going down the street, appear to leap, and waltz, and gyrate, as if he were possessed by several Devils'. It is funny, ridiculous, and unutterably sad.

Fanny cannot see Merdle plain because she too is locked into the prison of self. And again Dickens goes beyond the surface presentation in trying to understand and account for the damage that Fanny does to herself. He has a considerable admiration for her. He admires the pluck with which she sticks out Mrs Merdle's cool insults when that lady buys the girl off, as she hopes, from Edmund Sparkler. And he makes entirely credible her anguish of indecision about whether she should marry Sparkler at all. The handling of this scene perhaps derives from the moment in *Martin Chuzzlewit* where Mercy expresses her doubts about Jonas, though Fanny is far more consistently and finely rendered. She is a marvellous study in vacillation, and of particular concern to the present discussion because of Dickens's convincing demonstration of the fact that a person of Fanny's wit, vivacity and intelligence can become trapped by her desire to triumph socially. For she knows that Sparkler is an oaf (though even he is treated with considerate restraint). Fanny tells Amy that she has not the least intention of marrying Sparkler

'. . . to-night, my dear, or to-morrow morning either'.
'But at some time?'
'At no time, for anything I know at present,' answered Fanny, with indifference. Then, suddenly changing her indifference into a burning restlessness, she added, 'You talk about the clever men, you little thing! It's all very fine and easy to talk about the clever men; but where are they? *I* don't see them anywhere near *me*!'
'My dear Fanny, so short a time –'
'Short time or long time,' interrupted Fanny. 'I am impatient to change our situation. I don't like our situation, and very little would induce me to change it. Other girls, differently reared and differently circumstanced altogether, might wonder at what I say or do. Let them. They are driven by their lives and characters; I am driven by mine.'
'Fanny, my dear Fanny, you know that you have qualities to make you the wife of one very superior to Mr. Sparkler.'
'Amy, my dear Amy,' retorted Fanny, parodying her words, 'I know that I wish to have a more defined and distinct position, in which I can assert myself with greater effect against that insolent woman.' (Bk 2, ch 14)

Much of *Little Dorrit*'s greatness comes from its extraordinary sustained richness – of all the full-length novels it is the one with fewest expendable passages – so that to quote from only part of any dialogue is inevitably to offend against its worth. Still, this short extract does give some idea of how much more profound and sympathetic is Dickens's study of Fanny Dorrit than James's of Millicent Henning, fine though that undoubtedly is. For what James does not understand is the intense effect of class considerations that operate at every level of society and act as a sort of ceaseless yeast in people's lives. In trying to identify Millicent's desire to better herself James speaks of the 'ulcer of envy'. But the phrase does not do justice to the complex motives for human conduct that Dickens analyses. He knows that Fanny's 'burning restlessness' is a vitally conditioning factor in any number of lives; and he knows too that it perpetuates those social factors which bring it about. Samuel Smiles came nearer to the heart of the matter than James, when he spoke about the

> 'dreadful ambition for being "genteel." We must keep up appearances, too often at the expense of honesty; and though we may not be rich, yet we must seem to be so. We must be "respectable," though only in the meanest sense – in mere vulgar outward show.'

It is an observation that goes well with much in Dickens's novels, though Smiles spoils it all by adding that 'We have not the courage to go patiently onward in the condition of life in which it has pleased God to call us.'[1] Dickens would be unlikely to make that mistake. He knows only too well that the condition of life in which a man finds himself is man-made and therefore challengeable, as Fanny proves. The cost is terrible. Yet it at least has a vitality to it that makes it preferable to such habits of deference as Plornish exemplifies when he speaks to Clennam about William Dorrit:

> 'Ah! And there's manners! There's polish! There's a gentleman to have to run to seed in the Marshalsea Jail! Why, perhaps you are not aware,' said Plornish, lowering his voice and speaking with a perverse admiration of what he ought to have pitied and despised

[1] *Self-Help*, op. cit., p. 354.

'not aware that Miss Dorrit and her sister dursn't let him know that they work for a living. No!' said Plornish, looking with a ridiculous triumph at his wife, and then all round the room. 'Dursn't let him know it, they dursn't!' (Bk 1, ch 12)

And yet Plornish himself is desperately unhappy because he cannot get work. Dickens shows that Plornish does not suffer from the ulcer of envy but from that much more vicious malaise of the identification of class with worth, the belief that the class-system is good because it exists.

Meagles is also a victim of the disease. '"Aye, aye!" said Meagles. "A Barnacle is he? *We* know something of that family, eh, Dan? By George, they are at the top of the tree, though!"' (Bk 1, ch 17) And Meagles finds himself in the ludicrous position of abasing himself before a family whose incapacities for public office he justly hates. I think we do best by Dickens if we see the Barnacles as scum that the social yeast forces to the top. For we can hardly take them to represent an important satire in government. Their nepotism, their enemy 'the public', their watery-minded speaking habits: these compose a decent but limited satire which grew, we know, out of Dickens's rage at governmental bungling of the Crimean War and its sheer incompetence in home affairs. But the satire does not belong to the deepest and truest reaches of *Little Dorrit*.

Meagles's obsequiousness is a much greater matter than the satire on Barnaclism. Dickens does not merely show that Meagles's type of social fawning is a fact among 'good' men, but that it is an important part of the social process by means of which the Barnacles are kept in positions of authority and because of which people suffer. Indeed, it is remarkable that Dickens manages to keep sympathy with Meagles at all, considering how far he is prepared to go in showing his philistinism, his complacent insularity, his condescension to Tattycoram and Doyce, his deference to rank. And it is certainly part of *Little Dorrit*'s greatness that we should be made convincingly aware of Meagles's faults and yet be persuaded of his decency. His being good-hearted is not a cliché, because Dickens is able to show his capacity for suffering. He is deeply affected both by his daughter's marriage and by Tattycoram's disappearance. But Dickens does not soften his presentation. He shows us how culpable Meagles is. His attitude to Tattycoram is kindly meant but obtuse. We do not need to offer obvious suggestions about reification to see that his chosen name for the little girl is deeply offensive to her individuality. His determination never to know a foreign language is vulgar (it is echoed by the Bleeding-Heart Yarders' belief that 'every foreigner had a knife about him', and that any foreigner 'ought to go home to his own country'). And in addition Dickens has a very intense dislike for Meagles's 'curious sense of a general superiority to Daniel Doyce, which seemed to be founded, not so much on anything in Doyce's personal character, as on the mere fact of his being an originator and a man out of the beaten track of other men'. (Bk 1, ch 16)

Meagles's faults cause him to suffer, for they involve him in supporting a social process by which he can hardly hope to profit. Not that Dickens offers a simple moral rebuke. It is more that Meagles is bewildered into suffering; he does wrong without fully knowing it. But it harms him for all that. He is not unlike the Satan of Blake's *Milton*, 'Seeming a brother, being a tyrant, even thinking himself a brother/While he is murdering the just.' And although those words are perhaps too harsh for Meagles, it has to be admitted that in him as in so many other characters in *Little Dorrit*, Dickens scrutinizes behaviour and precept with an intensity that is quite new to him. That is why I have to speak at length about the novel's characters. For *Little Dorrit* provides a great creative criticism of the terrible damage done to human potentialities by beliefs, assumptions and social attitudes that seem to exercise a vast and growing tyranny over the finer possibilities of life. After all, Meagles knows that Gowan is an evil person, but Gowan comes from precisely that social class which it gives Meagles such satisfaction to contemplate and members of which he is so persistently keen to introduce into his household. How then should Meagles oppose the marriage of Pet and Gowan?

Gowan for his part is a man of great expectations. He tells Clennam that although he is lucky to have found Pet:

'Still, I had other prospects washed and combed into my childish head when it was washed and combed for me, and I took them to a public school when I washed and combed it for myself, and I am here without them, and thus I am a disappointed man.' (Bk 1, ch 34)

Gowan's dissolute aimlessness is fully part of the social process. Tip Dorrit echoes it. He asserts the family gentility 'by coming out in the character of the aristocratic brother', which requires him to tire of everything he does. As Fanny remarks, '"Edward is frightfully expensive and dissipated. I don't mean that there is anything ungenteel in that itself – far from it."' (Bk 2, ch 14) It is a vital part of the process that Henry Gowan and his mother should triumph over the Meagles. We see how brilliantly Dickens combines social probabilities with Meagles's sufferings in the great chapter, 'The Dowager Mrs. Gowan is Reminded That It Never Does'. And although it is quite impossible to do justice to the writing by tearing out a few sentences, the following give some idea of Dickens's mastery over his material. Mrs Gowan has just arrived at the Meagles's house:

'And how do you both do, Papa and Mama Meagles?' said she, encouraging her humble connexions. 'And when did you last hear from or about my poor fellow?'

My poor fellow was her son; and this mode of speaking about him politely kept alive, without any offence in the world, the pretence that he had fallen a victim to the Meagles' wiles.

'And the dear pretty one?' said Mrs. Gowan. 'Have you later news of her than I have?'

Which also delicately implied that her son had been captured by mere beauty, and under its fascination had foregone all sorts of worldly advantages.

'I am sure,' said Mrs. Gowan, without straining her attention on the answers she received, 'it's an unspeakable comfort to know they continue happy. My poor fellow is of such a restless disposition, and has been so used to roving about, and to being inconstant and popular among all manner of people, that it's the greatest comfort in life. I suppose they're as poor as mice, Papa Meagles?'

Mr. Meagles, fidgety under the question, replied, 'I hope not, ma'am. I hope they will manage their little income.'

'Oh! my dearest Meagles!' returned that lady, tapping him on the arm with the green fan and then adroitly interposing it between a yawn and the company, 'how can you, as a man of the world and one of the most business-like of human-beings – for you know you are business-like, and a great deal too much for us who are not –'

(Which went to the former purpose, by making Mr. Meagles out to be an artful schemer). (Bk 2, ch 8)

In an earlier novel Mrs Gowan would have been dealt her come-uppance. But here Dickens refuses all the chances for an explosion of righteous indignation. It is part of the social process that Meagles should be so helplessly humiliated. This is perhaps to labour the point, but I think that it is not sufficiently recognized how much more than satire *Little Dorrit* is, nor how it provides an exploration of a society whose essential movements are created by and so create the pervasive prison-taint of class and all that it involves: envy, vanity, wounded pride, the desire for power and dominance (Dickens is especially good at noting the sheer aggressiveness of people to each other), deference, money-lust, respectability and gentility: in short, all those elements which curb or thwart the decent human energies.

Yet Dickens probes deeper still. He enquires into prisons of self whose cause is certainly problematic and which may not have all that much to do with the social content. Mr F's Aunt clearly does not belong to the novel's social analysis, but she is no less relevant to its total concern:

The major characteristics discoverable by the stranger in Mr. F's Aunt, were extreme severity and grim taciturnity; sometimes interrupted by a propensity to offer remarks in a deep warning voice, which, being totally uncalled for by anything said by any-body, and traceable to no association of ideas, confounded and terrified the mind. Mr. F's Aunt may have thrown in these observations on some system of her own, and it may have been ingenious, or even subtle; but the key to it was wanted. (Bk 1, ch 13)

She is of course funny, but she is also part of Dickens's disturbed and disturbing enquiry into failures of communication. The enquiry shows itself in the study of Flora, pathetically and grotesquely imprisoned in a past that cannot be realized in the present. Mr F's Aunt is grotesque rather than pathetic, an unknowable comic mystery. She is reminiscent of some of Wordsworth's studies of incommunicability in the *Lyrical Ballads*. But like Wordsworth, Dickens is too aware of the horror and pathos of isolation to treat it as merely comic. Hence Maggy, also very near to a Wordsworthian perception. She is touching, pitiable, grotesque. Dickens does not sentimentalize her:

> Her large eyes were limpid and almost colourless; they seemed to be very little affected by light, and to stand unnaturally still. There was also that attentive listening expression in her face, which is seen in the faces of the blind; but she was not blind, having one tolerably serviceable eye. Her face was not exceedingly ugly, though it was only redeemed from being so by a smile; a good-humoured smile, and pleasant in itself, but rendered pitiable by constantly being there. (Bk 1, ch 9)

It is the constant qualifications that prevent us from taking a single or simple view of Maggy. The perceptions turn and turn again and unsettle us from a fixed view of the girl. Indeed the description of her is not only fine evidence of Dickens's sympathetic fullness of response to his characters, it also meets the requirements that George Eliot laid down for moral realism in *Adam Bede*. I shall have more to say about this in my last chapter, but it is worth quoting here her famous claim that

> these fellow-mortals, every one, must be accepted as they are: you can neither straighten their noses, nor brighten their wit, nor rectify their dispositions; and it is these people – among whom your life is passed – that it is needful you should tolerate, pity, and love: it is these more or less ugly, stupid, inconsistent people whose movements of goodness you should be able to admire. (ch 17)

It is difficult to see how these demands could be better met than in the study of Maggy. Not that they have always to be, given Dickens's interests. It would be quite irrelevant for him to bother about any individual movements of goodness in Mrs Merdle, since he is interested in her merely as a functional part of the social process. But with Maggy it is different, since for her the prison of self seems barely attributable to the process; the gin-drinking grandmother who brought her up is not essential to the case of her arrested growth. It is more that with Maggy, as with Mr F's Aunt and even Flora, Dickens testifies to the sombre mystery of lives that are broken or warped through accident or undiscoverable chance, though Maggy's life is made meaningful because of her effort to use to the full such gifts as she has. None of these people is a victim of the prison of society; and in presenting them for what they are Dickens resists any suggestion that there can be a simple equation between a healthy society and healthy individuals. And this brings us to Miss Wade.

I think it a mistake that Miss Wade should be spoken of as a lesbian. Dickens's daring does not lie in his suggestion of her sexual deviancy. Indeed, Miss Wade hates society as a whole, not just men. No, the study is great and terribly disturbing because of Dickens's ability to convince us of Miss Wade's intelligence and wit and the way these feed on chimera, so that she locks herself totally into a prison of paranoiac delusion. Faced with what Dickens shows us of Miss Wade we are likely to be reminded of Imlac's words: 'Of the uncertainties of our present state, the most dreadful and alarming is the uncertain continuance of reason.' It is impossible to quote the whole of the 'History of A Self-Tormentor', though nothing less will do if we are to begin to take the measure of Dickens's enquiry into Miss Wade's psychosis. But the following passage at least gives us some indication of how her prison has been painstakingly built up by an intelligence working on a thwarted need for love that perverts with monstrous cunning such offers of love as she receives. She is speaking of her time as governess at a house where she decides that the nurse has taken all the children's affection to herself:

The most crafty of her many subtleties was her feint of seeking to make the children fonder of me...

It became intolerable. Her ladyship my Mistress coming in one day when I was alone, and at the height of feeling I could support it no longer, I told her I must go. I could not bear the presence of that woman Dawes.

'Miss Wade! Poor Dawes is devoted to you; would do anything for you!'

I knew beforehand she would say so; I was quite prepared for it; I only answered, it was not for me to contradict my Mistress; I must go.

'I hope, Miss Wade,' she returned, instantly assuming the tone of superiority she had always thinly concealed, 'that nothing I have ever said or done since we have been together, has justified your use of that disagreeable word, Mistress. It must have been wholly inadvertant on my part. Pray tell me what it is.'

I replied that I had no complaint to make, either of my Mistress or to my Mistress; but, I must go.

She hesitated for a moment, and then sat down beside me, and laid her hand on mine. As if that honour would obliterate any remembrance!

'Miss Wade, I fear you are unhappy, through causes over which I have no influence.'

I smiled, thinking of the experience the word awakened, and said, 'I have an unhappy temper, I suppose.'

'I did not say that.'

'It is an easy way of accounting for anything,' said I.

'It may be; but I did not say so. What I wish to approach, is something very different. My husband and I have exchanged some remarks upon the subject, when we have observed with pain that you have not been easy with us.'

'Easy? Oh! you are such great people, my lady,' said I. (Bk 2, ch 21)

There is no doubt that Miss Wade is aided in building her prison by the social context in which she finds herself. But Dickens is far from suggesting that because she is an orphan and becomes a governess she is therefore victimized by her own mind. And his attitude to her is not prompted by simple resignation in the

face of what life does to such a person. His compassion is at one
with his effort to understand her. It is difficult not to sound glib
in suggesting that Dickens shows his own profound sanity and
humaneness in the way he treats Miss Wade, yet it has to be said.
And it applies equally to his study of Mrs Clennam.

There is a really fearful unnaturalness about Mrs Clennam. I
think, for example, of her threat to banish Arthur should he
attempt to enquire into the mysteries surrounding his father's
business. '"I will never see or know you more. And if, after all,
you were to come into the darkened room to look upon me
lying dead, my body should bleed, if I could make it, when you
came near me."' (Bk 1, ch 5) There is the gloomy pride with
which she speaks of being 'justly infirm and righteously in-
flicted'. And there is her unyielding rigidity of countenance and
posture. Yet in a sense there is no point in detailing the handling
of Mrs Clennam, for everything about it is so unerringly right
and just that we have simply to say that it is true. The collapse
of her house is sometimes criticized on the grounds that the
moment is too conveniently symbolic. Yet I think it fits perfectly into the folk-tale element of *Little Dorrit*. It has about it a
note of that inevitability which is first sounded in Miss Wade's
words about the inexorable patterns of life, and it symbolizes not
so much a sort of poetic justice as the unpreventable destructiveness of Mrs Clennam's life which her partial effort at atonement
cannot prevent. To object against the episode seems to me to
misunderstand Dickens's audacity, his unerring instinct for
taking advantage of all the means that allow him the fullest possession of his subject.

But what is his subject? Or rather, why is he so interested in
Mrs Clennam? We could offer some answers that would be
partial truths: that she is one more of the unnatural parents so
common to his novels, that she combines the disease of avarice
with the equally diseased desire to suffer. But this does not go to
the heart of the matter. Mrs Clennam is entangled in the social
process. And in a way that is admittedly difficult to pin down she
embodies destroyed possibilities and perverted energies which I

am sure Dickens fears may express a fundamental truth about his society. Mrs Clennam is no less a victim than is Meagles, but in a far more radical way, since the very root of her being has been poisoned. It is not that through her Dickens makes an accusation against mid-Victorian society. The nature of *Little Dorrit* would not permit so simple a confrontation. It is more that his study of her raises profoundly disquieting possibilities which, if they look inward to her own tormented way of life, also look outward to the society which seems to have much to do with creating it.

This point leads us to other prisons of self that the novel explores. For surrounding all the other prisons is a pervasive atmosphere of predatoriness. This is not entirely new. It is there already in *Oliver Twist*, although in that novel its cause is identified purely in economic and class terms. People who are starving or rejected by society do not owe it anything and therefore get what they can the nearest way. This notion is still present in *Bleak House* and it certainly has not disappeared from *Little Dorrit*. It is after all a truth. But there is a substantial difference between *Little Dorrit* and the earlier novels. For one has the feeling that where earlier Dickens is confident about having tracked down the causes of self-seeking, here he is more questioning, hesitant, and finally far more sombre. One way of explaining this new note would be to say that in *Little Dorrit* Dickens has come to accept both that there is a horrifying mystery about the prisons people build for themselves and that there may be such a thing as motiveless evil. And I do not think here of Rigaud so much as of Gowan, of Flintwinch, and of Casby: of all those who buy or sell people into captivity. '"The chances are that the more you give [a man], the more he'll impose on you,"' Gowan tells Clennam. '"But what a capital world it is."' (Bk 1, ch 26) It is part of Gowan's utter depravity that he should make no judgements at all. '"I am happy to tell you I find the most worthless of men to be the dearest old fellow too,"' he remarks to Meagles. (Bk 1, ch 17) Marriage is often the token of evil in the novel: Pet, Affery, even Flora ('"Mr. F. proposed with the full approval of Papa and what could I do?"'), are all the helpless victims of other people's wills. And we have to note that even William Dorrit in an irresolute, half-ashamed, half-self-pitying way, tries to persuade Amy to accept young Chivery, or at least to pretend to do so. The feeling of people's helplessness is very strong in the novel. It runs through the social satire and Doyce's inability to persuade Barnaclism to make use of his invention, through the study of self as appearance in which people become so trapped that they are made to behave in accordance with their appearances, through those who are victims of their own broken or warped minds, and finally to the many individuals who are imprisoned in the steely will of others. And how with this rage of self shall anything hold plea?

Will duty? '"She has done her duty,"' Frederick Dorrit says of Amy, and Dickens means it as high praise. Indeed, he is so determined to force the point about Little Dorrit that at one point he nods badly in allowing Meagles – of all people – to recommend duty to Tattycoram.

> 'Duty, Tattycoram. Begin it early and do it well; and there is no antecedent to it, in origin, or station, that will tell against us with the Almighty, or with ourselves.' (Bk 2, ch 32)

But what is duty? It defines Amy's worth. 'Everyone must find in his work the centre of his life,' Rilke wrote to Kappus, 'and thence be able to grow out radially as far as may be.' For Amy, duty is closely linked to work. '"Years of toil eh?" said Pancks, softly, touching [her hand] with his blunt forefinger. "But what else are we made for? Nothing."' (Bk 1, ch 25) Dickens makes such detailed use of hands in the novel that they almost plot his interests. Rigaud's are 'unusually small and plump' and unusually white, William Dorrit's are remarkable for their 'irresolute fingers', Merdle is 'anxious to hide his hands', Mrs Merdle's hands are not a pair, 'the left being much the whiter and plumper of the two' (the hand sinister is that of the lady), Miss Wade has a 'repressing hand', John Baptist has 'swart, knotted hands'; and Pancks has 'dirty broken hands and dirty broken nails'. For Pancks duty is degradation. '"I belong body and soul to my employer,"' he says, and it is so:

> '*Don't* I squeeze [the people]?' retorted Mr. Pancks. 'What else am I made for?'
>
> 'You are made for nothing else, Mr. Pancks. You are made to do your duty, but you don't do your duty. You are paid to squeeze and you must squeeze to pay.' (Bk 2, ch 31)

Dickens's success with Pancks depends on his not sentimentalizing him. He uses Pancks to challenge the bland recommendations for work that are so obvious a feature of even humane thought in the 1850s.

My remark may seem unfair to Ruskin, perhaps the most vocal champion of work as ideal fulfilment of the human potential. It was Ruskin who said that 'It may be proved with much certainty, that God intends no man to live in the world without working,' but he also added that 'it seems to me no less evident that He intends every man to be happy in his work'.[1] And in his analysis of the 'operative' in the famous section on the 'Nature of Gothic' in the *Stones of Venice*, Ruskin spent some time showing what was wrong with the concept of work in Victorian England. Certainly his argument comes very close to the case that Dickens explores in Pancks. If men are forced to operate in fixed patterns untrue to their own capacities and interests, Ruskin says, then their free spirit will be destroyed:

> It is verily this degradation of the operative into a machine, which, more than any other evil of the times, is leading the masses of the nations everywhere into vain, incoherent, destructive struggling for a freedom of which they cannot explain the nature to themselves.[2]

Pancks is 'like a little labouring steam-engine' and, if not an operative, can certainly stand for all those who are forced to accept that 'the kind of labour to which they are condemned is verily a degrading one, and makes them less than men'.[3] The

[1] From the Lecture on 'Pre-Raphaelitism', 1851. *Works*, Vol. XII, p. 341.

[2] *The Stones of Venice*, *Works*, Vol. X, pp. 193–4.

[3] Ibid., p. 194.

difference between Ruskin and Dickens lies not so much in their analysis of what happens to work in Victorian England, as in the fact that Ruskin is free to construct alternatives which are unavailable to Dickens's purpose. He cannot allow himself what would be the indulgence of imaging the 'free' life that Ruskin locates in the work of Gothic craftsmen. Do not mock Gothic gargoyles, Ruskin says:

> they are signs of the life and liberty of every workman who struck the stone; a freedom of thought, and rank in scale of being, such as no laws, no charters, no charities can secure: but which it must be the first aim of all Europe at this day to secure for her children.[1]

Great man though Ruskin is, it has to be said that his cast of mind all too readily leads him into the vague and unrealizable visions that take increasing hold on him in his later work. When we consider that Dickens's awareness of what was happening to England is even more appalled than Ruskin's, we can surely see that it is an essential part of his achievement that he should not seek release from social probabilities in what he shows. We are not meant to take Pancks's shearing of Casby's hair as symbolic of a representative act that typifies a struggle for freedom. Cathartic though the action is, it delivers Pancks from the representativeness that Dickens has achieved through him and might even be said to create a momentary flaw in the novel's social realism. But for the most part the realism is magnificently present:

> 'You lead such a busy life?'
> 'Yes, I have always some of 'em to look up, or something to look after. But what I like is business,' said Pancks, getting on a little faster. 'What's a man made for?'
> 'For nothing else?' said Clennam.
> Pancks put the counter question, 'What else?' It packed up, in the smallest compass, a weight that had rested on Clennam's life; and he had no answer....
> 'Here am I,' said Pancks ... 'What else do you suppose I think I am made for? Nothing. Rattle me out of bed early, set me going,

[1] *Stones of Venice, Works*, Vol. X, pp. 193–4.

give me as short a time as you like to bolt my meals in, and keep
me at it. Keep me always at it, and I'll keep you always at it, you
keep somebody else always at it. There you are with the Whole
Duty of Man in a commercial country.'

When they had walked a little further in silence, Clennam said:
'Have you no taste for anything, Mr. Pancks?'

'What's taste?' drily retorted Pancks.

'Let us say inclination.'

'I have an inclination to get money, sir,' said Pancks, 'if you
will show me how.' (Bk 1, ch 13)

Pancks of course is more than the mere machine that he pretends
to be, though it would be wrong to feel that Dickens deflects
the issue by not making him the sort of operative that Ruskin had
in mind. Pancks's work is degrading and meaninglessly cruel
right enough. But for all Casby's ownership of him, he manages
to keep open some loopholes for his spirit. His kindness to Little
Dorrit, his ability to communicate with John Baptist, and above
all his subversion of Casby's instructions to squeeze the Bleeding-
Heart Yarders – he 'squeezes' without taking their money –
demonstrate that his work is not literally soul-destroying. But
it might well be. Pancks's dry wit at Arthur's expense shows that
Dickens realizes how far belonging body and soul to your
employer can kill off all human capacities. But in inventing
Pancks he rejects the convenient deterministic simplicities of
Hard Times. And he does more. For through Pancks he also
demonstrates something that is true to the nature of social
change and implies a resourcefulness – optimism would be too
insistent a word – that Ruskin lacks. In Pancks's duplicitous
treatment of Casby's tenants we can see Dickens's imaginative
grasp of the inevitable failure of the capitalist dream of a country
united in aim and purpose. Pancks of course does not do much
harm to Casby's business. But it is not fanciful to suggest that
within the social realities that the novel entertains, he embodies
the promise of human resistance to a wicked system.

The point is important because it helps us become aware that
Dickens's concern with the prison of society is not settling for

a statement of bleak hopelessness. The possibilities and potentialities of change are allowed for, not so much in Pancks's shearing
of Casby as in his refusal to become a mere machine. Pancks is
not destroyed, for all that his destruction might be predicted from
the way he is meant to fit into the syndrome of the Whole Duty
of Man. He stands out, not necessarily as a typical example but
as an example none the less, against those helpless victims I have
already mentioned and of which I now need to say more.
Plornish is one. And Dickens's presentation of him testifies to the
wonderful complexity and comprehensive truthfulness of *Little
Dorrit*. Plornish is not a machine, but he accepts the process he
finds himself in far more readily than Pancks does. For him the
process might as well be a system. He admires Dorrit as a true
gentleman and Casby for being a landlord. Frederick Dorrit is
another and different kind of victim. He is, in fact, a terribly
disturbing image of a person whom years of meaningless toil
have all but drained of human identity: ' "I am merely passing
on, like the shadow over the sun-dial," ' he tells Clennam.
(Bk 1, ch 8)

Because Dickens can present us with Plornish, Pancks and
Frederick Dorrit, we gain some idea of the greatness of his novel.
And it has to be said that Pancks himself is far from being
intended as an entire answer to the sort of dark sense Ruskin
entertains, of destroyed human capacities in mid-Victorian
society. Quite apart from his being representative of only a small
resistant factor, Pancks's limitations are in themselves very real;
'taste' does not have any meaning for him. This is partly because
by the 1850s taste is often regarded as the 'badge of culture'
which Matthew Arnold was to distinguish from true culture.
Taste is a matter of class-identity, connected with leisure, and it
is part of Dickens's tactful awareness of the social process that he
should show Pancks as resisting it. If he were to aim at becoming a
man of taste, he would be in the way to destroying his own
identity.[1] Yet the possibilities of that identity are of course sadly

[1] I have written about the problem of taste and class in my essay on 'Mrs.
Gaskell and Brotherhood'.

diminished by what it may not include. This is one of the absurd tragedies of the social process.

Naturally, Meagles affects to be a man of taste. It goes with his desire to gain an identity that will put him on terms with the gentry. And Dickens is not philistinic about this. There is nothing crude about his dislike for Meagles's affectation. It springs from his awareness of how taste as the badge of class prevents true involvement with art:

> Of [his] pictorial acquisitions Mr. Meagles spoke in the usual manner. He was no judge, he said, except of what pleased himself; he had picked them up, dirt-cheap, and people *had* considered them rather fine. One man, who at any rate ought to know something of the subject, had declared that 'Sage, Reading' . . . to be a fine Guercino. As for Sebastion del Piombo there, you could judge for yourself; if it were not his late manner, the question was, Who was it? Titian, that might or might not be – perhaps he had only touched it. Daniel Doyce said perhaps he hadn't touched it, but Mr. Meagles rather declined to overhear the remark. (Bk 1, ch 16)

Meagles's interest in painting is of a piece with his interest in the Barnacles. It is the name, not the substance, which impresses him. And since to possess taste is to show yourself as a gentleman, Dickens pushed the point further in having Gowan marry Pet. For Gowan is nothing if not a man of taste:

> In his expressed opinions of all performances in the Art of Painting that were completely destitute of merit, Gowan was the most liberal fellow on earth. He would declare such a man to have more power in his little finger (provided he had none), than such another had (provided he had much) in his whole mind and body. If the objection were taken that the thing commended was trash, he would reply, on behalf of his art, 'My good fellow, what do we all turn out but trash. *I* turn out nothing else, and I make you a present of the confession.' (Bk 2, ch 6)

Taste is the possession of the gentleman, the Amateur. Mrs Gowan's remarks about her son's 'pursuit' are important here. It is, she says, '"a very respectable pursuit, I dare say, and some artists are, as artists, quite superior persons; still, we never yet in our family have gone beyond an Amateur."' (Bk 1, ch 26) To do so would of course be in bad taste. I imagine that I do not need to document the Victorian obsession with the artist as gentleman-dilettante, it is so obvious a feature of the time. Dickens's hatred of Gowan is no less obvious. And Meagles deeply distrusts him. Yet Meagles's attitude to art and class helps perpetuate the Gowans. And by the same token, it hampers the man who ought to be of great benefit to society. Which brings us to Doyce.

I think it is a mistake to jump too swiftly to the conclusion that since Gowan is the man of taste then Doyce is the true artist. It is more that Doyce's totally satisfying involvement in his work provides an image of fulfilment that is nearly unique in *Little Dorrit*. In an attempt to define what Dickens's interest in him is, we might say that he is something like an amalgam of Carlyle's ideal poet and Ruskin's thinking-worker. Carlyle's praise of Goethe is well known. He was 'a clear and universal *Man*', neither 'noble nor plebeian, neither liberal nor servile, nor infidel, nor devotee; but the best excellence of all these joined in pure union'.[1] Carlyle admired Goethe for holding governmental office, like Petrarch and Boccaccio, who 'though reverenced as Poets, were not supposed to have lost their wits as men; but could be employed in the highest service of the state, not only as fit, but as the fittest, to discharge these'.[2] Carlyle's recommendation of Goethe is close to Dickens's praise of Doyce for his 'composed and unobtrusive self-sustainment', his 'calm knowledge that what was true must remain true', and his determination to press for the acceptance of his invention since it is 'serviceable to the nation'. (Bk 1, ch 16) And the two come closer still in this crucial passage about Doyce:

> There was something almost ludicrous in the complete irreconcil-
> ability of a vague conventional notion that he must be a visionary
> man, with the precise, sagacious travelling of his eye and thumb
> over the plans, their patient stoppages at particular points, their

[1] *Critical and Miscellaneous Essays*, Vol. I, p. 214.
[2] Ibid., Vol. III, p. 200.

careful returns to other points whence little channels of explanation had to be traced up, and his steady manner of making everything good and everything sound, at each important stage, before
taking his hearer on a line's-breadth further. His dismissal of himself from his description, was hardly less remarkable. He never
said, I discovered this adaptation or invented that combination;
but showed the whole thing as if the Divine artificer had made it,
and he happened to find it. So modest was he about it, such a
pleasant touch of respect was mingled with his quiet admiration
of it, and so calmly convinced he was that it was established on
irrefragable laws. (Bk 2, ch 8)

It would be tempting to see in this passage a re-statement of the
Romantic concept of the artist: truth-teller through whom God
speaks and the unacknowledged legislator of mankind to boot.
Certainly Doyce's knowledge of the truth does not admit of
doubt on his part and is not meant to be doubted by us. Yet
Dickens also stresses his practicality, and if we take this to mean
that Doyce's genius is of use to the nation and that Meagles's
condescension is absurd, we must also recognize that Doyce
represents the sort of fusion of idea and work which Ruskin so
admired. We make a bad mistake, Ruskin claimed, when we
think 'that manual labour is degradation, when it is governed by
intellect'. Our trouble is that 'We want one man to be always
thinking, and another to be always working, whereas the work-
man ought often to be thinking, and the thinker often to be
working'.[1] True, Ruskin sees in such an aim the possibility of
breaking down class-distinctions; but he is just as much concerned that all men should lead the fullest lives of which they are
capable. And Doyce is the image of Ruskin's ideal fusion of
thought and labour in total creativity. He works 'for the work's
sake'. He may be linked to Rodin's cry, 'il faut toujours travailler',
or Forster's statement that for the artist 'the process of creation
is its own achievement'.

Yet even so, Doyce is not finally to be equated with the artist.
It is true that the artist is a persuasive instance of the fulfilment

[1] *Stones of Venice, Works*, Vol. X, p. 201.

that he embodies, but after all Dickens shows us that Doyce as the practical man is an employer with a small works: he is linked more nearly to the common experience of life than we can allow for if we call him 'the artist'. When he leaves for France, his workmen cheer him on his way, and one says that:

> 'Wherever you go, they'll find as they've got a man among 'em, a man as knows his tools and as his tools knows, a man as is willing and a man as is able, and if that's not a man where is a man.' (Bk 2, ch 22)

In this tribute to Doyce's intense practicality, there may be some reflection of Dickens's own proud and fierce involvement in the daily task of editorial work. Yet I think that by making Doyce an employer, his author endeavours to present him as less of an exception and more in the mainstream of Victorian life. And without doubt, his integrity, belief in work, dedication to his ideas, suggest much that is true of the best of middle-class manufacturers of the time. Doyce may be compared with Mrs Gaskell's Thornton and contrasted with Dickens's own Bounderby.

But for all that Doyce remains something of an exception. He is a genius, and very close indeed to Ruskin's definition of one:

> The fact is that a man of genius is always far more ready to work than other people, and gets so much more good from the work he does, and is often so little conscious of the inherent divinity in himself, that he is very apt to ascribe all his capacity to his work . . . in whatever field [genius] will always be distinguished by its perpetual, steady, well-directed, happy, and faithful labour in accumulating and disciplining its powers, as well as by its gigantic, incommunicable facility in exercising them.[1]

For Doyce work is meaningful, whereas for Pancks and Frederick Dorrit it is virtually meaningless, and it is typical of the great honesty of *Little Dorrit* that Dickens should face this issue. Ruskin, after all, deflects the problem by saying that a man needn't bother about whether he is a genius:

[1] *Works*, Vol. XII, p. 345.

Work he must, whatever he is, but quietly and steadily; and the natural and unforced results of such work will always be the things that God meant him to do, and will be his best.[1]

Those words have a decidedly hollow ring when they are placed against the actualities of what work means for Pancks and Frederick Dorrit. *Little Dorrit* has no room for Ruskin's comfortable pieties.

And there is another point. For although Doyce is praised for his proud championing of creative endeavour, Clennam represents something of the visionary dreariness that can and does come to great artists. Against Doyce's statement about the need to endure we may set Clennam's feeling of the possible pointlessness of endurance. The feeling comes to him during his solitude in prison, and in his mental state at this time we can detect an element of the cry implicit in Shakespeare's Sonnet 66, or of the Conradian horror of coming face to face with what may seem to be the desolate hollowness of the human condition:

> For a burning restlessness set in, an agonised impatience of the prison, and a conviction that he was going to break his heart and die there, which caused him indescribable suffering. His dread and hatred of the place became so intense that he felt it a labour to draw his breath in it. The sensation of being stifled sometimes so overpowered him, that he would stand at the window holding his throat and gasping. At the same time a longing for other air, and a yearning to be beyond the blind blank wall, made him feel as if he must go mad with the ardour of the desire. (Bk 2, ch 29)

We would not be wrong, I think, to see in this prose the heightened response of the artist to his conscious recognition that at certain times life itself seems a terrible imprisonment (to Shakespeare and Conrad we may add the name of Piranesi and much Romantic literature). And Dickens's greatness lies in his ability to cope with the recognition without luxuriating in it or dissembling it. We come back here to a point that I made earlier in the chapter, that there are no discoverable freedoms in *Little Dorrit*. Both

[1] Ibid., p. 346.

Clennam and Fanny feel 'a burning restlessness'. Yet neither can escape. The 'other air' for which Clennam longs is that of the 'free air and the free country swept by winds and wings of birds'; and it is beyond reach. Only once does what it stands for seem within grasp. There is the important episode of Clennam's attempt to persuade himself that he is in love with Pet Meagles. For him that is a dream of freedom, because it offers to release him from time. He walks towards the Meagles's house:

> A tranquil summer sunset shone upon him as he approached the end of his walk, and passed through the meadows by the river side. He had that sense of peace, and of being lightened of a weight of care, which country quiet awakens in the breasts of dwellers in towns. . . . Between the real landscape and its shadow in the water, there was no division; both were so untroubled and clear, and, while so fraught with the solemn mystery of life and death, so hopefully reassuring to the gazer's soothed heart, because so tenderly and mercifully beautiful. (Bk 1, ch 29)

But this would-be release into a freer world is denied Clennam. Pet comes to tell him that she is engaged to be married to Gowan.

Yet he finds it possible to endure his recognition of the inescapability of the prison condition. He does so because of Little Dorrit. And although putting it that way makes it seem crude, the way in which Amy becomes the symbol of endurance for Clennam, seems to me the most magnificent and deeply moving moment in the entire novel. I also think it one of the greatest moments of our literature. As indeed it should be. For the scene of Little Dorrit's appearance to Clennam is not so much great in the texture of the writing, fine and restrained though that is, as in its total import. She is not a leading from above, but she *is* the great transforming ordinary fact of endurance which counters Clennam's untoward thoughts:

> To see the modest head again bent down over its task, and the nimble fingers busy at their old work – though she was not so absorbed in it but that her compassionate eyes were often raised to his face, and, when they dropped again, had tears in them – to be

so consoled and comforted, and to believe that all the devotion of this great nature was turned to him in his adversity, to pour out its inexhaustible wealth of goodness upon him, did not steady Clennam's trembling voice or hand, or strengthen him in his weakness. Yet it inspired him with an inward fortitude, that rose with his love. (Bk 2, ch 29)

'Great nature.' It is a vast claim. Yet Dickens has earned the right to use it of her. We do not have to apologize for Amy as we do for Ruth Pinch, for Florence (occasionally), and for Esther. Dickens hardly ever falters with Amy because his perception of her worth is greater by far than anything he finds to praise in the earlier heroines. Little Dorrit really is the embodiment of selfless devotion, of duty, of endurance. Her 'weak figure with its strong purpose' is a wonderfully resourceful image of human potentialities opposed to the vast horror of the prison of society, for which London is the fit emblem and in which she can exist. There is a beautiful tact about Dickens's handling of the flowers she brings to Clennam:

> Nothing had ever appeared so beautiful in his sight. He took them up and inhaled their fragrance, and he lifted them to his hot head, and he put them down and opened his parched hands to them. (Bk 2, ch 29)

The flowers emblematize the restorative power that Little Dorrit offers Clennam and which can justly be opposed to the impossible dream of freedom that is associated with pastoral imagery and which William Dorrit pathetically pretends exists even within the Marshalsea. '"The air blows over the – ha – Surrey hills. Blows over the Surrey hills."' (Bk 2, ch 19)

I do not think that there is anything improperly prescriptive about Amy. Nothing could be more realistic than the misery she has to live through and survive against. As I have said before, she is not a mysterious figure of grace. She is unremarkable and ordinary. And in saying this, I think we need to recall Mrs Merdle's remark that 'we are not in our natural state'. In an important sense Mrs Merdle speaks the truth. It is not just that she parodies the Rousseauistic dream of freedom by her references to '"Savages in the Tropical seas (I should have been charmed to be one myself – most delightful life and perfect climate I am told)"'. (Bk 1, ch 20) Fundamentally, Little Dorrit's prison-birth signifies that Dickens regards her as the very opposite of the child of nature. But in her ability to 'grow out radially as far as may be' and communicate with so many otherwise self-imprisoned people (Maggy, Mrs Clennam, Arthur, her father, Fanny, her uncle), she represents a human possibility that stretches beyond the constrictions of class in which most are bound and which Mrs Merdle, speaking for most, thinks of as synonomous with an abandoning of 'our natural state'. And her very ordinariness makes her central as Doyce cannot be.

Of course, Little Dorrit is not meant to feed the novel with an optimism that in any way undercuts her own recognition that London is 'large, barren and wild'. (Bk 1, ch 14) The horror of what London represents cannot be dispelled. That is why the novel ends on so restrained a note. There is no escape. Clennam and Amy

> went down into a modest life of usefulness and happiness. Went down to give a mother's care, in the fulness of Time, to Fanny's neglected children no less than to their own, and to leave that lady going into Society for ever and a day. Went down to give a tender nurse and friend to Tip for some few years, who was never vexed by the great exactions he made of her, in return for the riches he might have given her if he had ever had them, and who lovingly closed his eyes upon the Marshalsea and all its blighted fruits. They went quietly down into the roaring streets, inseparable and blessed; and as they passed along in sunshine and in shade, the noisy and the eager, and the arrogant and the froward and the vain, fretted, and chafed, and made their usual uproar.

In the images of that final sentence we hear for the last time the balladic note which the novel has so often struck, and it provides exactly the right generalizing quality that the paragraph as a whole needs. For it is both a statement about individuals and a judgement on the qualities of life that they embody. It brings to a close the affirmative possibilities which Dickens has hinted at elsewhere in the novel as existing within the city-prison and which he has deliberately and comically associated with the language of pastoral. I think, for example, of Mrs Plornish enjoying old Nandy's singing: '[it] was a perfect pastoral to Mrs. Plornish, the Golden Age revived'; (Bk 2, ch 13) and of John Chivery's wandering among his mother's washing-lines 'as if it was groves'. Chivery and Mrs Plornish both belong to the possibilities that the last paragraph affirms. They are also constrained by the forces whose surrounding presence Dickens acknowledges. The uproar typifies the unavoidable prison, but it does not defeat the equally typical decency which Little Dorrit most fully represents. And for Dickens to be able to sustain his complex vision to the novel's very last words is the remaining evidence on which I would base my claim for *Little Dorrit*'s supremacy among the great novels of the language.

✳ 8 · GREAT EXPECTATIONS

If *Little Dorrit* is Dickens's greatest novel, the one that follows it is his worst. *A Tale of Two Cities* has patches of lively writing and it is by no means without interest. But for all that it is not very good. We may say that it picks up *Barnaby Rudge*'s concern with revolution, but we have to add that in the later novel Dickens seems almost to regard violence as the one way to bring about social change. It is as though a weary disgust with his society has led him into wishing it could be wiped out. No doubt that puts the matter too crudely, yet there is a perfunctoriness about the vision of the future at the end of the novel which suggests that Dickens is not really concerned with doing justice to the probabilities. Carton's prophecy of the 'long ranks of new oppressors, risen on the destruction of the old' who will themselves be destroyed, is near enough to the historical fact of Revolutionary France. But the same can hardly be said for his claim to envisage

> a beautiful city and a brilliant people arising from this abyss, and, in their struggles to be truly free, in their triumphs and defeats, through long years to come, I see the evil of this time and of the previous time of which this is the natural birth, gradually making expiation for itself and wearing out.

It is hardly possible that Dickens wants us to see in the Paris of the 1860s the beautiful city and brilliant people which Carton envisages. But nor can the vision be meant ironically. More likely, Carton is being wrenched from his role to become Dickens's spokesman about – but about what? Well, about violence in England and its outcome, perhaps. But really it is fruitless speculation, because at best *A Tale of Two Cities* provides a near desperate warning to the society Dickens had so deeply investigated in *Little Dorrit*. If it does not mend its ways then the revolution will come, and a good thing too (the *Tale* is full of the violent bursting of the bars of imprisonment and suffering). But Dickens knows that no such revolution will actually come. Hence the weary perfunctoriness that so marks and mars the book.

That at least is my own impression. But it is often enough suggested that the badness of *A Tale of Two Cities* is better explained in terms of Dickens's own domestic problems, which were certainly acute at the time. For he was engaged in the painful and emotionally exhausting process of separating from his wife, and there may be some truth in suggesting that he had little time or heart for writing. But if that is so, how shall we explain *Great Expectations*? For *Great Expectations* was begun in even worse circumstances than those that accompanied the writing of *A Tale of Two Cities*. The family affairs were still in a terrible mess, and the book had to be started in a great hurry to boost the sales of *All the Year Round*, which were rapidly falling with the serialization of Charles Lever's *A Day's Ride*. And since the magazine was a weekly publication, the writing of the novel had to be both speedy and carefully tailored for weekly instalments. Hardly ideal conditions in which to produce a masterpiece. And yet *Great Expectations* is a masterpiece. More, it is the most perfect and the most beautiful of all Dickens's novels. How was it done?

Because he was a genius, we might say, and leave the matter there. But some biographical circumstances are worth our consideration. With the break-up of his marriage Dickens decided to sell the family's London home, Tavistock House, and to move permanently to Gad's Hill. According to Johnson:

> During this time of breaking up Tavistock House, Dickens seemed torn with a mania for breaking with the past. In the field behind Gad's Hill he burned all the accumulated letters and papers of twenty years.[1]

[1] *Johnson*, Vol. II, p. 963.

We do not have to be very ingenious to see in this orgy of destructiveness an implicit ache to begin life again. Dickens was now in love with Ellen Ternan, the young actress who must have seemed the incarnation of those young and beautiful women of the novels who embody all the hope, love and sympathetic understanding which he felt that Kate had never supplied:

> Although Dickens was only forty-nine, his health was failing under the strain of the labours to which he subjected himself and the maniacal swift-paced walks in which he still indulged, but he touched up his grizzling hair, dressed as gaily as ever, and continued to act like a young man. It was as if he were under a compulsion to fight his body and deny the waning of his physical vigour.[1]

But his efforts to make time catch or to arrest it – shades of Mrs Skewton and of Turveydrop – came in face of his recognition that time was in fact hurrying up:

> The great old men whom he had known in his startling youth were almost all gone: Rogers dead, Hunt dead, Jeffrey dead, Sydney Smith dead, Landor far off in Italy, Carlyle growing ever more atrabilious and prophetically intolerant. Many of Dickens's closer associates were gone or scattered, too. Talfourd dead, Frank Stone dead, Stanfield enfeebled and ailing. Maclise isolated in an eccentric valetudinarianism, Cruikshank withdrawn to his fanatical teetotalism, Lemon estranged. Ainsworth, the close companion of the Cerberus Club days, the friend who introduced him to his first publisher, had vanished into obscurity.[2]

It is very nearly a lament for the makers, and without doubt Dickens's sad awareness of the irreversibility of time has much to do with the prevailing tone of *Great Expectations*. Yet the novel is not a lament for lost youth. Instead, it is an unflinching portrait of a man's life, and if it finally endorses the claim that you can't go home again, it does so without a trace of self-pity. The acceptance of time's irreversible nature is matched by an awareness of the irreparability of human action, and the novel as a

[1] Ibid., Vol. II, p. 970.
[2] Ibid. Vol. II, p. 970.

whole is built out of one man's effort to remember and thus make sense of and account for his life.

Great Expectations is a perfect example of the way in which, as Hans Meyerhoff points out:

> Time is charged with 'significance' for man because human life is lived under the shadow of Time, because the question, what *am* I, makes sense only in terms of what I have *become*, that is, in terms of the objective historical facts together with the pattern of significant associations constituting the biography or identity of the real self.[1]

In life the problem is, of course, that we can never be sure just which associations *do* constitute the biography or identity of the real self. Probably all great autobiographies are to some extent works of fiction, satisfying in their completeness and coherence, but problematic in relation to their creator. Hence the importance of the display of memory in art, for fictional autobiography is not subject to the same queries and doubts as must affect factual autobiography. All we require is the evidence by which the 'I' of the novel or poem shows us how he has become what he is. And although it is perhaps true that all great autobiographical writing, whether factual or fictional, is undertaken at a time of great personal crisis and in addition becomes a major form in the Romantic period because of new difficulties in defining identity, we do not need to know of Dickens's crises in order to make sense of *Great Expectations*, even though without their having forced themselves on him he probably could not have written the novel. The evidences that Pip provides of his own identity are the crucial events of his life which his memory calls up, and he constantly judges them from his present standpoint. Partly the judgement is in the very selection of what he regards as crucial. He has to give the appearance of telling us his life-history while at the same time making sure that its elements form a connected pattern. But partly the judgement lies in his attitude to the elements, his manner of response to their recall.

There are essentially two points of view in *Great Expectations*.

[1] *Time in Literature*, pp. 27–8.

One is that of the Pip who lives through the novel, the other belongs to the Pip who narrates it. And the second point of view is the authoritative one, commenting on, correcting, judging the earlier self (or selves). To take just one example. When Joe accompanies Pip to Miss Havisham's to speak about the boy's being apprenticed, we are told that he will not talk to Miss Havisham but addresses all his remarks to Pip:

> It was quite in vain for me to endeavour to make him sensible that he ought to speak to Miss Havisham. The more I made faces and gestures to him to do it, the more confidential, argumentative, and polite, he persisted in being to Me.
> 'Have you brought his indentures with you?' asked Miss Havisham.
> 'Well, Pip, you know,' replied Joe, as if that were a little unreasonable, 'you see me put 'em in my 'at, and therefore you know as they are here.' With which he took them out, and gave them, not to Miss Havisham, but to me. I am afraid I was ashamed of the dear good fellow – I *know* I was ashamed of him – when I saw that Estella stood at the back of Miss Havisham's chair, and that her eyes laughed mischievously. I took the indentures out of his hand and gave them to Miss Havisham. (ch 13)

It is a beautifully caught moment. On the one hand there is the boy's genuine and even perhaps excusable embarrassment. On the other, there is the narrator's self-accusation. And the fineness of the scene – its truth – depends on the way that the acknowledgement of shame is handled. 'I am afraid I was ashamed of the dear good fellow.' That is not shame. It has about it the clear hint of condescension which appeals to the reader to understand that there was every reason for shame. And of course Pip, the man who is launched into society, *does* feel superior to his country relatives, there is no helping it. But there is every helping the self-knowledge that can pass into self-congratulation. Hence the stern – 'I *know* I was ashamed of him.' The qualification acts as a rebuke to the previous lightly accepted culpability. It shows that the narrator is determined to get at the real truth.

I have made heavy weather of what is a fairly simple matter.

Yet it is worth emphasizing how sternly Pip wishes to judge himself and his life. All signs of self-pity and complacency are rooted out as they become identified.

But this brings us to an interesting point. The severity of Pip's self-judgement may eventually prove to be in excess of what he has to show us of his life. In other words, there is a third point of view that *Great Expectations* allows for – ours. Almost the best thing about the novel is that because of the self-excoriating quality with which Pip is determined to tell the truth about himself, we understand that his desire to atone for past errors leads him to identify error where none exists. There must be no hint of a desire for martyrdom about this, or the novel will be ruined. Dickens's success depends on his making Pip's desire for atonement plausible and honourable, not priggish or coy. And by and large the success is guaranteed because in spite of Pip's faults we are persuaded of his honesty, candour and essential likeability. Besides, although it is proper that *he* should regard the course of his life as dictated by faults, it is also proper that *we* should see the matter otherwise. In particular, the novel makes us understand that great expectations are highly problematic. Can one even be guilty of entertaining them, or are they inevitably fed into people's lives?

It is in *Great Expectations* that a theme which had begun to haunt Dickens from *Nicholas Nickleby* onwards comes finally to fruition. And although the novel's title may seem to indicate a rigorous moral concern, the sheer beauty of *Great Expectations* lies in its seamless development of the theme, so that we can hardly put our finger on any one point in order to say that it is *there* that the guilty ambition stems from, or *there*, or *there*. *Great Expectations* has very little moral stridency about it; and if Pip is an exemplary case it is not in a prescriptive manner. What James said of his admired Turgenieff applies almost perfectly to *Great Expectations*: '"It is life itself," we murmur as we read, "and not this or that or the other story-teller's more or less clever 'arrangement' of life."'

There is a very famous episode that will help show with what complexity Dickens handles the presentation of Pip's growth. It comes after the boy's first visit to Miss Havisham, when, in reply to his sister's and Mr Pumblechook's persistent questioning, he invents a whole series of incidents from the visit:

> 'She was sitting,' I [said], 'in a black velvet coach.'
>
> Mr. Pumblechook and Mrs. Joe stared at one another – as they well might – and both repeated, 'In a black velvet coach?'
>
> 'Yes,' said I. 'And Miss Estella – that's her niece, I think – handed her in cake and wine at the coach-window, on a gold plate. And we all had cake and wine on gold plates. And I got up behind the coach to eat mine, because she told me to.'
>
> 'Was anybody else there?' asked Mr. Pumblechook.
>
> 'Four dogs,' said I.
>
> 'Large or small?'
>
> 'Immense,' said I. 'And they fought for veal cutlets out of a silver basket.' (ch 9)

When we come to this scene our first response is to pay tribute to Dickens's wonderful and seemingly effortless ability to get inside the boy's mind. This is exactly the kind of story that a child *would* invent, it is so near to fairy-tale. But in addition, we notice that even in his fantasy Pip puts himself in an inferior position to Miss Havisham and Estella. He gets up behind the coach 'because she told me to'. And in addition to that, we notice that his story is a dream of riches: gold plates, silver baskets and the like. And this is where we have to be extremely tactful. It would be possible to say that in the boy's words we recognize the seeds of great expectations. But we can hardly make Pip culpable. He has already been exposed to Estella's scorn, has been introduced to an entirely new way of judging matters. '"Why, he is a common labouring-boy!"' How can Pip hear that contemptuous cry and not feel that it both tells the truth and is justified? And again. '"He calls the knaves, Jacks, this boy!" said Estella with disdain, before our first game was out. "And what hands he has! And what thick boots."' Can we blame Pip if he wants to ask Joe why he had ever taught me to call those picture-cards, Jacks, which ought to be called knaves. I wished Joe had been rather more genteely brought up, and then I should have been so too. (ch 8)

Pip the narrator may accuse himself of incipient snobbishness for thinking such thoughts, but we mustn't. Yes, the boy is wrong; but then Estella's unquestioning assumption of superiority and disdain make her seem right. She knows more, has no doubt that judgement must come from her vantage point, not his. Later, Pip admits that

> what I dreaded was, that in some unlucky hour I, being at my grimiest and commonest, should lift up my eyes and see Estella looking in at one of the wooden windows of the forge. I was haunted by the fear that she would, sooner or later, find me out, with a black face and hands, doing the coarsest part of my work, and would exult over me and despise me. (ch 14)

Coarse, common: Pip is using her words. 'You taught me language; and my profit on't Is, I know how to curse myself.' Who could *accuse* Pip of wrongful thoughts? He has simply become exposed to the subtle and insidious effects that class has on individuals. Pip's growth is to some extent the story of any Englishman. The social pressures to which he becomes exposed and which shape his response and attitude to his own way of life are common enough; and that their despicable nature is none the less sufficiently plausible to have a decisive influence over him, may well be less a criticism of him than of the fact and nature of English social life.

We cannot of course think that Pip's growing dream of being a gentleman is somehow to be freed from censure. His relationship with Biddy offers clear evidence of how badly he can behave. Yet even here matters are not simple. He is weak for preferring Biddy and then not acting on his preference. 'It was clear that Biddy was immeasurably better than Estella, and that the plain honest working life to which I was born, had nothing in it to be ashamed of, but offered me sufficient means of self-respect and happiness. (ch 17) And when he tells her he wants to be a gentleman on Estella's account, he secretly agrees with her when she says:

> 'If it is to spite her . . . I should think – but you know best – that it might be better and more independently done by caring nothing for her words. And if it is to gain her over, I should think – but you know best – she was not worth gaining over.' (ch 17)

But Biddy's words, judicious though they may be, do not meet the case. For there is the hope that Estella may be worth gaining in spite of her aloof disdain. Or just because of it. A foolish hope, no doubt, but then Pip's being wrong is not in question. His being culpable is. In short, we make a bad mistake if we agree with the narrator's harsh attitude to his earlier self. 'It was impossible to dissociate [Estella's] presence from all those wretched hankerings after money and gentility that had disturbed my boyhood – from all those ill-regulated aspirations that had first made me ashamed of home and Joe.' (ch 29) The severity is proper to him, but it would be improper to us.

Pip has good reason for such severity towards himself. Estella's influence has deeply conditioned his ways of seeing people, Biddy not excluded. Though he knows that she is better than Estella, it is Estella who becomes the ideal against which Biddy is measured. 'She was not beautiful – she was common, and could not be like Estella – but she was pleasant and whole-some and sweet-tempered.' (ch 17) And because he learns to see Biddy this way he builds up a life for himself that there can be no undoing. He cannot destroy the education that Miss Havisham has arranged for him through Estella. One of the saddest and most humanly convincing moments in the novel comes with Joe's visit to Pip in London. Pip admits that 'If I could have kept him away by paying money, I certainly would have paid money.' But Joe arrives, and is ill-at-ease:

> I had neither the good sense nor the good feeling to know that this was all my fault, and that if I had been easier with Joe, Joe would have been easier with me. I felt impatient of him and out of temper with him; in which condition he heaped coals of fire on my head.

'Us two being now alone, Sir,' – began Joe.

'Joe,' I interrupted, pettishly, 'how can you call me Sir.' . . .

'Well, Sir,' pursued Joe, 'this is how it were. I were at the Barge-
man t'other night, Pip;' whenever he subsided into affection, he
called me Pip, and whenever he relapsed into politeness he called
me Sir' . . . (ch 27)

We are bound to admire the narrator here. He is so determined
not to gloss over any of his earlier faults that he wins our
reluctant sympathy by the efforts of his own candour. On the
other hand, we can hardly *like* the person he is remembering
having been. And yet unpleasant though the younger Pip is, it
is not easy to see even here that he is entirely to blame for the rift
that has developed between Joe and himself. So many elements
have helped create it: his sister's and Pumblechook's vulgar
regard for expectations, Miss Havisham's single-minded malice,
Magwitch's gratitude for a small boy's act of kindness, Pip's love
for Estella – and, yes, Pip's growing vanity and determination
to realize his dream of being a gentleman, which does not cost
him our sympathy because of his obvious discomfort at what the
dream exacts from him in human terms.

Pip feels acutely guilty about Joe because in spite of his education and his ambitions he is basically a good man. More especially,
he feels guilt because he is aware of human ties that conflict with
social obligations and class distinctions. It is an old Dickensian
theme, but newly treated. Never before have we been con-
tinuously inside the mind of a Dickens character who has tried
to free himself from commitment to personal ties. The novelist's
concern is to explore the ways in which class-considerations
supervene upon human relationships, and Dickens was of course
very well positioned to make such an exploration. It is a moral
but not a moralized concern. On the one hand there are 'so many
ties' by which Pip frankly admits that he is linked to Joe; on the
other, there is the experience of growing away from first friends
which in some ways is perfectly natural though probably always
attended by a feeling of guilt. This is really a psychological
matter. For it happens that human ties may chafe against the

ambitious heart or any aspiration or purposeful dream. The trouble with Pip's aspirations is that they are not worth the effort. But suppose they were? Suppose he wanted to be a great novelist? The problem of Joe would not be lessened. Nor would the problem of Kate Dickens.

Bonds, ties. The novel makes much of them, but in a deeply questioning manner. What *are* the ties by which people are bound to each other? There is a clear and proper contrast between the ties by which Pip feels himself bound to Joe and the bonds by which he is legally tied to him as an apprentice. Legal ties can be severed. Can human ones? Which is the better condition, bondage or freedom? These are the sort of questions over which the novel broods and I do not think it possible to avoid recognizing how they bear back on Dickens's own life. But that does not mean he is attempting to excuse or justify his own life. Far from it. *Great Expectations* makes us aware that there are certain human ties which cannot be broken without impoverishment, no matter how casually they may be formed. For once they are formed an individual finds himself led into the labyrinth of another's being:

> Something clicked in his throat, as if he had works in him like a clock, and was going to strike. And he smeared his ragged rough sleeve over his eyes.
>
> Pitying his desolation, and watching him as he gradually settled down upon the pie, I made bold to say, 'I am glad you enjoy it.'
> 'Did you speak?'
> 'I said I was glad you enjoyed it.'
> 'Thankee, my boy. I do.' (ch 3)

That is how the relationship with Magwitch starts, prompted by Pip's unforced and entirely credible sympathy for the convict. But from now on he is to be inescapably linked to Magwitch because Magwitch is determined to repay the boy for his kindness. 'He gave me a look that I did not understand, and it all passed in a moment. But if he had looked at me for an hour or for a day, I could not have remembered his face ever afterwards, as having been more attentive.' (ch 5) The mysteriously indirect syntax of the second sentence suggests what difficulties the mature Pip has in accepting the unbroken bond which, as a child, he had not even understood was being formed. And the simple but deep truth that Dickens presents in the relationship of Magwitch and Pip is of how in the end we have to take responsibility for people to whom we may have felt no particular intensity of commitment.

The relationship means much more to Magwitch than it does to Pip. Pip is bound to Magwitch only by Magwitch's intensity of regard for him. Hence the mysterious gift of 'two fat sweltering one-pound notes that seemed to have been on terms of the warmest intimacy with all the cattle markets in the country'. (ch 10) And against that we see Pip's annoyance at Magwitch's haunting his dreams of great expectations:

> If I had often thought before, with something allied to shame, of my companionship with the fugitive whom I had once seen limping among those graves, what were my thoughts on this Sunday, when the place recalled the wretch, ragged and shivering, with his felon iron and badge! My comfort was, that it happened a long time ago, and that he had doubtless been transported a long way off, and that he was dead to me, and might be veritably dead into the bargain. (ch 19)

I think we shall mistake the importance of this passage if we see in it merely a proleptic irony. It is psychologically telling. Pip's memories of Magwitch have become quite cold and detached. We are a long way from the boy who pities the convict's desolation. And though of course Magwitch clearly isn't entirely dead to Pip, otherwise he would not remember him at all, the main weight of the moment rests on his indifference to the 'wretch' which will be shifted only because he will find out that there is no escaping from the ties by which Magwitch has bound himself to him.

Against the fact of bondage is inevitably the dream of freedom. When Pip goes with Joe to the marshes, to 'make him less ignorant and common' he recalls that

Whenever I watched the vessels standing out to sea with their white sails spread, I somehow thought of Miss Havisham and Estella; and whenever the light struck aslant afar off, upon a cloud or sail or green hill-side or water-line, it was just the same. (ch 15)

Freedom, escape, great expectations. They go together. But as soon as Pip decides to go to London he finds himself feeling guilty about Joe. For his relationship with Joe is one to which he himself is committed:

Looking towards the open window, I saw light wreaths from Joe's pipe floating there, and I fancied it was like a blessing from Joe – not obtruded on me or paraded before me, but pervading the air we shared together. I put my light out, and crept into bed; and it was an uneasy bed now, and I never slept the old sound sleep in it any more. (ch 18)

It is beautifully done, a most tactful way of praising Joe's worth, his gentleness, forbearance, kindness. And after it we have the great passage of Pip's departure:

I deliberated with an aching heart whether I would not get down when we changed horses and walk back, and have another evening at home, and make a better parting. We changed, and I had not made up my mind, and still reflected for my comfort that it would be quite practicable to get down and walk back, when we changed again. And while I was occupied with these deliberations, I would fancy an exact resemblance to Joe in some man coming along the road towards me, and my heart would beat high. – As if he could possibly be there! (ch 19)

It is about guilt and also about the irreparability of human action. It also foredooms Pip's dream of freedom. There is no way now he can recover the old relationship with Joe, but just because he carries this knowledge with him it troubles and effectively spoils his hope for breaking clean away from the past into a brave new world. And it is part of his decency that he should realize as much. 'I lived in a state of chronic uneasiness respecting my behaviour to Joe. My conscience was not by any means easy about Biddy.' (ch 34)

But what of the realized expectations? The dream of freedom turns slowly into a nightmare of dissipation, boredom and ennui, a life shared with the foolish and vicious and admired only by the sort of person whom Pumblechook personifies with his fawning 'May I?' Dickens's view of achieved expectations is of course a moral judgement. And it develops into a pattern, with Pip's expectations echoed by those of Mr Wopsle and the egregious Mrs Pocket, 'who in the nature of things must marry a title, and who was to be guarded against the acquisition of plebeian domestic knowledge'. (ch 23)

But Herbert Pocket hardly fits the pattern. He is very like Traddles:

> [He] had a frank and easy way with him that was very taking. I had never seen any one then, and I have never seen any one since, who more strongly expressed to me, in every look and tone, a natural incapacity to do anything secret and mean. There was something wonderfully hopeful about his general air, and something that at the same time whispered to me he would never be very successful or rich. (ch 22)

As with Traddles, so Herbert's decency is rewarded by his becoming rich after all. It is perhaps something of a mistake. And it is certainly difficult to reconcile Herbert's virtues with his pursuit of expectations. We may say that Dickens wants to show us a person who is not really contaminated by the pursuit, but it is difficult to see how this can be so, since the dream of expectations is also presented as fundamentally dangerous, and Herbert's fiancée rightly distrusts Pip. Still, it is not an important flaw.

The deep disaster of great expectations is the terrible human impoverishment to which they lead. They disturb and often destroy the dreamer's capacity for love and friendship. What saves Pip is that he finally discovers himself freely committed to Magwitch. He finds himself again as a worthwhile human being. When the convict first returns, Pip tries to dissociate himself. He lays a hand on Magwitch's breast to keep him away and he offers him clean money in exchange for those 'fat sweltering' notes he himself had been given. But the futility of keeping apart comes home to Pip when Magwitch mentions that he will be hanged if he is caught (as commentators have pointed out, the law affecting returned convicts had been altered by the date at which the novel is set, but Dickens is right to make use of it since it tautens Pip's dilemma):

> Nothing was needed but this; the wretched man, after loading wretched me with his gold and silver chains for years, had risked his life to come to me, and I held it there in my keeping! If I had loved him instead of abhorring him; if I had been attracted to him by the strongest admiration and affection, instead of shrinking from him with the strongest repugnance; it could have been no worse. On the contrary, it would have been better, for his preservation would then have naturally and tenderly addressed my heart. (ch 39)

It is important that the narrator should not intrude here. Instead, we directly witness Pip's immediate response, in all its bewildered muddle of self-pity, rage and straightforward disgust. There is no avoiding the disgust. Magwitch *is* revolting to the youth who has been educated into the acceptance of standards and manners of which the criminal in all his aspects is the most extreme violation. When Pip asks him what he was brought up to be, Magwitch replies "'A warmint, dear boy,'" and something of it comes out in his way of eating:

> He ate in a ravenous way that was very disagreeable, and all his actions were uncouth, noisy, and greedy. Some of his teeth had failed him since I saw him eat on the marshes, and as he turned his food in his mouth, and turned his head sideways to bring his strongest fangs to bear upon it, he looked terribly like a hungry old dog. (ch 40)

It also comes out in his pathetic determination not to be 'low'. And it shows most of all in his wish to create a 'gentleman', who shall be recognized by his money. "'I lived rough, that you should live smooth; I worked hard, that you should be above work.'" (ch 39) Coming to this moment from Dickens's other novels, we know precisely what is wrong about Magwitch's dream. It reminds us of Steerforth, of Rick, of Gowan.

It is a great stroke to make Magwitch so much the victim of respectable society that he determines to out-do it at its most ambitious. At this point Dickens exactly nails the absurdity that fed the Victorian idea of being or becoming a gentleman. 'By the by,' Hopkins wrote to Bridges in 1883, 'if the English race had done nothing else, yet if they left the world the notion of a gentleman, they would have done a great service to mankind.'[1] But of what service is the notion of a gentleman to Magwitch? Its final achievement is to make him seem abhorrent to the gentleman his money has created. And Pip's final victory comes when he breaks through the restraining bonds of his own gentle-manliness into an acceptance of Magwitch and the very different kind of bonds that tie them together. The great moment is Pip's sudden discovery that

> my repugnance to him had all melted away, and in the hunted wounded shackled creature who held my hand in his, I only saw a man who had meant to be my benefactor, and who had felt affec-tionately, gratefully, and generously, towards me with great constancy through a series of years. I only saw in him a much better man than I had been to Joe. (ch 54)

It is sudden because this is the first instance in many pages of Pip's having had anything to say about himself. As more than one critic has noted, Dickens manages with wonderful sureness Pip's gradual abandoning of self-consciousness as he unrehearsedly finds himself more and more drawn into the relationship of human complicity with Magwitch. When he finally accepts the convict's hand resting in his, we are carried back to his earlier revulsion from Magwitch's 'large brown veinous hands', and beyond that to his early shock over Estella's calling attention to his own 'coarse hands'. The acknowledgement of Magwitch's claims on him is a triumph of humaneness over the constricting dream of expectations, and nobody who has taken the measure of

[1] G. M. Hopkins, *Poetry and Selected Prose*, ed. W. H. Gardner, 1953, p. 196.

the novel will think the triumph lightly achieved, or that it possibly could be.

But it is less often noted that Pip's acceptance of Magwitch is the culmination of a process that has begun with his forgiveness of Miss Havisham. And his ability to win through to generous feeling towards her is the more important since there is every reason for him to hate her. It is she who has planned to ruin him. There is a technical difficulty, too. For Dickens can hardly have Pip draw attention to his act of forgiveness without making it seem a piece of blatant moralizing and self-recommendation. He has then to bless Miss Havisham unawares. But there is something about Pip that Dickens can now turn to advantage. We have already seen him becoming increasingly aware of the hideous nature of his own dream of expectations and its effect on him. He is therefore in a good position to understand what Miss Havisham has done to herself in denying claims that other human beings have on *her*. When in ch 49 he goes to see her in reply to her note, he finds her 'lost in the contemplation of the ashy fire'. The symbolism unobtrusively makes its point about her self-consuming desire to destroy, and it prepares us for Pip's remarking that 'there was an air of utter loneliness upon her, that would have moved me to pity though she had wilfully done me a deeper injury than I could charge her with'. We know that his perception of the old woman's isolation is authentic because we are aware of how much he knows about such isolation. We may, however, shift uneasily as we recognize Dickens's own voice beginning to edge into Pip's thoughts:

> I knew not how to . . . comfort her. That she had done a grievous thing in taking an impressionable child to mould into the form that her wild resentment, spurned affection, and wounded pride, found vengeance in, I knew full well. But that, in shutting out the light of day, she had shut out infinitely more; that, in seclusion, she had secluded herself from a thousand natural and healing influences; that, her mind, brooding solitary, had grown diseased, as all minds do and must and will that reverse the appointed order of their Maker; I knew equally well. And could I look

upon her without compassion, seeing her punishment in the ruin she was, in her profound unfitness for this earth on which she was placed, in the vanity of sorrow which had become a master mania, like the vanity of penitence, the vanity of remorse, the vanity of unworthiness, and other monstrous vanities that have been curses in this world? (ch 49)

The objection against this is not that it is unsound. What is said is perfectly just. But it is an intrusion. The voice is too much the author's, too little Pip's, and it awkwardly topples the scene towards a moralizing that loses touch with the psychological probabilities. But it is prevented from falling straight into easy pieties by Dickens's great dramatic sense, his unerring ability to invent the scene that will draw all the meanings of a theme into itself. The scene I have in mind is of Pip's act of forgiveness, and it provides the second way in which Dickens makes the entire episode credible:

> I looked into the room where I had left her, and I saw her seated in the ragged chair upon the hearth close to the fire, with her back towards me. In the moment when I was withdrawing my head to go away, I saw a great flaming light spring up. In the same moment, I saw her running at me, shrieking, with a whirl of fire blazing all about her, and soaring at least as many feet above her head as she was high. (ch 49)

It is somehow not enough to call this moment symbolic. For Miss Havisham's being finally consumed in the fire that expresses her self-destructive energies causes her appalling agonies. It also causes Pip to act quite unselfconsciously in an effort to save her. And it is marvellously tactful of Dickens to leave it until the next chapter for Pip to tell us how badly hurt he himself has been. There is no trace of self-pity or glorification about this. We do not normally praise Dickens for his restraint but we have to do so here. 'My hands had been dressed once or twice in the night, and again in the morning.' The flat, unemphatic manner of telling us this reinforces our awareness that all Pip's attention has gone out to Miss Havisham.

Yet his sufferings are considerable. They bear vivid testimony to his remark to Miss Havisham that it would have been better to have left Estella 'a natural heart, even to be bruised or broken'. They also precede his willing involvement with Magwitch's fate. And there is to be no underselling the intensity of how he will suffer for such involvement. The burns are the start of it. Orlick's very shocking torture of Pip emblematizes the probable consequences of commitment. It is an idea which Forster takes up in Gino's torturing of Philip Herriton. But the scene in *Great Expectations* is altogether more brutal. It both pinpoints Pip's agony of involvement and reveals Orlick as the most inhuman character in the novel because he is totally uncommitted. He recognizes no ties. '"I dropped your sister like a bullock"' he tells Pip. (One thinks in contrast of Joe's readiness to be '"a little ill-conwenienced myself"' rather than wrong his wife.)

Once Pip has accepted Magwitch he gives up his dream of clean money. But there are others in the novel who know that money is never clean, that it is, on the contrary, always dirty. For Wemmick and Jaggers life is never less than a dirty business. The two men are highly disturbing creations, products of Dickens's great moral and social realism. Wemmick, for example, is the good man who fully accepts the rottenness of a system by which he exists, but who manages not to be destroyed by it. Through Wemmick, indeed, Dickens explores an idea that he had half-glimpsed in Vholes and which he had pursued in Pancks. And even more than Pancks Wemmick is a great triumph because he is so unsettling a creation. There is no way of being at ease with him. We may say that in him Dickens provides a comic revivification of the cliché that an Englishman's home is his castle. We can point to his being totally secure in his domesticity. '"After I have crossed this bridge, I hoist it up – so – and cut off the communication."' And we know that he keeps his business and private lives totally distinct from each other. Jaggers has never seen his home:

'Never heard of it. Never seen the aged. Never heard of him. No; the office is one thing, and private life is another. When I go into the office, I leave the Castle behind me, and when I come into

the Castle I leave the office behind me. If it's not in any way disagreeable to you, you'll oblige me by doing the same. I don't wish
it professionally spoken about.' (ch 24)

It is a brilliant fancy. But Wemmick is undeniably worrying. It
is not just that he keeps all his decency and kindness at home, all
his hard-headedness for work, even though we are likely to be
uncomfortable with Dickens's ruthless insistence of such divi-
sions. The really disturbing fact is that Wemmick keeps the two
worlds apart because he knows that the virtues of the one cannot
flourish in the conditions of the other. And it is not straining too
hard to see in the fantastication of his Walworth castle a sort of
crazy exoticism that implies how much his imagination and more
impulsive and generous faculties are regularly frustrated by the
demands of business.

It is part of business to accept dirty money, or 'portable
property'. Walworth exists only because Wemmick deliberately
gets his hands dirty. This is shown in the astonishing scene where
he introduces Pip to Newgate, and is himself received by its
inmates on perfectly friendly terms. He arranges to receive two
pigeons from a man who is to be hung:

> They shook hands again, and as we walked away, Wemmick
> said to me, "A Coiner, a very good workman. The Recorder's
> report is made to-day, and he is sure to be executed on Monday.
> Still you see, as far as it goes, a pair of pigeons are portable property,
> all the same." With that, he looked back, and nodded at the dead
> plant, and then cast his eyes about him in walking out of the yard,
> as if he were considering what other pot would go best in its
> place. (ch 32)

Wemmick's hand-shake with the Coiner sets itself in clear contrast with Pip's not wanting to be touched by Magwitch. Yet as
a whole this scene is meant to be nearly baffling. For we are
likely instinctively to feel that Wemmick's behaviour is wrong,
his integrity somehow compromised by his readiness to take a
present from the condemned man. And the image of a 'dead
plant' is terribly close to suggesting a basic inhumanity about

Wemmick. But how can we accuse him of that? It is not just that we know about his Walworth life, but we see that the criminals themselves are his friends. In short, we do not know how to get our bearings with him. We do not even have the satisfaction of claiming that he is cynical about what he does. It is merely that he accepts the absurd contradictions of his position, presumably because life is for him a dirty business and it is as well to keep an area as free as possible from contamination. In the end we feel upset by the presentation of Wemmick because we expect Dickens to give us an indication of how we should respond to his two lives. We want to know where we are with him. And Dickens will not tell us.

Jaggers is even more disturbing. There is a real viciousness about him:

> 'If you talk of strength,' said Mr. Jaggers, '*I*'ll show you a wrist. Molly, let them see your wrist.'
>
> Her entrapped hand was on the table, but she had already put her other hand behind her waist. ''Master,' she said in a low voice, with her eyes attentively and entreatingly fixed upon him. 'Don't.'
>
> '*I*'ll show you a wrist,' repeated Mr. Jaggers, with an immovable determination to show it. 'Molly, let them see your wrist.'
>
> 'Master,' she again murmured. 'Please.'
>
> 'Molly,' said Mr. Jaggers, not looking at her, but obstinately looking at the other side of the room, 'let them see *both* your wrists. Show them. Come!' (ch 26)

There is no explaining away this moment, far less forgetting it. Still, Dickens tries at one point to explain Jaggers. The effort is misguided because it softens his study of the man. Jaggers is made to speak of how he is exposed to 'an atmosphere of evil', where nearly all the children he sees are regarded as 'so much spawn, to develop into the fish that were to come to his net – to be prosecuted, defended, forsworn, made orphans, bedevilled somehow'. (ch 51) It is not much of a fault, to be sure, but one regrets that Dickens should have felt the need to make obvious what is much better left implicit. The same is true of the moment where the man Mike is introduced:

'A man can't help his feelings, Mr. Wemmick,' pleaded Mike.
'His what?' demanded Wemmick, quite savagely. 'Say that
again!'
'Now, look here my man,' said Mr. Jaggers, advancing a step,
and pointing towards the door. 'Get out of this office. I'll have no
feelings here. Get out.'
'It serves you right,' said Wemmick. 'Get out.' (ch 51)

It is a little irritating, this explanation of what has been so marvellously rendered throughout the novel. But still, the rendering
is so fine that our objections have to be slight. And after all we
can never get away from the image of this ruthless, cool-headed,
hard man, whose awareness of what his commitment to the dirt
of life means comes out in the quite brilliant fact of his compul-
sive hand-washing. What other novelist, one wants to ask, could
have thought of that? It is so perfect and so obvious. As Christo-
pher Ricks shrewdly remarks 'The most important things about
Great Expectations are also the most obvious', and nothing could
be more obvious than Jaggers's 'washing his hands with scented
soap'. But then Dickens always does have this large obviousness
when he is at his best. And this is true from the moment when
Oliver asks for more to the moment when Riderhood and Headstone drown together. I can understand why so many critics and
readers should feel that such obviousness is the proof of Dickens's
lack of intellectual quality. It feels too true to be good. But the
response is unfair. It is not only that Jaggers's washing his hands
is dramatically unforgettable, it is a wonderfully resonant image.
It reaches out to touch the themes implicit in, for example: Pip's
dream of clean money, Magwitch's dirty money, Pip's not
wanting to be touched by Magwitch, Wemmick's handshake
with the dead plant, Molly's scarred wrists, Joe's work-grimed
hands. To invent an image that has such reverberative significance
is a sign of imaginative intelligence of the very highest order.

Jaggers's involvement with his professional life inevitably
differs from Wemmick's because it is total:

There was a bookcase in [his] room; I saw, from the backs of
the books, that they were about evidence, criminal law, criminal

biography, trials, acts of parliament, and such things. The furniture was all very solid and good, like his watch-chain. It had an official look, however, and there was nothing merely ornamental to be seen. In a corner, was a little table of papers with a shaded lamp: so that he seemed to bring the office home with him in this respect too, and to wheel it out of an evening and fall to work. (ch 26)

But Jaggers presents much the same problem as Wemmick. It is impossible to pin him down. We may want him to be heroic, but he will not become so. Dickens will not console our fears that Jaggers's deprivations are dreadful. Instead, we are forced to realize that his total absorption in the rottenness of his existence threatens a dire contamination. The disturbing note is sounded in his first interview with Pip and Joe:

> 'Lord forbid that I should want anything for not standing in Pip's way,' said Joe . . .
> 'Lord forbidding is pious, but not to the purpose,' returned Mr. Jaggers. 'The question is, Would you want anything? Do you want anything?'
> 'The answer is,' returned Joe sternly, 'No.'
> I thought Mr. Jaggers glanced at Joe, as if he considered him a fool for his disinterestedness. (ch 18)

And a little later in the same chapter we are told that Jaggers looks at Joe as though seeing in him 'the village idiot'. Such a moment may be linked to one much later, when Jaggers is said to be 'querulous and angry' with Pip, for having let Magwitch's fortune be lost. (ch 55)

Yet we also know that Jaggers is not entirely subdued to the element he lives in. And the greatness of Dickens's study depends on its demonstration that Jaggers, warts and all, remains a person for whom we feel sympathy. The study of the lawyer is a great example of emotional and imaginative generosity. If we except the rare and comparatively trivial moments I have mentioned, Dickens does not sentimentalize his views of Wemmick or of Jaggers, and yet he finds for them affirmative possibilities. They are convincing in their acceptance of a world which for them is corrupt and yet within which they find it possible to work, for good rather than evil, and knowing that such good has to be limited by their own complicity. It is hardly even possible to complain about Jaggers's seeing Joe as the village idiot, for it is part of his terrible acerbity of vision, true within its limits and both a judgement on him and an exoneration. And altogether the presentation of Jaggers manages almost miraculously to hold a balance between despair and optimism: the cost of his sort of involvement is enormous, but it is not definitive. Jaggers is deeply harmed by his commitment to the 'dirt' of life, yet his identification with it acts as a rebuke to Pip's dream of freedom and unsoiled expectations. The bonds that tie Jaggers chafe and disfigure. But they do not destroy.

Pip becomes disfigured by his acceptance of the bonds that tie him even to Miss Havisham, and in the breakdown that follows on Magwitch's death we see how deeply they cut into a person's life. It would be quite proper to see in this illness a sort of prolonged penance for earlier sins. But more importantly it images a radical psychological disordering. To realize his expectations, Pip has had to build an identity which the return of Magwitch threatens and finally destroys. As we might expect in Dickens, Pip's effort to create a new identity is imaged through clothes. When Jaggers comes to tell the youth of his expectations he also tells him that he must come to London in 'new clothes', and so Pip orders a suit from Trabb who remarks that it is 'an article much in vogue among the nobility and gentry'. And although the tailor already has Pip's measurements he re-measures him: ' "it wouldn't do under existing circumstances, sir – wouldn't do at all." ' (ch 19) Pip is that much of a new man. Throughout the second part of the novel his attention to dress is repeatedly shown and is given a comic twist when he returns to his home town to have his clothes-identity mocked by Trabb's boy:

> He wore the blue bag in the manner of my great-coat, and was strutting along the pavement towards me on the opposite side of the street, attended by a company of delighted young friends to whom he from time to time exclaimed, with a wave of his hand,

'Don't know yah!' . . . passing abreast of me, he pulled up his shirt-collar, twined his side-hair, stuck an arm akimbo, and smirked extravagantly by, . . . drawling to his attendants, 'Don't know yah, don't know yah, pon my soul don't know yah!' (ch 30)

Trabb's way with Pip is reminiscent of Crabbe's way with Daniel:

> And thus with clouded cane, a fop complete,
> He stalk'd, the jest and glory of the street.

Pip's effort to build a new identity for himself comes near to succeeding. We know as much from the narrator's insisting that his earlier self had become vain, hardened, appallingly self-regarding. But always there are the tugs towards another identity – the links with his past. The past can no more be denied than can Magwitch's true identity: 'The more I dressed him and the better I dressed him, the more he looked like the slouching figure of the marshes.' (ch 40) And Joe, we are told, looks 'natural' in his work-clothes.

We would be right to find in many of the references to Joe a hint of condescension. But I think that this is properly allowed for. Pip has learnt so deeply to live in terms of class-awareness that he cannot be other than condescending to Joe. As a result, he cannot return to the life they once shared. His breakdown manifestly images a broken identity. He remembers

> that I confounded impossible existences with my own identity; that I was a brick in the house wall, and yet entreating to be released from the giddy place where the builders had set me; that I was a steel beam of a vast engine, clashing and whirling over a gulf, and yet that I implored in my own person to have the engine stopped, and my part in it hammered off. (ch. 57)

No need to emphasize how much and with what marvellous directness that tells us how viciously Pip's efforts to become a gentleman have scarred him. Again, what is important is obvious.

But the greatest and most convincing victory Dickens wins from his writing of Pip's breakdown is the demonstration that you can't go home again. During the illness Joe comes to nurse

Pip, and indeed Pip first becomes conscious of the other man's 'holding his hand'. It is a detail whose unerring rightness typifies the sureness with which the entire episode is handled. So Pip remarks that

> we arrived at unrestricted conversation. I was slow to gain strength, but I did slowly and surely become less weak, and Joe stayed with me, and I fancied I was little Pip again. . . . I laid my head on Joe's shoulder, as I had laid it long ago when he had taken me to the fair or where not, and it was too much for my young senses . . . [Later he] carried me – so easily – across the court and up the stairs, [and] I thought of that eventful Christmas Day when he had carried me over the marshes.

The avenues to the past open up. Memory comes to reanimate a lost identity. But then Pip begins to recover:

> 'See, Joe! I can walk quite strongly. Now, you shall see me walk back by myself.'
> 'Which do not over-do it, Pip,' said Joe; 'but I shall be happy fur to see you able, sir.' (ch 57)

Obvious yet again. But how utterly right. No matter how strong Pip's ache to return to the past and undo his many mistakes, it cannot happen. There is no bridging the gap between himself and Joe. And so with his return to the village of his boyhood and his wish to marry Biddy:

> The June weather was delicious. The sky was blue, the larks were soaring high over the green corn, I thought all that countryside more beautiful and peaceful by far than I had ever known it to be. Many pleasant pictures of the life that I would lead there, and of the change for the better that would come over my character when I had a guiding spirit at my side whose simple faith and clear home-wisdom I had proved, beguiled my way. . . .
> The schoolhouse where Biddy was mistress, I had never seen; but, the little roundabout lane by which I entered the village for quietness' sake, took me past it. I was disappointed to find that the day was a holiday; no children were there, and Biddy's house was closed. Some hopeful notion of seeing her busily engaged in her

daily duties, before she saw me, had been in my mind and was defeated.

But, the forge was a very short distance off, and I went towards it under the sweet green limes, listening for the clink of Joe's hammer. Long after I ought to have heard it, and long after I had fancied I heard it and found it but a fancy, all was still. The limes were there, and their leaves rustled harmoniously when I stopped to listen; but, the clink of Joe's hammer was not in the midsummer wind. (ch 58)

I have quoted the passage at some length because otherwise its force cannot be communicated. Were *Great Expectations* a novel prior to *Little Dorrit* we would assume a passage such as this to be a certain prelude to the marriage of Pip and Biddy. The natural scene would provide the release from the terrible pressures of social life, and the forge and schoolhouse would be exactly the sort of properties which would provoke Dickens to an unfocused indulgence in Cockney pastoralism. But not now. However nearly the passage may seem to approach such an escapist dream, in fact the tone is perfectly sure. The prose, generalized and almost ballad-like, has a mythic air to it. This is a lost world to which there can be no return. Pip of course indulges a nostalgic pathos over the scene, but Dickens does not share it. He deliberately absents himself from any mood which might chime with Housman's blue remembered hills or Thomas's green and dying world. Pip has to learn that there can be no going back. It is Joe who marries Biddy, not he. And the passage as a whole returns us to his initial leave-taking of the village, so that we become finally aware of the novel's readiness to honour the irreparability of human action, the irreversibility of time:

We changed again, and yet again, and it was now too late and too far to go back, and I went on. And the mists had all solemnly risen now, and the world lay spread before me. (ch 19)

The echo of *Paradise Lost* does not require us to moralize Pip's expulsion from paradise. The moment is too humane and inclusive for that, especially when we consider it in the light of his attempted return: the dream of innocence, the fact of growth and maturity, the inevitable process of growing away from the security and warmth of childhood, the almost inevitable wish to leave the 'happy valley' in search of another life, and the sad consciousness of how all these things can never be undone: such elements find their place in the moments of faring forward and wished-for return. They give to *Great Expectations* a wise authority that is an essential part of its greatness. And although the revised ending is certainly a mistake because it qualifies exactly that sombre recognition of the irreparability of human action which is so wonderfully attested throughout the novel, it does no serious harm. It does not prevent *Great Expectations* from being the most unchallengeable of Dickens's novels. 'Properly speaking,' Goethe said, 'we learn only from those books we cannot judge.' The remark is perhaps too emphatic, but on the whole I feel about *Great Expectations* as I do about each of Dickens's great novels, that I would rather learn from it than judge it. At all events, when we recall the moment of Dickens's life at which it was conceived and written, we are likely to feel not just how marvellous a triumph the novel is, but how noble and sane an effort went into its composition.

✿ 9 · IN CONCLUSION: OUR MUTUAL FRIEND

Among the reviewers of *Our Mutual Friend* was the young Henry James, who took a strong dislike to Dickens's novel and said so in no uncertain terms. James's criticism seems to me quite mistaken but of considerable interest, because it puts very forcefully the case of all those who, like George Eliot and G. H. Lewes in the last century and critics too numerous to mention in this, have expressed deep reservations about Dickens's art. And without wanting to get myself entangled in the wrong sort of discussion here, it seems proper to try and end my book by taking up the issues that such criticism raises and attempting to answer them.

The basic objection to Dickens's novels, to put the matter as simply as possible without being unfair, is that life is not as he presents it. And *Our Mutual Friend* is especially liable to suffer from this general critical demand for realism. For the novel has always been something of a problem. James disliked it, Swinburne admired it. In our own day K. J. Fielding has said that it 'shows a sense of strain and a lack of coherence in its development',[1] while Arnold Kettle has endorsed Jack Lindsay's judgement that it is 'one of the greatest works of prose ever written, a work which finally vindicates Dickens's right to stand, as no other English writer can stand, at the side of Shakespeare'.[2] Kettle's view is perhaps the more widely held and it seems to me excessive. *Our Mutual Friend* is not so great a novel as either *Bleak House* or *Little Dorrit*. And this is not because of its obvious but trivial flaws – as for instance the scenes between Bella and her

[1] *Charles Dickens, A Critical Introduction*, 1958, p. 183.
[2] *Dickens and the Twentieth Century*, p. 225.

father and the presentation of Riah – for these can be matched by equally bad moments in the other two novels. No, the fact is that *Our Mutual Friend* has a tired perfunctoriness about much of its actual prose, a making-do with gestures towards the defining of characters rather than the inexhaustible energy that we customarily associate with Dickens. This is not necessarily a flaw, but it does entail a scaling-down of the imaginative energy we find in *Bleak House* and *Little Dorrit*. Inevitably, it limits the final achievement of *Our Mutual Friend*.

Edmund Wilson came near to the crux of the matter when he said that Dickens's last completed novel reflects the 'weariness, the fears and the definitive disappointments of this period' of his life.[1] *Our Mutual Friend* lacks the exuberance of *Bleak House* and the sustained depth of enquiry that makes *Little Dorrit* so great. It is as though Dickens has finally lost any belief in art's power to confront or disturb. Whether Wilson is quite right to say that Dickens is afraid of Podsnap I am not sure; but he certainly regards him as unsaveable. I think, for example, of Podsnap dismissing the poor. A meek man remarks

> that some half-dozen people had lately died in the streets of starvation. It was clearly ill-timed after dinner. It was not adapted to the cheek of the young person. It was not in good taste.
> 'I don't believe it,' said Mr. Podsnap, putting it behind him.
> The meek man was afraid that we must take it as proved, because there were the Inquests and the Registrar's return.
> 'Then it was their own fault,' said Mr. Podsnap . . .
> 'And you know; at least I hope you know,' said Mr. Podsnap, with severity, 'that Providence has declared that you shall have the poor always with you?'
> The meek man also hoped he knew that.
> 'I am glad to hear it,' said Mr. Podsnap, with a portentous air. 'It will render you cautious how you fly in the face of Providence.' (Bk 1, ch 11)

There is not about this the envigorating blaze of contempt that gives what would otherwise be similar passages in *Bleak House*

[1] *The Wound and the Bow*, p. 66.

their remarkable edge and power. The contempt is there all right, but it is curiously flat. It almost seems that Dickens is writing the book for himself. The novel's presiding tone might even be said to mark a turning away from an audience. Of course, this is something of an overstatement, but we may justifiably note that Dickens does not seem to have been unduly bothered by the fall in subscribers – it amounted to some 5,000 – after the first number had appeared. *Our Mutual Friend* is perhaps one of those works which are determined to succeed in spite of their audience. Such works feel as though they are deliberately taunting their readers, daring them to like and admire (*Paradise Regained* is another example).

All this is not to say that the novel fails. But it is to suggest that its achievement is problematic. And in trying to cope with the problems the novel presents it will help to start from the sort of objections made against it by Henry James. But before we come to those I must say a little of what the novel is about.

The title provides the clue. *Our Mutual Friend* is much concerned with sets of friendships, true and false. The false exhibit the near-impossibility of mutuality in a society where to take your place you need either money or the next best thing, respectability. The true imply that mutuality occurs only as the pressures of society are denied or surmounted. ' "Life," ' Mr Grewgious says in *Edwin Drood*, ' "is pounds, shillings and pence." ' The remark might well provide a questioning epigraph for *Our Mutual Friend*. 'Friend' is a key word of the novel, and it seems to be inextricably connected with money. I suggested that in *Great Expectations* we have a wonderfully resourceful exploration of the difficulties and problems that surround selfless personal relationships. In *Our Mutual Friend* selflessness is rare. Instead we have the Veneerings and their bran-new friends whom money buys, Mr Lammle's friendship with Fascination Fledgeby which Lammle makes in order to ease himself out of money difficulties, Fledgeby's friendship with Mr Twemlow which he makes to ease him into them, Silas Wegg's friendship with Venus and Boffin, Mrs Lammle's friendship with Miss Georgiana Podsnap, the partnerships of Hexam and Riderhood and Riderhood and Headstone, all made with money in mind. From Lady Tippins down to Riderhood, true friendship is sacrificed to money. ' "Shall I invest in a bow," ' Wegg asks himself, when he sees Boffin for the first time. And where money isn't the conditioning factor, respectability is. Its pressures show themselves even in so decent a person as Miss Abbey Potterson who renounces Gaffer, but suggests to Lizzie that she ' "come under my direction . . . and be respectable and happy" '. (Bk 1, ch 6) And the pressures are resisted by the characters who choose or are brought to accept selfless friendships, made in despite of money interest or the claims of respectability.

Now so much might be given the novel by a hostile critic. And he might even agree that as with *Dombey, Bleak House* and *Little Dorrit, Our Mutual Friend* has the sort of echoic pattern and structure that can allow Dickens to spread his vision over so wide a range of society as to suggest that it is truly comprehensive. But he would then go on to say that the trouble with the novel is that in its presentation of character it fails to convince. At least, if he were Henry James he would say that. 'There is no humanity here,' James remarked of *Our Mutual Friend*. 'Humanity is nearer home than the Boffins, and the Lammles, and the Wilfers and the Veneerings.'[1] A few years later G. H. Lewes made very much the same objection, though with the whole of Dickens's work in mind. Dickens's characters are 'caricatures and distortions of human nature. . . . It may be said of Dickens's human figures that they are wooden, and run on wheels'.[2] It is a familiar enough protest. And so is James's complaint that humanity

is in what men have in common with each other, and not in what they have in distinction. The people just named have nothing in common with each other, except the fact that they have nothing in common with mankind at large. What a world were this world if the world of *Our Mutual Friend* were an honest reflection of it.[3]

[1] *The House of Fiction*, ed. Edel, 1962, p. 255.
[2] 'Dickens in Relation to Criticism' in *The Dickens Critics*, p. 62. Lewes's essay was written in 1872.
[3] *The House of Fiction*, p. 255.

What a world indeed. But how seriously are we meant to take the word 'reflection'? Does James mean it literally? If so, we can agree without fuss that *Our Mutual Friend* is not a reflection. It is concerned with penetrative judgement, not mere surface image, though it may and does use surface images. After all, Podsnap's ideas on art come dangerously near to an 'honest reflection'. 'Literature; large print, respectively descriptive of getting up at eight, shaving close at a quarter past, breakfasting at nine, going to the City at ten, coming home at half-past five, and dining at seven.' (Bk 1, ch 11) We do not want to identify James with *that* view of art. Yet there is a sense in which Dickens's own scornful dismissal of Podsnap art looks back – as surely do James and Lewes – to George Eliot's prescriptive demands of the novelist, as it is made in Chapter 17 of *Adam Bede*. At least, if Dickens did not have George Eliot in mind, I do not see why we should not feel that she lends herself uncomfortably to his contempt. George Eliot tells her readers that her strongest effort as a novelist is

> to give a faithful account of men and things as they have mirrored themselves in my mind. The mirror is doubtless defective; the outlines will sometimes be disturbed, the reflection faint or confused; but I feel as much bound to tell you as precisely as I can what that reflection is, as if I were in the witness-box narrating my experience on oath.[1]

We might of course object against this that no mind is a mirror, pure and passive; and that perception always implies some sort of judgement. On the other hand, it has sometimes been the case that Dickens's critics have defended his distorting mirror of art that on the grounds that since art is art because it is not nature there is no need for his work to do other than answer to internally consistent rules. The defence has a measure of justness and it inevitably leads to his name being coupled with that of Ben Jonson. For both, it can be and is argued, art provides an insight into life by the very fact of its radical distortions, for what these do is to create a pared-down presentation of types. And it can

---

[1] *Adam Bede*, op. cit., p. 171.

further be insisted that there is absolutely no reason why Dickens should be judged by standards that were invented to account for a very different sort of fiction. The only trouble is, that this sort of defence comes near to the manner by which Dr Johnson chose to defend Shakespeare. 'The palaces of Peru or Mexico are certainly mean buildings if compared with the houses of European monarchs,' Johnson says, 'yet who could forbear to view them with astonishment, who remembered that they were built without the use of iron?' Undoubtedly, there are critics for whom Dickens is a great novelist considering that he did not have the advantage of knowing the work of George Eliot and Henry James. And underlying this condescension is an assumption that he could not cope with human probabilities as they could. My own belief is that Dickens's greatness allows him to perceive and write about subjects which George Eliot's and Henry James's investment in realism – at least as it affects what they take to be human probability – prevents them from recognizing.

In writing about *Little Dorrit*, I quoted part of Chapter 17 of *Adam Bede* to show how Dickens could, when he wanted, amply fulfil the sort of demands George Eliot makes of the novelist. It must be quoted again, this time at slightly greater length, and with the remembrance that George Eliot is pretending to address an unspecified friend:

> These fellow-mortals, every one, must be accepted as they are; you can neither straighten their noses, nor brighten their wits, nor rectify their dispositions; and it is these people – amongst whom your life is passed – that it is needful you should tolerate, pity, and love: it is these more or less ugly, stupid, inconsistent people, whose movements of goodness you should be able to admire – for whom you should cherish all possible hopes, all possible patience.

It is a famous passage, of course, and it owes a good deal to George Eliot's entirely honourable doctrine of altruism, which a little later she identifies as 'the secret of deep human sympathy'. Her demand is for a selflessness that recognizes an integrity in human identity; people as they are, not as you would have them be. Her remarks may be linked to Kant's statement that 'man . . . *exists* as an end in himself, *not merely as a means* to be arbitrarily used by this or that will.'[1] But there is a problem about George Eliot's words, depending on who the good friend is whom she addresses. If he is a novelist then it is clear how he can accept his characters; after all, he has created them. If, on the other hand, he is a man in the street, acceptance is not nearly so easy. He can, of course, accept bent noses and dull wits. But such acceptance is not qualitatively different from Boffin's acceptance of Wegg's wooden leg. Yet to get beyond this sort of superficial recognition of other people is not an easy matter. George Eliot knows that. Indeed, her novels are aesthetic teachings partly because they try to show how different are the outer and inner characteristics by which people are recognized and know themselves. But the deep and valuable acceptance of people-as-they-are is mere question-begging for the non-creator of those people. If human probability in art has simply to do with bent noses and thick wits then it is trivial, and it can easily be mirrored. And in a way this is what Dickens does in *Our Mutual Friend*. But he also shows how unlikely it is that one man-in-the-street will 'accept' other men-in-the-street 'as they are' for the excellent reason that in any deep sense he doesn't *know* who they are. It is all very well for George Eliot to speak of acceptance, but who *is* Harmon/Handford/Rokesmith, who *is* Boffin, who *is* Wrayburn, who *is* Wegg, who *is* Headstone, etc. etc? How, for example, can Boffin accept Wegg as he is when Wegg projects an image of himself that is different from the self that schemes to get Boffin's money from him? 'What a world were this world if *Our Mutual Friend* were an honest reflection of it.' Not reflection, certainly, but judgement on relationships and the inevitable ignorance of one person about another it may well be. Its characters are wooden because fundamentally that is how they appear to each other. And there is nothing humanly improbable in that.

[1] *Fundamental Principles of the Metaphysic of Ethics*, 1955, p. 55. The italics are Kant's.

But how is it made probable? By Dickens's manner of presenting us with a world that the novel investigates in which
there are, so we are made to feel, countless examples of deceived
and deceiving friends of whom we are offered a mere sample, and
because of the examples of buying and selling in marriage and
other relationships, all of which presuppose a total indifference
to the freedom and integrity of individuals who are bought or
otherwise deceived. And here *Our Mutual Friend* deepens into
its most worthwhile concern. If it were merely concerned to show
that money dictates relationships then it would provide the sort
of satire that we find in *Martin Chuzzlewit*. But in addition, *Our
Mutual Friend* continues *Great Expectations'* concern with identity
and the difficult and problematic ways by which it is assembled,
recognized or denied. For in this novel Dickens is writing about
a society that has become largely incapable of mutuality and in
which individuals treat each other objectively, as things or instruments to their own ends. 'Rational beings,' Kant said, 'are
called *persons*, because their very nature points them out as ends
in themselves, that is as something which must not be used
merely as means, and so far therefore restricts freedom of action
(and is an object of respect).'[1] But the characters of *Our Mutual
Friend* typically *do* use each other as means; and because freedom
of action is not at all restricted, we have Dickens's terrible study
of people being turned into one-dimensional objects. His
figures, Lewes protested, are 'merely masks'.[2] But the characters
of *Our Mutual Friend* can be nothing else to each other. Properly
speaking, Lewes's criticism should be directed against the society
Dickens renders, not Dickens's art. For in a very radical sense,
the people of his novel are forced to see themselves from the
outside. Identity rests on class-consciousness and its promoted
images. You are what you are seen to be. The notion goes all the
way back to *Oliver Twist* but it has now a different – and one
almost wants to say final – bleak certainty of perception. In a
really terrible sense the society of *Our Mutual Friend* can be

[1] *Metaphysic of Ethics*, op. cit., p. 55.
[2] *The Dickens Critics*, p. 61.

honestly reflected, since it has turned itself into stiff inhumaness. It has become reified:

> The great looking-glass above the sideboard reflects the table and the company. . . . Reflects Veneering; forty, wavy-haired, dark, tending to corpulence, sly, mysterious, filmy – a kind of sufficiently well-looking veiled-prophet, not prophesying. Reflects Mrs. Veneering; fair, aquiline-nosed and fingered, not so much light hair as she might have, gorgeous in raiment and jewels, enthusiastic, propitiatory, conscious that a corner of her husband's veil is over herself. Reflects Podsnap; prosperously feeding, two little light-coloured wiry wings, one on either side of his else bald head, looking as like his hair brushes as his hair. . . . Reflects Mrs. Podsnap . . . quantity of bone, neck and nostrils like a rocking-horse, hard features, majestic head-dress in which Podsnap has hung golden offerings. Reflects Twemlow; grey, dry, polite, susceptible to east wind. . . . Reflects mature young lady; raven locks, and complexion that lights up well when well-powdered – as it is – carrying on considerably in the captivation of mature young gentleman. . . . Reflects charming Lady Tippins on Veneering's right; with an immense obtuse drab oblong face, like a face in a tablespoon, and a dyed Long Walk up the top of her head, as a convenient public approach to the bunch of false hair behind, pleased to patronise Mrs. Veneering opposite, who is pleased to be patronised. (Bk 1, ch 2)

I have quoted this at some length, though the passage as a whole is considerably longer, because I think it important we note how Dickens hates nearly all the people he is writing about. The tone is very largely one of unrelieved disgust. It may seem to lay him open to the charge of non-acceptance. But it is possible to argue that Dickens *is* accepting the characters. The characteristics he touches on are all that is necessary in order to know them. For the great looking-glass is an honest reflection of people who have turned themselves and others into essences. I borrow the word from Sartre because it so perfectly explains Dickens's concern:

> If one considers an article of manufacture – as, for example, a book or a paper-knife – one sees that it has been made by an artisan who had a conception of it; and he has paid attention, equally, to the

324 · *The Melancholy Man*

conception of a paper-knife and the pre-existent technique of production which is a part of that conception and is, at bottom, a formula. Thus the paper-knife is at the same time an article producible in a certain manner and one which, on the other hand, serves a definite purpose, for one cannot suppose that a man would produce a paper-knife without knowing what it was for.[1]

Much of *Our Mutual Friend* is devoted to a study of how people are turned into essential objects by other people's desire that they should serve a definite purpose. Indeed, it would not be wrong to suggest that Dickens shows class-consciousness as creating a consciousness of something like a pre-existent technique of production. People know what they ought to make of other people. When Bradley Headstone meets Riderhood by chance, he thinks 'Here is an instrument. Can I use it?' And a good deal of the novel's amazing resourcefulness springs from Dickens's bitter demonstration of how people are reduced to essences through improper relationships. They are turned into things. It is so with Twemlow:

> There was an innocent piece of dinner-furniture that went upon easy castors and was kept over a livery stable-yard in Duke Street, Saint James's, when not in use, to whom the Veneerings were a source of blind confusion. The name of this article was Twemlow. Being first cousin to Lord Snigsworth, he was in frequent requisition, and at many houses might be said to represent the dining-table in its normal state. Mr. and Mrs. Veneering, for example, arranging a dinner, habitually started with Twemlow, and then put leaves in him, or added guests to him. (Bk 1, ch 2)

Dickens's language shows how the case is the same for many others. Thus, when Mr and Mrs Podsnap give a dinner-party for 'seventeen friends of their souls' they hire 'a well-conducted automaton' to play quadrilles. The party is for their daughter Georgiana, a 'young rocking horse' who is 'being trained in her mother's art of prancing in a stately manner without ever getting on'. (Bk 1, ch 11) There is the ubiquitous and appalling

[1] *Existentialism and Humanism*, 1948, pp. 25–6.

old Lady Tippins, 'dyed and varnished' who may possess some fragment of a real woman about her although

> you could easily buy all you see of her, in Bond Street; or you might scalp her, and peel her, and scrape her, and make two Lady Tippinses out of her, and yet not penetrate to the genuine article. (Bk 1, ch 10)

And there is Alfred Lammle, who has a 'pasty sort of glitter, as if he were constructed for candlelight only, and had been let out into daylight by some grand mistake.'

Jenny Wren's dolls are fittingly modelled on the society with which Dickens is concerned:

> 'There was Lady Belinda Whitrose. I made her do double duty one night. I said when she came out of the carriage, "*You*'ll do, my dear!" and I ran straight home and cut her out and basted her. . . . That's Lady Belinda hanging up by the waist, much too near the gaslight for a wax one, with her toes turned in.' (Bk 3, ch 2)

Jenny speaks of her dolls as Dickens speaks of many of the characters of *Our Mutual Friend*. The human is indistinguishable from the artificial. No wonder he was so struck when Marcus Stone told him about the articulator of human bones who lived in St Giles's.[1] The novel was already under way, but Dickens was right to put Mr Venus in, because his trade so aptly symbolizes the bizarre construction of identities which the society of *Our Mutual Friend* is shown to expend its energies on.

But Dickens's demonstration of fixed identities is not merely a matter of language. Much of the novel's presentation of its society depends, it is true, on the assertions carried by the novelist's imagistic powers; but as we would expect, the theme of dehumanization or reification is also and perhaps more importantly made a matter of dramatic presentation. Scene after scene testifies to the fact that people deny each other's humanity. To take just one example. Eugene Wrayburn is visited by Jenny's father, whom he nicknames Mr Dolls and whom he fumigates:

> [Wrayburn] took the shovel from the grate, sprinkled a few live

[1] *Forster*, p. 572.

ashes on it, and from a box on the chimney-piece took a few pas-
tilles, which he set upon them; then, with great composure, began
placidly waving the shovel in front of Mr. Dolls, to cut him off
from his company. (Bk 3, ch 10)

And having turned Dolls into an object, Wrayburn offers him
money to tell him where Lizzie is, although he knows the old
man will use it to buy the drink that is rapidly killing him.
'"Eugene, Eugene,"' Lightwood asks, '"can you stoop to the
use of such an instrument as this?"' In a very radical way, the
scene demonstrates Eugene's refusal to honour any demand for
accepting people 'as they are'.

Because identities are improperly created through vicious
relationships, many of the individuals of *Our Mutual Friend* come
to have split identities. The point is fairly simply made in the
case of Riah and Fascination Fledgeby, which takes to its extreme
an idea that makes its first appearance in the characters of Spen-
low and Jorkins, and which is immeasurably advanced in the
study of Casby and Pancks. Riah is the good man who is made
to look bad, Fledgeby the bad man made to look good. Riah,
indeed, is made to submit to Fledgeby much as Jenny Wren's
father submits to Wrayburn, and as Harmon apparently submits
to Boffin. Just how damaging submissiveness is, hardly needs
emphasizing, but it is worth quoting a note from Kant's *Observations on the Beautiful and Sublime*, because it is so fine an expression
of an idea that we also find in Dickens's novel:

> In submissiveness there is not only something exceedingly danger-
> ous, but also a certain ugliness and a contradiction, which at the
> same time indicates its illegitimacy. An animal is not yet a com-
> plete being, because it is not conscious of itself . . . it knows
> nothing of its own existence. But that man himself should stand in
> need of no soul and have no will of his own, and that another soul
> should move his limbs, this is absurd or perverse. Such a man is like
> the mere tool of another. . . . The man who stands in dependence
> on another is no longer a man, he has lost his standing, he is
> nothing but the possession of another man.[1]

[1] Cassirer, *Rousseau, Kant and Goethe*, pp. 17–18.

It would be difficult to find a better statement than Kant's about an idea that is central to *Our Mutual Friend*, where individuals constantly become the possession of others and are consequently turned into mere tools. It is perhaps not surprising that James did not understand what Dickens was demonstrating in the novel; for James could not really know about the way in which, given the conditions of English society, lives are circumscribed by the inevitable and inescapable pressures of the social arrangement and its process.

There are also, however, those characters whose divided identities are to some extent their own responsibility. And inevitably this brings us to Bradley Headstone. Headstone is the most pitiable and horrifying case of a split identity that the novel has to show. He has struggled for respectability, tried to raise himself out of the abyss by sheer dogged effort and hard work; he *wants* society to give him an identity – that of a schoolmaster. The hideous result is that this identity costs him any coherent or unified life.

> Composedly smoking, [Wrayburn] leaned an elbow on the chimneypiece, at the side of the fire, and looked at the schoolmaster. It was a cruel look, in its cold disdain of him, as a creature of no worth. The schoolmaster looked at him, and that, too, was a cruel look, though of the different kind, that it had a raging jealousy and fiery wrath in it. . . .
>
> 'In some high respects, Mr. Eugene Wrayburn,' said Bradley . . . 'the natural feelings of my pupils are stronger than my teaching.'
>
> 'In most respects, I dare say,' replied Eugene, enjoying his cigar, 'though whether high or low is of no importance. You have my name very correctly. Pray what is yours?'
>
> 'It cannot concern you much to know, but –'
>
> 'True,' interposed Eugene, striking sharply and cutting him short at his mistake, 'it does not concern me at all to know. I can say Schoolmaster, which is a most respectable title. You are right, Schoolmaster.' (Bk 2, ch 6)

Of this scene James says that it is clever but insufficient. It is, he adds, vulgar, because of the 'essentially small character of these personalities. In other words, the moment, dramatically, is great, while the author's conception is weak'. And James goes on to remark that such a scene demonstrates Dickens's inability to see beneath the surface of things. He is, James says, 'the greatest of superficial novelists'.[1] I have no particular wish to attack James, but his views have a currency which make them worth challenging. And the fact is that he is staggeringly innocent of any understanding as to what Dickens shows us in the interview between Eugene and Bradley. For it is not their 'personalities' but their identities which matter, identities which are fixed for them by the social process and which condemn them to an imprisonment within the identities that are given and which they give to themselves. It is part of Eugene's indifference to people that he should objectify his relationship with them by renaming them: Jenny Wren's father becomes Mr Dolls, Riah becomes Brother Aaron, and Headstone becomes Schoolmaster. There is nothing in the slightest superficial about Dickens's understanding of Eugene's superficial way of treating people. Nor in his recognition that Headstone has laid himself open to such treatment. Bradley wants to be accepted as a respectable schoolmaster. And he sacrifices everything to his yearning. At one sad and revealing moment he tells Riderhood, '"I have absolutely no friends,"' (Bk 4, ch 15) and his terrible loneliness results from his passion to achieve what Riderhood calls a ''spectable calling'. '"I tell you sir,"' he says to Eugene, '"I have worked my way onward, out of both [my origin and my bringing-up], and have a right to be considered a better man than you, with better reasons for being proud."'

Yet the real anguish of Bradley's condition is his fear that he has not even achieved respectability:

> 'You think me of no more value than the dirt under your feet,' said Bradley . . .
> 'I assure you, Schoolmaster,' replied Eugene, 'I don't think about you.'

[1] *The House of Fiction*, p. 256.

'That's not true,' returned the other; 'you know better.'

'That's coarse,' Eugene retorted; 'but you *don't* know better.'

That is superficial? Bradley's respectability sits as uneasily on him as his dress, which he wears with a certain stiffness; we are told that he is never quite at his ease. And finally the identity is destroyed. Riderhood turns up at Bradley's school after the schoolmaster's murderous attack on Wrayburn and asks him to write his name on the blackboard. The class shrills out the name 'Bradley Headstone'. Riderhood reveals his knowledge of Bradley's crime. '"They looked at each other. Bradley, slowly withdrawing his eyes, turned his face to the black board and slowly wiped his name out."' (Bk 4, ch 15) The moment provides one of those great dramatic images which crystallize a theme. It is marvellously apt and it is, of course, terrible. For Bradley's wiping out his name is a final admission that he has not been able to achieve the identity for which he sacrificed his life (literally, as it turns out). He becomes a kind of nothing.

Most commentators have felt that in the presentation of Bradley Dickens taps dark and deep agonies in himself. His career, too, had been a struggle against background and bringing-up, had involved him in the effort to achieve the respectability which the affair with Maria Beadnell had suggested to him he lacked. And in those fearful suppressed energies that occasionally burst out in Bradley there may well be a reflection of Dickens's own violent powers and emotional intensities. If so, it has to be said that he never slackens his sane understanding of the cost involved in the struggle to achieve an identity by which a man can be socially placed. And this does not mean that in effect he proposes a moralizing acceptance of the poor man at his gate since God ordered his estate. Dickens knows only too well the unavoidable social pressures that force people into the struggle for 'betterment'. But he never loses sight of the cost. And his dislike of Charley does not spring from any feeling that Charley should not have been educated, but from his understanding of what can happen to people for whom education is, as it almost inevitably must be, a part of class-consciousness. The scene in

which Charley renounces Lizzie may be melodramatically
rendered, but there can be no question of the intelligent understanding Dickens shows in his recognition of its human probability:

> 'But you shall not disgrace me,' doggedly pursued the boy. 'I'm
> determined that after I have climbed up out of the mire, you shall
> not pull me down. You can't disgrace me if I have nothing to do
> with you, and I *will* have nothing to do with you.' (Bk 2, ch 15)

Charley's final break with Headstone is equally credible. He
bursts into tears when Bradley confesses to the attack on Wrayburn and says that it is ' "an extraordinary circumstance attendant
on my life, that every effort I make towards perfect respectability, is impeded by somebody else through no fault of mine" '.
(Bk 4, ch 7) The credibility is, admittedly, more in the social
probabilities than in the actual words that Charley is made to
use, and one of the reasons that *Our Mutual Friend* isn't as fine as
its predecessors is that Dickens seems often not to bother about
doing more than present characters who can stand for his interests.
He has little interest in them. Charley, Riah, Jenny Wren, Lightwood and even Venus are all cases in point. But this does not
mean that Dickens is unable to see beneath the surface of things.
On the contrary, he is so absorbed in the primary and essential
pressures by which people function that he gives little time in
Our Mutual Friend to the richness of surface texture to which his
work accustoms us. The novel is no less intelligent than *Little
Dorrit*, but it is certainly less attractive.

But what of the Boffins? It might easily seem that they are an
indulgence, a relapse into the world of Cheerybles and Pickwick.
Dickens seems to like them because they are cheerful old phili-
stines. Mrs Boffin makes an attempt to become fashionable. She
is, her husband informs Wegg, 'a highflyer at fashion'. And
Boffin himself decides to become educated, to learn about the
decline and fall off the Rooshan Empire. Neither succeeds. And
it is often said that their failure demonstrates Dickens's own
middle-class complacency. I do not think so. His point may be

simple, but it is not that simple. The Boffins provide in themselves evidence that the purposes to which education and appearance are often put in the society they inhabit cannot define human worth, though both may be, and frequently are, used to define social identity. Dickens does not say that education and taste do not matter; he says that there is no reason to suppose the educated man better than the uneducated, given that education is liable to be a badge of attainment. The idea may be obvious – though it is usually ignored because like most of Dickens's 'obvious' ideas it is rather too uncomfortable to live with – but there is nothing philistinic about it, any more than there is anything philistinic about his praise of the Boffins:

> These two ignorant and unpolished people had guided themselves so far on their journey of life, by a religious sense of duty and desire to do right. Ten thousand weaknesses and absurdities might have been detected in the breasts of both; ten thousand vanities additional, possibly, in the breast of the woman. But the hard, wrathful and sordid nature that had wrung as much work out of them as could be got in their best days, for as little money as could be paid to hurry on their worst, had never been so warped but that it knew their moral straightness and respected it. (Bk 1, ch 9)

The nature in question is that of the dead Jailor of Harmony Jail, who has shown his respect for Boffin by turning him into the Golden Dustman. And of course much of the novel turns on the apparent effect this has on Boffin, making him into a 'bad' man. I shall come back to this point later. For the moment I want to note only that Dickens's praise of the Boffins is reminiscent of his praise of Charley Neckett and of Pancks, and that there is nothing either complacent or anti-intellectual about it. It merely testifies to his willing acceptance of people as they are, and his understanding of the affirmative possibilities of the human spirit under stress.

But the other possibilities are more insistent. Surrounding the Boffins in their new-found wealth are 'all manner of crawling, creeping, fluttering, and buzzing creatures'. (Bk 1, ch 17) The dehumanizing imagery includes Wegg and his lust after money.

Indeed, at one moment he is seen in quite grotesquely comic orgasmic excitement as he thinks he is about to unravel the secret of Boffin's dust-heaps.

> Mr. Wegg's wooden leg started forward under the table, and slowly elevated itself as he read on . . . On the way to this crisis Mr. Wegg's wooden leg had gradually elevated itself more and more, and he had nudged Mr. Venus with his opposite elbow deeper and deeper, until at length the preservation of his balance became incompatible with the two actions, and he now dropped over sideways on that gentleman, squeezing him against the settle's edge. Nor did either of the two, for some few seconds, make any effort to recover himself; both remaining in a kind of pecuniary swoon. (Bk 3, ch 6)

In addition, there is the amiable lunacy of Mrs Wilfer's appearance, her determination not to be condescended to or to appear as anything other than possessed of the gentility that she feels her husband lacks. And there is her daughter, Bella, yearning to be free of the degrading poverty which surrounds her.

Here we come across the old theme, the search for freedom and the belief that money or position will buy it. The whole of Bella's education is taken up with showing this to be a delusion, and the presentation of Eugene shows it even more decisively. It also shows, I think, where Dickens emerges as a decisively greater novelist than either Henry James or George Eliot, who are both equally exercised over the problem of freedom. I think one might put George Eliot's position simply but not unfairly by saying that for her freedom seems to be impossible within the web of society, so that the search for it is either doomed to failure or, if it is to succeed, presupposes that there can be a disentangling of self from the web. But since she also shows that such disentangling is impossible, her only 'free' characters are those who are offered impossible escapes. In James's case, freedom becomes an illusion because he shares the point of view which Dickens exposes through various characters. Arnold Kettle's words put the point best. James's books are tragedies, Kettle says, 'precisely because their subject is the smashing of the bourgeois illusion of freedom in the consciousness of characters who are unable to conceive of freedom in any other way.'[1] But James himself is so deeply involved in the illusion that he cannot escape from it.

It is part of Dickens's greatness that he should see clearly what George Eliot and Henry James see only imperfectly, that the dream of freedom which they entertain is and must be an illusion. And in Eugene we are presented with the man who, more than anyone else in *Our Mutual Friend*, vindicates Dickens's method with character and denies where it does not make utterly irrelevant the criticisms levelled against him by George Eliot, G. H. Lewes, James and their literary heirs.

In the *Divided Self* R. D. Laing offers a definition of a type of personality that is of considerable help in any consideration of Dickens's study of Eugene. A basically ontologically secure person, Laing says, 'will encounter all the hazards of life, social, ethical, spiritual, biological, from a centrally firm sense of his own and other people's reality and identity.' Such a person has an 'integral selfhood'.[2] But the ontologically insecure person lacks this sense of selfhood and the assurances that go with it. ' "I know less about myself than about most people in the world," ' Eugene tells Lightwood (Bk 2, ch 6), and to judge from his treatment of Riah, Lizzie, Headstone, and Mr Dolls he has precious little knowledge of who they are. I am not about to suggest that Eugene should be treated as a pathological case; it is more that he symbolizes a terrible malaise at the heart of the society with which Dickens is concerned and which makes it impossible for people to accept each other as they are. Eugene quite simply believes he is free. Or rather, he thinks himself independent of human claims. His money, social position and intelligence all offer him a freedom which turns out to be a delusion. He calls himself a 'bad, idle dog', freed from the necessity to work; and he has all the typifying qualities that could make him one of the Arnoldian elite. He has a multiplicity of talents

[1] *An Introduction to the English Novel*, 1953, Vol. II, p. 32.
[2] *The Divided Self*, Penguin edn., p. 39.

and an indifference as to how they are used. He might be an anticipation of Will Ladislaw.

Eugene, however, suffers from a debilitating ennui. When Jenny Wren asks him why he doesn't reform and become a good dog he tells her that 'there's nobody who makes it worth my while'. He is intelligent enough to see that the social class with which he is identified has nothing about it that can appeal to him; but he lacks the moral courage and honesty to break out of the identity he is given and which he uses. The classic liberal solution to his problem would be to find him a cause. But Dickens rejects this:

> 'Then idiots talk,' said Eugene . . . 'of Energy. If there is a word under any letter from A to Z that I abominate, it is energy. What the deuce! Am I to rush out into the street, collar the first man of wealthy appearance that I meet, shake him, and say, "To the law upon the spot, you dog, and retain me, or I'll be the death of you?" Yet that would be energy.'
> 'Precisely my view of the case, Eugene. But show me a good opportunity, show me something really worth being energetic about, and I'll show you energy.'
> 'And so will I,' said Eugene.
> And it is likely enough that ten thousand other young men, within the limits of the London Post-Office town-delivery, made the same hopeful remark in the course of the same evening. (Bk 1, ch 3)

It is deftly done, and it establishes Dickens's awareness that the 'cause' is no solution to the problem that faces Eugene. He is and remains for most of the novel trapped in the identity that he wryly accepts though he knows it is stupid and vicious.

The break-through – it is almost a literal one – occurs when his face is smashed by Bradley's murderous attack. His being 'free' to taunt the Schoolmaster makes him Bradley's victim and it also smashes what seems most to demonstrate his class identity. What Dickens had in mind here is both important to an understanding of his novel and to a proper appreciation of his stance towards the dogma of class or race as it so frequently shows itself in Victorian England. When Disraeli published *Lothair* in 1870, he added a preface in which he spoke of how his famous trilogy *Coningsby, Tancred* and *Sybil* had asserted 'the doctrine of race' and were thus 'entirely opposed to the equality of man, and similar abstract dogmas'. And in *Sybil* itself we are referred to the portrait of a certain Aubrey St. Lys:

> He was distinguished by that beauty of the noble English blood, of which in these days few types remain; the Norman tempered by the Saxon; the fire of conquest softened by integrity; and a serene, though inflexible, habit of mind.

Ruskin time and again spoke of the upper classes as being of 'purer race than the lower'; and he claimed that

> a gentleman's first characteristic is that fineness of structure in the body, which renders it capable of the most delicate sensation; and of structure in the mind which renders it capable of the most delicate sympathies – one might say simply, 'fineness of nature.'[1]

George Eliot described Felix Holt's face as having

> the look of habitual meditative abstraction from objects of mere personal vanity or desire, which is the peculiar stamp of culture, and makes the very roughly-cut face worthy to be called 'the human face divine.' (ch 30)

Admittedly, what lies behind George Eliot's sentence is an idea of greater subtlety and decency than anything that Ruskin or Disraeli based their words on, yet in the end it is equally abstracted from the social realities. Felix is a free man. He becomes removed from his social context into a world of the elite.

Dickens will have none of this. It is only after Eugene has been terribly wounded that he accepts Lizzie and marries her. Headstone's attack has destroyed the identity on which he had built the pretence of being a 'free' man, someone too fine and pure to accept the girl as anything other than an object. He had intended her to be his mistress. ' "I think of setting up a doll," ' he says to Jenny Wren.

---

[1] *Modern Painters, Works*, Vol. VII, p. 345.

'You had better not,' replied the dressmaker.

'Why not?'

'You are sure to break it. All you children do.' (Bk 2, ch 2)

Eugene's language is that of a man who wishes to be free to treat people as instruments. And for all his better feelings we are repeatedly told that his freedom is basically a matter of self. When he follows Lizzie to her hide-out and discovers how distressed she is by his visit, Dickens notes that although he feels pity for her 'it was not strong enough to impel him to sacrifice himself and spare her'. (Bk 4, ch 6) It is the same with his attitude to Jenny Wren. 'He was sorry, but his sympathy did not move his carelessness to do anything but feel sorry.' (Bk 3, ch 10) Eugene, in fact, suffers from a sort of paralysis of will brought on by his indolent loathing of the identity which he has fixed to him, which causes him to see others in fixed terms, and which he half-perceives is foolish and wicked. Only half-perceives, because total acceptance of people as they are is impossible to him given the framework of perception within which he lives.

When he eventually comes to accept Lizzie, Eugene is rescued from the class self-consciousness in which he has been bound and which he has mistaken for freedom. The marriage should not be compared with that of Sybil and Egremont. Disraeli had offered the marriage of his hero and heroine as a way of knitting-up the two nations (except that he couldn't quite bring himself to have a nobleman marry a commoner, so he allowed Sybil to be a noble lady in disguise). Dickens has no such intention, no such hope; and if it comes to that, no such interest. For him the marriage is redemptive at least for Eugene, because it frees him from the false and crippling belief that he is a free man. True freedom turns out to be commitment. The paradox is not a slight one.

And here we have to note the use made of pastoralism in the novel. Lizzie tries to escape from the agony of her relationship with Eugene and so flees from the city up-river. But Eugene follows her, and Bradley follows him, and Riderhood follows *him*. There is no escape. Dickens returns to an important idea of

Oliver Twist, the rottenness of society that creeps out to infect the free natural world. When Betty Higden wanders out from the city she too is trying to escape. She finds her way upstream:

> In these pleasant little towns on the Thames, you may hear the fall of the water over the weirs, or even, in still weather, the rustle of the rushes; and from the bridge you may see the young river, dimpled like a young child, playfully gliding away among the trees, unpolluted by the defilements that wait for it on its course. (Bk 3, ch 8)

The yearning for escape is genuine enough, and nature here has all the mythic power and significance which it has in *Little Dorrit* and *Great Expectations.* But as in those two novels, so in *Our Mutual Friend,* the dream of escape into a natural world of innocence is unavailing. That Eugene should be half-killed in natural surroundings, that Betty should die there and that Headstone and Riderhood should be drowned together at the Lock, sufficiently indicate Dickens's powerful insistence on the impossibility of escape from the human condition which is circumscribed by social realities.

We come back here to the marriage of Eugene and Lizzie. What sort of social reality does it represent? Does Dickens condescend to the girl? In the last chapter of the novel the Voice of Society makes itself heard, and Twemlow says:

> 'If this gentleman's feelings of gratitude, of respect, of admiration, induced him (as I presume they did) to marry this lady . . . I think he is the greater gentleman for the action, and makes her the greater lady.'

Humphry House remarks of this speech that

> it is impossible not to take the voice of Twemlow . . . as the voice of Dickens . . . But the application is solely to Eugene: and how can any action of his make a 'greater lady' of a girl whose moral superiority to him has been hammered in with such unremitting emphasis, except on the assumption that she gains in status by becoming his wife? . . . Twemlow's ingenious phrasing very imperfectly conceals a sort of satisfaction that Eugene is really

doing a very generous thing in marrying Lizzie, and that she is doing very well for herself by marrying him.[1]

This criticism has been too often quoted with approval not to demand some show of opposition. For House is, I think, quite wrong. Wrong, in the first place, to feel that Twemlow's voice is Dickens's (when was ever a novelist more prepared than Dickens to intercede in his own voice whenever he felt like it?). I agree with what House has to say about Twemlow's concealed satisfaction, but then Twemlow, for all his decency, is as much trapped in class-consciousness as anyone in the novel. And of course Twemlow is right to say that Eugene makes Lizzie a greater lady, if he means by that raising her status. It is no more than a fact of social life. But Twemlow is quite wrong to think that Eugene's action makes him the greater gentleman, and House is quite wrong to think Dickens is endorsing Twemlow's remark, except as we understand gentleman in the sense in which it is used of John Chivery – to mean innate goodness and human decency – or in the sense Herbert Pocket implies when he says that his father believes that the only true gentleman is the gentleman at heart. ' "He says, no varnish can hide the grain of the wood." ' (G.E., ch 22) Not that this sense matters very much to Dickens; it merely lets him deny the assumption that the capacity for delicate sensations and delicate sympathies are dependent on the accident of birth.

Lizzie herself thinks that Wrayburn is above her. But there is nothing improbable in that. It is what she would feel, since the whole social process insists it is so. She says to Bella:

'I have no more dreamed of the possibility of *my* being his wife, than he ever has – and words could not be stronger than that. And yet I love him. I love him so much and so dearly, that when I sometimes think my life may be but a weary one, I am proud of it and glad of it. I am proud and glad to suffer something for him, even though it is of no service to him, and he will never know of it or care for it.' (Bk 3, ch 9)

[1] *The Dickens World*, p. 163.

Lizzie's words have an immediate relevance to Bella because they contrast her selfish love with the other's selfless regard for Wrayburn. They may also seem to support House's idea that Dickens feels that really Wrayburn is doing a very generous thing in marrying Lizzie. But the next chapter opens with what must be – it inevitably is – an ironic contrast between Lizzie's exalted love of Wrayburn and Wrayburn's attitude to her and others. The first words of Bk 3, ch 10 are these:

> 'And so, Miss Wren,' said Mr. Eugene Wrayburn, 'I cannot persuade you to dress me a doll?'
>
> 'No,' replied Miss Wren, snappishly; 'if you want one, go and buy one at the shop.'

Wrayburn is shown at his worst in this chapter. Cruelly arrogant in his attitude to Jenny and her father, selfish, ruthlessly contemptuous. And by juxtaposing Lizzie's view of him with the one we are offered, Dickens shows how she as much as anyone else in the novel is trapped in class-consciousness. Her thinking Wrayburn far above her is both right, since she clearly cannot expect him to marry her, and wrong, since she thinks his social superiority guarantees his moral superiority. And her mistake about him is of a piece with her wanting Charley to be educated into respectability, believing that as a result he will be better. But as the chapters 9 and 10 of Book 3 show, Dickens in no way endorses Lizzie's view of Wrayburn. Nor Twemlow's.

Yet the marriage is one of the ways in which *Our Mutual Friend* finds it possible to provide images of human decency and change within the social process. The marriage frees Eugene in that it makes him a more committed and hence more integrated person. And it seems reasonable to suppose that the same will hold true of Lizzie. At all events, their relationship signifies a triumph of human possibilities over the Voice of Society in much the same way as Amy and Clennam's marriage asserts itself against those who make 'their usual uproar'. It is the more important to note this because although there is absolutely no facile optimism in *Our Mutual Friend*, neither it nor *Little Dorrit* is fairly characterized in Lukacs's verdict that after 1848 'the really great writers of the period sank into a profound depression and hopelessness – like Flaubert and in his later years, Dickens'.[1]

Critics reluctant to settle for an account of Dickens as a pessimist have not infrequently argued that *Our Mutual Friend* is a symbolist novel in which the River and the Dust stand for opposed values: the River affirmative, Dust negative; and that in some way or other the river symbolizes a transcendence or quality of life existing beyond the humanized dust world and partially glimpsed through death and its regenerative possibilities. The river houses dead bodies, but it can be seen as a purifying agent or, if not that, then a medium of release to another life. This seems to be Hillis Miller's view and it is shared by many others. It is not Dickens's. When Rogue Riderhood is nearly drowned, his daughter has the idea that

> if affairs could remain thus for a long time it would be a respectable change. . . . Also some vague idea that the old evil is drowned out of him, and that if he should happily come back to resume his occupation of the empty form that lies upon the bed, his spirit will be altered. In which state of mind she kisses the stony lips, and quite believes that the impassive hand she chafes will revive a tender hand, if it revive ever.

> Sweet delusion for Pleasant Riderhood. (Bk 3, ch 3)

It would be possible to quote an astonishingly varied set of opinions as to what the river is supposed to symbolize. They cover all the possibilities, from life to death. But I do not think that Dickens intended any of them. The river is the river is the river. As Ernst Fischer has said, symbolism is really a product of naturalism: it wells up as a desire to 'discover the mysterious whole, the meaning of life, behind and beyond social realities'.[2] *Our Mutual Friend* has nothing of this kind of symbolism to it. Dickens's concern is not to find 'the meaning of life' but to offer a creative criticism of probable individual lives and relationships, given the social realities from which the novel starts.

---

[1] *Studies in European Realism*, 1964, p. 98.
[2] *The Meaning of Art*, Penguin, p. 80.

It would be convenient to see these realities as grouped around the dust. For the dust means money, and money is certainly a basically conditioning factor of the way people behave in the novel. Yet if we try to see the dustheaps as symbols we again run into trouble. K. J. Fielding is at least honest when he says that Dickens confuses the issue by making money both good and bad:

> The foul dust-heap, composed of vast quantities of refuse, does represent wealth. But not only are its more unsavoury aspects glossed over, but we are not allowed to forget that the golden-hearted Boffin also helped to build them up, that he inherits them, and that they are passed on to Bella Wilfer and the miser's son with the evident approval of the author.[1]

But what is wrong with that? Dickens hasn't an essential objection against money, only against the uses to which it is put and the ways in which people destroy themselves to get hold of it. Of course, he knows that there is no such thing as clean money, and his audience would know all about dust-heaps, so that glossing-over doesn't come into it. But he also knows that there are people whose involvement with money is not totally degrading, though it is always troubling, as Bella has to learn. That is his case about Boffin, and given an especial twist through the duplicitous plotting of the dustman's apparently going down-hill into miserliness and inhuman hardness. Many of Dickens's critics seem to feel he has betrayed his trust when he keeps to the social realities. They feel he should set himself against money, for example, and recommend an entirely different way of life. But as a mimetic novelist Dickens is not free to offer such recommendations. Besides, he sees that the large dismissals of Victorian society are a luxury which no sane man can afford, not just because they lead to nihilism or vatic escapism, to Carlyle or to Ruskin, but because they are too easy. And Dickens will not settle for easy answers: easy positives, easy negatives. One might reflect on the story *Dust or Ugliness Redeemed*, which appeared in the first volume of *Household Words*. It is about a man who loses

[1] *Charles Dickens, A Critical Introduction*, p. 189.

342 · *The Melancholy Man*

a paper claim to money, throws himself into the Thames, and is rescued by some people who are sifting among a dust-heap and bring him back to life by burying him up to his neck in the heap, the warmth of which quickly restores him. As a tale it is not very good, but in providing all the hints of the complexities by which *Our Mutual Friend* becomes a great novel it is worthy of note.

Because Dickens's view is so complex, Orwell's often-quoted and widely approved criticism of him is hopelessly wide of the mark. Admirable and clear-minded though Orwell is, he does not really understand Dickens. Or, what is more likely, he simply hadn't re-read the novels before writing his essay. Whatever the reason, he misses the point entirely in suggesting that it was beyond Dickens to 'grasp that, given the existing form of society, certain evils *cannot* be remedied'.[1] In so far as it applies to *Our Mutual Friend* – and it often has been applied to the novel – the remark must mean that Dickens as a determined optimist decides to squash his criticisms against money and give it to the deserving people at the end of the novel so that their success will imply that the good always triumphs. Whereas, the critics imply, he ought really to have admitted that money always corrupts or that it does not help solve all evils that society throws up. And he didn't do that because he couldn't. 'The truth is', Orwell adds, 'that Dickens's criticism of society is almost exclusively moral. Hence the utter lack of any constructive suggestion anywhere in his work.' I imagine that there is not much need to defend Dickens against the charge of his criticism being almost exclusively moral. All the great novels are concerned with the social process. But constructive suggestion? This is, of course, a misunderstanding of the nature of the novelist's task. But it is more than that. It falsifies the issue. Dickens knew perfectly well that given the existing form of society certain evils cannot be remedied, if for no other reason than that the evils usually *are* the existing form. But he also shows human potentialities and affirmative possibilities which reveal that the form is not a rigid fixity but a process. It is not a matter of constructive suggestion

[1] *A Collection of Essays*, p. 58.

so much as his understanding of the nature of change and a refusal to settle either for a deterministic pessimism or bland prescriptive optimism. Dickens is the greatest of all our novelists to the extent that he is the one who has been able most fearlessly and fully to confront society as a process, to explore its evils and the cost in human terms to those who make up the process, and yet see how elements in it change it and therefore guarantee it will not become the solid and unbudgeable framework that Orwell and others seem to take for granted he saw it as. Boffin's goodness, the marriage of Lizzie and Wrayburn, the education of Bella – these are not extrapolations from the process but a viable part of it. It is in Dickens's ability to imagine those people and not in any 'constructive suggestions' that one sees how truly great he is.

And there is Betty Higden. She also is part of the process. She represents that resilient element which refuses to be coerced – objectified – into an identity by the efforts of class-conscious philanthropy or Charity. Dickens is not making a simple-minded attack on Charity. Indeed, he shows that by no means all of Betty's suspicions are well-founded. That is not the point. For what concerns him about Betty Higden is her determination to maintain an integrity of identity that would be taken from her, she feels, if she were seen in terms of what Charity would make of her. And it is when we contemplate what Dickens could imagine for Betty Higden that we see finally how he emerges as greater than George Eliot.

I have already quoted George Eliot's criticism of Dickens's presentation of the decent poor, her judgement of his 'miserable fallacy that high morality and refined sentiment can grow out of harsh social conditions, ignorance and want; or that the working-classes are in a condition to enter at once into a millenial state of altruism.' Admittedly, those words were written before *Our Mutual Friend*, but it is hardly likely that Dickens's last novel would have caused her to alter them. More likely, she would regard it as confirming them. For, great artist that she is, George Eliot's realism in the end implies a withdrawal from certain social actualities into a series of assertions whereby accepting people as they are in fact means imposing identities on them that are derived from her own class-consciousness. This does not affect the solid core of her achievement, but it does draw attention to the fact that such elements of her novels as the stage-jews of *Daniel Deronda* and the appallingly bad pub-scenes of *Silas Marner* represent more than a failure of superficial mirroring of people-as-they-are. They spring from a determined (one might really say predetermined) attitude towards human probabilities that shows itself as a failure of imaginative intelligence.

For in the last analysis, George Eliot understands less about the social process than Dickens does, just as she understands less about the nature of identity in social relationships. Such terms as high morality and refined sentiment have nothing to do with the matter of Dickens's novels. They belong to a world of constructive suggestions, together with James's notionalizing of humanity. They are prescriptive rather than truly mimetic. And for all that critics might protest that *Our Mutual Friend* is somehow not like life, it is a truly mimetic novel. When George Eliot, when Lewes and James protest about Dickens's view of humanity, what they are really doing is to protest against his method of showing human probabilities, since it upsets their own calculations or judgements of the probable. And it is because of his method that Dickens can discover truths hidden from them. His techniques do not require apologizing for. They are an essential part of his vision. Indeed, without them there would be no vision.

We cannot apply to Dickens's novels terms invented for other novelists and expect to do him justice, or see how truly great he is. Throughout this book I have tried not to use many formal terms because I am acutely aware of how they can distort what Dickens offers us. The only word I have invoked with any frequency is mimetic, because that seems to me true to his greatest art and sufficiently flexible not to tie it down unfairly or restrict its scope. But I imagine it is clear that by mimetic I do not mean realistic in the sense in which that word is mostly used, and as it is used by critics who wish to attack Dickens. Which is not to say that Dickens is free from faults, large as well as small. But the small seem to me too obvious and harmless to bother about, while the large are not frequent. And although they have to be noted I think it proper to apply to Dickens the words Goethe used of Schiller, that before so great a man one should make one's criticisms on bended knees.

INDEX

✳ INDEX